Sweet Thunder
Duke Ellington's Music in Nine Themes

Jack Chambers
Sweet Thunder
Duke Ellington's Music in Nine Themes

MILESTONES
MUSIC & ART

SWEET THUNDER

copyright © 2019 by Jack Chambers

ALL RIGHTS RESERVED. Photographs and other illustrations, where applicable, are the property of the artist and are used by permission. No part of this book may be reproduced by any means without the prior written consent of the author with the exception of passages in reviews. Requests for copying or reproduction for educational or other purposes must be directed in writing to the author.

MILESTONES logo © 2018 Jack Chambers and Bruce Lynn

This book was created with the assistance of CanamBooks selfpublishing services

Library and archives Canada Cataloguing in Publication

Library of congress Cataloguing Data

Chambers, Jack. 1938-

Sweet Thunder: Duke Ellington's Music in Nine Themes/Jack Chambers
includes bibliographical references, playlists and index

1. Duke Ellington 1899-1974   2. Composers – Biography

3. Musicians – United States

ISBN (print) 978-1-9990585-0-0
ISBN (EPUB) 978-1-9990585-1-7
ISBN (MOBI) 978-1-9990585-2-4

Cover design and chapter titles: Jack Chambers
Cover photo: © Herman Leonard
Author photo: Norie Yazu
Interior design: Ted Sancton/Studio Melrose

This book was set in Plantin MT Pro Light 11/14

First Impressions of Duke Ellington
Worlds and Years Apart

"I remember probably better than anything the time we were tied up in Shanghai alongside a ship that had come out later, and somebody on it had a record of *Black and Tan Fantasy* – played, as I did not learn at the time,… by Duke Ellington. That was a world heard through a porthole, and never to be forgotten."
– *Otis Ferguson, Seaman First Class (later journalist), ca. 1928*

"His music has a truly Shakespearean universality, and as he sounded the gamut, girls wept and young chaps sank to their knees."
– *reviewer at the London Palladium, 1933*

"The Ellingtonians played with startling existential freshness, heartfelt profundity, and an interlinked unity of various individual skills. They played for people in love. The performance was a triumph for the band in its high-pressure harmony and hallelujah of groin-grinding surrealistic tension."
– *reviewer in Madras, India, 1963*

Sweet Thunder

CONTENTS

Introduction
Black and Tan Fantasies   1

Acknowledgements   8

Abbreviations   10

1 Ellington's Harlem...
   "...the world's most glamorous atmosphere"   11

2 Sweet and Pungent
   Duke and the Plunger Mutes   45

3 The Fifth Reed
   Ben Webster and the Tenor Ascent   81

4 Lotus Eaters Unite!
   The Spectral Alliance of
   Johnny Hodges and Billy Strayhorn   127

5 Panther Patter
   Duke Ellington at the Piano   163
   Appendix A: Piano in the Foreground   197
   Appendix B: Piano Recitals Annotated   199

6 Bardland
   Shakespeare in Ellington's World   201

7 Afro-Eurasian Ellington   245

8 Duke Ellington's Parallel Universe: The Stockpile   265
   Appendix: The Stockpile So Far   295

9 Three Steps into *The River*   299

Index of People and Places   337

Index of Compositions and Songs   343

SWEET THUNDER

Introduction

Black and Tan Fantasies

Edward Kennedy (Duke) Ellington (1899-1974)

This book invites readers to explore the music of Duke Ellington (1899-1974) by pursuing nine themes that recur in his music. The themes have been pieced together selectively from Ellington's voluminous output and show how he developed them, picking and choosing images, ideas and predilections that intrigued him. The themes that I discuss here are organized in ways that make them coherent and accessible, and tracking them can bring great satisfaction to listeners of diverse tastes and backgrounds. I know this because I have tested all of them with audiences. I have presented them all and seen them work.

I hope the organization into themes will bring new insights to listeners who already know Ellington's music. Most of all, I hope it will provide an entry-point for relative newcomers to Ellington's 50-year creative journey. Previous presentations of each of the themes (or chapters, in this context) are listed at the end of this Introduction; it is a scholarly appendage that can be easily skipped but giving it a glance might be encouraging for readers who might harbor doubts.

Duke Ellington's music is in danger of being ignored. He is not alone, of course. Serious music of all kinds faces the same threat. Ellington poses a formidable task for listeners who might be attracted to him because of the sheer volume of his work. The numbers defy credulity – more than 2,000 compositions, including songs, soundtracks, revues, hymns, big-band jazz, ballets, tone poems, and concert pieces. He was at least a hundred times more prolific in his output than Bach, Beethoven, Richard Strauss, Erik Satie, Thelonious Monk, Miles Davis, or other musicians who might entice listeners looking for substantial musical experiences. What really counts has nothing to do with the numbers, of course. Ellington's works resound with memorable melodies, fascinating rhythms and, above all, splendid harmonies. That is what counts.

Where does one begin? The themes in this book make very good starting points.

Not only is the sheer volume formidable, but most of his music, nearly all of his greatest music, is music without words. He wrote at least a hundred songs, including the standards "Sophisticated Lady," "Satin Doll," "I'm Beginning to See the Light," "Just Squeeze Me (But Don't Tease Me)," and dozens more. His songs seem like confections in the company of the masterful instrumental compositions. Happily, Ellington's first astute critic, the classicist R. D. Darrell, in a prescient critique in 1932, made exactly the same point. "Ellington writes naturally for instruments alone," Darrell wrote. "The human voice is not disdained" but "Ellington has emancipated American popular music from text for the first time since the Colonial days of reels and breakdown." In our day the inextricable mating of words with music has come not from Tin Pan Alley (as in Darrell's day) but from rock music in its many guises, including hip hop, perhaps the most doggedly prosaic pop music of all time. For more than half a century the most common music to which three generations of young people have been exposed is almost exclusively music with words, music dominated by lyrics. It envelops us in elevators, shopping malls, on iPods and web streams. The quality of the lyrics can be poetic or pathetic. No matter. The quality is less important than the fact that the words predominate. Words are the common coin of our daily existence; words are the stuff of shopping lists, invoices, memos, want ads, newspapers, e-mail messages, tweets, Harlequin romances....

Words in a song affix music to our conscious experience, our daily lives. Music, in its essential form, is nonverbal. Music without words, if it is inspired, bypasses experience that is rooted in the verbal and infiltrates a more mysterious human domain, a place that can be eloquent though wordless, expressive though uncanny, intelligent though rooted in feeling. So the generations who have heard only music with words must learn to discover the thrill of music *without* words, music that is not burdened by verbal messages but has a deeper reality.

Obviously, songs are music too. Music with words has its own distinguished place. Most of my chapters discuss songs.[1] Those songs range from the playful, such as "Drop Me Off in Harlem" (in chapter 1) to the dramatic, as in Billy Strayhorn's stunning "Lush Life" (in chapter 4). One chapter discusses songs that have Shakespeare's words set to Ellington's music (chapter 6). But mostly I discuss music without lyrics, and I hope listeners will discover that it carries the sensual thrill of an experience that goes deeper. It carries the sensation E.E. Cummings captured in his famous stanza –

> since feeling is first
> who pays any attention
> to the syntax of things
> will never wholly kiss you

Symphony-goers, opera buffs and modern dance aficionados – people who have had the curiosity to look beyond word-laden pop music – will need much less persuading to take this guided tour through Ellington's music.

Duke Ellington's music is rich and various. Chosen with care, it has the breadth of Shakespeare, but Ellington is four centuries closer

---

[1] Indeed, one of the themes I have traced through Ellington's music, though it is not included in this book, is his creative use of the voice; it is called (quoting R.D. Darrell) "The human voice is not disdained." For details, go to <torontodukeellingtonsociety.com> and click on "Archives."

to us than Shakespeare. Judiciously selected, it has the depth of Bach, but Ellington is two hundred years closer to us than Bach. Ellington's music is grounded in times and places and situations more or less familiar to us and yet sublimated so that we see them freshly, as if for the first time. His music has its roots in dance-band rhythms, blues harmonies and pop-song melodies but it is, at its best, so much more than any of those things. It literally rose out of them.

Listeners with preconceptions will lose those preconceptions as we make our straightforward trip through the themes in this book. Readers who come to it saying, "I don't like jazz," will be consoled to discover that Duke Ellington also didn't like jazz. Those who come to it saying, "I don't understand jazz," will have the inestimable advantage of hearing the music fresh and unfettered.

The themes in this book trace evolutions and configurations in the way Ellington used instruments (the plunger-muted trombone, the tenor saxophone, the piano), and the way he expressed emotion (sensuality, melancholy, comedy, tragedy), and the astonishing ways he used tones as evocations of the world around him (flora and fauna, cityscapes, a river flow, wise guys, nobility). The themes explore some of Ellington's "black and tan fantasies," as he put it in the title of his first great composition (1927). In tracing these themes in Ellington's music, I have sometimes encumbered the text with scholarly trappings (tables, figures, discographies, an occasional footnote) but they are easily ignored by those who don't want them or need them. Ellington's music speaks for itself, of course, and I hope it speaks all the louder by allowing each piece to shine in its place and time.

Duke Ellington's music deserves your attention. All it asks of you is an open mind and a willing spirit. With good planning and a little luck, it will make its way into the part of your mind where feeling is first.

Each chapter is intended to be self-contained. (Because of that, there is occasionally some repetition, but, I hope, not annoying.) Each chapter, including this one, ends with the list of References (with page references to direct quotations *in italics*) and the Playlist (the recorded works in order of their appearance in the chapter). The order of the chapters is not arbitrary. I start with "Ellington's Harlem" (chapter 1) because that theme more than any other follows the major peregrinations of Ellington's first 50 years. I want the music to be the focal point, not the biography. (There are many biographies, some better than others.[2]) Starting with themes that take in a span of time will provide enough biography, I think, to satisfy most music lovers whether they come to the book knowing something or nothing about Ellington's life. I end with "Three Steps into *The River*" because the strangely imperfect form of that masterpiece of Ellington's last years necessarily implicates the frenetic pace at which Ellington felt compelled to live those years. *The River* is often overlooked even by specialists (and, as I show in the chapter, by Ellington himself) at least partly because of the hurly-burly surrounding it. The hurly-burly makes a striking contrast to the grace and serenity of the music that came out of it.

Reading the chapters in sequence is not required or expected. From my experience in presenting these themes to audiences, the ones that audiences seem to find most entertaining are "Bardland: Shakespeare in Ellington's World" (chapter 6) and perhaps "Panther Patter: Duke Ellington at the Piano" (chapter 5). They appear near the middle of the book. According to the sequencing strategy people are taught in marketing classes, they should have been placed last and first, respectively. Readers should feel free to apply this sequencing strategy or any other.

In whatever sequence you choose, I know you will find a rich, rewarding, sensual experience. Edward Kennedy "Duke" Ellington (1899-1974) had the uncanny ability to convey the world around him in melody and harmony and rhythm. It is a world of color and grace and pulsations, at once novel and wry and yet strangely familiar.

Previous Iterations of the Chapters

All chapters have been refined, updated and corrected from earlier versions. All of them have been presented as talks and several of them have been published as articles. Texts and playlists for these talks (and others) can be found at <torontodukeellingtonsociety. com> and click on "Archives."

1 Ellington's Harlem "...the world's most glamorous atmosphere"
   2013 "Ellington's Harlem – the world's most glamorous atmosphere." Presentation to Duke Ellington Society, Chapter 40 (12 February)

2 Sweet and Pungent: Duke and the Plunger Mutes
   2014 "Sweet and pungent: Ellington's plunger trombones." Presentation to Duke Ellington Society, Chapter 40 (11 February)

3 The Fifth Reed: Ben Webster and the Tenor Ascent
   2016 "The Fifth Reed: Ben Webster and the Tenor Ascent." *IAJRC Journal* (Summer 2016): 50-60.
   2015 "Ben Webster Plays Ellington for 37 Years." Presentation to Duke Ellington Society, Chapter 40 (10 February)
   2011 "Not Ben, not Mex: Ellington's Other Tenors." Presentation to Duke Ellington Society Chapter 40 (8 February)

4 Lotus Eaters Unite! The Spectral Alliance of Johnny Hodges and Billy Strayhorn
   2007 "Lotus Eaters Unite! The Unholy Alliance of Billy Strayhorn and Johnny Hodges." Presentation to Duke Ellington Society, Chapter 40 (13 February)

5 Panther Patter: Duke Ellington at the Piano
   2018 "Duke Ellington at the piano." Presentation to Duke Ellington Society, Chapter 40 (13 February)
   2017 "Panther Patter: Duke Ellington at the Piano." *Blue Light* 24 (Summer 2017): 6-15.
   1999 "Panther Patter: Duke Ellington at the Piano." *Coda* 287 (September/October): 32-36.

---

2 John Edward Hasse's *Beyond Category: The Life and Genius of Duke Ellington* (Smithsonian 1993; Da Capo pbk 1995) is comprehensive and reliable. My personal favorites, the ones I go back to most often, are less comprehensive but more intimate. Richard O. Boyer's "The Hot Bach" originated as a two-part profile of Ellington in mid-career in *The New Yorker* in 1944; it is reprinted in *The Duke Ellington Reader*, ed. Mark, Tucker (Oxford University Press, 1995, pp. 214-245). Stuart Nicholson's *Reminiscing in Tempo: A Portrait of Duke Ellington* (London; Pen Books, 1999) ingeniously arranges quotations from dozens of Ellington's associates into an oral history of his life and times.

6 Bardland: Shakespeare in Ellington's World
2009 "Sweet Thunder: Duke Ellington Swings Shakespeare." Sound Unbound: Conference on Poetry and Sound. Jackman Centre for Humanities, University of Toronto (17 November)
2009 "The Duke and the Bard: Kindred Spirits 400 Years Apart." Friends of Linguistics at the University of Toronto. (FLAUT, 28 May)
2007 "Duke Ellington and William Shakespeare: Kindred Spirits 400 Years Apart." Academy for Lifelong Learning, University of Toronto. (21 March)
2005 "Bardland: Shakespeare in Ellington's world." *Coda* 319 (March/April 2005): 10-17, 38. Reprinted DEMS Bulletin 05/1 (April-July 2005): www. depanorama.net/dems/051f.htm (scroll down to 1-43)
2004 "Bardland: Shakespeare in Ellington's World." Presentation to Duke Ellington Society, Chapter 40 (10 February)

7 Afro-Eurasian Ellington
2009 "Afro-Eurasian Ellington." Presentation to Duke Ellington Society, Chapter 40 (10 February)

8 Duke Ellington's Parallel Universe: The Stockpile
2016 "Duke Ellington's stockpile: The posthumous heritage." *IAJRC Journal* (Spring 2016): 30-38.
2015 "Duke Ellington's Parallel Universe: the Stockpile." *Blue Light* 22 (Spring 2015): 7-16.
2006 "Duke Ellington's Parallel Universe: the Secret Stockpile." *Coda* 328 (July/Aug 2006): 13-21.
2006 "Duke Ellington's Parallel Universe: the Secret Stockpile." Presentation to Duke Ellington Society, Chapter 40 (14 February)

9 Three Steps into *The River*
2017 "Duke Ellington's Three Steps into *The River*." *IAJRC Journal* (Spring 2017): 9-17.
2016 "Duke Ellington's Three Trips Down *The River*." Presentation to Duke Ellington Society, Chapter 40 (9 February)

Reference (page numbers to direct quotations are shown *in italics*)
Darrell, R.D. 1932. "Black Beauty." *Disques* III: 152-161. Reprinted in *The Duke Ellington Reader*, ed. Mark Tucker. New York: Oxford University Press. 57-65. *p. 57*

ACKNOWLEDGEMENTS

My first debt is to the members of the Toronto Duke Ellington Society, Chapter 40, who have provided me with receptive audiences annually for over 20 years when I presented the themes in this book and many others to them. They were an irreplaceable sounding board, knowledgeable on many matters but capable of wonder at pieces they had heard before in different contexts and delighted with unfamiliar ones discovered among the unplumbed riches. With their help I became aware of the strengths of the themes and the weaknesses. The Society fulfills its mandate of keeping Duke Ellington's music current. Executive members take on their responsibilities with passion and commitment. Individual members have left an impression on this book. At the risk of inadvertently forgetting someone, I applaud Bruce Barton, Irene Barton, the late Jim Brackley, Tim Elliott, Gerry Lazare, Martin Loomer, Mel Manley, Chris McEvilly, the late Ernie Mills, Jim Northover, Stan Schiff, Alan Shiels, Judy Shiels, David Stimpson, and other fellow members.

John Hornsby has served the Toronto Duke Ellington Society in all executive positions but he has been especially indispensable in his capacity as archivist, keeping voluminous records for the Society and for jazz music generally. He has supplied me with sometimes unknown and otherwise unavailable recordings and interviews, news items, scrapbook clippings and other material. More than a data source, he has been consultant, fact checker and friend for many years.

Mark Miller is also an archivist but as an accidental by-product of his work as the most prolific of all jazz biographers. On this book, he was also a willing advisor on the 21st-century publishing process it went through. The book was prepared for publication by CanamBooks; I am grateful to Jordan Dessertine, my consultant, and Ted Sancton of Studio Melrose, for the interior design.

Ted O'Reilly, producer and host of Duke Ellington's 75th Birthday Concert on 29 April 1974, the radio broadcast which included the definitive (though as yet unissued) recording of *The River*, graciously made the studio-quality taping of that concert available to me. More generally, he is a fount of knowledge for the whole span of the music, and a tactful corrector of names, dates and places.

I have been blessed with astute editors throughout the long gestation of this book. The late Sjef Hoefsmit reprinted "Bardland" in the DEMS Bulletin and supplied resources and minutiae on several of my articles, as he did for countless other authors. Ian Bradley, editor of *Blue Light*, journal of DESUK, and Ian Thiele, editor of *IAJRC Journal*, gamely met formatting and other challenges in preparing some chapters for a wider audience. My association with *Coda* magazine (d. 2009) began even before the idea of this book came into being. My editors there – Bill Smith, John Norris, Stuart Broomer, Daryl Angier and Andrew Scott – gave me the kind of encouragement in their *very* different ways that, I hope, comes to fruition in this book.

I am grateful to the Toronto Duke Ellington Society for their generous grant toward the production costs of *Sweet Thunder*, in keeping with their mandate of preserving the musical legacy of Duke Ellington and his musical colleagues. The Duke Ellington Society of Sweden also provided aid in recognition of their commitment to that legacy. These two Duke Ellington Societies and their sister societies around the world are devoted to keeping Duke Ellington's music alive by providing occasions for public performances and fresh interpretations by contemporary musicians. They hope, as I do, that *Sweet Thunder* might contribute to that initiative.

ABBREVIATIONS

as	alto saxophone
b	bass, string bass
bjo	banjo
bs	baritone saxophone
CBC	Canadian Broadcasting Corporation
CBS	Columbia Broadcasting System
CJRT	Toronto radio station
cl	clarinet
DEMS	Duke Ellington Music Society
DESNY	Duke Ellington Society New York
DESUK	Duke Ellington Society United Kingdom
d	drums
fl	flute
flg	flugelhorn
g	guitar
IAJRC	International Association of Record Collectors
MiMM	*Music Is My Mistress* (1973 memoir by Ellington)
NAACP	National Association for the Advancement of Colored People
NYC	New York City
org	organ
ORTF	*Office de radiodiffusion-télévision française* (National broadcast corporation of France)
p	piano
tb	trombone
tp	trumpet
ts	tenor saxophone
voc	vocal

Chapter 1

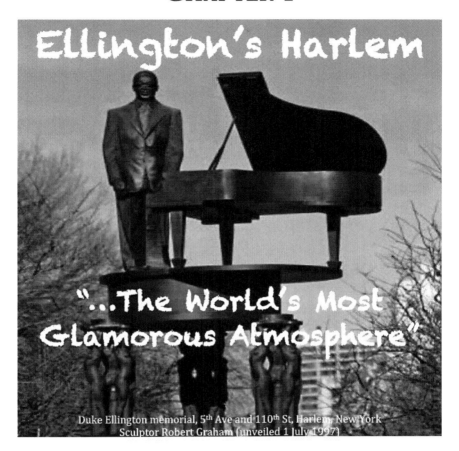

Duke Ellington memorial, 5th Ave and 110th St, Harlem, New York
Sculptor Robert Graham (unveiled 1 July 1997)

When Duke Ellington arrived in Harlem in 1923 he was simply dazzled. Not that he was a bumpkin by any means – he was 24, and back home in Washington, D.C. he was a hotshot well beyond his years, a contractor of dance bands for all occasions, often their nominal leader and piano player, the best-dressed man at any gathering, a pool shark, a "world champion drinker" (as he would later fancy himself, years after he had lost interest in the charms of alcohol), a husband and father at the age of 19 and redoubtable lady's man who cruised the nightspots in his Chandler town car, "going nowhere," he said, "as fast as we could" (Nicholson 18). But to Ellington, Harlem represented a higher league altogether. "It was New York that filled our imagination," he recalled 50 years later. "We were awed by the never-ending roll of great talents there.... Harlem, to our minds, did indeed have the world's most glamorous atmosphere. We had to go there" (*MiMM*, pp. 35-36).

Harlem, the upper Manhattan neighborhood whose stately brownstones were built by the Knickerbockers and other Dutch-American gentry in the 19th century, was, by the 1920s, almost exclusively African-American, and conspicuous among its citizens was an upstart class of cultural bellwethers including political theorists W.E.B. DuBois (1868-1963) and Marcus Garvey (1887-1940), Broadway orchestrator Will Vodery (1885-1951), composer and conductor William Grant Still (1895-1978), poets and novelists Zora Neale Hurston (1891-1960), Langston Hughes (1902-1967) and Countee Cullen (1903-1946), artists Aaron Douglas (1899-1979) and Romare Bearden (1911-1988), contralto Marian Anderson (1897-1993), hit songwriters Eubie Blake (1883-1983), Noble Sissle (1895-1975), Andy Razaf (1895-1973) and Henry Creamer (1879-1930), piano virtuoso and composer James P. Johnson (1894-1955), tap dancer and movie star Bill "Bojangles" Robinson (1878-1949), singer/dancer and entrepreneur Ada "Bricktop" Smith (1894-1984), world heavyweight boxing champion Jack Johnson (1878-1946), star athlete, actor and operatic baritone Paul Robeson (1898-1976), among others. It was a teeming meritocracy bringing amazing vigor to American culture two generations after Abraham Lincoln's Emancipation Proclamation.

Duke Ellington would quickly carve out his own space among these bellwethers. Like him, they all came from some other corner of the country and converged in Harlem. He reveled in their company. He could match their swagger from the start and, most important, he quickly learned to emulate their strivings.

"In Harlem," Ellington wrote in 1931, "we have what is practically our own city; we have our own newspapers and social services, and although not segregated, we have almost achieved our own civilization." Harlem was the focus of his orchestra's theme song from 1940 onward, its theme stated in Billy Strayhorn's opening couplet –

Hurry hurry hurry, take the 'A' train,
You'll find it's the quickest way to get to Harlem.

How to get to Harlem was the first of many lessons Strayhorn, the young provincial from Pittsburgh, learned from Ellington, directing him to the subway line that would take him to the place where he would hang his hat for the rest of his days. By the time Strayhorn wrote his one and only tribute to Harlem in 1940, Ellington had already written no fewer than 14 compositions with "Harlem" in the title. There would be 17 in all, culminating in 1951 with *A Tone Parallel to Harlem*, widely recognized as the pinnacle of Ellington's extended compositions. His Harlem songs leading up to that pinnacle run the gamut from trite to terrific, and because of that they make an entertaining and occasionally enlightening preamble to the majestic *Tone Parallel to Harlem*. (Ellington's "Harlem" songs with discographical details are listed at the end of the chapter with other compositions discussed here.)

"The Cotton Club, the Aristocrat of Harlem"

It took a couple of years for young Duke Ellington to gain street-corner recognition in the Harlem pantheon. He may have been a local hero in D.C., but when he arrived in New York he lacked the street-smarts to get him into the nightspots run by mobsters and the moxie to get past the 'we'll-call-you' indifference of bookers and agents. As always, his impeccable grooming and decorous manners helped him win the kind of friends who could get him in the front door of musical establishments. One of his early champions was Willie the Lion Smith, the piano wizard who welcomed him into his Harlem nightspot, the Capitol Palace, where he could rub shoulders with the established New York crowd. Another was the singer/dancer/vaudevillian Bricktop (nee Ada Beatrice Louise Virginia Smith), who touted Ellington's band, the Washingtonians, to the mobsters who ran Barron's Club, where she performed. The Broadway orchestrator Will Vodery agreed to answer Ellington's importune questions on composing and arranging, and found himself spending so many hours with the young man that he became, Ellington later said, his personal tutor.

Mainly, though, Ellington's good luck was self-made. Even Otto

Duke Ellington, the Aristocrat of Harlem, in 1929

Hardwick, who grew up with Ellington in Washington and played saxophone in his bands until 1946, was awed by him. "The amazing thing about him is that the language, the slant, everything, didn't rub off from someone else, and it wasn't a legacy either," he said. "He went inside himself to find it. He's an *only*, that's for sure" (reported by Balliett). Ellington's mother had told him, "Edward, you are blessed," and he never doubted her in this or anything else.

He soon took over the leadership of the Washingtonians, replacing banjo-player Elmer Snowden in 1924. Two years after that their records came out with his name attached, as "Duke Ellington and His Washingtonians," and a year after that, in 1927, it was simply "Duke Ellington and His Orchestra." It would take a few more years, until 1929, for the first records under the name "Duke Ellington and His *Famous* Orchestra."

The big break came in April 1927 when the Duke Ellington Orchestra won the job as house band of the Cotton Club. Entertainment reporter Archie Seale, writing in the *New York Age* in 1935, dubbed the club "the aristocrat of Harlem," and gave Duke Ellington full credit for making it noble. "When Duke Ellington wrote 'Black and Tan Fantasy,' little did he realize that this was the beginning of country-wide recognition for himself and the Cotton Club," Seale wrote. "The Cotton Club then began to entice the silk hats and ermines – the class people of Park Avenue and Riverside Drive."

Jungle Nights in Harlem
"Black and Tan Fantasy," Ellington's early breakout composition, was first recorded in April 1927, one month after "East St. Louis Toodle-Oo," its companion in harmonic sophistication. By then, Ellington had already tried his hand at exalting Harlem with the first of his 17 "Harlem" titles. He called that first piece "A Night in Harlem," and we can imagine from Ellington's descriptions of the raucous uptown nightlife at the time that a composition about a night in Harlem must have been raucous in its own right. Unfortunately we will never know. The record was never issued. It was recorded by "Duke Ellington and His Kentucky Club Orchestra" on the Vocalion label on 29 November 1926, and that same date produced the incipient brilliance of "East St. Louis Toodle-Oo" and "Birmingham Breakdown." Both of those

titles would soon be accorded more masterful recordings on other labels but even compared to these first takes, "A Night in Harlem" was sure to lack luster, no matter how good or bad it might have been. "East St. Louis Toodle-Oo" and "Birmingham Breakdown" were issued as the A and B sides of a Vocalion single, but "A Night in Harlem" and another tune by Ellington recorded on that day, "Who is She?" have never surfaced.

The disappearance of "A Night in Harlem" meant that the real inauguration of Ellington's Harlem tributes came few months later, after the orchestra established itself as the heartbeat of the uptown community at the Cotton Club. It was called "Harlem River Quiver," a jittery little number by Dorothy Fields and Jimmy McHugh, the writers of the Cotton Club revues for which Ellington's orchestra provided the onstage accompaniment. It was probably designed as a showcase for the kick-line of beautiful young dancers (which may account for its alternate title, "Brown Berries"). The composition is not Ellington's but the arrangement contains his imprints, with the simple melody stated and restated by Joe "Tricky Sam" Nanton's

The Cotton Club, "the aristocrat of Harlem," where Duke Ellington led the house band from April 1927 until 1932

trombone, muted but not plungered, a chorus on open trumpet by Louis Metcalf, a bass saxophone chorus by Otto Hardwick and the "giddyap" sound of drummer Sonny Greer plonking away on wood blocks.

A month later Ellington recorded "Harlem Twist," and it proved to be anticlimactic among the Harlem titles because it was merely a new name for "East St. Louis Toodle-Oo," which Ellington had recorded under its own title twice before, once for Vocalion and once for Brunswick, and would record yet a third time for Cameo a month later. "Harlem Twist" was recorded for Okeh, and the change of title may have been a subterfuge in case the record company was unhappy about buying used goods, though that did not seem to bother the other companies.

Ellington finally wrote a piece commensurate with his high regard for Harlem in March 1929, two years into his five-year tenure at the Cotton Club. He called it "Harlem Flat Blues," and it was his first attempt at evoking the rhythms and harmonies of the tenement life of Harlem. Ellington had spent his Washington youth in the spacious surroundings of houses and he seemed to be fascinated by the vertical swirl of humanity all around him in Harlem's crowded apartment blocks. He would evoke Harlem tenements more indelibly, as we shall see, in later compositions "Harlem Air Shaft" and *A Tone Parallel to Harlem*; the progression from "Harlem Flat Blues" in 1929 to the polytonal swing of "Harlem Air Shaft" in 1940 or the self-assured concert grandeur of the *Tone Parallel* in 1951 provide revealing landmarks for Ellington's musical evolution.

Harlem was a magnet not only for Ellington's Washingtonians but for thousands of African-Americans in the southern Diaspora. From 1899, when Ellington was born, until 1923, when he first set foot in Harlem, the population of this seven-square mile neighborhood increased by 150 percent, from 60,000 to 150,000 (Lawrence, 37). Overcrowding would prove to be ominous in a few more years but in these early years – before it reached critical mass – Ellington obviously found it enchanting.

"Harlem Flat Blues" is an ambitious arrangement that provides a frame for striking solos by Joe Nanton on plunger trombone and Barney Bigard on clarinet. The arranged sections at the opening and the closing spotlight the reeds for eight bars and then the brass with plungers for eight more making a parallel in the ensemble for the featured solos, with Nanton stepping out of the brass ensemble and Bigard out of the reed ensemble. The lithe arrangement and bright solos make the steady, unvarying clunk of the rhythm section all the clunkier, a minor blemish under the sparkling surface.

The rhythm is much more supple a year later on "Jungle Nights in Harlem," a jive number in which Ellington pulls out all the stops. Every player in the band except the bassist and drummer gets a turn in the spotlight, however brief, so that all the main attractions of the rapidly maturing Cotton Club orchestra are on display, including the piano player who leads with eight bars to establish the sprightly dance rhythm. The stars are Freddy Jenkins on muted trumpet, who exchanges flashy call-and-response with the brass section, and Barney Bigard on clarinet, in a repeated cascading run. With all the orchestral flash, it is easy to imagine the long-limbed Cotton Club chorus line stealing the show at the nightly performances. Ellington caps the piece with a theatrical diminuendo ending with a showy long chord sounding the climactic ending.

Cotton Club dancers backed by Duke Ellington and the Cotton Club Orchestra, with drummer Sonny Greer perched above Duke Ellington as he conducts from the piano

"More than the beginning"

Ellington's preoccupation with celebrating Harlem in musical terms may have come about by emulating a Harlem hero as much as from a heartfelt homely urge from the transplanted provincial. Although jazz tradition was still a work in progress when Ellington moved to New York, there were already a few crowning figures recognized far and wide as the fountainhead of a burgeoning musical movement. Top of the list, for Ellington and everyone else, was James P. Johnson, piano player extraordinaire, songwriter, and composer of rags, symphonies and operas. He was born in 1894, five years before Ellington, but he was precocious where Ellington was methodical. James P recorded a rag called "Carolina Shout," on piano rolls in February 1918 and in May 1921; the 1921 version, widely distributed by a company called QRS, became a pop sensation. Piano rolls were one of the technological marvels of the nascent recording industry, and they worked by revolving a prerecorded cylinder that depressed the keys on a specially equipped "player piano." Perforations in the revolving cylinder tripped the keys that made the music.

A generation of would-be piano players studied James P's technique as the piano roll ran its course. One of them was the 22-year-old Ellington. He scrupulously studied the fingering of "Carolina Shout" in his Washington home, slowing the cylinder and turning it back,

James P. Johnson, ca. 1928

until he gained enough mastery to dazzle his friends with its syncopated runs. A year later, he would meet another up-and-coming piano whiz, Thomas 'Fats' Waller, and discover that he had put himself through exactly the same routine in his Harlem parlor. "Carolina Shout" became the indispensable étude for modernistic piano students.

To Ellington and every other musician his age, James P. Johnson was the world's greatest piano player and the embodiment of the Harlem spirit. In Ellington's mind, those two attributes, spirited piano and spiritual Harlem, were inseparable. In his memoir, Ellington mixed them without blinking:

> "Harlem had its own rich, special folklore, totally unrelated to the South or anywhere else. It's gone now, but it was tremendous then. So there in that atmosphere I became one of the close disciples of the James P. Johnson style.... James, for me, was more than the beginning. He went right on up to the top.... [At late-night jams] it was me, or maybe Fats, who sat down to warm up the piano. After that, James took over. Then you got real invention – magic, sheer magic."

James Price Johnson was born in New Jersey. His parents nurtured his precocious musical talent by exposing him from an early age to symphony concerts, Broadway revues and church recitals across the river in New York City. By the time his family moved to New York in 1908, when James was 17, he was already acquainted with the musical venues and many of the musicians. His highly original piano style, a merger of ragtime and blues with an awareness of classical voicings and a gift for melody and ambidextrous countermelody, became known as "Harlem stride piano." It was the formative style of a coterie of hot piano virtuosi that included Luckey Roberts (given name Luckyeth), Willie the Lion Smith and of course Fats Waller and Duke Ellington, all of them striving to match Johnson's technical adroitness. (More on Ellington's piano styles from stride onward can be found in Chapter 5 "Panther Patter.")

The Harlem connection that Ellington finds inextricable from James P's music shows itself in a tradition that Ellington obviously emulated. Several of James P's compositions celebrate Harlem in their titles. The first one came in 1921, the same year as "Carolina Shout," when Johnson cut a piano roll with his composition "Harlem Strut." (See "James P. Johnson's Music Cited" at the end of this chapter.) It is, as its title suggests, a brash, prancing melody that seemingly invites listeners to strut along until Johnson introduces countermelodies that complicate the strut. At that point strutting becomes a dare, and only the most gifted strutters should take it up. Maybe this is what Ellington sees as part of the "rich, special folklore" of Harlem, this individualistic cockiness. James P treats us to a taste of the Harlem flair, by capturing its very strut.

Following "Harlem Strut" (1921), James P would turn out a long list of homages to Harlem in the 1920s and 1930s: "Harlem Choc'late Babies on Parade" (1926), "Go Harlem" (1930), "Harlem Hotcha" (1932), *Harlem Symphony*, with "April in Harlem" as its 2nd movement (1932), "Christmas Night in Harlem" (1934), "Harlem Number Man" (1938), and "Harlem Woogie" (1939). Like Ellington's Harlem songs (starting five years later and carrying on a few years longer), Johnson's Harlem songs range from minor rhythm numbers to more ambitious compositions.

Johnson's most ambitious homage is *Harlem Symphony*, a 20-minute orchestral work in four movements. The movements make a kind of kaleidoscopic view of Harlem in its heyday. "Subway Journey," the opening movement, attempts to capture the soundscape (according to Johnson's notes) as the subway train pulls out of "Penn Station," passes "110th St. – The Jewish Neighborhood," through "116th St. – Spanish Neighborhood" and "125th St. Shopping District," then cruises into "135th St. – Negro Neighborhood," down "7th Ave. Promenade" and returns to Penn. The second movement, "April in Harlem," is peaceful and rhapsodic, an interjection of the quiescence Johnson felt on a spring day walking down the avenues that were set apart from the bustle of shoppers and traffic. "Night Club," as the title suggests, rings in the excitement of the entertainment district, with dancing rhythms and whirling melodies. The fourth movement, "Baptist Mission," evokes a spiritual feel, with sonorous chords imitating a Sunday meeting place. Johnson's structure alternates the lively and swinging in the first and third movements with the reverent and stately, a simple, effective structure with mood swings from rhythmic intensity to quiet reverence.

Conceptually, Johnson's *Harlem Symphony* is the direct precursor of Ellington's Harlem masterpiece some twenty years later, the *Tone Parallel to Harlem*, which is his final composition in the tradition and its crowning glory (as we shall see). Structurally, the two could hardly be more different. But Johnson's conception, using musical intervals to evoke settings and situations from streetscapes and cabarets to churches is exactly the esthetic impulse that many listeners might be inclined to call "Ellingtonian." Like Ellington, Johnson's musical imagination in *Harlem Symphony* works functionally rather than formally, stimulated by the world outside, by Penn Station and flower gardens and children dressed in their Sunday best. Consciously or not, Ellington's memory of *Harlem Symphony* must have inspired him to realize, years later, the conceptual basis for *A Tone Parallel to Harlem*.

Johnson composed *Harlem Symphony* in 1932 but he had to wait until 1939 before finding an orchestra that would perform it. (It can now be heard with Johnson's other orchestral works in a 1992 performance by the Concordia Orchestra conducted by Marin Alsop, listed at the end of the chapter in the works cited.) The seven-year interval between composition and performance was the kind of artistic frustration that plagued Johnson's larger ambitions in his lifetime. In his last decades he saw his disciples eclipse him notwithstanding their continued lip service. It was partly a personality matter, as Johnson was a family man with a conservatory bent (though no conservatory). As his biographer Scott Brown observed, "He was not a uniquely colorful individual like many of his friends, such as Willie 'The Lion' Smith, Fats Waller, and Duke Ellington." And then Brown adds, wistfully, "In a tradition of nicknames, he had none." His pioneering role was resuscitated posthumously, and nowadays his recordings are readily available and a handful of his compositions are counted among the jazz standards. Most fittingly he is revered for making a leap forward in the development of American piano music. One small thread of James P's influence survives in Duke Ellington's perpetuation of his homages to Harlem.

Taxi Uptown

In the Harlem heyday, money flowed uptown and most of it came from the deep pockets of the midtown habitués of Harlem's playhouses and speakeasies, from "the silk hats and ermines," as Archie Seale put it, "the class people of Park Avenue and Riverside Drive." The Cotton Club attracted the glitterati – politicians, business magnates, racketeers and their molls, Broadway headliners, Hollywood stars, boxing champions, literary giants, all the fashionable people – all well-to-do and all necessarily white.

The financial benefits were obvious. Barry Ulanov, Ellington's first biographer, tells about an evening when the rum-runner Legs Diamond repeatedly requested "St. Louis Blues." When he finally departed in the small hours of the morning, he pressed "a thousand dollar note" into the obliging bandleader's hand. "Go buy yourself a cigar," he said, and when Ellington replied that he didn't know where he could find a cigar that expensive, Diamond gave him another thousand dollar bill for giving him "a good laugh." Occasionally there were artistic benefits. Ulanov recounts another night when Leopold Stokowski, conductor of the Philadelphia Orchestra, sat alone at a corner table. When Ellington approached, Stokowski quietly told him, "I have always wanted to meet you and hear you conduct your compositions." Ellington repaid the compliment by attending a concert at Carnegie Hall the next night as Stokowski's guest.

While it lasted, the nightly rush of midtown A-Listers was a social phenomenon, and Ellington, with his unerring instincts, wrote a piece that caught the derring-do of the slumming fur coats and white ties. "Drop Me Off in Harlem" is a fox trot with a sinuous lope as its rhythm. Ellington's arrangement of his composition leaves the infectious melody unadorned all through with smooth trombonist Lawrence Brown stating the A melody and trumpeter Arthur Whetsel the bridge. When Ellington jazzes up the piece in the second chorus he does it conservatively by having the orchestra reprise the melody with tasteful embellishments by Cootie Williams on muted trumpet and Barney Bigard on clarinet. With the instincts of a hit maker, Ellington never lets the pop-style melody recede.

"Drop Me Off in Harlem" practically cried out for a lyric, and it soon got one. Nick Kenny, popular columnist for the *New York Daily Mirror* and occasional contributor of light verse, was one of those midtown A-Listers who made nightly forays to the Cotton Club.

Legend has it that Kenny and Ellington shared a taxi and the song title came into being when Ellington announced his drop-off point to the driver (Lawrence 189). Kenny took Ellington's phrase as the starting point and finished the lyric with plain-spoken hyperbole:

> Drop me off in Harlem,
> Any place in Harlem,
> There's someone waiting there
> Who makes it seem like
> Heaven up in Harlem
>
> If Harlem moved to China
> I know of nothing finer
> Than to stow away on a plane some day
> And have them
> Drop me off in Harlem

The most abiding vocal version came years later when Ellington and Louis Armstrong spent two days recording together in an inevitable, if belated, meeting of musical patriarchs. Ellington finds himself among Armstrong's band members along with the ingenious addition of Barney Bigard, the only musician who had played a featured role in both men's bands.

Ellington, true to form, serves as much more than the piano player. All 17 of the tunes they recorded are his own compositions and the arrangements, though largely predictable, often show his touch. On "Drop Me Off in Harlem," Armstrong plays the melody on his trumpet with characteristic brilliance and then sings the lyric with seemingly impromptu variations undoubtedly scribbled down by Ellington. At the bridge, Armstrong sings –

> There's Duke Ellington up in Harlem
> He writes all his tunes in Harlem
> And ol' Satchmo is still swingin'
> Way up in Harlem

It is a performance that endures, predictably, on its charm rather

Duke Ellington and Louis Armstrong recorded together in 1961 in a small-band session released as The Great Summit (photo Arnold Meyers, Roulette Records)

than artistic merit, long after the social phenomenon that inspired it was forgotten and, truth to tell, by 1961, when Armstrong recorded these lines, Harlem was undergoing social turmoil that made it almost unimaginable.

Harlem Speaks in London

In 1933, the Ellington Orchestra undertook a tour of Europe that proved to be an eye-opener for Ellington and his musicians, and indeed a watershed for the global spread of American music. (The exported music was jazz in the first instance, but successively throughout the 20th century other blues-based genres were exported, including Delta blues, big-band swing, Broadway pop, country and western, bluegrass, and rock 'n' roll in all its iterations from rock to hip-hop.) Ellington performed for two weeks in London at the vast Palladium as part of a bill with a dozen other acts and also starred with the orchestra in a monumentally influential jazz concert at the Trocadero. From London, he shepherded the band to several provincial capitals all the way to Edinburgh, and then on to Paris. His impact in the boom years of the Jazz Age was colossal. "On this trip," Mercer Ellington wrote, "Ellington's composure, wit and innate dignity had 'commanded respect' – to use a phrase he always liked – in the two most sophisticated capitals of the world, London and Paris."

The attentive, knowledgeable crowds in England, including many record collectors and amateur discographers, a scholarly fan base all but unknown at home in the United States at the time, was partly the legacy of a well-connected enthusiast with the unlikely name Spike Hughes (née Patrick Cairns Hughes). In his early twenties, Hughes fancied himself a composer and musician but his enduring contribution came as a vociferous advocate of the upstart jazz emanating from the New World. In 1933, he had sailed to New York and persuaded high-caliber musicians including Coleman Hawkins and Benny Carter to record his compositions. The gap between sophisticated Europe and thrill-seeking America was not lost on him. Reporting on a performance by Ellington at the Cotton Club for England's *Melody Maker*, he opens by saying, "It has recently been on my mind that America does not honestly know or appreciate the real treasure she possesses in Duke Ellington." In July, when Ellington arrived in England, the whole band understood exactly what Hughes meant. "In Europe, we were royalty," Harry Carney said, "in Texas, we were back in the colored section." Hughes proceeded to show his appreciation with single-minded devotion. He attached himself to the entourage and wrote articles about almost every note they played.

One of Hughes's vibrant impressions of America on his visit was the spirit of Harlem. In a newspaper report extolling the arrival of the orchestra in London, he refers to Ellington as "the Aristocrat of Harlem" (two years before the American journalist dubbed the Cotton Club with that same phrase). Midtown Manhattan, weighed down by the Great Depression, came out second-best in Hughes's eyes. "Nowhere in Harlem," he wrote, "did I see the sullen, depression-conscious faces that haunt Broadway."

It was a view that Ellington undoubtedly found gratifying, and it inspired him to compose a piece called "Harlem Speaks" for his one and only record session of the 1933 tour. Ellington makes "Harlem Speaks" a kind of display piece in which six of the distinctive voices in the orchestra take turns strutting their Harlem stuff for a chorus. Ellington frames his star soloists in a kind of boogaloo rhythm, an infectious, sprightly tempo. Cootie Williams states the bright melody on his open trumpet and then steps aside for variations by Johnny Hodges on alto saxophone, Freddy Jenkins on muted trumpet, Harry Carney on baritone saxophone, Tricky Sam Nanton on tightly muted trombone, Lawrence Brown on melodious open trombone, and finally, with the band in full swing behind him, Nanton returns on the raucous plunger-muted trombone that had become the most eccentric signature of Ellington's orchestra (as discussed further in Chapter 2, "Sweet and Pungent"). In a little over three minutes, Ellington makes "Harlem Speaks" into a kaleidoscope of the band's range from melodic highs to rhythmic lows, conservatory intonation and muted rumblings.

Face to face with a brand-new audience, Ellington was obviously reveling in their raised eyebrows and delighted smiles. "Harlem Speaks" is a simple concept perfectly executed (in two complete takes) that showcases the lighter side of the Harlem Renaissance. Here is the aristocrat of Harlem strutting his stuff before the dazzled highbrows of the Old World.

Two Concertos for Cootie

Ellington's compositional genius has its roots, as everyone agrees, in his sensitivity to the individuality of his star soloists and in his ability to enfold their personal sounds in settings that give them collective integrity. It comes from a deep affinity between composer and musician, a kind of symbiosis inexplicable by science or psychology, comparable perhaps to the great impressionist painters, to Monet especially, who used the same palette as his contemporaries but somehow visualized idiosyncratic blends that made unique, individualist, inimitable paintscapes.

Sometimes it is possible to catch glimpses of it as it develops, this profound affinity between Ellington and his virtuoso characters. Best of all, I think, with Cootie Williams. He joined the band as an emergency replacement for Bubber Miley, who was Ellington's first star soloist on his plunger-muted trumpet and also the co-composer of Ellington's first great compositions. Miley appeared to be indispensable in the first flowering of the band, but he was alcoholic, a binge drinker who soon began missing more engagements than he showed up for (a story told in more detail in Chapter 2, "Sweet and

Pungent"). Ellington suffered Miley's erratic behavior with characteristic patience but finally, in 1929, was forced to replace him. He hired Cootie Williams (given name Charles, but never called that except by his mother, who died when he was eight), a Southerner who had made his way to New York with an obscure band in 1928, when he was 17, and impressed all the city slickers with his rich, confident trumpet sound in the manner of the nonpareil Louis Armstrong.

Williams was not hired because he could fill Miley's role but simply because he was the best young trumpet player available. Ellington recalled, "Cootie had been playing open horn all that time, and when the guys heard about the change he was making, he got kidded a lot.... Everybody told him he'd have to use the plunger and growl all night long. How was he going to make out, they all wanted to know. But he didn't pay them any mind. He caught onto a lot from Tricky Sam [Nanton, the band's plunger specialist on trombone], and before you knew it everyone was saying nobody could work with a plunger like Cootie" (Shapiro 1955).

As it happens, two of Ellington's Harlem tributes show off both sides of Cootie Williams. "The Boys from Harlem" provides a handsome workout for his dexterous open trumpet, and "Echoes of Harlem," one of Ellington's masterworks, an inevitable entry on anyone's list of his 20 or 30 great compositions, showcases his mastery of the plunger mute.

"The Boys from Harlem" was recorded by an octet called Cootie Williams and His Rug Cutters, one of a series of small-band spinoffs intended to keep an entrepreneurial foot in the more modest side of the record-buying market. It is a lively, jive-worthy confection (hence the "rug-cutters" designation in the band name, bobby-soxer slang for the acrobatic dancers whose moves required hard surfaces even if it meant taking scissors to the wall-to-wall rug). "The Boys from Harlem" is based on "Tiger Rag," one of the first jazz tunes ever recorded (1918, by the Original Dixieland Jazz Band) and for decades the epitome of 'jazzy' spunk. Jazzy it is, though Ellington's reinvention of it in "The Boys from Harlem" is considerably removed from the cornball antics of its first incarnation, as might be expected 20 years later. Williams plays the opening melody over the jump rhythm but the beauty of his open trumpet sound and the impeccable control of the lively melodic leaps are truly revealed in his extemporaneous last choruses with the rhythm section playing freely behind him. Williams's long turns at the opening and the closing are separated by a two-chorus interlude composed by Ellington for two deep-throated reeds playing rapidly (though limited in range) in unison. The horns are baritone saxophone (Harry Carney) and bass saxophone (Otto Hardwick). It is a strangely guttural combination, seldom, perhaps never, replicated, but Ellington gives it life. It is one more sign of Ellington's inventive spirit that he would insert such a challenging segment into an otherwise enjoyable, toe-tapping piece of froth. "The Boys from Harlem" is a plain-spoken demonstration of Cootie Williams's bold control on the open trumpet but it happens to include a gee-whiz duet in the middle like the jelly in a donut.

"Echoes of Harlem," the other Harlem title that Ellington composed for Cootie Williams, is one of the treasures among Ellington's compositions and arguably the pinnacle of Cootie Williams trumpet artistry, though there were many. In later renditions it was often introduced as "Concerto for Cootie," a more fitting title (though one that does not fit our Harlem theme). It was first recorded in 1936, a debut that was impressive but uncharacteristically tentative compared to many of its later recordings. Admittedly, tentative is a relative term when it comes to Williams; the original is lively but certainly his virtuosity and his ebullience, an inseparable trait of his virtuosity, are realized more fully in later performances. Happily, there are many to choose from because the number was a fixture in Ellington's repertoire from 1934 until 1941, when Williams left the band, and then it was revived with a difference (as we shall see) in 1963, when Williams returned, and played occasionally until 1967.

Of its many iterations, almost all of them striking, the masterwork (in my hearing) survives on a radio broadcast from a club deceptively called the Cotton Club. The original Cotton Club, the Harlem aristocrat where Ellington effectively honed his art, closed in 1936, but an enterprising group opened a club with the famous name downtown about a year later in the vicinity of the theater district. It proved to be a shadow of the old Cotton Club. This ersatz Cotton Club would close forever in 1940, faded and unloved, but in its first year it

Charles Melvin "Cootie" Williams (1910-1985) (photo Jan Persson)

was a boon for Ellington. In an attempt to recreate its old glory, the owners installed the Duke Ellington orchestra on its bandstand fairly regularly from May 1937 to May 1938.

This masterful version of Cootie's concerto "Echoes of Harlem," as a live recording from the 'other' Cotton Club, gets a small lift from the audience as they recognize Ellington's piano vamp that sets the stage for Williams's grand entry. Williams crafts the beautiful blues melody plaintively at first, carefully placing his notes in syncopation with the vamp. After the first chorus, Williams rests as the saxophone section takes over with a handsome interlude (actually an interpolation from a minor 1932 composition called "Blue Mood"). In the Cotton Club performance, Williams intones colorful phrases on top of the ensemble as if he is impatient to get on with his starring role. Then the piano vamp returns and sets the mood for Williams's climactic variation on the theme, this time raucous and wailing.

Williams is bold and assertive with or without the mute, attributes that befit his large stevedore frame, but beneath this gruff exterior he expresses a plaintive sorrow, a kind of melancholy that he seemingly cannot hide.

When a reporter asked Ellington about the sources of his inspiration, Ellington said, "You look at the same melancholy again and again from a different perspective" (Boyer 1944). "Echoes of Harlem" frames that melancholy in a rare kind of perfection, the more so because it is a seamless meeting of the minds of the composer and his soloist. It is a striking instance of the ineffable symbiosis between the composer and the eccentric virtuoso, one of the many in his band.

When Williams returned to the Ellington orchestra after an absence of 22 years, Ellington revived "Echoes of Harlem" with a striking difference. The arrangement was now sparser and the melancholy more emphatic. Williams's departure from Ellington's front line in November 1940, at the crest of the Swing Era, had made news in the entertainment pages of every major American newspaper; his return in late 1962, with the Swing Era a distant memory, may have received a column-inch in the jazz press but was otherwise unheralded. Like so many other Ellingtonians, Williams's successes in his years away from the band were few. Williams joined the popular Benny Goodman orchestra as featured soloist (with Ellington's blessing), and left after a year to front a dance band under his own name at the Savoy Ballroom. He became a trivia answer among devoted beboppers when he was listed as co-composer with Thelonious Monk on the great jazz standard "Round About Midnight," but everyone knows that it is Monk's composition and Williams gets his name on it, in the venerable swing-era tradition, simply because he is the bandleader on its first recording. As the dance-bands waned, Williams traveled with a quartet and in the end found himself playing with local rhythm sections in small cities when the opportunities arose.

On his return to Ellington after 22 years, Williams must have wondered why he had waited so long. To Ellington's audience, young and old, as to Ellington himself, Cootie Williams was still the star soloist he had been when he left. At an outstanding concert in Paris in 1963, soon after Williams's return, Ellington starts the piano vamp that signals the introduction to "Echoes of Harlem" and the audience erupts. The gap of 22 years seems to be wiped away in an instant. Williams had probably not experienced such adulation since he left. In this Paris rendition and in other revivals, Ellington extends the vamp allowing for the time it takes for the 52-year-old to wend his way from the back riser where the trumpet section sits to the microphone on the proscenium. Ellington plays the vamp markedly slower, perhaps giving the soloist time to re-acquaint himself with phrases he had not played for decades, but perhaps for a more salutary reason, to allow this mellow veteran to wring out the melancholy that was always there and which has now, in this incarnation, become the focus of Cootie's concerto. In this new arrangement, the saxophone interlude (the "Blue Mood" interpolation) has disappeared; most of the saxophone players who had played it in the 1930s were still present in the band and could no doubt have revived it, but its absence is deliberate. This "Echoes of Harlem" is all Cootie Williams, somewhat quieter though far from taciturn, somewhat less intense on the high notes though still hitting them, and somewhat pensive, maybe musing about the bygone days when it all seemed so easy. Both the composer and the soloist are different people now, decades after they first played these notes, but somehow they are still perfectly in sync. Here we have perfection on a different scale.

"Essence of Harlem in an Air Shaft"
Duke Ellington's orchestra attained one of its creative peaks in 1939 to 1942, with an aggregation of musicians who had been with him for a decade or more and, surprisingly, a couple of newcomers who injected new spirit into the band. The newcomers were bassist Jimmy Blanton, only 20 when he joined in late 1939 (and profiled more fully below in Chapter 5, "Panther Patter" on Ellington as pianist), and tenor saxophone player Ben Webster (the main subject of Chapter 3, "The Fifth Reed"). This version of the orchestra is often called "the Blanton-Webster band" in homage to their presence.

Ellington's romance with Harlem received its due in a composition he called "Harlem Air Shaft," a brilliant example of the seemingly reckless precision that characterized the Blanton-Webster band. "Harlem Air Shaft" gained further distinction because it was accorded a rhapsodic description of its content – or, more accurately, its composer's *intent* – in an interview with Richard O. Boyer for a two-part profile that appeared in the *New Yorker* in 1944, a profile that is, to this day, perhaps the most perceptive insight into the elusive Ellington. An "airshaft," also known architecturally as a ventilation shaft, is a small enclosed opening that runs the height of a tall building and allows air flow (ventilation) from otherwise enclosed spaces. Airshafts have fallen out of use with the invention of air conditioning and other technologies. They were a feature of many of Harlem's overcrowded tenements (though not, of course, of Ellington's expansive West Harlem penthouse). Asked by Boyer about his fanciful title, Ellington explained that he saw the airshafts as "one great big loudspeaker" in which all the vitality of the community could be captured. Here is Ellington's remarkable description:

> "So much goes on in a Harlem air shaft. You get the full essence of Harlem in an airshaft. You hear fights, you smell dinner, you hear people making love. You hear intimate gossip floating down. You hear the radio. An airshaft is one great big loudspeaker. You see your neighbor's laundry. You hear the janitor's dogs. The man upstairs' aerial falls down and breaks your window. You smell coffee. A wonderful smell, that smell. The airshaft has got every contrast. One guy is cooking dried fish and rice and another guy's got a great big turkey. Guy-with-fish's wife is a terrific cooker but the guy's wife with the turkey is doing a sad job. You hear people praying, fighting, snoring. Jitterbugs are jumping up and down always over you, never below you. That's the funny thing about jitterbugs. They're always above you."

"I tried to put all that in 'Harlem Air Shaft'," Ellington said.

It is a tall order, obviously, but the time was right. With Ellington's compositional genius at its peak and his orchestra stunningly sensitive to every nuance he set down, "Harlem Air Shaft" managed to slot a hundred impressions into its three-minute space.

Numerous commentators have noted that Ellington's composition actually invokes no noticeable sound parallels – no barking dogs, no "praying, fighting, snoring" humans or any other mundane sound. Does it matter? "Rather than ponder the meaning of the title," the annotator of the definitive Blanton-Webster compilation says, "it's much more enjoyable to be swept away by the sheer exuberance of the Ellington orchestra." The rhythm is an insistent thump in straightforward quarter time. The composition is built on an equally insistent riff, a phrase repeated over and over, serving as the underpinning for ensemble statements by the trumpets on one iteration and by the reeds on another. Adding yet another layer to the complex orchestration are soaring solo statements played over the riff by Tricky Sam Nanton on trombone, Cootie Williams on trumpet and Barney Bigard on clarinet. The master's touch, adding yet another fillip to the rich texture, comes through clearly when the tune's powerful forward motion – its swing – is stopped dead at the end of each 32-bar chorus while the reeds fill with an out-of-time two-bar phrase.

"Harlem Air Shaft" may have been constructed for acrobatic dancers in the first place – the "jitterbugs" Ellington mentions prominently at the end of his remarkable description. It is easy to imagine those jitterbugs catching their breath in the two-bar interludes before resuming their acrobatics.

But for Ellington's inspired title, air shafts might be completely forgotten. The composition occupies a special niche for its exuberant invocation of the Harlem that used to be, the bygone days of the old Cotton Club spirit and the all-night rent parties and the artistic flowering of the Harlem Renaissance – all of which were disappearing in the 1940s when Ellington wrote it. "Harlem Air Shaft" would have been a worthy consummation for Ellington's long obsession with the "glamorous atmosphere" he found on his arrival, a fitting finale for a moment of history that was rapidly slipping away. As Ellington himself said, recalling the "rich, special folklore," "It's gone now." Harlem was now suffering through hard times, and after "Harlem Air Shaft" Ellington seemed to give up on it as a musical stimulus. But, unpredictable as he always was, Ellington's consummation of his theme was yet to come, in a monumental final bow to the Harlem that, by then, existed only in his imagination.

A "Kaleidoscopic, Marvelously Descriptive Tour"

Eleven years after "Harlem Air Shaft," in 1951, Duke Ellington visited his Harlem theme one last time. He was 52, and the epic composition that resulted, called *A Tone Parallel to Harlem*, recaptures the vigor and joy and pride he felt when he arrived there in his twenties and thrived there in his thirties. *A Tone Parallel to Harlem* is (as his biographer Hasse puts it) "this kaleidoscopic, marvelously descriptive tour of Harlem." It is long, almost 14 minutes, and it was conceived as a symphony but it works at least as well in the big-band version. Paradoxically, this consummation, this celebration of "the world's most glamorous atmosphere," was conceived and performed at the very moment that Harlem was going through the most desolate and dispiriting time in its history.

Harlem was already overcrowded when the Great Depression hit in 1929. The influx of African-American immigrants from the dustbowl South and smaller northern cities multiplied, seeking work where there was almost none to be had. Housing, employment, education, sanitation, welfare and other services practically collapsed under the weight. Many people thought, with statistical backing, that the situation was caused by a lack of will among politicians because of the monochromatic blackness of the place. Poverty increased, the crime rate soared, and policing became brutal. Civil rights protests sometimes ended in riots and looting, with the spiraling of violent retaliation. By the 1940s the streets were inhospitable places for people who appeared affluent and dangerous for non-blacks, affluent or not. East Harlem became a ghetto. West Harlem, where the Ellingtons lived, may have felt the tensions less forcibly but even there they were inescapable. The tensions were felt vividly one night in 1954 when Billy Strayhorn was mugged after leaving his taxi late at night; his wallet was stolen after he was punched in the face, kicked in the ribs and shoved into a sandpile at a renovation site (Hajdu, p.149-50).

None of these tensions found their way into the *Tone Parallel*. It was an artistic decision on Ellington's part, not naïveté. Ellington was well aware of what was happening. He singled out "civil rights" protesters, among others, in his description of the urban landscape he was seeking to capture, and the first performance of the work, a gala one at the Metropolitan Opera House in January 1951, was a benefit concert for NAACP (National Association for the Advancement of Colored People, Hasse 297). For all that, Ellington was not writing protest music. The Harlem he captured in his music was the one imprinted in his mind, not the one then smoldering on the streets below. All these years later, with Harlem's equilibrium restored, that con-

Harlem street scene in the 1930s (courtesy Ray Carman, DESNY)

ception is fully justified. The music, as Ellington knew, would outlive the turmoil.

Ellington seems to have gone to some lengths to invest this composition with romantic trappings that removed it further from the momentary distress. In *Music Is My Mistress* (p. 189), he talks about composing it on the Île de France, the transatlantic luxury liner, as he was returning with the rest of the orchestra from a European tour. It was commissioned, he says, as "a concerto grosso for our band and the symphony" by the NBC Symphony when Arturo Toscanini was its conductor. Ellington used the occasion of its 1951 premiere at the NAACP benefit to introduce *A Tone Parallel to Harlem* with lengthy remarks about the Harlem he was interested in portraying musically (reprinted in his memoir, published in 1973, when Harlem was still seething). He wrote, in part,

> "We would now like to take you on a tour of this place called Harlem. It has always had more churches than cabarets. It is Sunday morning. We are strolling from 110th Street up Seventh Avenue, heading north through the Spanish and West Indian neighborhood towards the

125th Street business area. Everybody is nicely dressed, and on their way to or from church. Everybody is in a friendly mood. Greetings are polite and pleasant, and on the opposite side of the street, standing under a street lamp, is a real hip chick. She, too, is in a friendly mood. You may hear a parade go by, or a funeral, or you may recognize the passage of those who are making Civil Rights demands."

Somehow, he manages to get it all in – the decorum of Sunday churchgoers, the dash of Spanish rhythm, the glimpse of the earthy hipster, the passing funeral....

A Tone Parallel to Harlem is built around two short motifs. The first is a two-note phrase stated at the opening on trumpet (by Ray Nance) that seems to sound out the word "Harlem."

Har - lem

The second motif, a kind of hymn, is introduced later by a solo trombone, and recurs with different voicings, most notably by a clarinet trio grounded magisterially by Carney's bass clarinet. The climax melds the two motifs over an insistent rhythmic crescendo leaving the impression of chest-beating pride and confidence.

Ellington brings in his two motifs repeatedly but they are always nuanced and fresh. (In the second studio recording by the band in 1951, generally reckoned the most inspired among many wonderful performances, I counted 16 repetitions of the "Harlem" motif in the first half, about seven minutes, but the count is hardly definitive when its guises are so bountiful.) The contexts in which the motifs recur are so rich in texture and varied in instrumentation that there is no sense in which they seem excessive. On the contrary, they unify the composition perfectly, providing the listener with melodic touchstones as Ellington's longer works did not always succeed in doing. *A Tone Parallel to Harlem* stands as his greatest achievement in extended composition.

Ellington performed *A Tone Parallel to Harlem* frequently with the band for the rest of his days, often springing it on the musicians unexpectedly at concerts whenever he received a request and watching them scramble to unearth their complex scores in the playbook. He recorded the band version in studios five times, including what might be considered the definitive version in December 1951 and a lively, seemingly more spontaneous version in 1963 (both listed in the discography). He also recorded it twice with symphony orchestras (also in the discography). Since his death, it has been performed by symphony orchestras all over the world <musicsalesclassical.com/composer/work/2311/27667>.

Ars longa...

Ellington's sensitivity to the plight that had overtaken his glamorous Harlem in the decades since his arrival in 1923 comes clear in a revealing incident at the time (also due to John Edward Hasse, 297). Ellington presented a signed score of *A Tone Parallel to Harlem* to Harry S. Truman, President of the United States, in 1950, with a note about the upcoming NAACP benefit concert. In the note Ellington expressed the hope that the proceeds from the concert "will be used to help fight for your civil rights program – to stamp out segregation, discrimination, bigotry and a variety of other intolerances in our American society." Ellington asked if Margaret Truman, the President's daughter and a classical singer, might serve as chairwoman of the event. He never received a reply. The note, discovered by Hasse in the Truman archives, shows that "somebody wrote an emphatic 'No!' in inch-high letters, underlined twice."

By the time Ellington composed this consummate Harlem tone parallel, the glory days of Harlem had been overwhelmed by social issues of many kinds. Harlem's half-century as the nurturing ground of African-American – nay, of distinctively American – music, dance, literature, entertainment, athletics, civil rights and political debate was buried in its abrasive present. Historically, the abrasive present seemed to obliterate recognition of the creative pinnacle that preceded it. Not for Duke Ellington's contemporaries, of course, the generation that witnessed its glory days and reveled in it. For them, Harlem's nurturing role was simply a matter of fact. One of those contemporaries, George F. Frazier, reflecting in 1933 on Ellington's impact on his European audiences, said, "The British and the French publics realized that here was American music undiluted, music unblemished by foreign tinctures, music that had come many generations past from Africa to New Orleans and Harlem." Simplistic though Frazier's genealogy may be in the light of what we now know, it gives due prominence to Harlem alongside New Orleans. Harlem, after all, was the place where New Orleans rhythms and rudiments were invested with the harmonic depth and formal extensions that turned them into a music that could be admired internationally, and ultimately globally. All jazz histories, the best and the worst, maintain New Orleans' primacy but Harlem has been largely undervalued for its role in its upward mobility. Harlem today, decades after reconciling the most pressing social and political issues that briefly made it a forbidding place, still awaits the historical restitution. For a moment in time, it really was, as one of its most gifted habitués put it, "the world's most glamorous atmosphere."

References (page numbers to direct quotations are shown *in italics*)
Balliett, Whitney. 1988. "Selfishness is essential." Originally *New Yorker*. In *Collected Works: A Journal of Jazz 1954-2001*. 2002. New York: St. Martin's Griffin. 521-525. *p. 522*.
Boyer, Richard O. 1944. "The Hot Bach." *The New Yorker*. 24 June -1, 8 July. Reprinted in *The Duke Ellington Reader*, ed. Mark Tucker. New York and Oxford: Oxford University Press, 1995. 214-245. *p. 234, p. 235*
Brown, Scott E. 1986. *James P. Johnson: A Case of Mistaken Identity*. Metuchen, New Jersey: The Scarecrow Press. *p. 7*
Ellington, Duke. 1973. *Music is My Mistress*. New York: Doubleday. *pp. 35-36, pp. 94-95, p. 189*
Ellington, Duke. 1931. "The Duke Steps Out." Reprinted in *The Duke Ellington Reader*, ed. Mark Tucker. New York and Oxford: Oxford University Press, 1995. *p. 49*
Ellington, Mercer, with Stanley Dance. 1978. *Duke Ellington in Person: An Intimate Memoir*. Boston: Houghton Mifflin. *pp. 60-61*
Feather, Leonard. 1977. Liner note to *The Duke Ellington Carnegie Hall Concerts January 1943*. Prestige 2CD.
Frazier, George F., Jr. 1933. "Music and Radio" (column). *Playhouse Magazine*. Cited by Harvey G. Cohen (2010) *Duke Ellington's America*. University of Chicago Press. *pp. 126-27*.

Hajdu, David. 1996. *Lush Life: A Biography of Billy Strayhorn*. New York: Farrar Straus Giroux. *pp. 149-150.*

Hasse, John Edward. 1993. *Beyond Category: The Life and Genius of Duke Ellington.* Washington: Smithsonian; New York: Da Capo pbk 1995. *p. 323, p. 297.*

Hughes, Spike. 1933. "The Duke – In Person." *Melody Maker* (May). Excerpt in *The Duke Ellington Reader*, ed. Mark Tucker. New York and Oxford: Oxford University Press, 1995. *p. 69*

Hughes, Spike. 1933. "Meet the Duke!" *Daily Herald* (13 June). Reprinted in *The Duke Ellington Reader*, ed. Mark Tucker. New York and Oxford: Oxford University Press, 1995. *p. 72, p. 75*

Lawrence, A.H. 2001. *Duke Ellington and His World*. New York: Routledge. *p. 37, p. 189*

Nicholson, Stuart. 1999. *A Portrait of Duke Ellington: Reminiscing in Tempo*. London: Pen Books. *p. 18.*

Seale, Archie. 1935. "The Cotton Club, the Aristocrat of Harlem." *New York Age*. n.p.

Shapiro, Nat, and Nat Hentoff, eds. 1955. *Hear Me Talkin' to Ya: The Story of Jazz as Told by the Men Who Made It*. New York: Rinehart. *p. 215*

Ulanov, Barry. 1946. *Duke Ellington*. New York: Creative Age Press. *p. 118, pp. 188-89*

Playlist

James P. Johnson's Music Cited

1921 "Harlem Strut" 2:59 and "Carolina Shout" 3:32 May 1921. QRS piano rolls, New York City. Biograph CD (1988).

1932 *Harlem Symphony*. "Subway Journey" 3:55, "April in Harlem" TIME, "Night Club" TIME, "Baptist Mission" TIME. February 1992, New York City. *James P. Johnson, Orchestral Works*. The Concordia Orchestra conducted by Marin Alsop. Nimbus CD (2011).

Ellington's "Harlem" Songs

original recordings 1926-1951 plus later recordings cited in the text. Duke Ellington composer unless otherwise noted

1926 "A Night in Harlem" 29 November 1926 (Vocalion unissued)
Duke Ellington and His Kentucky Club Orchestra
Bubber Miley, Louis Metcalf tp; Joe Nanton tb; unknown cl;
Otto Hardwick ss, as, bs; unknown cl, as, bs; Duke Ellington p,
Fred Guy bjo, Mack Shaw tuba, Sonny Greer d

1927 "Harlem River Quiver" 2:41 (aka "Brown Berries," comp Dorothy Fields and Jimmy McHugh) 19 December 1927

Bubber Miley, Louis Metcalf tp; Joe Nanton tb; Rudy Jackson cl;
Otto Hardwick ss, as, bass sax; Harry Carney cl, as, bs;
Duke Ellington p, Fred Guy bjo, Wellman Braud b, Sonny Greer d
Solos: Nanton, Hardwick bass sax, Metcalf

1928 "Harlem Twist" 3:15 (= "East St. Louis Toodle-Oo") 18 Jan 1928
Okeh Records. Same as "Harlem River Quiver" except Barney Bigard cl replaces Rudy Jackson.

1929 "Harlemania" (comp Jimmy McHugh and Dorothy Fields) 18 February 1929 Arthur Whetsel, Freddy Jenkins tp; Joe Nanton tb; Barney Bigard cl, Johnny Hodges, Harry Carney reeds; DE p, Fred Guy bj, Wellman Braud b, Sonny Greer d [Note: This record is often said to mark the debut of Cootie Williams as Bubber Miley's replacement, but he is not present.]

1929 "Harlem Flat Blues" 3:07 1 March 1929 *Early Ellington* Decca GRP
Same as "Harlemania" but ADD Cootie Williams, tp.
Solos: Nanton, Bigard

1930 "Jungle Nights in Harlem" 4 June 1930
Cootie Williams, Arthur Whetsel, Freddy Jenkins tp; Joe Nanton, Juan Tizol tb; Barney Bigard cl, Johnny Hodges, Harry Carney reeds; DE p, Fred Guy bj, Wellman Braud b, Sonny Greer d
Solos: Ellington, Jenkins, Bigard

1932 "Blue Harlem" 16 May 1932 Cootie Williams, Arthur Whetsol, Freddy Jenkins tp; Joe Nanton, Juan Tizol, Lawrence Brown tb; Barney Bigard cl, Johnny Hodges, Otto Hardwick, Harry Carney reeds; DE p; Fred Guy g; Wellman Braud b; Sonny Greer d.

1932 "Harlem Romance" (usually "Clouds in My Heart") 19 September 1932. Same as "Blue Harlem."

1933 "Drop Me Off in Harlem" 3:06 17 February 1933, revived 1957, 1958, 1961, 1965, 1967. *Original Masters 1932-1939*
Arthur Whetsel, Cootie Williams, Freddy Jenkins tp; Joe Nanton, Juan Tizol, Lawrence Brown tb; Barney Bigard cl, Johnny Hodges, Otto Hardwick, Harry Carney reeds; DE p; Fred Guy g; Wellman Braud b; Sonny Greer d.
Solos: Brown, Whetsel, Williams, Bigard

"Drop Me Off in Harlem" 3:50 (Ellington/Nick Kenny) 3 or 4 April 1961 *Louis Armstrong & Duke Ellington* (Roulette) NYC.
Louis Armstrong tp, Trummy Young tb, Barney Bigard cl, DE piano, Mort Herbert b, Danny Barcelona d.

1933 "Harlem Speaks" (take 1) 3:14 13 July 1933. Chenil Galleries, London. *The British Connexion 1933-1940* (Jazz Unlimited 1999) Arthur Whetsol, Cootie Williams, Freddy Jenkins tp; Joe Nanton, Juan Tizol, Lawrence Brown tb; Barney Bigard cl, Johnny Hodges, Otto Hardwick, Harry Carney reeds; DE p; Fred Guy g; Wellman Braud b; Sonny Greer d.
Solos: Cootie, Hodges, Freddy Jenkins, Carney, Nanton (muted), Brown (open), Nanton again (plunger-muted)

1934 "Harlem Rhythm" (from *Symphony in Black*, aka "Merry Go Round") December 1934

1936 "Echoes of Harlem" 3:00 (aka "Cootie's Concerto") 27 February 1936. *The Chronological Duke Ellington 1935-1936*. Classics 659. Arthur Whetsol, Cootie Williams, Rex Stewart tp; Tricky Sam Nanton, Lawrence Brown, Juan Tizol tb; Barney Bigard cl, Johnny Hodges, ss, as; Harry Carney cl, bs; DE p; Fred Guy g; Hayes Alvis b; Sonny Greer d

"Echoes of Harlem" 4:40 broadcast 15 May 1938 *DE at the Cotton Club*. Storyville [2010]. Wallace Jones, Cootie Williams tp; Rex Stewart cor; Joe Nanton, Juan Tizol, Lawrence Brown tb; Barney Bigard, Johnny Hodges, Otto Hardwick, Harry Carney reeds; Ellington p; Fred Guy g; Billy Taylor b; Sonny Greer d.

"Echoes of Harlem" (3:32) 23 February 1963, Olympia Theatre, Paris. *The Great Paris Concert*. 2 CD. Atlantic [1989].
Ray Burrowes, Ray Nance, Cat Anderson, Cootie Williams tp; Lawrence Brown, Buster Cooper, Chuck Connors tb; Johnny Hodges as; Russell Procope cl, as; Jimmy Hamilton cl; Paul Gonsalves ts; Harry Carney bs; DE p; Ernie Shepard b; Sam Woodyard d.

1937 "Harmony in Harlem" 3:12 (Ellington/Hodges/Mills) 20 September 1937. *Original Masters 1932-1939* Same as "Echoes of Harlem" (1936) except Freddie Jenkins replaces Wallace Jones.

"Harmony in Harlem" 3:18 6 January 1965, New Jersey. Johnny Hodges and Wild Bill Davis *Compact Jazz* (Verve) Lawrence Brown tb, Hodges as, Davis org, Bob Cranshaw b, Grady Tate d

1938 "The Boys from Harlem" 2:16 (aka "Cat Rag") 21 December 1938 *Complete 1936-1940... Small Group Sessions* (Mosaic). Cootie Williams and His Rug Cutters
Cootie Williams tp, Barney Bigard cl, Johnny Hodges as, Otto Hardwick bass sax, Harry Carney bs, Duke Ellington p, Billy Taylor b, Sonny Greer d [based on *Tiger Rag*]

Solos: Williams, Carney/Hardwick, Williams

1940 "Harlem Air Shaft" 2:57 (orig "Rumpus in Richmond" 1930) 22 July 1940, frequent to 1967. *The Blanton-Webster Band* (RCA). Wallace Jones, Cootie Williams tp; Rex Stewart cor; Joe Nanton, Juan Tizol, Lawrence Brown tb; Barney Bigard, Johnny Hodges, Ben Webster, Otto Hardwick, Harry Carney reeds; Ellington p; Fred Guy g; Jimmy Blanton b; Sonny Greer d.
Solos: Nanton, Williams, Bigard, Williams, Bigard

1943 "Blue Belles of Harlem" 6:03 23 January 1943 Carnegie Hall, New York. *Carnegie Hall Concerts January 1943* [2CD 1977]. Rex Stewart, Wallace Jones, Harold Baker, Ray Nance tp; Joe Nanton, Lawrence Brown, Juan Tizol tb; Johnny Hodges as; Chauncey Haughton cl, ts; Otto Hardwick as; Ben Webster ts; Harry Carney cl, bs; DE p; Fred Guy g; Junior Raglin b; Sonny Greer d.
Composed 1938, and never recorded in the studio by Ellington, though several concert performances survive. Paul Whiteman commissioned Ellington and five other composers (Ferde Grofé, Raymond Scott, Bert Shefter and Walter Gross) to write pieces that use bell tones (according to Leonard Feather, liner note).

1951 *A Tone Parallel to Harlem* 13:47 (orig *Harlem Suite*, title often shortened as *Harlem*) 7 December 1951, *Ellington Uptown* (Columbia).
Francis Williams, Shorty Baker, Willie Cook, Clark Terry, Ray Nance tp; Quentin Jackson, Britt Woodman, Juan Tizol tb; Willie Smith as; Russell Procope cl, as; Jimmy Hamilton cl, ts; Paul Gonsalves ts; Harry Carney bs, bcl; Duke Ellington p, Wendell Marshall b, Louie Bellson d.
Performed frequently to 1972; studio recordings with orchestra 1951 twice, 1952, 1955, 1963; with symphonies 1963 Paris Symphony with Ellington orchestra, 1970 Cincinnati Symphony.

Chapter 2

Sweet and Pungent
Duke and the Plunger Mutes

angel with trombone, detail Cristoforo Roncalli, Sant'Andrea della Valle, Rome, ca. 1590

Billy Strayhorn's composition "Sweet and Pungent" appears on a 1959 recording called *Blues in Orbit* (Columbia), a record that is entirely made up of earthy, intense, often rollicking blues tunes. Blues structure is the oldest jazz form but the blues on *Blues in Orbit* are in the decidedly modern style that Duke Ellington evolved after much soul-searching at the start of that decade. The mood is urbane, the harmonies are sophisticated, the solos are boppish, and the rhythms are supple. Those revisions hoisted Ellington out of his doldrums in the waning days of the Swing Era and resulted in the spectacular rebirth of his music at the 1956 Newport Jazz Festival. "Sweet and Pungent" is a nuanced blues though definitely earthy. Its earthiness is fixed by the leading solo voice. That voice is trombone played in a style that might have seemed to be a throwback in this modern context. It is played by Booty Wood, a new man in the section who had just replaced the redoubtable Quentin Jackson. Wood is the only soloist on the four-minute composition. He is thus the latest link in a venerable Ellington tradition, for Wood plays his long, rich, dazzling trombone solo through the homely old-time filter called a plunger mute.

How Sweet? How Pungent?

The plunger mute is literally a toilet plunger, the bell-shaped rubber fixture that one affixes to a short broomstick and plunges into the mire of a plugged-up toilet. Duke Ellington made capital use of the plunger's musical applications in his compositions, and in his wry way invented a more refined genealogy for it. On a television performance that featured a trumpet solo with a plunger mute, Ellington's host, Dick Cavett, highly amused, asked, "Wasn't that a toilet plunger he used?" Ellington coyly replied, "Well, aaah, yes, it was a toilet plunger but, you see, it was made for the trumpet first and since then they've found other uses for it."[1]

The plungers used as mutes by trombone players and trumpet players may never (we trust) have been pressed into domestic use but they are exactly the same objects, the same humble tools, usually dull red, that can be found at any hardware store. As Ellington appreciated more than any other composer, the musical application of the toilet plunger came into being as a flash of genius by some homespun hero whose name is now lost. It was a sound that Ellington appreciated, even reveled in. Many of the greatest practitioners of plunger-muted brass instruments plied their trade in Ellington's orchestra.

"Sweet and Pungent," Ellington's oxymoronic title for Booty Wood's spectacular debut with his orchestra, suits the composition perfectly. The sound of the plunger-muted trombone, in an inspired performance like Booty Wood's, is *sweet* in a plaintive, highly vocalized

---

[1] Ellington appeared on The Dick Cavett Show on 17 February 1971. Cavett's interview with Ellington was interspersed with musical interludes which featured Ellington and trumpeter Cootie Williams with the house band. The dialogue about the plunger mute was reported in the *Bulletin* of the Ellington Society of Sweden (April 2018).

An early album cover (X series, 1954) graphically emphasizes
the role of the plunger mute in Duke Ellington's music

way, like the voice of wise old sage at peace with the world, and it is at the same time *pungent*, slightly blurty, verging on rudeness when it gets enthused, and always guileful, always on the verge of saying something witty, at times even hilarious. An old-fashioned word for the sound of a plunger-muted instrument is "gutbucket." One of Ellington's primary exponents of the plunger mute in his orchestra, the trumpeter Bubber Miley, said, "If it ain't got swing, it ain't worth playin'; if it ain't got gutbucket, it ain't worth doin'" (Shapiro 1955). That sentiment may overstate the case somewhat but it works perfectly as the theme of this chapter.

In expert hands like Booty Wood's and all the other plunger specialists who came before and after him in Ellington's orchestra, the plunger mute lends an eerily vocal, decidedly human sound to the brass instrument. That is no accident. It does so by simulating the human vocal apparatus. Speech sounds are made by modulating the flow of air from the lungs through the resonating vocal cords (the 'Adam's apple') and then shape-shifting the oral cavity with tongue, teeth and lips. The brass instrument, an extension of the lungs, carries the flow of air, the mouthpiece supplies the resonating sound wave like ersatz vocal cords and the plunger, manipulated around the bell of the horn, simulates the modulating oral cavity. Technically, the plunger can simulate only vowel sounds, not consonants. Vowels depend on opening the oral area wide (for "ah," which is why doctors ask you to say "ah" when they peer into your throat) or constricting it (for "ee" or "oo"). The "wa" sound that we use in describing the "wa-wa" effect of the plunger mute is made by starting the plunger tight to the bell and gradually opening it so that it goes from closed "oo" to open "ah"; the transition from "oo" to "ah" produces the semi-vowel "w" ("oowaaa" in speech as in tromboning). Most musicians insert a straight mute in their horns in order to increase the turbulence of the airstream (and not incidentally to compel themselves to blow harder). The plunger's crude replication of speech is at once the source of its novelty and the source of its charm.

Playing a trombone is hard because it requires moving a slide into intervals that make scalar pitches (notes), and playing it with a plunger mute is harder because it requires manipulating the plunger on the bell of the horn with the hand that is not moving the slide (usually the left). Art Baron, the last of Ellington's plunger-mute specialists, said, "It's a whole emotional thing. You really have to want to speak through the horn.... If you listen to the great plunger trombone masters, it's full of conversation. It's a talking instrument."

"A dark, intense music" from the wah-wah mute

Ellington fell under the spell of the plunger mute around 1923 when he was exposed to the brash brass sounds of the New York city-slickers soon after he arrived in that city. True to form he immediately seized on its potential for adding colorful highlights to his music. Never mind its vaudeville history of comic noise-making. Never mind its limitations in range and dynamics. Those were challenges that Ellington relished. "Here is a guy who uses a mute and he can only get seven good notes out of it," he once said (according to Stanley Dance). "The problem [for the composer] is to use those seven." Plunger-muted trombones and trumpets became a trademark of Ellington's music for all his days. One of Ellington's first American boosters, the journalist Otis Ferguson, explained it this way: "he got music out of the use of a wah-wah mute which had formerly been used for laughs, a dark intense music.... He introduced these effects into the entire brass and reed sections to achieve a whole style."

"Sweet and pungent" describes Booty Wood's solo perfectly. It describes equally perfectly all of Booty Wood's predecessors and successors in the Ellington orchestra who played plunger-muted trombone solos. Those solos form a continuous tradition, a "whole style" as Otis Ferguson put it. Its first blossoming in Ellington's music came in 1926, not coincidentally at the very moment that he emerged as a world-class composer. It suited his esthetic perfectly. "The band is a combination of personalities, tonal devices," he explained in an interview with Jack Cullen in 1962. "As a result of certain musicians applied to certain instruments, you get a definite tonal character." Few tonal devices contributed more to Ellington's distinctive sonic character than plunger-muted brass.

Ironically, the showy 1959 plunger masterpiece "Sweet and Pungent" came into being at a moment in jazz history when the top trombonists of the day – J.J. Johnson, Slide Hampton, Eddie Bert, Frank Rosolino, Melba Liston, Kai Winding – would rather split their lip than be caught with a plunger in their trombone cases. It was a period of jazz history that lasted about 25 years, from 1945 to around 1970, when the plunger had the same cornball reputation among jazz musicians as banjo rhythms and cowbell accents. "Pungent" was putting it mildly. To the bebop and post-bop modernists, it reeked of old mold.

If Duke Ellington noticed how hopelessly passé the plunger was in 1959 when he recorded "Sweet and Pungent," he never let on. For him, the plunger trombone was no fad or fancy. It was one if his signature sounds from start to finish. His instinct was infallible. Unlike banjos and cowbells, plunger-muted brass sounds outlasted their bebop stigma. Now, once again, the best brass players in jazz carry the humble toilet plunger in their cases.

Charlie Irvis, shadowy pioneer

Ellington had moved to New York in 1923 as the piano player with the Washingtonians, the collective band led by banjo player Elmer Snowden with Arthur Whetsol on trumpet, Otto Hardwick on saxophone and Sonny Greer on drums. Snowden went his separate way a few months later over a dispute about the way he was dividing up the earnings, meager though they were, and Ellington assumed the leader's role (Hasse. p. 78). Under Ellington, the band's fortunes improved immediately with a long-term booking at the Kentucky Club in midtown Manhattan. Ellington hired Fred Guy, on guitar and banjo, as Snowden's replacement and then, at the urging of pianist Willie the Lion Smith, his mentor in the big city, he hired trombonist Charlie Irvis. Ironically, Fred Guy would stay with Ellington for 24 years, until 1949, and leave no lasting mark whatever on the music; after he retired, he was never replaced. Charlie Irvis stayed only about a year, but Irvis's influence would become an indelible, lifelong component of Ellington's style.

Irvis, a shadowy figure in jazz history, was the impetus for Ellington's use of extravagant brass effects. Ellington's first biographer, Barry Ulanov, said, "Whether it was an accident, a charming trick of fate, or simply Ellington's sly, innocent-appearing way of doing things, shortly after the band moved into the Kentucky [Club] the first of the 'jungle' sounds moved onto the bandstand with them, the first of the growls which have typified Duke's music ever since."

Ulanov credits Irvis with introducing pungency into Ellington's naïve sweetness. "Duke's palette was committed to a pale impression-

The Washingtonians: Sonny Greer, Charlie Irvis, Bubber Miley (seated), Elmer Snowden, Otto Hardwick, Duke Ellington

ism in the first years of his stay at the Kentucky," Ulanov says. "But Charlie Irvis ruffled the placid surface of Ellington's 'conversation music' with a series of doo-wa's and rrr-ump's which were like injections of a nasty word, a saucy phrase, wonderful touches of musical innuendo. They added a fillip to the Washingtonians' music which made an already out-of-the-way band unique.... The sounds he made with his trombone were, as Duke says, 'jungle-istic'." Ulanov's enthusiasm for Irvis impels him into onomatopoeia decades before Tom Wolfe made it fashionable in non-fiction writing: "He used the cap of a bottle for a mute and played all around the bottom of his horn, growling elfishly, oafishly, suggestively, jungle-istically at the Kentucky customers. He ... rolled off long cadences of clear notes, broken by those exquisite shivers of sound, a bleat, a brump, a yawp.... "

Irvis soon had an ally. The next year, when Arthur Whetsol returned home to Washington to attend Howard University, Ellington replaced him with Irvis's friend and fellow New Yorker, cornetist Bubber Miley. By the time Miley arrived, in Ulanov's account, Ellington's use of "growling" brass was already established. Beyond a doubt Miley gave it a further nudge, but Ulanov is adamant that it was Irvis who was the prime mover. "Bubber turned up in late 1924, cut musically, emotionally from Irvis's cloth," Ulanov says. "Like Charlie, he didn't worry much, played what he wanted to. Like Charlie, he growled."

Ulanov's crediting of Irvis as the prime mover in the stylistic shift has generally been overlooked by later commentators. The general consensus credits Miley, not Irvis, for this shift. Circumstantial evidence is certainly in Miley's favor. Though he joined the band a year after Irvis, Miley immediately became Ellington's principal soloist, playing leads and taking solos on almost everything the band recorded while he was in it. He is credited as co-composer with Ellington on "East St. Louis Toodle-Oo," "Creole Love Call," "Blues I Love to Sing" and "Black and Tan Fantasy," Ellington's greatest works to that time. "Our band changed its character when Bubber came in," Ellington said, looking back on these days some three decades later. "Bubber used to growl all night long, playing gutbucket on his horn," he told Nat Shapiro in 1955. "That was when we decided to forget all about the sweet music."

Charlie Irvis, prime mover of Ellington's growling brass

Willie the Lion Smith, who often hosted Miley and Irvis on his stage at the Capitol Club in Harlem, and sent both of them to Ellington in the first place, had a more balanced view. Smith said, "It was the team of Miley and trombonist Irvis that later developed Ellington's 'jungle style', when Duke had a band at the Kentucky Club near Times Square."

Charlie Irvis, mysteriously, left behind very little evidence of his prowess with the plunger mute. Though he is fairly well represented on records with Ellington and others, one listens in vain for the "elfish, oafish, suggestive… shivers of sound" that Ulanov described. Irvis's growling is nowhere on display. If the credit for ruffling Ellington's placid surface really belongs to Irvis, at least in the first instance, we have to take Ulanov's word for it, keeping in mind that Ulanov had access to living memories of Ellington's orchestra at the Kentucky Club (as very few later biographers did). It is not even clear from the evidence we have that Irvis even used a plunger mute. Ulanov talks about him using the "cap of a bottle" (presumably actually from a large jar) for a mute. Otto Hardwick, who was in the band at the time, told Inez Cavanaugh, "The word gutbucket must have stemmed directly from Irvis's style and his use of a real bucket for a mute." This much is certain, whatever Irvis used to make his "oafish" sounds, he was definitely present at the "ruffling" of Ellington's orchestral style, and for the first flowerings of his genius for composition.

In the long run, neither Irvis nor Miley stayed around very long. Miley suffered from debilitating alcoholism that made his appearances with the band uncertain and they were never sure from one night to the next whether he would show up. Even when he did, he could not always play. Ellington said, "Bubber was very temperamental, and liked his liquor, [and] he used to get under the piano and go to sleep when he felt like it" (Shapiro 1955). Ellington put up with him for a few erratic years and finally replaced him in 1929. Arthur Whetsol had returned the year before but he was incapable of playing with the plunger, or perhaps unwilling to play it because of its low repute. Miley's real replacement, Cootie Williams, had no experience with it when he was recruited but proved more than willing, and he would leave an everlasting impression on Ellington's music.

Miley died on Welfare Island three years later, in 1932, only 29 years old. Charlie Irvis left the band before Miley, in 1926, and freelanced around New York with some success, but he inexplicably quit playing altogether in the early 1930s, soon after making some records with Miley, who was by then destitute. Irvis apparently died in 1939, at 40, absent from the music scene for six or seven years and forgotten. His Ellington tenure, momentary though it was, gained momentum because his replacement in the orchestra was his disciple and friend Joe Nanton, and Nanton was destined to become an iconic Ellingtonian.

Enter Joe 'Tricky Sam' Nanton
(1904-1948, with Ellington 1926 to 1948)

When Charlie Irvis stopped showing up for band dates in 1926, Ellington turned to Irvis's good friend, Joe Nanton, five years younger (b. 1904) and at that moment very much in Irvis's shadow. At first Nanton refused Ellington's offers, fearing he was taking his friend's job, but Ellington prevailed and Nanton joined Ellington's orchestra for what would turn out to be 20 years, until 1946, when Nanton died on the job. For someone who seemed reluctant to join at the start, Nanton's devotion to Ellington was single-minded. He alone among the hardcore Ellingtonians refused to record outside the band for all

Joe 'Tricky Sam' Nanton, fountainhead of Ellington's plunger tradition

those years. The sound of his particular wa-wa trombone is thus unique to Ellington's orchestra, and it is the true fountainhead of the plunger tradition. Nanton was shy and self-contained. In the only revealing interview he ever gave, he told the journalist Inez Cavanaugh about finding his way with the plunger. In 1921, after seeing a trumpet player named Johnny Dunn use the plunger, he decided to try it with the trombone. "I got the plunger, all right, but it sounded so terrible everybody howled.... I kept on trying until I got it to sound in tune.... It takes a helluva lot of experimentation and above all the *ears* have to be in tune. It's not all slide, you have to use your lip too, and work it out until the desired effect is obtained. After doing this over a period of years, that's all you're good for."

By his own account, Nanton may have elevated the technique for plunger-muted trombone. Kurt Dietrich, the encyclopedic chronicler of Ellington's trombonists, summarizes Nanton's contribution succinctly: "Charlie Irvis and Bubber Miley may have initiated the important brass component of Ellington's 'jungle sound,' but after replacing Irvis, and outliving the unfortunate Miley, it was Nanton who was destined to bring this art to its peak." Nanton's nickname, Tricky Sam, was pinned on him by Otto Hardwick soon after he joined the band as a tribute to his virtuosity with plunger effects.

Nanton made his record debut with the plunger mute on a ditty called "Li'l Farina," a pop song recorded soon after he joined the band (21 June 1926). More than a year passed before he made his first auspicious contribution. "Black and Tan Fantasy" was composed by Ellington and Bubber Miley in 1927. Ellington obviously realized how special it was because he recorded it four times that year for three different labels (Brunswick, RCA Victor and Okeh). Listening to the recordings in chronological order might encourage someone to invoke the old witticism about "sticking with it until you get it right." Except that, in this case, the first recording (in April) was already recognized as a masterpiece, and it is hard to conceive of re-recording a masterpiece and getting it 'righter'. Amazingly, that is what happens. On the fourth recording of the piece, for Okeh in November, Miley pulled one of his disappearing acts. In his absence, Nanton gets to state the opening melody in harmony with Miley's replacement, a fiery, technically adept trumpeter named Jabbo Smith. Perhaps it was Jabbo Smith's nervousness as the last-minute replacement that makes this version extra special: he contributes mightily, not only in the shared melody statement at the start but also in his solo (after Otto Hardwick recites the 'sweet' second melody on alto saxophone) and again when playing the lead in the final blues chorus that ends with the somber coda from Chopin's "Funeral March." Nanton precedes Smith's final melody statement with his own solo, constructing a clever crescendo that starts with relatively subdued muted trombone, intensifies with ever-more-extravagant plunger effects and culminates in a wild laughing jag, setting the stage for Smith's dramatic return. This solo chorus was given to Nanton because of Miley's absence and he makes dramatic capital of his scant twelve bars.

As Nanton's plunger effects became a show-stopping attraction, Ellington sometimes exploited the sound by voicing the entire brass section with plungers. "Echoes of the Jungle," with the expanded band in 1931, written by Cootie Williams, sets Nanton and alto saxophonist Johnny Hodges on a lush background of wa-wa brass in the final choruses. Leading up to the wa-wa backgrounds, Nanton solos after Hodges and Williams in a mellow mood that belies the "jungle" of the title. ("Echoes of the Jungle" was one of four titles that invoked the jungle in these Cotton Club years, along with "Jungle Jamboree" [1929], "Jungle Blues" [1930], and "Jungle Nights in Harlem" [1930], in what we would now call a branding exercise by Irving Mills, Ellington's agent; we know that Ellington's mother despised the term "jungle music" applied to her son's music and so it is not hard to guess how Ellington felt about it, but of course he said nothing.) Ellington's richly textured arrangement of "Echoes of the Jungle" is somewhat marred by Fred Guy's mechanical four-to-the-bar banjo strums, but it is possible to ignore them unless someone points them out. (Whoops.) More important are the confident, personal solos by Cootie Williams and Johnny Hodges, two musicians added to the band for the Cotton Club expansion and destined to be Ellington's front-line soloists for decades. Joe Nanton, an old hand already in his fifth year with the band, stands tall alongside them.

Nanton's ability to invest the plunger mute with rich, blues-based sobriety in melancholy performances such as "Black and Tan Fantasy" and "Echoes of the Jungle" firmly established it in Ellington's orchestral palette forever more, but it was impossible for Ellington or anyone else of his vintage to forget that the history of the plunger mute begins in vaudeville. Tricky Sam Nanton was well aware of its extravagant side, a hint of it showing in the hyena laugh that capped his solo in "Black and Tan Fantasy." Eventually, as he became established as one of the band's attractions, Ellington allowed him to indulge its comic extravagances in a parody of a teary old ballad called "In the Shade of an Old Apple Tree" (written in 1905, when Ellington was six, and, he said, the first popular song he remembers hearing). Ironically, the lyric croons about "sweet music":

> "In the shade of an old apple tree
> When the love in your eyes I could see
> When the voice that I heard, like the song of the bird
> Seemed to whisper sweet music to me."

That sweet music sours slightly under Ellington's baton in 1933. Ellington's arrangement opens with sweet reeds that were a staple of society bands at the time but were anathema to jazz bands. After that, Ellington leaves Nanton to his own extravagant devices. The performance demonstrates the exhibitionistic side of the plunger-muted trombone.

By the time the orchestra recorded "In the Shade of the Old Apple Tree" in 1933, Ellington had expanded his trombone section so that Nanton, after eight years sitting by himself in the lower brass tier, was joined by not one but two other trombonists. The new configuration was in fact the foundation that Ellington would stick with for the rest of his days, though it was peculiar to him in the annals of jazz band instrumentation. The lead trombonist, who joined the band in 1932, was Lawrence Brown, who was destined to occupy that chair for many years. He was a smooth, technically impeccable player, capable of playing the highest trombone parts in ensembles, and a smooth, laid-back soloist, good on ballads and capable at faster tempos. Two years before Brown was hired, in 1929, Nanton had been joined by Juan Tizol, a light-skinned Puerto Rican who played valve trombone, pitched the same as the slide trombone but incapable, obviously, of slurring the transition between notes and other sliding effects, and, as Tizol liked to say, more exacting in intonation and timbre (a boast that did not endear him to his section mates). Tizol, who was also destined to occupy his chair more often than not for many decades, was a reluctant improviser whose solo parts, like his ensemble parts, were written out. Ellington prized him for the Latin tinge he brought to the band with his colonial roots in Puerto Rico. (He would be co-composer with Ellington of "Caravan," "Perdido, "Conga Brava," "Bakiff" and other Latin staples in the band's repertoire.) With the additions of Brown and Tizol, Nanton now occupied the third trombone chair, playing middle register parts in the ensembles and soloing almost exclusively on plunger features. For the remaining 41 years of the orchestra's existence, whenever Ellington had to replace a trombone player he sought replacements who filled exactly the same roles as the three originators – the technically brilliant, intonation-conscious lead player, the ensemble stalwart valve trombonist, and the plunger specialist. Ellington was not interested in clones, of course. Personalities changed, for better or worse, but the functions stayed exactly the same.

Tricky Sam Nanton, Harry Carney (clarinet), and Wallace Jones intone the melody of "Mood Indigo." The trombone and trumpet use plunger mutes

Trombonists who specialized in playing with the plunger mute make an unbroken thread throughout the 50-year history of Ellington's orchestra. Although they used basically the same equipment, they brought with them different strengths and weaknesses, personal quirks and individual styles. Ellington, of course, revelled in their differences. He wrote character parts for them that were as different as Falstaff and Hotspur and Prince Hal. Tracing Tricky Sam's long and varied legacy is one of the treats in the canon.

"Ko-Ko," the Classic and the Revival

The different personalities who occupied the plunger-trombone chair are dramatically illustrated in two versions of Ellington's "Ko-Ko," recorded (and conceptualized) 16 years apart. The original "Ko-Ko" (in March 1940) is unanimously acclaimed among his greatest compositions, and it is a showcase for the plunger trombone. The piece is a raucous, hyperactive romp, perhaps the culmination the 'jungle style' that came to the fore with "East St. Louis Toodle-Oo" more than a decade earlier. Ellington described it to his audience at Carnegie Hall in 1943, as "a little descriptive scene of the days that inspired jazz... in New Orleans [at] a place called Congo Square, where the slaves used to gather and do native and sensuous dances –

religious dances." Its mood is definitely sensuous and, if not conventionally spiritual, undeniably spirited

In the original recording, Ellington uses Juan Tizol's straight round tone in a repeated one-bar phrase as a kind of call that is answered by two-bar responses from the ensemble in the opening 12-bar blues chorus. The call-and-response, the main motif of the piece, is not a melody so much as an insistent rhythmic cadence. Tricky Sam Nanton wades into this roiling atmosphere with two full choruses (24 bars) of edgy improvisation that sustain the rhythmic insistence of the opening. Ellington allots himself a chorus on piano, and then composes a big-band chorus with space for fillers by bassist Jimmy Blanton, a kind of orchestrated bass solo. Nanton then returns and leads the final chorus on his muted trombone.

"Ko-Ko" lasts two-and-a-half minutes, seven blues choruses at a medium-fast tempo, and its cohesion is remarkable. One of Ellington's astute critics, the French composer and theorist André Hodeir, said, "The 1940 version of *Ko-Ko* was splendidly strange and violent. The introduction seemed to come from another world, while Tricky Sam's solo had a wail that was more than merely exotic." Much of the credit for the brilliance of "Ko-Ko" must go to Nanton, spotlighted in three of its seven choruses, for so flawlessly sustaining his leader's collective conception.

Sixteen years later, in 1956, Ellington recorded "Ko-Ko" in a new arrangement. He may have been inspired to revive "Ko-Ko" because of his high regard for Quentin Jackson, who had inherited Joe Nanton's role. Jackson brought to the muted-trombone chair virtuoso technical capabilities along with the earthiness that was a prerequisite for his role in the band. In the new arrangement, Ellington retains the prominence of the plunger mute by bringing in Jackson for the blues chorus after the opening ensemble, just as Nanton had done earlier. Otherwise, Ellington's arrangement differs, with the slick clarinet of Jimmy Hamilton providing the contrasting voice to Jackson's raunchy plunger muted trombone. The mood of the new "Ko-Ko" is more refined than its original; it is a much more genteel dance. The difference, needless to say, drew criticism. André Hodeir was so disheartened by the differences that he declared, "This is not just another bad record; it is the sign of a dereliction which confirms once and for all the decadence of a great musician."

Hodeir, it must be said, was operating in a time warp. In the five years before he published his critique, Ellington had been struggling to find personnel and to develop repertoire; the recordings that reached Hodeir in France were often woeful, some of them undeniably "bad" (Hodeir's adjective). Hodeir could not know (even people closer at hand hardly realized) that Ellington had finally assembled what would turn out to be one of his greatest orchestras. Indeed, just four months after recording the new "Ko-Ko" this orchestra would dazzle the jazz world at the Newport Jazz Festival, put Ellington's face on the cover of *Time* magazine (a considerable coup at the time), and begin a ten-year recording contract at Columbia that resulted in several brilliant records. some of them among his most brilliant. We can concede that the new "Ko-Ko" is gentler than the original but with the advantage of hindsight in no way a "dereliction" (Hodeir's other word). In fact, for our purposes in trying to get our bearings on fifty years of plunger-muted trombone, the existence of two versions of "Ko-Ko" with key roles given to (spoiler alert) the two greatest practitioners on that instrument offers the kind of instructive comparison that is too good to pass up.

The revived "Ko-Ko" is played faster and lacks the orchestral density of its classic counterpart. Quentin Jackson's plunger solo is more controlled than Tricky Sam's, and perhaps because of that less 'jungle-istic', but he is articulate in his own special way. His beautiful chorus brings fresh assurance that the legacy of Tricky Sam carries on and in fact is enriched.

Granted, the two "Ko-Ko"s are moods apart. One is acclaimed as a masterpiece and the other is mostly ignored. But there is no accounting for taste, and I suspect there are listeners – intelligent, thoughtful, serious listeners – who might even choose the later refined "Ko-Ko" over the ebullient original. Best of all, there is no need to choose, of course, when we have both.

Duke's Choice, Tyree Glenn
(1912-1974, with Ellington 1947-1951)
Tricky Sam Nanton's immediate successor was Tyree Glenn, a Texan who had a wealth of experience by the time he started substituting

for Nanton in the days when Nanton's health was failing. Glenn had played in Europe and all over the United States in top-flight bands led by Benny Carter, Don Redman and Cab Calloway. A versatile musician, Glenn played vibraphone as well as trombone, an exotic combination, and he would be Ellington's one and only vibraphone soloist, albeit an infrequent one. His main role was the third trombone chair. Thanks to internet gossip, we know that Glenn occupied a special place in his leader's pantheon. Steve Voce, the personable reviewer and critic for the British *Jazz Journal*, once confided: "In a discussion with Stanley Dance I suggested that Quentin Jackson was my favorite re-creator of the Nanton role. Stanley preferred Booty Wood and told me that Duke's favorite was Tyree Glenn."

With such an experienced replacement for Nanton, Ellington apparently felt no need for a breaking-in period. He provided Glenn with solo space soon after he joined the band, in August 1947, when ailing Joe Nanton was still the nominal holder of the third chair. Glenn's debut came on a piece called "Hy'a Sue," an extraverted riff piece that might have been written for acrobatic dancers in the waning days of the jitterbug era, when they still commandeered the ballroom floor. Glenn is assigned the first solo chorus, and he displays his trademark "ya-ya" plunger sound, distinctively different from the more typical "wa-wa" sound. Linguistically, "ya-ya" is formed in the transition from the "ee" vowel to the "ah" vowel (eeyaaaa), with the "ee" formed by holding the plunger snug against the bell and then opening it abruptly to form "ah." The semi-vowel "y" is formed in transitioning between closed "ee" and open "ah" (in speech as in tromboning). The title "Hy'a Sue," not accidentally, obliquely includes the "ya" syllable in its title, a nod from Ellington to Glenn's uniqueness.

The riff structure of "Hy'a Sue" makes a very comfortable setting for improvisers and it gets spirited choruses not only from Glenn but also from Jimmy Hamilton on tenor saxophone and Johnny Hodges on alto saxophone. (In live performances of "Hy'a Sue" later on, Ellington left Glenn's chorus intact but he took to giving Hamilton several choruses, so that this piece is the prime exhibit for the clarinetist Hamilton's very appealing, if reluctant, tenor style, discussed further in Chapter 3, "Fifth Reed.")

Tyree Glenn, said to be Ellington's favorite of his plunger trombonists

Ellington's affection for Tyree Glenn's plunger stylings undoubtedly led him to prepare two striking performances toward the end of Glenn's relatively short tenure with the band. One of them comes in Ellington's *Liberian Suite*, an extended work commissioned by the government of the African republic of Liberia to mark the centennial of its founding as a homeland for repatriated American slaves. The commission was symbolic for Ellington (and for American music) because it bestowed international political recognition on the liberating aesthetic of jazz, the African-American musical genre, which was then less than half a century old. Ellington's six-part *Liberian Suite* has its attractive moments, to be sure, but it came at a time when his orchestra was more unsettled than at any other time in its 50-year history and Ellington's writing, though prolific as always, often lacked direction and sometimes conviction. (This is the period, by the way, that André Hodeir deplored in his critique of the revised "Ko-Ko.") Stanley Dance, reviewing the premiere performance of *Liberian Suite* at the December 1947 Carnegie Hall recital, labels it "one of the lesser Ellington extended works." The first movement of *Liberian Suite* is a pop song, "I Like the Sunrise," espousing a kind of trite optimism in the repetitive sunrise metaphor. The other five movements are called dances (methodically "Dance No. 1," "Dance No. 2," and so on), all rhythmically mobile with some fine ensembles and solos but difficult to distinguish from one another without close study. (Neither the song nor the dances had a notable afterlife with Ellington or with anyone else though the song makes an obligatory appearance on anthologies of Ellington's songs by, for instance, Ella Fitzgerald and Frank Sinatra.) The dances are attractive individually but they do not leave an impression collectively.

Tyree Glenn, as it happens, is responsible for two of the more memorable individual moments. On "Dance No. 2," he solos on vibraphone with a fine, ringing solo that fits snugly into the feeling of elation that appears to be the main impression Ellington hopes to convey with the suite. Then on "Dance No. 5," the suite's finale, Glenn and cornetist Ray Nance concoct a celebratory feast with their plunger mutes. "Dance No. 5" opens with a declamatory chorus by Harry Carney on his baritone saxophone that sets the stage, so to speak, for the plunger players who take up the rest of the five-minute 'dance'. Nance plays first and then Glenn plays his chorus, and on the final chorus Nance and Glenn dance around one another in a spontaneous improvisation of notable ingenuity and feeling. This movement brings the suite to a close not as its climax but at least as a rousing crowd-pleaser.

The high point of Glenn's work with Ellington (and, as it turned out, of his career) came on another of the orchestra's moderately interesting performances. In 1950, beguiled by the extended playing time afforded by the new medium of 33-rpm long-play (LP) high-fidelity records, Ellington and Billy Strayhorn dressed up four of his famous melodies in arrangements that were four or five times longer than the 3-minute originals, and collated them as "concert arrangements" on an LP titled *Masterpieces by Ellington*. One of them was "Mood Indigo," one of Ellington's most celebrated arrangements in its 1930 original. Stretching it to 15 minutes could hardly improve on it, and Ellington elongates it simply by having a succession of soloists pay homage to its haunting melody. One of the soloists, the fifth, is a vocalist, Yvonne Lanauze, who renders a smooth and plainspoken rendition of the lyric that is in perfect sync with the four smooth and plain-spoken instrumental soloists who went before her. Mercifully, the placid mood is relieved by a resounding chord from Ellington that brings on the sixth soloist, Tyree Glenn, for what turns out be a plunger extravaganza. His dramatic entry nine minutes into the piece begins with a chorus that reshapes the melody in "wa" and "ya" syllables, and a second chorus that raises the temperature further with growls and slurs. It is a virtuoso display of plunger technique, all the more powerful because it roils the surface with a blast of fresh air. It became a fitting valedictory for Glenn's time in the band.

By the time Tyree Glenn played his choruses on "Mood Indigo" in December 1950, he had already been out of the band for several months. Ellington brought him back for the *Masterpieces* recording, a move that proved to be a strategic gem for both of them. Glenn's departure provides a poignant aside about the way life and art sometimes clash. The Ellington orchestra was booked for a European tour from April to June 1950, an occasion that was widely publicized as one more sign of the return to normalcy in Europe after World War II. Glenn had toured the continent before the war with Don Redman's orchestra and, as fate would have it, he had a dalliance with a French woman while he was there. Now, with Glenn slated to return to Europe with Ellington, Glenn's wife issued a travel ban – there would be no more European tours for her husband, ever. Glenn, shamefaced, tendered his resignation.

Though Glenn would return to the band intermittently as a substitute (in 1972, for instance, when Booty Wood broke a finger) he never stayed long. It would take Ellington almost a year to find his replacement – hence Glenn's momentary recall for the *Masterpieces* date. Ironically he found the replacement right in his orchestra, in fact, sitting on the chair beside the one that Glenn had occupied.

Quentin 'Butter' Jackson
(1909-1976, with Ellington 1948-1959)

Quentin Jackson, called 'Butter' by everyone, had joined Ellington's orchestra a year after Tyree Glenn, occupying the second chair that was the province of a valve trombonist. Whether Jackson actually played the valved instrument in the first two years when he was relatively inconspicuous (as the second-chair trombonists always were) seems unlikely but Dietrich, in his comprehensive study of Ellington's trombonists, found a photograph of the band with Jackson holding what appears to be a valve trombone, so apparently he did, at least once.

Jackson's career was closely tied to Tyree Glenn's. They were section-mates in Cab Calloway's band for several years, and Glenn recommended him to Ellington when Juan Tizol quit the band. Two years went by without Jackson making an impression on his boss and he might have simply faded away if fate had not intervened. His break came on the European tour when Glenn was forced to quit the band. When the band reached Europe, Lawrence Brown, Ellington's primary trombone soloist all his years in the orchestra, fell ill. With Glenn gone and Brown indisposed, Jackson was the only experienced player in the section. Suddenly he was called on to play Brown's swing solos and Glenn's plunger solos as well as his own second-chair parts. He was inconspicuous no longer. Jackson was one of the most technically gifted trombonists who ever played with Ellington, and now, after two years as mainly an ensemble player, his solo gifts were suddenly on display. Ellington took to introducing him affectionately to his sold-out European audiences as *Monsieur le Beurre* ("Mister Butter"). When the band returned from Europe in 1951, Jackson's luck held. Juan Tizol rejoined the band, taking over the second chair that he had founded, and Jackson slid over into Glenn's vacated chair, where he would leave his own indelible mark as the most upbeat, devil-may-care growler of them all, and perhaps the most artful.

One of Jackson's roles in the band, as for all the band members, was to fill the familiar spaces of his predecessors on the old hits that Ellington played nightly at his concerts. Usually those spaces went by quickly, as mere moments in a ten-minute medley of eight or ten titles. Jackson's time in the third chair happened to encompass two full-

Quentin 'Butter' Jackson, a lighter, more azure sound with the plunger

length rearrangements of classic recordings. His positive outlook really comes clear when he plays the parts made familiar by Tricky Sam Nanton, his darker, bluer prototype. We have already seen the contrast in their styles in "Ko-Ko," with Jackson taking his turn 16 years after Nanton's classic original. Jackson may play the same notes as Tricky Sam – he sometimes does – but his feeling is always lighter, more azure. "Black and Tan Fantasy" provides another contrast. Ellington re-recorded "Black and Tan Fantasy" along with several other decades-old hits for Capitol Records in what was viewed by critics at the time as a desperate attempt at recapturing past glories. With hindsight, it looks more like Ellington was purposefully displaying the new talents that he had gathered in his band in the early 1950s and putting their own stamp on its sound. Butter Jackson was one of those ascending talents, obviously, as the muted trombone specialist.

The new "Black and Tan Fantasy" is stretched out. Along with

Jackson, Ellington uses it to display the assertive style of Russell Procope on both alto saxophone and clarinet. Procope, a big-band journeyman who joined Ellington in 1946, brought back the woody sound of New Orleans clarinet that had been lost when Jimmy Hamilton replaced Barney Bigard. Procope's solos on "Black and Tan Fantasy," first on alto saxophone and later on clarinet, evoke the jungle style of the classic version. Ray Nance states the melody at the start on plungered trumpet, in Bubber Miley's stead, but the rest of the arrangement belongs to Procope and to Butter Jackson, with two solos each, separated by a stride chorus by Ellington that sounds like a parody of his older style. Jackson's plunger style showcases his mastery of the technique and it also has a mellowness that must have seemed, to listeners familiar with the classic recording, like a slowing of the pulse. To listeners less familiar with the 1927 version, it brings an understated melancholy all its own.

Tricky Sam came to Ellington with his plunger technique intact. Everyone who followed him had to learn it on the job. Several of them initially objected to it, but not Jackson. "I've always been a melodic trombone player… with the exception of when I get that plunger in my hand," he told the Jazz Oral History Project. "Then my mind goes filthy."

As the Ellington orchestra gelled in the 1950s, Ellington's ambitions soared, and his virtuoso instrumentalists were given fresh opportunities to show their mettle. One of Ellington's more ambitious projects, and in some ways the least promising, was a record project that would merge his orchestra with Count Basie's, the only other jazz band that had survived the decade following the collapse of the Swing Era. The encounter with Count Basie in 1961 was the first of a sequence of recordings initiated by Ellington with musicians outside his band that would eventually include recordings with Louis Armstrong (also in 1961) and Coleman Hawkins, John Coltrane, Charles Mingus and Max Roach (all in 1962). Those other meetings were manageable small-band recordings, but the Basie affair defied the odds by bringing together both bands, 35 musicians in one studio, with twice the usual number of instrumentalists including two pianists (three with Billy Strayhorn), two drummers and two bassists. Some of the logistics of the arrangements were dealt with beforehand but the details were mainly worked out in the studio by Ellington, Strayhorn and Basie's arranger and trumpeter Thad Jones. It turned into an all-night session with considerable party time for the musicians and, against all odds, some interesting results.

One of the pieces is a Thad Jones composition, "To You," in which Quentin Jackson takes the only solo in front of a veritable squadron of his peers. Jackson, as it happened, was an unofficial liaison between the two bands. He had recently left Ellington and joined Basie so that at the time of the joint recording session he had a foot in both camps. Thad Jones's arrangement is dreamy and dance-like, not the fare that Jackson typically got to show his skills on. Dense brass harmonies (5 trombones, and as many as ten trumpets) are the focus of the arrangement and Jackson's 43-second chorus brings a momentary ripple to the surface. Jackson's moment at the front of the assembled crowd is perhaps a token of the esteem he had gained in this outsized company.

Jackson's virtuosity with the plunger mute put him in demand outside of the Ellington orchestra as the bebop stigma began to unravel. He appeared on records in orchestras led by Oliver Nelson, Quincy Jones, Milt Jackson, Charles Mingus and Thad Jones/Mel Lewis, among others. On a recording with Dinah Washington, the raunchy, blues-based diva, Jackson is accorded a showpiece that, though unconnected to his Ellington association, is irresistible in any discussion of the machinations of the plunger mute. On *Dinah Washington Sings Bessie Smith*, a tribute to the "Empress of the Blues" who had died in 1937, Washington revives an old chestnut by Fletcher Henderson originally called "Trombone Cholly." It was originally written as a tribute to Charlie Irvis, the patriarch of Ellington's plunger trombone lineage, but Washington retitles it "Trombone Butter" in Jackson's honor. With Jackson's growls ringing in her ears, Washington belts out this everlasting homage to plunger-muted trombonists:

> He wails and moans, he grunts and groans,
> He moos just like a cow.
> Nobody else can't do his stuff
> Cause he won't teach em how.
> Make it talk, make it sing,

Lordy, where did you get that tone?
If Gabriel know'd how you could blow
He'd let you lead his band I know.

Amen to that.

There is a considerable distance between the frippery of "Trombone Butter" and the technical consummation of all plunger-mute trombone playing, which also belongs to Jackson. Not surprisingly, the consummation originated in Duke Ellington's uncanny imagination. Ellington's masterpiece *Such Sweet Thunder*, also known as the Shakespeare suite, includes four compositions called sonnets. They are literally musical transpositions of the rigid Shakespearean sonnet form, with 14 lines of iambic pentameter, that is, ten beats representing ten syllables in each line, organized as four quatrains that rhyme ABAB and a final rhyming couplet (as discussed at length in Chapter 6, "Bardland," on the Shakespeare suite). Sonnets are challenging as literary forms because of their formal rigidity; transliterated into musical forms, they are almost impossible. In the Shakespeare suite, Ellington recognized the challenges they posed for his musicians and assigned each of the four sonnets to one of his most technically adept musicians: clarinetist Jimmy Hamilton, trombonist Britt Woodman, bassist Jimmy Woode and trombonist Quentin Jackson.

The literary form of the sonnet had no equivalent in musical form before Ellington, so that Ellington's musicians had no precedents to guide them. The intricacies of Ellington's musical sonnet include sustained notes every tenth beat (representing rhymes) as well as the controlled beats and formal pauses. Jackson's colleagues struggle playing their sonnets on open horns and plucked strings, and for Jackson the challenges are multiplied by adding the movement of the slide with the right hand and the manipulation of plunger mute with the left. On Jackson's specialty, "Sonnet for Sister Kate," he is masterful if not exactly flawless. His sonnet, like the others, is melodically mechanical and rhythmically stodgy (the sonnets do not swing). They are necessarily technical *tours de force*.

Quentin Jackson's "Sonnet for Sister Kate," a musical analogy to *The Taming of the Shrew*, represents Shakespearean comedy, and Jackson conveys not only facility beyond reckoning, wending his way through the contrary manipulations of slide and plunger, but also through it all he somehow manages to convey the high spirits of the Shakespearean rom-com. Both attributes – technical facility and high spirits – seemed to come naturally to *Monsieur le Beurre*.

The "Deacon," Lawrence Brown
(1907-1988, with Ellington 1932-1951, 1960-1970)

No trombone player devoted as much of his career (and life) to Ellington as Lawrence Brown, and Ellington reciprocated by making Brown his lead trombonist in perpetuity whenever he was in the orchestra, as well as his principal trombone soloist. From the moment he joined in 1932 until his retirement in 1970 (with a hiatus from 1951 to 1960), Brown's smooth tone and melodic facility were featured on countless ballads and swing numbers. Notwithstanding the romantic flair in his playing, Brown was a prickly character, antisocial and close-mouthed. He guarded his solo space jealously. His band-mates called him the Deacon. Alone among them, he neither smoked. drank nor cursed. Pete Welding, a *Down Beat* editor, rode the band bus in 1962 and neatly captured the man's insularity amid the card-playing and hard-edged banter of men trying to make a tedious, bone-rattling ride seem shorter: "Brown, aloof, dignified, a seeming refutation of the aphorism 'no man is an island,' quickly became absorbed in a copy of *Popular Mechanics*."

After 20 years, in 1951, Brown quit the band along with Johnny Hodges and Sonny Greer, played for a while in Hodges's small band, and then freelanced for a few years mainly in California, with middling success. During his nine-year absence from Ellington's band, the trombone section actually thrived, with Britt Woodman in Brown's chair, John Sanders on valve trombone, and first Quentin Jackson and then Booty Wood in Tricky Sam Nanton's chair. In the absence of the taciturn Brown, the trombonists became a brotherhood. Together, Woodman, Sanders and Jackson put in extra hours perfecting their group sound. They took pride in their intricate, well-drilled interplay, and Ellington recognized their collective strength and wrote several pieces that exploited their finely calibrated background harmonies, best displayed on *The Cosmic Scene* (1958), featuring the trombone trio in a nine-man band Ellington called the Spacemen. During this

Lawrence Brown, with plunger: "It can really mess your lip"

nine-year recess from Brown, there was coherence and fellowship in the trombone section as never before or afterwards. Then in 1960 Brown rejoined the band and reclaimed most of the solo space. The tight-knit trombone players of the Brown-free years soon departed.

Brown, predictably, disdained the plunger mute. "It can really mess your lip so that you won't be able to play straight at all," he told Stanley Dance. In that, Brown was not being merely petulant. Art Baron, the last of Ellington's plunger specialists and the most pedagogical, explained it this way:

> "That little mute ... creates a lot of back pressure. It messes with your chops. You've got to build up your stamina to play it. So you don't want to play a hard, plunger solo and then go play some soft, high lead stuff. If you're a real precision, quiet player, used to playing very soft, it's maybe not for you, because you're adding a lot of resistance putting that mute in there. That's why Lawrence Brown, although he sounded great with the plunger, didn't like playing it. And the bell of the horn rests in the palm of your left hand, which also puts an undesirable pressure on your mouth. But that's part of the deal."

It was that "part of the deal" that Brown despised (as did, for the same reasons, all of those post-bop trombonists mentioned earlier, who made the plunger mute nearly extinct in their generation). Brown, like every other trombonist in the band and also every trumpeter, had to learn the rudiments of plunger technique for those ensembles in which all of the brass instruments were muted.

Ironically, soon after Brown rejoined the band in 1960, Ellington found himself without a plunger specialist for a recording project called *Recollections of the Big Band Era*. He prevailed upon Brown to play the plunger solo on "Minnie the Moocher," the hoary old theme song of Cab Calloway. Ellington knew, of course, that the technically impeccable Brown "sounded great with the plunger" (as Art Baron said). To no one's surprise, certainly not Ellington's, the meticulous Brown acquitted himself nobly.

From then on, Brown occasionally played plunger parts, albeit grudgingly. "I did it first as a favor," he told Stanley Dance, "but I guess it developed into a saving, as when you've got one man who can do two things. So long as Ellington had his music, something has to revert to the first, basic type, and the plunger is the connection between the beginning and the band now." To Brown's credit, he made the connection when he had to.

Mitchell 'Booty' Wood
(1919-1987, with Ellington 1959-60, 1963, 1970-1972)

It is hard to imagine that "Sweet and Pungent," the iconic 1959 plunger trombone solo that I used as the introduction to this illustrated history, was the first plunger solo Booty Wood ever recorded. It is even harder to imagine that Ellington sprung it on him in the recording studio. Wood, taken by surprise, was not pleased. Stanley Dance, who was present, reported Wood's succinct reaction: "'Why would he have *me* play that?' he asked disgustedly." Despite Wood's initial misgivings, after playing it he knew he had excelled at it. "Sweet and Pungent," by anyone's standard, is a masterful example of plunger trombone style, and from that moment Wood settled into his new role. As Dance says, "It is a different story today [in 1970]. Wood declaims the dramatic plunger roles with zest and artistry.... 'Booty Wood is one of the best plunger trombonists I've ever heard,' said Ellington."

Mitchell 'Booty' Wood

Wood was destined, of course, to play Tricky Sam's parts on the old favorites, as all of the third-chair trombonists had done. After his dazzling start, he might have hoped that his presence in the orchestra in its later years would inspire Ellington to exploit his talents by writing new material for him but, if so, he was destined to be disappointed. Inexplicably, new features for trombone players grew scarce in Ellington's final decade, and for the plunger trombonist they grew even scarcer. The last tailor-made feature for Booty Wood seems to have come in 1960, though he hung on in the band off and on for another decade. The specialty number came in one of Ellington's more oblique inspirations, when he and Strayhorn arranged five melodies from Edvard Grieg's *Peer Gynt Suite*. (Grieg's suite originated as incidental music for Henrik Ibsen's play of the same name, and Ellington may have listened to it as a reference point when he himself was commissioned to compose incidental music for Shakespeare's *Timon of Athens* for the Stratford Festival in 1963.)

On one of Grieg's melodies, "Solvejg's Song," Ellington pits

Wood's raucous, throaty plunger against Jimmy Hamilton's sweet, careening clarinet in an opposition so diametric that it gives an unsettling, otherworldly feeling. The melodrama suits the plot. Hamilton's clarinet conveys the lament of Solvejg, Gynt's lover, as she pines for her long-lost wandering soul-mate, and Wood's growling trombone conveys Gynt's manic travels through deserts, madhouses and shipwrecks. The music hovers somewhere between jazz and symphony without committing itself to either; it is more truly third stream, a term that Ellington had no use for, than many compositions that branded themselves with that name. It is weird and fascinating.

Unluckily for Booty Wood, it had a short shelf life. After this haunting composition was recorded in June 1960, it was never played again. In one of the more bizarre chapters of Ellington's career, the Grieg Foundation in Bergen, Norway, banned performances of Ellington's reinterpretation on grounds that it was "copied in a manner which damages the author's reputation." That verdict was greeted abroad with some derision and gave rise to a heated debate in Norway. When the Grieg Foundation upheld their verdict, Ellington took umbrage. "We shall never play it again," he told a Norwegian newspaper reporter. "Billy Strayhorn made it with so much love that there is no fun in playing it now that it has been vetoed" (Cooke 2002, p. 165). So Booty Wood never had the good fortune of recreating his dazzling performance in "Solveig's Song" before a live audience.

Art Baron
(1950- , with Ellington 1973-1974)

Art Baron tags himself as "the last trombonist Ellington ever hired" and he took a special interest in coming to grips with the tradition that he had joined at the tag-end. He was far and away the youngest musician who ever inherited Tricky Sam's chair – 31 years younger than Booty Wood, his immediate predecessor, and 41 years younger than Butter Jackson, with whom he studied for a while. He was younger by about ten years than those post-bop players who disdained the plunger mute, and even though they were the pace-setters in his formative years, he somehow did not inherit their disdain. He was a schooled musician, a graduate of the Berklee College of Music in Boston, the prestigious jazz incubator, an experience that Tricky Sam

Art Baron, Ellington's "last trombonist"

Nanton would undoubtedly have found unfathomable.

Baron's tenure in Ellington's third trombone chair turned out to be Ellington's last year, 1973-1974. It was the one in which Ellington spent the least time in recording studios for 40 years or more, with few commercial recordings and apparently no private, self-funded stockpile sessions. As a result, Baron never got to display his prowess with the plunger in studio conditions. Luckily, some of Ellington's live performances that year catch him wielding the plunger to good effect on pieces designed specifically for him. One of the best finds him playing a chorus on "St. Louis Blues" with Ellington in Stockholm, Sweden. Happily, it is more than a perfunctory performance of W.C. Handy's 1914 warhorse. Ellington turns it into a small spectacle by adding showy flourishes in his piano solo for his Nordic admirers, with Baron showing off his plunger mastery after an open trombone chorus by the Swede Åke Persson, a local favorite of the Maestro's and a special guest on the occasion.

Duke Ellington died nine months after Art Baron joined the band. Baron stayed on when Mercer Ellington stepped in to finish the band's commitments and afterward when Mercer tested the public appetite for a shadow band in his father's name. After that, Baron himself led a small band of Ellington alumni called the Duke's Men. He remains active in studio sessions and pit bands. He has also been active in clinics and classrooms keeping the plunger tradition alive by passing on his knowledge to young players. His tenure was brief but he has been a proud member of the exclusive company.

Finding the "good notes"
As the last of Tricky Sam's rightful heirs, Art Baron knows details that those of us who simply revel in the music could not otherwise appreciate. For instance, playing with the plunger affects the pitch of the instrument. "Now when you're using that little mute, it makes the horn very sharp," Baron says. "After you play a while, you learn how to compensate…, adjust with your chops and your slide positions." The plunger also limits the range. "There are a couple of funny little pedal tones you can use with the mute, but you rarely play below middle C with it," he says. "You can go down to A and G below it, but it doesn't speak as well, and you can go up to the C and D in the staff. So the range is about an octave…."

And then he adds, "… but if you listen to Tricky Sam, he said a lot in an octave." And so of course did all the men who succeeded him in one of Duke Ellington's most idiosyncratic traditions. Actually, the limitations Baron describes suited Ellington perfectly. As he himself put it, suppose you have "a guy who uses a mute and he can only get seven good notes out of it. The problem [for the composer] is to use those seven."

No one ever did it better.

References (page numbers to direct quotations are shown *in italics*)
Baron, Art (as told to Bob Bernotas). 1996-2013. "Masterclass with Art Baron: An Introduction to the Plunger." *Online Trombone Journal.* http://trombone.org/articles/library/viewarticles.asp?ArtID=14 [accessed April 2017]
Cavanaugh, Inez M. 1945. "Three Interviews: Tricky Sam Nanton." Reprinted in *The Duke Ellington Reader*, ed. Mark Tucker. 1993. New York: Oxford University Press. 462-471. *p. 463, pp. 466-467*
Cooke, Mervyn. 2002. "Jazz among the Classics, and the case of Duke Ellington." In *The Cambridge Companion to Jazz*, ed. Mervyn Cooke and David Horn. Cambridge, UK: Cambridge University Press. 153-173. *pp. 164-165.*
Cullen, Jack. 1962. "Ellington on the Air in Vancouver." Interview on

CKNW, 30 October 1962. In *The Duke Ellington Reader*, ed. Mark Tucker. 1993. New York: Oxford University Press. 338-341. *p. 339.*

Dance, Stanley. 1978. Booklet with "Duke Ellington." *Time-Life Giants of Jazz* (3-LP box set). Alexandria, Virginia: Time-Life Books. *p. 4.*

Dance, Stanley. 1977. Liner note for Duke Ellington, *Carnegie Hall Concerts, December 1947*. Prestige 2-CD [1977].

Dance, Stanley. 1970. *The World of Duke Ellington*. London: Macmillan. *p. 114, p. 194*

Dietrich, Kurt. 1995. *Duke's 'Bones: Ellington's Great Trombonists*. Rottenburg, Germany: Advance Music. *p. 21, p. 125.*

Ferguson, Otis. 1982. *In the Spirit of Jazz: The Otis Ferguson Reader*, ed. Dorothy Chamberlain and Robert Wilson. New York: Da Capo Press [1997 reprint]. *p. 54.*

Hasse, John Edward. 1993. *Beyond Category: The Life and Genius of Duke Ellington*. New York: Simon & Schuster. *p. 78.*

Hodeir, André. 1962. *Toward Jazz*. New York: Grove Press. *p. 28, p. 32*

Shapiro, Nat, and Nat Hentoff, eds. 1955. *Hear Me Talkin' to Ya: The Story of Jazz as Told by the Men Who Made It*. New York: Rinehart. *p. 231, p. 238*

Smith, Willie the Lion, with George Hoefer. 1964. *Music on My Mind: The Memoirs of an American Pianist*. New York: Doubleday. Foreword by Duke Ellington. *p. 144*

Ulanov, Barry. 1946. *Duke Ellington*. New York: Creative Age Press. *pp. 44-45, p. 45, p. 47*

Voce, Steve. n.d. "The Duke's in Bed: The Ellingtonians as Encountered by Steve Voce." http://ellingtonweb.ca/Hostedpages/Voce/Voce.html [accessed February 2014]

Welding, Pete. 1962. "On the road with the Duke Ellington orchestra." Reprinted in *The Duke Ellington Reader*, ed. Mark Tucker. 1993. New York: Oxford University Press. 326-332. *p. 328.*

Playlist (recordings cited in order of appearance in the chapter)

"Sweet and Pungent" (4:02) NYC, 2 Dec 1959 *Blues in Orbit* (Columbia [2004]) Ray Nance tp; Britt Woodman, Booty Wood, Matthew Gee tb; Johnny Hodges as, Russell Procope cl, as; Jimmy Hamilton cl; Paul Gonsalves ts; Harry Carney bs; Ellington p; Jimmy Woode b; Jimmy Johnson d.

"Black and Tan Fantasy" (3:23) NYC 3 Nov 1927 *Okeh Ellington* (Columbia 2CD [1991]) Jabbo Smith, Louis Metcalf tp; Joe Nanton tb; Harry Carney cl, bs; Rudy Jackson cl, ts; Otto Hardwick ss, as; DE p; Fred Guy bjo; Wellman Braud b; Sonny Greer d.
Solos: Jabbo + Nanton (1st melody), Hardwick as (2nd melody),

Jabbo, Hardwick, Ellington, Nanton, Jabbo

"Echoes of the Jungle" (3:27) Camden, NJ June 16, 1931 *Early Ellington* (Bluebird 1989). Arthur Whetsol, Cootie Williams, Freddie Jenkins tp; Joe Nanton tb, Juan Tizol vtb, Barney Bigard cl, ts, Johnny Hodges cl, ss, as, Harry Carney cl, as, bs, Duke Ellington p, Fred Guy bjo, Wellman Braud b, Sonny Greer d
Solos: Hodges, Williams, Nanton/Hodges, Hodges, Bigard

"In the Shade of the Old Apple Tree" (3:12) NYC 15 Aug 1933 (Classics 646) Arthur Whetsol, Freddie Jenkins, Cootie Williams tp; Tricky Sam Nanton, Lawrence Brown, Juan Tizol tb; Johnny Hodges, Harry Carney, Otto Hardwick, Barney Bigard reeds; DE p; Fred Guy g; Wellman Braud b; Sonny Greer d.
Solos: 'sweet' reeds, Jenkins, Nanton

"Ko-Ko" (2:39) 6 March 1940 *Blanton-Webster Band* (RCA Victor 3CD). Wallace Jones, Cootie Williams tp; Rex Stewart cor; Lawrence Brown, Tricky Sam Nanton, Juan Tizol tb; Barney Bigard cl, Johnny Hodges as, Harry Carney bs, Otto Hardwick as, Ben Webster ts; DE p; Fred Guy g; Jimmy Blanton b; Sonny Greer d.
Solos: Tizol, Nanton, Ellington, Blanton, Nanton

"Ko-Ko" (2:19) Chicago, 7 Feb 1956 *Historically Speaking* (LoneHill [2004], orig Bethlehem) Cat Anderson, Clark Terry, Willie Cook, Ray Nance tp; Britt Woodman, John Sanders, Quentin Jackson tb; Johnny Hodges, Russell Procope, Paul Gonsalves, Jimmy Hamilton, Harry Carney reeds; DE p; Jimmy Woode b; Sam Woodyard d
Solos: Quentin Jackson, Jimmy Hamilton

"Hy'a Sue" (2:54) Hollywood 14 Aug 1947 *Complete Duke Ellington 1947-1952* Vol. 1 (CBS Fr)
Shelton Hemphill, Ray Nance, Francis Williams, Shorty Baker, Dud Bascomb tp; Lawrence Brown, Claude Jones, Tyree Glenn tb; Johnny Hodges, Russell Procope, Jimmy Hamilton, Al Sears, Harry Carney reeds; DE p; Fred Guy g; Oscar Pettiford b; Sonny Greer d.
Solos: Glenn, Hamilton (ts), Hodges

"Dance No. 5" (5:08) *Liberian Suite* 24 Dec 1947 *Ellington Uptown* (Columbia [2004]), also *Complete DE 1947-1952* Vol. 5 (CBS Fr). Shelton Hemphill, Ray Nance, Francis Williams, Shorty Baker, Al Killian tp; Lawrence Brown, Claude Jones, Tyree Glenn tb; Johnny Hodges, Russell Procope, Jimmy Hamilton, Al Sears, Harry Carney reeds; DE p; Fred Guy g; Oscar Pettiford, Junior Raglin b; Sonny Greer d.
Solos: Carney, Nance (muted), Glenn (plunger chorus, then simultaneous with Nance)

Excerpt from "Mood Indigo" (2:54, from 8:50 to 11:34, of 15:25). 18 Dec 1950. *Masterpieces by Ellington,* on *Complete DE 1947-1952* Vol. 5 (CBS Fr).). Harold Baker, Ray Nance, Francis Williams, Fats Ford, Cat Anderson tp; Lawrence Brown, Quentin Jackson, Tyree Glenn tb; Johnny Hodges, Russell Procope, Jimmy Hamilton, Paul Gonsalves, Harry Carney reeds; DE p; Wendell Marshall b; Sonny Greer d, Yvonne Lanauze voc

"Black and Tan Fantasy" (5:10) Chicago, 29 Dec 1953 *Ellington '55* (Capitol) Clark Terry, Cat Anderson, Willie Cook, Ray Nance tp; Quentin Jackson, Britt Woodman, Alfred Cobbs tb; Russell Procope, Rick Henderson, Paul Gonsalves, Jimmy Hamilton, Harry Carney reeds; DE p; Billy Strayhorn celeste; Wendell Marshall b; Dave Black d
Solos: Nance (tp plunger), Procope (as), Ellington, Jackson (plunger), Procope (cl), Jackson (plunger)

"To You" (3:53) Thad Jones comp, arr NYC, 6 July 1961 *Duke Ellington Meets Count Basie* (Columbia [1999]) orchestras of Ellington (right channel) and Basie (left channel)
Solo: Quentin 'Butter' Jackson

"Trombone Butter" (3:36) Chicago, 30 Dec 1957 *Dinah Washington Sings Bessie Smith* (EmArcy) Flip Ricard, Clark Terry tp; Butter Jackson tb; Eddie Chamblee ts; McKinley Easton bs; James Craig p; Robare Edmonson b; Jim Slaughter d comp Fletcher Henderson (as "Trombone Cholly").

"Sonnet for Sister Kate" (2:24) NYC, 24 April 1957 *Such Sweet Thunder* (Columbia) Clark Terry, Cat Anderson, Willie Cook, Ray Nance tp; Quentin Jackson, Britt Woodman, John Sanders tb; Johnny Hodges, Russell Procope, Paul Gonsalves, Jimmy Hamilton, Harry Carney reeds; DE p; Jimmy Woode b; Sam Woodyard d
Solo: Quentin (Butter) Jackson

"Minnie the Moocher" (2:47) NYC, 13 Dec 1962 *Recollections of the Big Band Era* (Reprise). Cootie Williams, Cat Anderson, Roy Burrowes, Ray Nance tp; Lawrence Brown, Chuck Connors, Buster Cooper tb; Johnny Hodges, Russell Procope, Paul Gonsalves, Jimmy Hamilton, Harry Carney reeds; DE p; Ernie Shepard b; Sam Woodyard d.
Eddie Barefield arr
Solo: Lawrence Brown (plunger)

"Solvejg's Song" (3:59) Hollywood, 29 June 1960 *Grieg: Peer Gynt Suite* (Columbia) Ray Nance, Willie Cook, Andres Merenguito, Eddie Mullins tp; Lawrence Brown, Booty Wood, Britt Woodman tb; Johnny Hodges, Russell Procope, Paul Gonsalves, Jimmy Hamilton, Harry Carney reeds;

DE p; Aaron Bell b; Sam Woodyard d.
Solos: Hamilton, Wood

"St. Louis Blues" (3:57) Stockholm, 25 Oct 1973 *Duke Ellington in Sweden* (Caprice [1999]) Harold Money Johnson, Johnny Coles, Barry Lee Hall, Mercer Ellington, Rolf Ericson tp; Vince Prudente, Art Baron, Chuck Connors, Åke Persson tb; Russell Procope, Geezil Minerve, Harold Ashby, Percy Marion, Harry Carney reeds; DE p; Joe Benjamin b; Rocky White d
Solos: Ellington, Persson, Baron (plunger)

Chapter 3

THE FIFTH REED

Ben Webster & the Tenor Ascent

uncredited illustration *Hear Me Talkin' to Ya* ©1950 Doubleday Co.

One of the overlooked mysteries of Duke Ellington's well-scrutinized career is why he was so tardy in latching onto the solo power of the tenor saxophone. From the beginning, Ellington included tenor parts in his ensembles, where it was played as a double by the man whose solo instrument was the clarinet. That combination – clarinet doubling tenor in ensembles – became a fixture in Ellington's reed section at the outset and lasted 43 years. There was astounding longevity in the men who occupied that chair. Table 1 makes a graphic illustration of that longevity with the long, almost unbroken grey span on the left side. It was overwhelmingly the domain of two musicians: Barney Bigard for 14 years (from 1928 to 1942) and Jimmy Hamilton for 25 years (from 1943 to 1968). Before

Bigard, Ellington employed a couple of fill-ins. Prince Robinson got the call whenever the Washingtonians, as the band was called in his day, added a fourth reed player for record dates or dances. Rudy Jackson filled the chair regularly for six months in 1927, until the arrival of Bigard.

The fourth reed, doubling clarinet and tenor with primary clarinet solo duties, became permanent with Rudy Jackson's hiring in June 1927, and became a fixture with Bigard six months later. When Bigard left in 1942, Chauncey Haughton filled his chair for a year until he was drafted into the war effort, and Jimmy Hamilton took it over.

Ellington clung doggedly to the clarinet solo role, writing elaborate parts for Jimmy Hamilton until 1968, more than a decade after the clarinet had fallen out of favor as a solo instrument in modern jazz groups. Other big-band arrangers had pretty much abandoned it in the 1950s and small-band leaders had no room for it. The swing stars who had momentarily given it swagger had faded; Benny Goodman was semi-retired and Artie Shaw had quit. ("When in doubt do nothing," Shaw wrote in one of his philosophical memoirs that passed for 'doing nothing' in his retirement.) Ellington only gave up on it when Hamilton retired.

This fact is a little deceptive in Table 1 because it might appear that Norris Turney carried on in Hamilton's place. Although Turney sometimes played tenor saxophone and occasionally clarinet, his solo instruments were mainly alto saxophone and, for the first time in Ellington's orchestral palette, flute (a change considered in detail in Chapter 7, "Afro-Eurasian Ellington").

After Hamilton retired in 1968, the clarinet solos were usually taken by Russell Procope, the Ellington veteran who had sat alongside Hamilton since 1946 and would stay in the band until Ellington's death in 1974. Procope had occasionally been featured in clarinet solos as well as alto saxophone solos throughout his tenure. After 1968 he became in effect the custodian of parts originally written for Bigard and Hamilton as well as his own, though those features were played infrequently in these years.

The other reed chair outlined chronologically in Table 1 is the solo tenor saxophone chair, historically the fifth chair in Ellington's reed

	Clarinet (Tenor Sax in ensemble)		Tenor Sax (solo, ensemble)
1925	Prince Robinson	1925- 1927 occasional	
	Rudy Jackson	1927 June- 1927 Dec	
1930	Barney Bigard	1928 Jan - 1942 July	
		1933 9 May	Joe Garland
		1935 19 Aug / 36 29 July	Ben Webster
1940		1940 Feb- 1943 Aug	Ben Webster
	Chauncey Haughton	1942 July- 1943 July	
	Jimmy Hamilton	1943 June- 1968 July	
		1943 Aug- 1944 May	Elbert (Skippy) Williams
1945		1944 May- 1949 May	Al Sears
		1948 May- Nov	Hal Singer
		1948 Nov- 1949 June	Ben Webster
		1949 May- 1950 Mar	Charlie Rouse
		1949 June- 1950 Feb	Jimmy Forrest
1950		1950 Feb-Sept	Alva Beau McCain
		1950 April-June	Don Byas
		1950 Sept -1953 Feb	Paul Gonsalves
		1953 Feb- March	Tony Scott
1955 *1962 1965		1953 Mar-1972 Sept	Paul Gonsalves
		1968 July- 1974 April	Harold Ashby
1970	Norris Turney (mainly alto sax, flute)	1969 May- July 1969 Oct -1973 Feb	
		1972 Sept.-Nov.	Russ Andrews
		1972 Dec- 1974 April	Paul Gonsalves
1974		1973 Oct. -1974 April	Percy Marion

*Ellington featured tenor saxophonists Coleman Hawkins (18 August 1962) and John Coltrane (26 September 1962) with small groups on Impulse! recording sessions

TABLE I – Chronology of two chairs in Duke Ellington's reed section: Clarinet doubling Tenor Saxophone (left column) and Tenor Saxophone (right column)

section, shown in the right column. The graphic contrast between the two sides of the table is striking, and goes some distance toward setting the tone for the rest of this chapter. The simplicity of the chronology of Duke Ellington's solo-clarinet chair on the left side contrasts with the hodge-podge that marks the history of the tenor saxophone chair on the right side. Various facets of that turbulent history come up in later sections. I begin with the mystery that I mentioned at the beginning, the late blooming of Ellington's accommodation of a tenor saxophone soloist – graphically indicated by the long blank space in the top right quadrant interrupted only by a couple of one-night stands.

Minding the Gap

From the beginning of his bandleading career in 1925 until his creative flowering with the 1940 band, Duke Ellington was content to ply his trade without the help of a permanent, big-toned tenor saxophone soloist. He got the sound of the tenor into his ensembles because his clarinet soloist Barney Bigard was adept at doubling. Occasionally, but not very often, he asked Bigard to take a solo turn on tenor, as we will see. The fact that he gave Bigard a few tenor solos was surely a sign that Ellington was not oblivious to the impact that the tenor saxophone was making on other bandstands. An even surer sign was that on a couple of occasions in this fifteen-year stretch Ellington hired tenor saxophone specialists to join his orchestra in studios for specific assignments.

The first of these imported specialists was Joe Garland who joined the band for one record session on 9 May 1933. "Happy as the Day is Long," Garland's feature, is a pop song with words by Ted Koehler and music by Harold Arlen sung by Ivie Anderson. Garland wrote the arrangement, and he made the most of his guest stint by writing a conspicuous part for his own instrument. As Bruce Talbot remarks (2008), "Significantly, Joe gave himself the first hot tenor solo in the band's recorded history, predating Ben Webster by several years." Not only did Garland give himself a solo but he also plays the lead on the *A* melody in this AABA song (with Freddie Jenkins's trumpet playing the bridge). Garland's solo may qualify as a "hot tenor solo" but it lasts only eight bars in the final chorus before the reprise of the melody.

Exactly why Garland got to write the arrangement will never be known, but it is probably safe to say that if Ellington had written it the tenor would not have been assigned the featured role, given his

Joe Garland (1903-1977)

indifference to it at the time. Garland's solo is "hot" because Garland was a regular member of the Mills Blue Rhythm Band led by Lucky Millinder, as hot a band as there was at the time. Garland was a rising talent, and he went on to play in Louis Armstrong's orchestra starting in 1939, serving as his musical director in 1940-1941 and again in 1945-1947. He is probably best remembered as the composer of Les Brown's theme "Leap Frog" and (with some dispute) Glenn Miller's theme "In the Mood." In the backrooms of the Swing Era, Joe Garland was a figure to be reckoned with, and his inaugural solo with Ellington adds another point of interest to his now-forgotten accomplishments.

Barney Bigard's occasional tenor solos could hardly be called "hot." He soloed, for instance, on "Bugle Call Rag," the first record he ever made with Ellington's Washingtonians (9 January 1928). The deployment of instruments on this early record seems bizarre knowing how the instruments would soon be parceled out for posterity. Otto Hardwick plays baritone saxophone and Harry Carney, destined to become the master of the baritone saxophone, plays clarinet both

Young Barney Bigard (1906-1980)

in the ensemble lead and in a solo. The master clarinetist Bigard plays tenor saxophone. As one soloist among eight in the two-and-a-half minute recording, Bigard's tenor contribution is barely noticeable.

That was Bigard's fate as tenor soloist – when Ellington does let him solo he gives him little space. This despite the fact that, according to Lambert (1998, 30), Bigard "had gained a reputation in Chicago as a tenor saxophonist in the days before he joined Ellington." If Ellington was beguiled by Bigard's reputation on tenor saxophone when he first joined the band, as his solo debut on "Bugle Call Rag" suggests, it did not last long. When the band recorded Joe Garland's tenor-rich arrangement on "Happy as the Day is Long," Bigard was given the day off.

Teaching the Tenor to Swing

It may not have been Bigard's tenor saxophone playing that Ellington disliked but, more generally, the tenor saxophone itself. After Adolphe Sax's new invention finally caught on around the turn of the twentieth century, some forty years after Sax invented it and went bankrupt, it was mostly used as a novelty instrument in music halls, for tongue-slapping sound effects and bumble-bee flights. Then in the 1920s the mighty virtuosity of Coleman Hawkins dispelled the stigma attached to the instrument. In nightly displays with the Fletcher Henderson orchestra at the popular Roseland Ballroom, Hawkins fashioned linear melodies on the tenor saxophone with grace and power, modeled on the melodic and rhythmic sense that Louis Armstrong was displaying on trumpet. Hawkins's connection to Armstrong was face-to-face. For a year starting in September 1924, Armstrong had left Chicago for New York so he could play in Henderson's orchestra. The orchestra boasted talented individuals in every section and the genius of Armstrong made them even better. His impact is audible in every part of the band as it soon would be in the whole jazz genre. It shines through in the swing of Henderson's rhythm section, in the intricacy of the arrangements that Henderson and Don Redman wrote for the band, and in the fluency of the principal soloists. Within a year or so, Louis Armstrong's playing would have that impact on everyone who played the music.

Coleman Hawkins was the first one to grasp the impact and make it his own. He was well schooled on his instrument and, at least as important, he was proud and competitive. He transliterated Armstrong's melodic inventiveness and rhythmic swing to the tenor saxophone. On an instrument of such dubious lineage, it was an unexpected turn, but Hawkins brought dauntless mastery to it. His big-toned sound became the model for dozens of musicians, and the tenor saxophone rose swiftly into the front ranks of jazz instruments. Hawkins is revered as the father of the tenor saxophone well beyond the confines of jazz.

All of this was going on during Duke Ellington's formative years, as he made his way to New York in 1923, ascended to the leader's role with the Washingtonians in 1924, and worked out the elements of his style as leader of the house band at the Kentucky Club in 1924-1927. By the time he reached his first artistic plateau at the Cotton Club, where the billing was Duke Ellington and His Famous Orchestra, Ellington must have been keenly aware of the Henderson orchestra, the house band downtown at the Roseland Ballroom and the stan-

Coleman Hawkins (1904-1969)

dard-bearer in the field. At the very moment that Ellington was allotting Bigard his meager half-chorus on "Bugle Call Rag," Fletcher Henderson was dazzling New Yorkers with the likes of "King Porter Stomp" (recorded 14 March 1928), Jelly Roll Morton's ditty impeccably arranged by Henderson (and destined in his arrangement to be a hit again ten years later for Benny Goodman), which owed much of its iconic success to Hawkins's brawny tenor solo.

Ellington knew about it and, surprisingly, ignored it. Prince Robinson, Ellington's occasional tenor player in the Washingtonians before Bigard joined, mainly played clarinet for Ellington although he was known elsewhere as one of the new breed of tenor players. Lambert (1998, 17) writes, "Coleman Hawkins regarded Robinson as among the keenest of his early rivals." Ellington gave Robinson few opportunities to show off what he had picked up from Hawkins; instead, he became the founding member of the clarinet-doubling-tenor role that would come to fruition with Barney Bigard.

By the time Joe Garland played his eight-bar tenor solo with Ellington, Coleman Hawkins was being showcased nightly in tenor saxophone masterpieces with Henderson's orchestra including "The Stampede" (recorded 14 May 1926, Hawkins's breakthrough), "Whiteman Stomp" (11 May 1927, composed by Fats Waller) and "Queer Notions" (18 August 1933, Hawkins's own composition, his tour de force). Undoubtedly it was the clamor for these recordings that provided the stimulus for Ellington to try his hand at writing dedicated tenor saxophone parts, though he never said so. Two years after Joe Garland's guest shot, in 1935 and again a year later in 1936, Ellington again added a fifth reed to his section and brought in a tenor saxophone player to record with his orchestra. The resulting pieces are not in themselves especially noteworthy, but they take on long-term significance because the tenor player Ellington hired for both occasions was Ben Webster, a newcomer from the Midwest. Webster had gained swift recognition among the New York cognoscenti because Fletcher Henderson chose him as Coleman Hawkins's replacement when Hawkins took off in 1934 for a prolonged stay in England. But Webster's destiny would be attached to Ellington, not Henderson, as the man who finally filled Ellington's fifth-reed chair and filled it so successfully that he became its prototype.

It did not happen overnight. Even after he heard what Webster could bring to the sound of his band, Ellington was apparently in no hurry. On the first session with Webster as guest, in August 1935, he was allotted good solo space on "Truckin'," a pop song with lyrics by Ted Koehler and music by Rube Bloom. (Coincidentally or not, Joe Garland had also been imported to play tenor saxophone on a Ted Koehler song.) Ivie Anderson's vocal occupies one chorus in the solo sequence, following Cootie Williams on trumpet, and Tricky Sam Nanton on trombone takes a chorus and then Webster gets his turn. Years later, Webster remembered the date vividly. "Barney Bigard took a vacation in 1935 and I had a chance to sit in the band for two or three weeks," he said. "And we went out on the road for a little while. Then we made this record 'Truckin'.'... Then Barney came back, so I had to leave, naturally. But I sure hated to leave, because I'd enjoyed that music and hearing those guys play. That was such a great band."

The playing on "Truckin'" is spirited – the title refers to a new dance and the lyric describes its moves. Lambert (1998, 60), the only critic who ever wrote about this number, praises the arrangement extravagantly, saying it is "outstanding in its integration of soloists and orchestra and in the way it inspires the band to give such a driving, urgent performance." That praise seems more fitting for Webster's next guest shot, eleven months later (July 1936), especially on the piece called "In a Jam," which is undoubtedly Ellington's arrangement. "In a Jam" is a kind of blowing session, as the title suggests, but with the choruses reined in as duets (first Nanton/Bigard, and then Hodges/Williams) before Webster and Rex Stewart take unbridled solo choruses. Webster does not yet have the sound and style that would so readily identify him a few years later, but the potential is easy to hear.

Ellington apparently remained unconvinced, or at least he showed no signs of urgency about adding the fifth reed permanently. He would wait four more years, until February 1940, before hiring Ben Webster full time. By then he really had no choice. Coleman Hawkins, after his four-year sojourn in Europe, from 1934 to 1939, returned to the United States and scored a huge hit with "Body and Soul," a popular success destined to be a jazz classic, on RCA Victor, Ellington's label. At almost the same moment, Count Basie's orchestra stormed out of the Midwest with not one but two tenor sax stars, Herschel Evans and Lester Young. Cab Calloway, Ellington's relief band at the Cotton Cub, boasted Chu Berry on tenor. Swing bands were suddenly all the rage, and all of them featured tenor players – Vido Musso with Benny Goodman, Georgie Auld with Bunny Berigan and later with Benny Goodman, Tex Beneke with Glenn Miller, Tony Pastor with Artie Shaw, Eddie Miller with Bob Crosby, Joe Thomas with Jimmy Lunceford, Dick Wilson with Andy Kirk. The absence of a tenor star in Ellington's band had been noticeable for years but now seemed glaring.

Tardy though he was, Ellington's luck held. Though Ben Webster was gainfully employed and in demand, Ellington got word to him that he was planning to add a fifth reed to the section, and Webster leapt at the chance.

Making Space for Webster

Webster was 30 when he joined Ellington's orchestra. He was born in Kansas City, and his aptitude for music, as he recalled in an interview for the Smithsonian archive, makes his apprenticeship sound almost magical. "I studied on violin in grade school," Webster said. "I liked piano, but I didn't study on it. I'd left home and gone to Amarillo, Texas, playing piano with a band called Bretho Nelson .... Shortly after, Budd Johnson [a tenor saxophone player] and his brother Keg came through with Gene Coy's Aces. I met them and we started buddying around right away. So one day I just asked Budd, like, 'How do you run a scale on that thing?' So he showed me and I just went from there."

Webster joined the Young Family Band alongside Lester Young, son of the leader, Webster's age-mate (both born in 1909), and destined to become a major influence on the instrument. Webster was 21 at the time, and a novice on the saxophone. "It was Lester Young's daddy who taught me the notes on the horn," he said. "He played and taught all the instruments." Webster made his first records with Benny Moten's talented Kansas City band in 1931, and was already good enough to be given solo space. He then went to New York and played the field – besides Fletcher Henderson, he appeared with Teddy Wilson, Billie Holiday, Cab Calloway and other top bands, though never for long.

Physically, he was hard to miss. He was broad and bear-like, with bulging eyes; one of his nicknames was "Frog," bestowed by Ellington's young bass player (and Webster's protégé) Jimmy Blanton. He was a binge drinker, and he could be gruff and destructive when he binged; another of his nicknames was "Brute." He was also sentimental. He had been raised in a home bereft of males, supported staunchly by his mother, Mayme, a schoolteacher, and his great-aunt, Agnes Johnson. They catered to his every wish, and his devotion to the matriarchs was boundless. His sentimental side came through brilliantly in his ballad playing. In his later years, he took to playing the old Irish ballad "Danny Boy," a favorite of his deceased mother and great-aunt, and a tear would sometimes curl down his cheek.

Ellington, with a mother-fixation of his own, seems to have recognized that Webster's personal demons would be sublimated

Ellington's saxophone section in 1940: Barney Bigard (partly cut off), Johnny Hodges, Otto Hardwick, Ben Webster, Harry Carney

creatively in the framework of his orchestra. That, after all, was Ellington's gift. As Barney Bigard said, "He always studied a person's style, to make it comfortable for him to play. He knew the guy's limitations and his exceptional qualities" (as told to Stanley Dance, p. 85). How Ellington might have discerned all that from Webster's guest appearances four and five years earlier is hard to guess, but there is no doubt that when Webster joined he brought a spark that ignited the whole band.

Why Ellington chose Webster as the man to inaugurate what would be the final expansion of his orchestral instrumentation was never stated, but circumstantial evidence points to Willie the Lion Smith as go-between. One of Webster's obsessions was stride piano. His first professional job was providing the live soundtrack for silent films on a honky-tonk piano in Amarillo, Texas. All his life he gravitated toward empty piano benches, and when he was in his cups he was known to remove piano players bodily from their benches. When the mood took him, he played like a man possessed. According to Rex Stewart, his bandmate with Ellington and thereafter his eloquent apologist (1972), when Webster decided to leave Kansas City and try his fortunes in New York, Count Basie gave him some valuable guidance. He told Webster to seek out the Lion, major domo of the Harlem stride piano players, and ply him with cigars and whisky in order to gain entry into the music scene. Webster took his advice and quickly became a regular in the Lion's den. Ten years earlier, Duke Ellington had done exactly the same thing when he arrived in New York, and Willie the Lion Smith became his life-long idol and mentor (discussed more fully in Chapter 5, "Panther Patter"). It is not hard to imagine the Lion advocating on young Webster's behalf and Ellington giving it total credence. In any case, the mutual respect of Ellington and Webster for the Lion was surely a good omen, a convergence of tastes rooted in their very different characters.

Ellington explained his delay in bringing Webster into the band as a matter of economics. "After he made a record date with us in 1935, I always had a yen for Ben," he said (*MiMM* 163). "So as soon as we thought we could afford him, we added him on." The delay might have been partly due to scruples. One of Webster's high-profile jobs before joining Ellington was with Cab Calloway's orchestra, and because Calloway served as Ellington's relief band at the Cotton Club, Ellington considered Calloway's musicians to be off limits (Hasse 1993, 229). Under the circumstances, all Ellington could do was let Webster know that if he ever found himself unemployed he would make a place for him. Some time after that Webster gave Calloway his notice. Ellington then let a discreet interval go by. Webster was subbing in Teddy Wilson's orchestra immediately before joining Ellington (DEMS 2004-2005).

When Webster joined Ellington's orchestra, it was mostly made up of veterans, loyal to their leader well beyond the norms of their nocturnal habitat. Among them were a few notably prickly characters whose loyalty brought with it a sense of entitlement. They ferociously guarded not only their solo space but also their ensemble space. Thad Jones talks about sitting in as a substitute in Ellington's trumpet section as a young man and finding himself without a written score: "Looking over at a nearby player's part, he began blowing along, making up harmonies as he went, only to hear Cootie Williams growl, 'Get offa my note!'" (Peress, 189). Webster, fortunately, was not likely to be intimidated by anyone other than Ellington himself. He called Ellington "the Governor," and he said, "If Duke likes you, you're home free" (Dance, 122). Apart from the Governor, no one in the band carried a carried a bigger stick.

Webster's way was made smoother because there were a few other changes in the band around the time he arrived. Billy Strayhorn had joined the year before, in January 1939, preparing the way for those who came after him because of his benign temperament, and also because, as arranger/ composer and (briefly) lyricist, he did not displace anyone on the bandstand. Jimmy Blanton joined the band in

"Blanton-Webster Band" – Duke Ellington with reeds and rhythm. Ben Webster seated behind him, Jimmy Blanton standing at right

November 1939. The young bassist was destined to set the technical standards for all the jazz bass players who came after him, and the veterans recognized his extraordinary gifts, but Ellington eased Blanton's entry into the band by retaining his predecessor Billy Taylor in a unique two-bass configuration until Taylor gave up of his own volition. Webster joined a few months after Blanton, in late January 1940 (DEMS 2004-2005). Later that year, in November 1940, Cootie Williams, after 11 years with Ellington, left to play with Benny Goodman, thus removing a decidedly prickly presence from the band. His replacement was Ray Nance, slightly younger and upon his arrival nearly unknown.

These personnel shifts were few, but they carried considerable weight. Cumulatively, they proved potent enough to crack the cocoon of the old guard and make way for new life. Their impact is neatly encapsulated by the fact that the 1940-1942 orchestra is often referred to as "the Blanton-Webster band" (by RCA Victor, for instance, as the title of their definitive reissue of the 66 master takes that are the band's sumptuous legacy). Blanton and Nance would revitalize two of Ellington's longstanding strengths, and Webster would bring brand-new musculature. For Ellington as for Webster, the time was ripe.

"Out-and-Out Blowing" and So Much More

From his first notes as a regular with Ellington's orchestra, Ben Webster plays with the broad-toned swagger that would characterize his playing for the rest of his days. The metamorphosis from the generic sound in the earlier guest shots to the distinctive, individualistic, instantly identifiable style at all tempos is striking, but it is hardly unique. Many of Ellington's greatest soloists sound most distinctively personal in the context of Ellington's band – more so, paradoxically, than when they are on their own. Webster seems to have required no probationary period. By temperament, he was not a man who sat quietly and waited his turn. Harry Carney said, "Ben brought new life to a section that had been together a long time. He was inspired and he inspired us so that we worked together and tried to improve the section. We used to rehearse all alone, just the sax section" (Hasse 1993, 230).

Webster's stylistic advances were partly due to his nightly exposure to Johnny Hodges. Webster assimilated Hodges's flair in his solos, especially in ballads, using the full range of his horn, gliding up to notes and holding them for an extra beat, tendencies that can edge toward melodrama but, used tastefully, can communicate rapture and sensuality. Balliett (2001: 405) said, "His early style… stemmed directly from [Coleman] Hawkins, but it went through a subtle reshaping during the three years he spent with Duke Ellington in the early forties. He fell under the lyrical sway of Johnny Hodges, and this released a poetic outpouring that continued the rest of his life." Webster freely acknowledged what Hodges taught him, though the 'lessons' were non-verbal and diffident. "I learned a lot from him," he told Stanley Dance (1970, 122), "but you know what his only advice to me was when I came in the band? 'Learn your parts!'"

It was a highly productive time – many commentators consider these years to be Ellington's creative peak. New music was abundant with Strayhorn, Juan Tizol and Mercer Ellington also contributing charts. With the new charts, Ellington could allot solo space as he saw fit, and Webster got a full share. In his first year, the band made 31 records in the Victor studios and Webster soloed on 13 of them.

At first, Ellington clearly saw Webster's strength in his brawny, big-toned power. "Conga Brava," one of the early recordings with a Webster solo (15 March 1940), exploits that power masterfully. The latin-tinged piece of exotica by Tizol and Ellington has the orchestra navigate gracefully through the first chorus with Tizol on valve trombone and Bigard on clarinet over undulating rhythms. When Webster enters in the second chorus the rhythms straighten and the mood rises by calculated degrees from sultry to hot. Webster's solo is insistent from the start but its intensity grows so that Webster seems to modulate the opening mood rather than disrupting it. At the end of Webster's chorus the band is swinging infectiously. Rex Stewart on cornet picks up on Webster's swing and guides it back down, summoning the latin tinge in the end and making way for the return to the theme and Tizol's re-statement of the opening melody. The arrangement has a stunning symmetry with Webster's improvised accelerando framed by Tizol's stately latin beat. Ellington's arrangement is a prime example of his remarkable talent for capitalizing on the

Ben Webster in 1941

natural proclivities of his musicians, in this instance fusing Tizol's conservatory smoothness with Webster's ebullient swing.

Ellington's masterwork for Ben Webster came soon after. "Cotton Tail" (recorded 4 May 1940) is an uptempo romp, and Webster is the only soloist. The first chorus opens in full flight stated by the brass sections with saxophone counter-melody. The structure is AABA using the chord sequence of George Gershwin's "I Got Rhythm," a structure now known generically in jazz as "rhythm changes," one of the conventional structures of jazz composition. "Cotton Tail" is one of the first examples. On the first chorus, Cootie Williams plays the eight-bar bridge on muted trumpet; on the final chorus (the sixth), when the orchestra restates the theme, the bridge is played at high volume by the entire trumpet section. The progression from muted trumpet in the first chorus to full-throated brass at the end is an indicator of the crescendo thrust of this ingenious arrangement. The second and third choruses are assigned to Webster. He plays with unbridled enthusiasm pushed by the rhythm section, except on the *B* section where the trumpets riff behind him and urge him onward. In the fourth chorus Webster steps aside for a romping brass arrangement, and in the fifth for a remarkable saxophone choir. The last chorus reprises the opening lines but with much greater intensity and amplitude, capped by the brass shout in the final bridge. "Cotton Tail" is a climactic piece, a show-stopper, bold and defiant.

Ben Webster was destined to replicate his performance on "Cotton Tail" for the rest of his days, nightly with the Ellington orchestra for the next few years and, after that, in every other context, small or great, that he played in for the thirty-odd years after he left the orchestra. He never complained. It pleased crowds everywhere he went, but his feeling for it may go deeper than the thrill of pleasing crowds. Though Duke Ellington is credited as sole composer, Rex Stewart (1972, 129) wrote, "As a composer and arranger, Ben's most significant contribution was *Cotton Tail*, for which he also wrote the now-famous saxophone-section chorus," that is, the stunning fifth chorus. That reed ensemble is one of the glories of the piece, set off perfectly in Ellington's many-layered arrangement. Webster apparently developed the 32-bar ensemble in those reed-section rehearsals Carney talked about. He would have started with the rhythm changes as the harmonic underpinning. For the intricate voicings of the various reeds Webster was undoubtedly inspired by the tight reed ensembles composed by Benny Carter that he had played in the Henderson orchestra. Ellington evidently took Webster's 32-bar chorus as the starting-point and built the complex six-chorus "Cotton Tail" around it. It was part of Ellington's composing technique to take improvised lines and melodic figures developed by his musicians as starting points and develop full orchestrations, sometimes crediting the band member who gave it impetus and sometimes not, as in this case. Webster, star witness to Ellington's architectonics, never complained.

"Cotton Tail" earned ovations from critics as well as audiences.

The composer/critic Schuller (1989, 129-30) said, "It changed the face of jazz and foretold in many way where the music's future lay," and he elaborated thus:

> Never before had Ellington opened up a piece for out-and-out blowing .... *Cotton Tail* and Webster's solo loosened, ever so slightly, the compositional harness that Ellington had been constructing for over a decade. *Cotton Tail*, particularly in its execution, let in a gust of spontaneity, of freshness, of flexibility, which the Ellington band was never to lose again and which offered a whole new way of integrating composition and improvisation.

Schuller hears "Cotton Tail" as a precursor of bebop, the ascendant jazz style that was still a year or two away when it was recorded. If Schuller is correct, there is considerable irony in the struggles that Ellington would have in accommodating those new currents, which in the early 1950s would result in the lowest point of his musical life. Undeniably, "Cotton Tail" resembles the bebop-to-come in a couple of fairly superficial aspects. It is based on pre-existing chord changes imported from the American songbook, notably the rhythm changes, a practice that reached its apogee in bebop. And it is played at rapid-fire tempo, as bebop typically was. In other respects, there is little resemblance. "Cotton Tail" is through-composed in four of its six choruses and it provides orchestral frames for Webster's improvisations in the other two choruses, where bebop essentially stated the melody and loosed soloists to play over rhythm accompaniment while the other soloists looked on, waiting their turn. This bebop pattern persisted even in the few attempts at big-band bebop, best exemplified by Dizzy Gillespie's short-lived orchestra. Essentially, bebop was small-band music and solo-centric, the antithesis on both counts of "Cotton Tail." Boppers may have admired "Cotton Tail" but it was not an Ellington number that they themselves played (as they did "Perdido" and "It Don't Mean a Thing"). Schuller is surely right in pointing out that boppers sought the "spontaneity" and "freshness" that "Cotton Tail" flaunted, but more specific links do not really work.

Ben's Nocturnes

Although Webster's first solos with Ellington pegged him as the band's jive bomber, Ellington soon discovered that he was also an effective ballad soloist, investing his manly sound with a sentimental tinge. Ellington made him the featured instrumentalist on his romantic ballad "All Too Soon" (recorded 22 July 1940). The heartbreak theme would be made explicit when lyrics were added for a pop song version by Ellington and Carl Sigman – "All too soon/We had to part/The moment you had touched my heart...." But the heartbreak is every bit as eloquent when Webster embellishes the melody with a crooning, breezy tone. His solo invokes Johnny Hodges, a point that was surely not lost on Hodges himself, sitting in his shadow as Webster rose for his solo. Webster found himself in a context that Ellington had usually given automatically to Hodges, or occasionally to trombonist

Ben Webster at rest

Lawrence Brown in his 'sweet' ballad mode.

A glorious example of Webster's ballad mastery was preserved under extraordinary circumstances when two students received permission to record the Ellington orchestra at a dance date in Fargo, North Dakota, in November 1940. In spite of the grueling bus rides required for weeks on end to play one-night stands in the Upper Midwest, the band played with uncanny spirit whenever they were in the presence of swaying dancers in a ballroom, even on a night when many musicians wore gloves against the cold. The Fargo dance date is the most celebrated of all Ellington dance dates because it caught the band at its spontaneous best in surprisingly sharp sound fidelity. One of the highlights – perhaps the best moment of many good ones – comes near the end of the evening, after more than two hours of music and two intermissions. Ellington announces "Star Dust," Hoagy Carmichael's hit song of the day, a mega-hit in today's jargon. The song was hitherto unknown in Ellington's repertoire. It turns out that it was a head arrangement of the familiar melody specifically intended to give the band a break from reading scores all night long. "The band had never heard it before," said Jack Towers, one of the students who recorded the concert (and later an esteemed audio engineer in the music business). "It was something that Ben [Webster] and [Jimmy] Blanton had worked up as roommates" (2002). Blanton set the tempo for the rhythm section on his bass, and Webster launched into an extemporaneous recital of Carmichael's melody with subtle variations. Webster sustains the ballad mood with free-flowing, uninhibited affection for over four minutes. The rhythm section, buoyed by Ellington's embellishments, provides sympathetic accompaniment. It is surely a tribute to Webster's remarkable performance that his bandmates, technically on 'recess' while he works, lay down an underscore for him at several points. Webster treats Carmichael's handsome melody reverently, wonderfully relaxed and inventive at every turn. It is a remarkable ballad performance, treasured all the more for the small miracle that resulted in its preservation on a frigid night in a dance-hall in the Upper Midwest.

Webster maintained his role as Ellington's broad-toned swinger on uptempo numbers but his role as balladeer grew apace. Ellington continued to place him in contexts that formerly went to other musicians. One of those contexts, an Ellington specialty, almost a uniquely Ellingtonian genre, is the impressionistic ballad, a kind of dream sequence in which the soloist rides the sinuous melody over lush, textured chords (the subject of Chapter 4, "Lotus Eaters Unite!"). The genre was the exclusive domain of Johnny Hodges with the momentary exception of one number in Ben Webster's time in the band. "Chelsea Bridge" (2 December 1941), composed by Billy Strayhorn under the inspiration of James McNeill Whistler's fogbound impression of Battersea Bridge (Whistler's "Nocturne in Blue and Gold," ca. 1875; Strayhorn's title apparently commemorates Chelsea Church in the background). The piece is a nocturne, a slow-motion glide over rich chords. Like "Warm Valley" and "Day Dream" before it, "Chelsea Bridge" seems tailor-made for Hodges, but in its inaugural recording the solo role was assigned to Ben Webster. He plays it with consummate grace and poise, a kind of sublimation of the quiescence he displayed on "Star Dust" now heightened significantly in the controlled studio atmosphere. Webster's debt to Hodges is never more obvious – it is easy to imagine the notes he chooses as they would sound on Hodges's alto saxophone – but Webster brings to it his own rich depths. It is a triumphant performance, and one that Webster would reprise countless times both with Ellington and in his afterlife as an itinerant jazzman. Webster put his own stamp on "Chelsea Bridge," and in Ellington's repertoire it remained forever after the province of the tenor saxophone soloist.

So it went with most of Webster's precedents as the first holder of the fifth-reed chair. The men who succeeded Webster in Ellington's orchestra as tenor saxophone soloists, even the best of them – Al Sears, Paul Gonsalves and Harold Ashby – all came into the band knowing Webster's solos by heart. Being conversant with Webster's solos and Webster's sound became the credentials for the occupant of the fifth reed chair. Webster's successors knew they would be called on to play "Conga Brava," "Cotton Tail," "All Too Soon" and "Chelsea Bridge," and every one of them arrived knowing how Webster had played them before them.

Webster in Absentia

Ben Webster put his stamp on the fifth-reed chair although his tenure was, by Ellingtonian standards, short lived. He left in 1943, after fewer than four years. One account claims that his departure was forced when Webster, in one of the brutish moods that bedeviled him from time to time, refused to stop noodling at the piano and surrender the bench to his leader. Digby Fairweather gives the story mythic proportions with this account: "Webster left Ellington because one night he had been allowed to play piano with the band, stayed too long at the keyboard, and when Ellington took offence and refused to discuss the matter, Webster cut one of Ellington's best suits to bits" (Carr, Fairweather and Priestley 1988: 531). Other accounts of his leaving ignore the violence and say that he simply felt the pull of Fifty-Second Street, where small-band modern jazz was suddenly thriving. This version gains credence because, in the immediate aftermath of his leaving, Webster himself thrived on Fifty-Second Street, buoyed by the reputation that followed him from his time with Ellington. The brutish version gains perhaps more credence because Webster always cherished his time with Ellington and regretted leaving, which he treated as a kind of exile.

Though Webster would return to the Ellington orchestra for short stays on numerous occasions, Ellington always maintained a kind of distance. In 1948, five years after leaving, Webster sat in with the band for seven months. His 'official' stature is not altogether clear. Al Sears, Webster's successor, had settled into the fifth chair with considerable distinction, so that Webster seems to have been an adjunct, a kind of long-term guest. Exactly how Ellington might have fit Webster into ensembles with Sears in the chair is a mystery because the band made no studio recordings in these months due to a Musicians' Union strike. Most likely Ellington did not fit him into ensembles at all. In live performances from these days, when Ellington introduced Webster for his solo features he took some pains to set him apart from the others. At the Carnegie Hall concert in November 1948, for instance, Ellington announced, "And now, [as] a special extra added soloist tonight there's one of our former members who is identified with many of our outstanding things." He makes it eminently clear that Webster is an adjunct.

If Ellington showed some reserve on his guest appearances, Webster, for his part, made no secret about missing the band. In an

Ben Webster in 1967

interview for the Smithsonian archive late in his life he said, "The height of my ambition was to play with Duke.... Duke has always been way out front. He was then and he still is now."

Webster, Byas and "How High the Moon"

Ellington's aloofness probably accounts for the tune he selected as Webster's feature at Carnegie Hall and elsewhere, which was not one of Webster's tried-and-true specialties – not one of "our outstanding things," as Ellington put it. Instead, he called on Webster to solo on "How High the Moon." Unexpectedly, this old ballad from an obscure 1940 Broadway play became a bebop anthem in the mid 1940s. So Ellington, struggling to carve his niche among the young turks who were stealing the limelight from him and so many other old established names, called on Webster, the man who had rubbed elbows with the 'other side' on Fifty-Second Street, to give it a go. At Carnegie Hall, Webster responds with a smart solo that is not patently bebop but also not straight swing. Setting Webster in this context suggests that Ellington brought him back into the band in hopes of importing some Fifty-Second Street pizzazz without bending too far in that direction. Ultimately, he would have to bend further.

Ellington's inclusion of "How High the Moon" in his concerts reflects the peculiar tensions that were rocking the jazz world in the latter half of the 1940s, and were specifically rocking Ellington. The bebop revolution, spearheaded by the brilliance of Dizzy Gillespie and Charlie Parker, was beguiling the best young musicians and diverting the jazz audience. For Ellington, "How High the Moon" represents an oblique nod in their direction. In the accelerated pace of change at the time, it soon became passé. "The boppers clearly liked the chord changes better than the melody," as Ted Gioia observed in his jazz history, "and when Charlie Parker composed his oft-played 'Ornithology,' he kept the former and discarded the latter." "Ornithology" was just one of the bop anthems based on the chord changes of "How High the Moon." Later on, Coleman Hawkins used them as the underpinning for his "Bean at the Met," and Miles Davis for his "Solar." In 1948, at Carnegie Hall, the original melody still had its cachet; after all, the Dizzy Gillespie orchestra had played it in that same setting a year before. By the late 1940s and into the 1950s, Ellington was scuffling to hold his place in the jazz pecking order against the young, aggressive revolutionaries like Parker and Gillespie.

With his Old-World manners and a string of undistinguished dance numbers and pop tunes for Columbia Records, for the only time in his life Ellington looked like yesterday's news. Because Ben Webster had established himself in the company of the hipsters on 52nd Street, Ellington apparently looked to him to bridge the gap by playing the bop anthem at Carnegie Hall and elsewhere. It did not work.

"How High the Moon" became a kind of fetish for Ellington, and the pains he took with it over a six-year period crystallize his travails with bebop. He had recorded it in November 1947 in the same arrangement that Webster played a year later at Carnegie Hall. The studio recording is conventional swing, jazzy and uptempo, suitable for jitterbugging at the very moment when that acrobatic dance style was a dying art. The arranger, surprisingly, was neither Ellington nor Strayhorn nor anyone involved with the new music, but Dick Vance, who had played lead trumpet and arranged scores in the last incarnation of the Fletcher Henderson Orchestra (from 1935 to 1939). Vance now made his living in Broadway pit bands and on the side he sold arrangements to the few remaining dance bands. Ellington's studio recording of Vance's chart is a throwback – conventional swing, with several short, lackluster solos.

At Carnegie Hall, Ben Webster gave the chart a livelier reading than the studio version, but any real hope of tapping into the bop animus with that arrangement was doomed from the start.

Two years later, from April to June 1950, Ellington was digging out "How High the Moon" for another special guest. The fifth chair in the reed section was still very much in flux at the time (as Table 1 graphically shows), and it was momentarily occupied by one Alva Beau McCain, its most anonymous occupant ever. In a brainwave, Ellington conscripted Don Byas to join the orchestra as a guest for their European tour. Byas, an expatriate American living in Amsterdam, had genuine bop credentials, having worked in the house band at Minton's Playhouse in Harlem along with Charlie Christian, Thelonious Monk and Kenny Clarke, where bebop is said to have been born. After that, in the mid-1940s, after stints with Count Basie and Coleman Hawkins, Byas was a regular in Dizzy Gillespie's band at the Onyx Club on 52nd Street. In September 1946, he joined Don Redman's orchestra for the first post-War jazz tour of Europe and he remained behind when the tour ended. He stayed there for the rest of his life. (He died in Amsterdam in 1972.) Byas was well settled in Europe and playing at the peak of his powers in 1950, when Ellington recruited him for the same adjunct role that Webster had occupied almost two years earlier.

Ellington resuscitated "How High the Moon" as Byas's nightly feature, as it had been Webster's, but with a striking difference. For Byas, Ellington reconceived "How High the Moon" as a kind of concerto, with Byas ruminating on the melody over thick hymn-like chords for three minutes and then exploding into a wild improvisation over crackling brass for three more minutes. It is not bebop but it is

Don Byas (1912-1972)

certainly a tour de force, and – finally – it comes in an arrangement imbued with Ellington's ingenuity and spirit. Byas's performance is preserved in spectacular performances from Zurich (2 May 1950) and other European venues. The contrast between Webster's and Byas's performances of "How High the Moon" a year and a half apart make a graphic progress report on Duke Ellington's growing confidence in the new musical paradigm he was building from the ashes of the Swing Era.

Don Byas effectively bailed out Ellington on the European tour as the right man in the right place. In terms of the chronology of the fifth-reed chair, the tenor saxophonists Ellington had left behind when he embarked on the European tour were two aspirants who would go on to make their names elsewhere. In his search for the new, Ellington had momentarily filled the fifth chair with two young tenor players, Jimmy Forrest and Charlie Rouse (as shown in Table 1). Rouse stayed for almost ten months (May 1949 to March 1950) and Forrest overlapped with him for seven of them (June 1949 to February 1950). Exactly how Ellington deployed two tenors in a six-person reed section is unclear. In the expansion to six reedmen with the guest appearances of Webster and later of Byas, they had served as soloists, either coming out of the wings for their turn at the mic or sitting silently in the section until their names were called.

Neither Rouse nor Forrest qualified as a featured guest at this stage of their careers. They were novices, presumably hoping a stint with Ellington would get them started. Ellington's plans for integrating both into the section remains a mystery. He never talked about it, and the one recording session with both men in the band, a nondescript Columbia session in September 1949, offers no clues as to how they worked together, if indeed they did. Rouse does not solo at the recording session and is not discernible in the ensembles though he was apparently present. Forrest solos on one of the four titles, "The Greatest There Is," a blues with words and music by Ellington that seems to be a limp homage to bebop. Ellington's lyric is sung by one Lu Elliott, whose tenure in the band was even shorter than Forrest's. The sentiments of Ellington's song are strained and its humor falls flat. Ellington's lyric yokes together hipster slang and Gillespie-style bop syllables: "My man sends me, I don't know how far/Yes, my man sends me I don't know how far/ With a sha-ba ool-ya-oo and skoo-dap-da!" Jimmy Forrest plays the opening and closing choruses, and if they are not exactly memorable they are still better than anything else on the record.

Rouse and Forrest were soon gone. Both men would prove their worth elsewhere. Charlie Rouse (1924-1988) became the constant presence in Thelonious Monk's Quartet from 1959 until 1970, Monk's most productive and successful years. Jimmy Forrest (1920-1980) worked steadily as a leader of small bands and recording sideman with a blues edge. He is notorious in the Ellington annals for lifting the second theme of Ellington's "Happy-Go-Lucky Local" and recording it as his own composition under his own title, "Night

Train," a hit record in 1952. The plagiarism prompted one of Ellington's iconic rejoinders. When was asked about it, he replied, "We must be flattered and just go write something better." Years later Mercer Ellington admitted that they had sued Forrest and ultimately accepted a cash settlement (Nicholson 1999: 322).

Don Byas was their replacement on the three-month European tour. The circumstances of their leaving are as unmarked as were their arrivals. They left nothing behind. Byas suited Ellington's purposes better than either of them, but he was strictly on loan. No one, not even Duke Ellington, would persuade him to return home.

"Hey, sweetie…."
It took a few more years before Ellington finally reconciled bebop and "How High the Moon." Paul Gonsalves moved into the fifth reed chair in 1950, in what turned into a lifelong appointment that would stabilize that position for more than twenty years. Though Gonsalves's appointment looks like it was made in heaven, it came about as a kind of happy accident. Ellington was playing at Birdland and Gonsalves, out of work with (he says) $7.20 to his name, went to hear the band. Ellington surprised Gonsalves by saying, "Hey, sweetie, I've been looking for you. Why don't you come to the office tomorrow?" Gonsalves came, and Ellington hired him to fill the tenor saxophone chair on a road trip. It was the specter of Ben Webster that turned it into a permanent appointment. Gonsalves told Stanley Dance:

> Secretly, I was thinking, 'I've got this job because I know all of Ben Webster's solos from the records.' The first thing that Duke played was "C Jam Blues," and then "Settin' and a-Rockin'." So I asked him if he still had "Chelsea Bridge," and as I stood up to play my solo I overheard him say to Quentin Jackson, 'This so-and-so sounds just like Ben!' So I got the job.

Gonsalves became the talisman for a turn of fortunes for the band. The next year he was joined in the orchestra by trumpeters Clark Terry and Willie Cook, and trombonist Britt Woodman. It was 1951, and Ellington finally had a coterie of sidemen who were devoted to his esthetic and had absorbed the rudiments of bebop in their formative years. Until then, that combination – fluency in Ellingtonia and facility in bebop – had proven elusive. As the dismal 1940s ended, the Ellington orchestra's fortunes took an upward swing, not all at once but in steps that would, in the fullness of time, erupt into their 1956 triumph at the Newport Jazz Festival.

One of the small steps that foretold that moment was a raucous new arrangement, the third, of "How High the Moon." In the early 1950s Ellington started calling that title again after a hiatus of about three years. The new version bore no resemblance to Dick Vance's jive arrangement or to the concerto-like extravaganza that Don Byas had played in Europe. In fact, it bore little resemblance to "How High the Moon." Instead, the band roared into "Ornithology," Charlie Parker's signature tune written for him by Little Benny Harris. Ellington avoids the bebop title in favor of the title of the Broadway tune, by now an old warhorse, that supplied its chord changes but the

Paul Gonsalves (jazzploration.com)

melody they are playing is unmistakably "Ornithology." In some performances by the Ellington orchestra it is possible to pick out phrases from the original melody in solo statements by Jimmy Hamilton and Paul Gonsalves. This arrangement was never recorded in a studio, and the arranger is not identified. If it is a head arrangement, worked out on the fly, it is remarkably polished, with a chorus of four-bar exchanges by the trumpet players and great gusto in the rollicking ensembles. And, most important, it brought audiences to their feet night after night. After one performance in Hamilton, Ontario (8 February 1954), perhaps the best that has survived, Ellington finally quiets the rambunctious applause by announcing, "Thank you!! That was *supposed* to be 'How High the Moon'!" In truth, it was much better than that. After eight years of trying Ellington had finally extricated that old song from the Swing Era. And himself with it.

After Ben, the Deluge

If Ellington was initially wary of the tenor saxophone as a solo voice, his reservations disappeared with Ben Webster. From 1940 on, the orchestra was never again without a tenor soloist, and in the hierarchy of Ellington's solo voices the tenor man got as much solo space as any wind instrument and more than most. Indeed, it became a growth area. After clarinetist Jimmy Hamilton retired in 1968, Ellington replaced him not with a clarinetist who doubled on tenor but with a second tenor saxophone soloist (thus, viewed obliquely, catching up to Count Basie's trend-setting example thirty years after the fact). That was still a few years off when Webster departed in August 1943.

Al Sears (1910-1990), Webster's successor after the nine-month trial of one Skippy Williams, left his own impression in a five-year stint that lasted until 1949. Sears had been on the road with bands since he was 17, and he learned the value of strutting his stuff. For all his experience, he had to pass through an initiation rite with the Ellington band. "I'm the newest man in the band and I just haven't caught on to the system yet," he told George T. Simon in *Metronome*. "Instead of starting at the top, the whole band starts at 'H' – that is, everybody except me. ...If it weren't for Johnny [Hodges] I'd be completely lost. He cues me.... The other night on a broadcast he practically pushed me to the mike to make sure I'd come in right on

Al Sears playing to the jitterbugs

Al Sears (1910-1990)

my chorus, and then, when it was all over, he yanked me back by my coat to make sure I'd stop."

It did not take long for Ellington to exploit Sears's earthy R & B appeal. "I was a salesman for Duke," Sears told Joe Goldberg in 1960. "I played two or three notes, and stomped my foot, and I stopped the show for him every night." Ellington paid Sears the compliment of giving him his own nightly feature, "Carnegie Blues" (excerpted from *Black, Brown and Beige*), and unleashing his bawling tenor on novelty songs such as "(Otto Make That) Riff Staccato" (10 May 1945, arranged by Mary Lou Williams, and sung by Ray Nance) in a vain attempt at getting a hit record.

Al Sears left Ellington under strange, perhaps hurtful circumstances, though Ellington of course would never admit the hurt. Sears hoped to make his name as a leader in his own right, and when that ambition faltered he joined a small band formed by Johnny Hodges, Ellington's lead saxophone player and most admired soloist from 1928 until 1951, when Hodges left Ellington abruptly (discussed further in Chapter 4, "Lotus Eaters Unite!"). Sears became Hodges's straw boss in the band, looking after bookings and travel plans for the administratively feckless Hodges. He also gave Hodges his one taste of success by composing and soloing on the only hit record the band had, "Castle Rock," a minor sensation in the growing rhythm 'n' blues genre (and precursor of the rock 'n' roll boom). The success proved illusory. Sears left Hodges after about a year and spent the rest of his days playing minor clubs and supplying back-up honking on records by doo-wop groups and the like. Hodges scuffled for a few years and returned to Ellington in 1955, where he reclaimed his star status and stayed until his death in 1970.

Immediately following Sears, Ellington went through the most unsettled period of his 50-year career. One of the elements in conspicuous flux was the fifth reed chair. Some of the travails have been hinted at above with Ellington's failure to integrate young Charlie Rouse and Jimmy Forrest, and the conscription of Webster at Carnegie Hall in 1948 and the expatriate Don Byas to bolster the inconspicuous Alva Beau McCain on a European tour in 1950 (shown graphically in Table 1).

Stability was eventually restored with the enlisting of **Paul Gonsalves** (1920-1974). He joined after the European tour in 1950 and it took a few years for him to work his way into Ellington's charmed inner circle, as much because of Ellington's unsettled esthetics in these years as Gonsalves's personal diffidence. A true Ellingtonian not only for his unflinching loyalty but for his impact on the sound of the orchestra both in ensembles and solos, Gonsalves rightly merits a chapter of his own. (Gonsalves would die just ten days before Ellington and the news was kept from Ellington in hospital for fear of compounding his infirmity.) Gonsalves's career highlight by all accounts came at the Newport Jazz Festival in July 1956 when his rollicking interval between "Crescendo in Blue" and "Diminuendo in Blue" set the audience dancing in the aisles and upsetting the curfew of the upper-crust town. It was a performance that gave Ellington a contemporary profile unrivalled by any American musician (*Time* cover story, best-selling LP *Ellington at Newport*, a favorable contract with Columbia Records – all amply documented at book-length by Morton 2008).

Gonsalves's true worth was audible both before and after his Newport watershed. Close listening reveals Ellington experimenting with the rollicking side of Gonsalves on his arrival, six years before he let it loose at Newport, in an obscure recording called "The Happening." And in the end there was so much more than rollicking sax when Gonsalves was showcased on ballads and blues especially on the stockpile recordings (discussed at length in Chapter 8, "Ellington's Parallel Universe"). From the day he joined, he was a constant presence. Unlike some of his bandmates, he was a benign presence, and he shared his tenor saxophone role on the occasions that the Maestro asked him to with grace and dignity.

When **Jimmy Hamilton** took over Barney Bigard's clarinet chair in 1943, he inevitably inherited the other obligation that went with that role, doubling on tenor. He was not amused, at least not at first. He told Stanley Dance (1970: 137):

> Right off the bat, Duke told me I'd have to play tenor. Clarinet was my instrument, but on saxophone I was more of an alto player. That didn't matter to him. ... I took the job and everything was nice, except that I didn't like the tenor. I thought it was holding me back, because of the difference in mouthpiece.... [I]t was a handicap to my clarinet study. The characters of the two instruments are quite different. The tenor is more flexible so far as bending notes is concerned, and it is very easy to play, so you are less tense and can take more liberties.

Those differences – shucking off tension and taking liberties – worked wonders for Hamilton. His tenor soloing had vigor and rough grace that gave him a distinctive voice even among all the full-time tenor players. It could hardly have been less like his conservatory-based clarinet virtuosity. Dance (1998) made the obvious point: "Hamilton's approach to his two instruments was so astonishingly different that it is hard to credit their being played by the same man."

Ellington could hardly resist using that distinctive voice, despite Hamilton's objections. He assigned Hamilton tenor solos as often as he thought he could without ruffling Hamilton's sensibilities. At a Cornell University concert (10 December 1948), with both Al Sears and Ben Webster in the orchestra, Ellington keeps Hamilton on his feet soloing on "Hy'a Sue" for five choruses, the longest solo by an Ellington tenor saxophonist until Gonsalves's marathon 37-chorus solo at the Newport Jazz Festival in 1956.[1] Among the many high points of Hamilton's undervalued, almost unnoticed, tenor role, his

---

1 The studio recording of "Hy'a Sue" (Columbia 1947) featured Tyree Glenn on plunger trombone with Hamilton's tenor obbligato, and then a chorus by Hodges. At the Cornell concert, Ellington could take certain liberties and keep Hamilton on his feet for as long as he wanted.

Jimmy Hamilton (1917-1994) on tenor with Louie Bellson, 1951

Duke Ellington conducting with tenor saxophonists Paul Gonsalves and Jimmy Hamilton and alto saxophonist Johnny Hodges

solo on the rollicking studio recording of "Happy-Go-Lucky-Local" (2 January 1954) on *Ellington 55* (Capitol) was a conspicuous gem among several others. This performance made it very clear that the orchestra's doldrums were coming to an end.

When Jimmy Hamilton retired in 1968 he was replaced by **Harold Ashby,** who did not play the clarinet at all but played tenor saxophone very much in the style of Ben Webster. When Ashby first arrived in New York from Kansas City to try his luck on the music scene in the 1950s, Webster took a liking to him and found some work for him. His first recordings were with a small band assembled by Webster ten years before Ashby joined Ellington (*The Soul of Ben Webster* on Verve, 1958). Notwithstanding Webster's help, Ashby remained a fringe player around New York until he joined Ellington.

Harold Ashby's hiring spelled the end of the clarinet specialist

Duke Ellington with Harold Ashby (1925-2003)

chair after 40 years, a change that was hardly noticed and little lamented. Most other big bands had eliminated the clarinet as a solo voice at least 15 years earlier. The orchestra now had both Gonsalves and Ashby as tenor soloists and Ellington gave them more or less equal space. By the late 1960s, Gonsalves was ailing and often unreliable, and sharing the tenor chores with Ashby was a godsend. Ashby was featured on "Thanks for the Beautiful Land on the Delta" (27 April 1970) in the *New Orleans Suite* (Atlantic Records) and several other compositions in what turned out to be an extraordinarily vital period for Ellington in 1970-1972, before cancer slowed him and ultimately killed him in 1974. In live performances, Ellington often accorded Ashby the ultimate tribute of a solo feature, sometimes in a fairly casual head arrangement (such as "B.P. Blues" at Ellington's 70th birthday concert in Manchester, England), where Ashby gets to show off his smooth tone and easy swing in a joyous context.

One critic credits Ashby as "the last man to join the band whose personality Duke used in the old way as a specific element within his compositions" (Lambert 1998: 312). Technically that distinction really belongs to another reed player, **Norris Turney**, who joined the orchestra in 1969, a few months after Ashby. In an eerie development, Ellington hired Turney, an alto saxophonist, several months before Johnny Hodges's sudden and unexpected death in a dentist's chair in 1970. His addition added a sixth player to the reed section, and for the months in which he and Hodges overlapped, Turney sat in the trombone section. After Hodges died, Turney simply moved down a row and took his place behind Hodges's music stand. Many observers at the time wondered if the orchestra could survive at all without Hamilton and Hodges, but Ashby and Turney brought positive energy to the decades-long stability of the reed section and clearly stimulated Ellington's creative juices. Turney inherited the role of the main alto saxophone soloist, and he could emulate Hodges well enough, as he did on "Checkered Hat" (23 February 1971) written by Turney as a tribute and named by him for Hodges's characteristic headwear. His major solo instrument, however, became the flute, a belated discovery in Ellington's instrumental palette and one he obviously relished (as discussed in Chapter 7, "Afro-Eurasian Ellington").

Paul Gonsalves, Harold Ashby and Ben Webster "In Triplicate"

Besides alto and flute, Turney also played tenor saxophone with great flair. The convergence of three gifted tenor saxophone players in the reed section was not an accident that Ellington could long resist. From 1969 until 1973, as long as Turney was in the orchestra, Ellington took uncommon delight in herding his three tenors onto the proscenium and giving them their head on a bumptious tenor battle called "In Triplicate." After Turney left, he encouraged Ben Webster to join the fray and kept on beaming.

The spectacle of three tenor saxophone players vying for attention in a kind of jam session with Ellington beaming his approval takes on high irony for listeners with an historical bent. It had taken Ellington 15 years, from 1925 to 1940, to accord the tenor saxophone a full voice in his music. Once he admitted Ben Webster into the fold in 1940 his feeling for it never wavered, and his enthusiasm kept on growing until, in the end, he may have had one or two more tenor saxophones than he really needed.

Webster Plays Ellington in Perpetuity
As for Ben Webster, he had 30 very active years after he left Elling-

ton's full-time employ. On at least six occasions in those 30 years he appeared with the orchestra as a special guest, sometimes for weeks at a time. He made studio recordings with Ellington in April 1958 and with Mercer Ellington in July 1958, when Mercer tried his hand at leading a band of his own. His live appearances with Ellington were recorded at Carnegie Hall, Cornell University and other venues in 1948. After Webster moved to Europe in 1965, settling first in Amsterdam and then in Copenhagen, he joined Ellington whenever their paths crossed. He appears on live recordings with the band in Antibes, France, in 1966 and in several Scandinavian cities on a 1971 tour. Those guest spots were high points in his long and winding itinerary.

Even when they were oceans apart Ellington was a constant presence in Webster's music. Webster played Ellington compositions, along with songbook standards and blues, at every concert, club date and recording session wherever he traveled. His repertoire of Ellington's music ventured well beyond the compositions he had been assigned to play in his three years in the orchestra. In a long discography thanks to his association with Norman Granz's Verve label in the 1960s and the seemingly insatiable appetite for his music on European labels in the last nine years of his life, he left behind perceptive readings of numerous Ellington compositions that he was never called upon to perform when he was actually with Ellington, including "Come Sunday," "Bojangles," "The Single Petal of a Rose," "I'm Beginning to See the Light," "Things Ain't What they Used to Be," "Do Nothin' Till You Hear From Me," "Rocks in My Bed," "Stepping into Swing Society" and "Stompy Jones," as well as new settings of the compositions that were indelibly associated with him, "Conga Brava," "All Too Soon," "Just A-Sitting and A-Rocking," "Chelsea Bridge" and countless versions of "Cotton Tail" – a cornucopia of Ellington's music rooted in the taste that was shaped once and for all from 1940 to 1943. (The Playlist for this chapter ends with "Webster Plays Ellington – A Selection.")

Almost all of Ellington's iconic soloists – the branded Ellingtonians – spent much more of their careers beside Ellington rather than away from him. Webster was the notable exception. He was destined to ply his trade away from the orchestra for most of his professional life, which spanned 37 years. But in a sense he never left Ellington. His style became fully formed while playing in Ellington's orchestra and it remained unchanged for the thirty years afterwards. He did not really need the refresher courses that his intermittent guest encounters with the Ellington orchestra provided for him. The fifth reed chair belonged to him – it was his legacy – no matter who was sitting in it at the moment. For Webster, it was a matter of self-esteem. He needed to know that the Governor would let him sit in whenever he showed up at whatever theater or nightclub or concert hall the orchestra was booked into. Home, as the old saying goes, is the place where, when you show up there, they cannot turn you away.

References (page numbers to direct quotations are shown *in italics*)
Balliett, Whitney. 2001. "Big Ben," in *Collected Works: A Journal of Jazz 1954-2001*. New York: St. Martin's Griffin. 405-406.
Carr, Ian, Digby Fairweather and Brian Priestley. 1988. *Jazz: The Essential Companion*. London: Paladin Grafton Books. 529-531. *p.531*
Dance, Stanley. 1970. *The World of Duke Ellington*. London: Macmillan.
Dance, Stanley. n.d. "Conversation with Paul Gonsalves."
 http://www.paulgonsalves.org/articles.html. [Retrieved May 2016]
Dance, Stanley. 1998. Liner note to Ellington, *Cornell University Second Set 1948*. MusicMasters CD.
DEMS Bulletin 04/3 December 2004-March 2005.
 http://www.depanorama.net/dems/043b.htm. [Retrieved 12 June 2015]
Ellington, Duke. 1973. *Music is My Mistress*. New York: Doubleday.
Gioia, Ted. 2012. *The Jazz Standards: A Guide to the Repertoire*. New York: Oxford University Press.
Goldberg, Joe. 1960. Liner note to Al Sears, *Swing's the Thing*. Swingville [Prestige]
Hasse, John Edward. 1993. *Beyond Category: the Life and Genius of Duke Ellington*. New York: Simon & Schuster.
Lambert, Eddie. 1998. *Duke Ellington: A Listener's Guide*. New York: Scarecrow Press.
Nicholson, Stuart. 1999. *A Portrait of Duke Ellington: Reminiscing in Tempo*. London: Sidgwick & Jackson.
Morton, John Fass. 2008. *Backstory in Blue: Ellington at Newport '56*. New Brunswick, New Jersey: Rutgers University Press.
Peress, Maurice. 2004. *Dvořák to Duke Ellington: A Conductor Explores America's Music and Its African American Roots*. New York: Oxford University Press.
Schuller, Gunther. 1989. *The Swing Era: The Development of Jazz 1935-*

1945. New York: Oxford University Press.

Shaw, Artie. 1952. *The Trouble with Cinderella: An Outline of Identity*. New York: Collier Books. Reprint 1963. *p. 13*.

Simon, George T. 1944. "It's Like Nothing Else [Al Sears]." *Metronome* (July). Reprinted in *The Duke Ellington Reader*, ed. Mark Tucker. New York: Oxford University Press, 1993. 460- 461.

Stewart, Rex. 1972. "The Frog and Me." *Jazz Masters of the Thirties*. NY: Macmillan. 120-29.

Talbot, Bruce. 2008. Liner notes in *The Best of Duke Ellington 1932-1939*. Columbia/RCA Original Masters. 4 CD.

Towers, Jack. 2002. Quoted in liner note to *The Duke at Fargo 1940: Special 60th Anniversary Edition*. Storyville Records 2 CD.

Playlist (in order of appearance in the chapter)

"Happy as the Day is Long" (2:39) 9 May 1933. *The Best of Duke Ellington 1932-1939* (Columbia/RCA Original Masters 4 CD [2008]) Cootie Williams, Arthur Whetsol, Freddie Jenkins tp; Joe Nanton, Juan Tizol, Lawrence Brown tb; Johnny Hodges, Otto Hardwick, Harry Carney, Joe Garland reeds; Ellington p; Fred Guy g; Wellman Braud b; Sonny Greer d; Ivie Anderson voc. (Ted Koehler words, Harold Arlen music) Garland arr.
Solos: Garland ts lead on A, Jenkins tp bridge, Anderson voc; Jenkins; prob. Brown; **Garland 8 bars**, Jenkins.

"Bugle Call Rag" (2:37) New York, 9 January 1928. *The Okeh Ellington* (Columbia 2 CD) The Washingtonians, Duke Ellington, leader, p, arr Bubber Miley, Louis Metcalf tp; Joe Nanton tb; Harry Carney cl, as, bs; Barney Bigard cl, ts; Otto Hardwick ss, as, bs; Fred Guy bjo; Wellman Braud b; Sonny Greer d.
Solos: Hardwick bs, Metcalf tp, Nanton tb, Hardwick bs, Carney cl, ensemble, DE p, Metcalf tp, **Bigard ts**, Nanton tb, ensemble with cl lead (Carney)

Fletcher Henderson Orchestra, "King Porter Stomp" (3:09) (comp. Jelly Roll Morton) New York, 14 March 1928.
Bobby Stark, Russell Smith, Joe Smith tp; Benny Morton, Jimmy Harrison tb; Don Pasqual as, bs; Buster Bailey cl; Coleman Hawkins ts; Fletcher Henderson p, Charlie Dixon banjo, June Cole tuba, Kaiser Marshall d.
Solos: Stark, Hawkins, J. Smith, Bailey Harrison

Fletcher Henderson Orchestra, "Queer Notions" (2:47) New York, 18 August 1933. *A Study in Frustration: The Fletcher Henderson Story* (Columbia 3 CD)
Bobby Stark, Russell Smith, Henry Red Allen tp; Dicky Wells, Sandy

Williams tb; Hilton Jefferson as; Russell Procope as, cl; Coleman Hawkins ts; Henderson p; Bernard Addison g; John Kirby b; Walter Johnson d. Hawkins comp, Horace Henderson arr.
Solos: Hawkins, Allen, Hawkins, Allen, Hawkins

"Truckin'" (2:57) New York, 19 August 1935 (comp. Koehler- Bloom) *Duke Ellington Classics 1935-36* Arthur Whetsol, Cootie Williams, Rex Stewart, tp; Tricky Sam Nanton, Lawrence Brown, Juan Tizol tb; Johnny Hodges, Otto Hardwick, Ben Webster, Harry Carney reeds; DE p; Fred Guy g; Hayes Alvis & Billy Taylor b; Sonny Greer d; Ivie Anderson voc
Solos: Cootie Williams, Ivie Anderson, Tricky Sam, Webster

"In a Jam" (3:02) New York, 29 July 1936. *Original Masters 1932-39*
Same as *Truckin'* but omit Alvis and add Barney Bigard cl
Solos: Nanton/Bigard (duet), Hodges/Williams (chase), Webster, Stewart (liner note: Webster "still finding his feet, stylistically")

"Conga Brava" (2:54) (comp. Ellington – Tizol) Chicago, 15 March 1940. *Blanton-Webster Band*. Bluebird [RCA] 3CD.
Wallace Jones, Cootie Williams, Rex Stewart tp; Tricky Sam Nanton, Lawrence Brown, Juan Tizol tb; Barney Bigard, Johnny Hodges, Otto Hardwick, Ben Webster, Harry Carney reeds; DE p; Fred Guy g; Jimmy Blanton b; Sonny Greer d.
Solos: Tizol, Bigard, Webster, Stewart, Tizol

"Cotton Tail" (3:08) Hollywood, 4 May 1940 *Blanton-Webster Band*. Bluebird [RCA] 3CD. Wallace Jones, Cootie Williams, Rex Stewart tp; Tricky Sam Nanton, Lawrence Brown, Juan Tizol tb; Barney Bigard, Johnny Hodges, Otto Hardwick, Ben Webster, Harry Carney reeds; DE p; Fred Guy g; Jimmy Blanton b; Sonny Greer d.
Solo: Webster

"All Too Soon" (3:28) New York, 22 July 1940. Personnel as for "Cotton Tail."
Solos: Ellington, Brown, Webster

"Star Dust" (4:16) Crystal Ballroom, Fargo, North Dakota, 7 November 1940.
Rex Stewart, Wallace Jones, Ray Nance tp; Joe Tricky Sam Nanton, Juan Tizol, Lawrence Brown tb; Barney Bigard cl, ts; Johnny Hodges as; Otto Hardwick as, cl; Ben Webster ts; Harry Carney bs; Duke Ellington p; Fred Guy g; Jimmy Blanton b; Sonny Greer d.
Solo: Webster

"Chelsea Bridge" (2:52) comp. Strayhorn. Hollywood, 2 December 1941. Same as "Cotton Tail" except Ray Nance replaces Cootie, Junior Raglin

replaces Blanton, Billy Strayhorn replaces Ellington
Solos: Strayhorn, Webster, Strayhorn, Tizol

"How High the Moon" (4:51) Carnegie Hall, 13 November 1948
(Vintage Jazz Classics [1991])
Al Killian, Shelton Hemphill, Harold Baker, Francis Williams tp;
Lawrence Brown, Tyree Glenn, Quentin Jackson tb; Jimmy Hamilton,
Johnny Hodges, [Russell Procope?] Al Sears, Ben Webster, Harry
Carney reeds; DE p, Fred Guy g, Wendell Marshall b, Sonny Greer d.

"How High the Moon" (6:25) 2 May 1950, Kongresshaus, Zurich. *Live in Switzerland* (TCB [Austria 2007]).
Ernie Royal, Harold Baker, Al Killian, Nelson Williams, Ray Nance tp;
Lawrence Brown, Quentin Jackson, Ted Kelly tb; Jimmy Hamilton cl;
Russell Procope cl, as; Johnny Hodges as; Don Byas, Alva Beau
McCain ts; Harry Carney bs; Duke Ellington p, Wendell Marshall b;
Sonny Greer, Butch Ballard d.

"The Greatest There Is" (2:43) New York, 1 September 1949. *Complete Duke Ellington 1947-1952*, Vol. 3. Harold Baker, Al Killian, Nelson
Williams, Dave Burns, Ray Nance tp; Lawrence Brown, Quentin
Jackson, Tyree Glenn tb; Jimmy Hamilton cl; Russell Procope cl, as;
Johnny Hodges as; Charlie Rouse, Jimmy Forrest ts; Harry Carney bs;
Duke Ellington p, comp and lyric; Wendell Marshall b; Sonny Greer d,
Lu Elliott voc

"How High the Moon" (5:14) The Forum, Hamilton, Canada,
8 February 1954. *Duke Ellington in Hamilton* (Radix Music 2CD).
Clark Terry, Willie Cook, Cat Anderson, Ray Nance tp; Quentin Jackson,
Britt Woodman, George Jean tb; Rick Henderson as; Jimmy Hamilton cl,
ts; Russell Procope cl. as; Paul Gonsalves ts; Harry Carney bs;
Duke Ellington p, Wendell Marshall b, Dave Black d.
Solos: Gonsalves, Nance/Terry/Cook, Hamilton, Woodman, Gonsalves.

"Carnegie Blues" (2:46) New York, January 1945. *Complete RCA Victor 1944-46* (3 CD RCA [2000]).
Taft Jordan, Shelton Hemphill, Cat Anderson tp; Rex Stewart cnt;
Ray Nance tp, vln; Claude Jones, Lawrence Brown, Joe Nanton tb;
Jimmy Hamilton cl, ts; Otto Hardwick, Johnny Hodges as; Al Sears ts;
Harry Carney cl, bs; Ellington p; Fred Guy g; Junior Raglin b; Sonny
Greer d. Comp Ellington, orig. "The Blues" from *Black Brown and Beige*.
Solos: Sears, Brown, Raglin.

"(Otto Make That) Riff Staccato" (3:02) New York, 10 May 1945.
CD issue and personnel as for "Carnegie Blues." Arranged by Mary
Lou Williams.

Solos: Sears, Jordan obbligato, Nance voc

Johnny Hodges, "Castle Rock" (2:48) New York, 3 March 1951.
Johnny Hodges, *Four Classic Albums* (Avid Jazz 2CD [2010]).
Emmett Berry tp, Lawrence Brown tb, Hodges as, Al Sears ts,
Leroy Lovett p, Lloyd Trotman b, Sonny Greer d.
Solo: Sears (also composer, arranger)

"Diminuendo in Blue and Crescendo in Blue" (14:20) Newport
Jazz Festival, Newport, R.I., 7 July 1956. *Ellington at Newport 1956
Complete* (Columbia 2CD [1999])
Cat Anderson, Clark Terry, Willie Cook, Ray Nance tp; Quentin Jackson,
Britt Woodman, John Sanders tb; Johnny Hodges as; Jimmy Hamilton cl,
ts; Russell Procope cl. as; Paul Gonsalves ts; Harry Carney bs; Duke
Ellington p, Jimmy Woode b, Sam Woodyard d.
Solo: Gonsalves

"The Happening" (2:38) New York, 17 April 1950. *Billy Strayhorn
All Stars* (Prestige CD [1992]), originally Mercer Records.
Cat Anderson tp, Juan Tizol tb, Willie Smith as, Oau Gonsalves ts,
Strayhorn p, Wendell Marshall b, Louie Bellson d.
Solo: Gonsalves (also composer)

"Hy'a Sue" (4:48) 10 December 1948. *Cornell University Second Set*
(MusicMasters [1996]).
Ray Nance, Shelton Hemphill, Francis Williams, Harold Baker, Al Killian
tp; Lawrence Brown, Quentin Jackson, Tyree Glenn tb; Johnny Hodges as;
Russell Procope as, cl; Jimmy Hamilton, Al Sears, Ben Webster ts; DE p;
Fred Guy g; Wendell Marshall b; Sonny Greer d.
Solos: Glenn, Hamilton ts.

"Happy-Go-Lucky-Local" (5:33) Chicago, 17 January 1954. *Ellington '55*
(Capitol CD [1999]).
Clark Terry, Willie Cook, Cat Anderson, Ray Nance tp; Quentin Jackson,
Britt Woodman, George Jean tb; Rick Henderson as; Jimmy Hamilton cl,
ts; Russell Procope cl. as; Paul Gonsalves ts; Harry Carney bs;
Duke Ellington p, Wendell Marshall b, Dave Black d.
Solos: ....Hamilton ts, ...Anderson

"Thanks for the Beautiful Land on the Delta" (3:38) New York, 27 April
1970. *New Orleans Suite* (Atlantic).
Cootie Williams tp; Money Johnson, Mercer Ellington, Al Rubin, Fred
Stone tp, flugel; Booty Wood, Julian Priester tb; Dave Taylor b-tb; Russell
Procope as, cl; Johnny Hodges as [his last recording]; Norris Turney as, cl,
flt; Harold Ashby ts, cl; Paul Gonsalves ts; Harry Carney bs, cl, b-cl;
Ellington p; Joe Benjamin b; Rufus Jones d.

Solo: Ashby

"B.P. Blues" (4:15) Free Trade Hall, Manchester, England, 26 November 1969. *DE's 70th Birthday Concert* (Blue Note 2CD [1995]).
Cat Anderson, Cootie Williams, Rolf Ericson, Mercer Ellington tp; Lawrence Brown, Chuck Connors tb; Johnny Hodges as; Norris Turney as, ts, flt, cl; Russell Procope cl, as; Harold Ashby ts, flt; Paul Gonsalves ts; Harry Carney bs, cl, bcl; Ellington p; Wild Bill Davis org; Victor Gaskin b; Rufus Jones d.
Solo: Ashby

"In Triplicate" (6:15) Place and personnel same as "B.P. Blues."
Solos: Ellington, Davis, Gonsalves, Turney, Ashby.

Addendum: Webster Plays Ellington – A Selection

"Cotton Tail" (3:23) Los Angeles, September 1957 *Ella Fitzgerald Sings the Duke Ellington Songbook* (Verve 3CD)
Ben Webster ts, Stuff Smith vln, Paul Smith p, Barney Kessel g, Joe Mondragon b, Alvin Stoller d, Ella Fitzgerald voc
Solos: Fitzgerald novelty scat, Webster trades fours in coda

"Rocks in My Bed" (3:54) as above
Solos: Fitzgerald, Webster blues chorus

"Be Patient" (2:16) (comp Mercer Ellington) 17 July 1958 Mercer Ellington Orchestra, *Stepping Into Swing Society* (Fresh Sound CD [2008])
Cat Anderson, Shorty Baker, Clark Terry tp; Britt Woodman, Quentin Jackson, John Sanders tb; Jimmy Hamilton, Russell Procope, Johnny Hodges, Ben Webster, Harry Carney reeds; Jimmy Jones p, Carl Lynch g, George Duvivier b, Sam Bailey d
Solo: Webster ballad feature

"I'm Beginning to See the Light" (2:44) New York, 10 January 1960. Webster, *Warm Moods* (Reprise) Webster ts, Donn Trenner p, Don Bagley b, Frank Capp d + string quartet, arr Johnny Richards.

"Come Sunday" (5:10) New York, 1963. Ben Webster and Joe Zawinul, *Soulmates:* (Riverside). Webster ts, Zawinul p, Richard Davis b, Philly Joe Jones d

"Do Nothing 'til You Hear From Me" (3:33) New Jersey, 3 March 1964 *The Happy Horns of Clark Terry* (Impulse!)
Clark Terry flugl, Phil Woods as, Ben Webster ts, Roger Kellaway p, Milt Hinton b, Walter Perkins d.

Solos: Kellaway, Ben Webster, Terry, Terry/Webster

"The Single Petal of a Rose" (3:18) New Jersey, 11 March 1964. Webster, *See You at the Fair* (Impulse!)
Webster ts, Hank Jones p, Richard Davis b, Osie Johnson d.

"Bojangles" (3:07) Copenhagen, 22 November 1971. Danish Radio Big Band, *Ben Webster Plays Duke Ellington* (Storyville)
Solos: Allan Botchinsky tp, Jesper Thilo cl, Webster ts [last recording of an Ellington composition]

Chapter 4

Lotus Eaters Unite!

The Spectral Alliance of Johnny Hodges and Billy Strayhorn

photo montage Johnny Hodges (Herman Leonard photo) and Billy Strayhorn (unknown)
© 2017 Jack Chambers and Craig Diegel

In 1956, nine of Duke Ellington's virtuoso sidemen banded together and recorded an album of music, 40 minutes, without Ellington. They called the album *Duke's in Bed*, a sly wink of a title, as if they were making music while the boss wasn't looking. Billy Strayhorn, Ellington's longtime co-composer, played piano in Ellington's stead, and Johnny Hodges, Ellington's star saxophonist, was the nominal leader of the band. Ellington may or may not have actually been in bed at the time, but he is certainly not absent from the music they made. As in dozens of instances when Ellingtonians got together in a recording studio, the leader's imprint is unmistakably etched onto the proceedings. On this occasion, three of the tunes they played were written by Ellington (including an obscure one called, with another sly wink, "Duke's in Bed"). A fourth track, "Take the 'A' Train," though written by Strayhorn, was indelibly associated with Ellington as his orchestra's theme song for the 16 years leading up to 1956 (as it would be for the remaining 18 years of the orchestra's – and Ellington's – life). Those four tracks make up half the album's length. The other tunes consist of an old pop song, three riff-based jump tunes by Johnny Hodges, and one brand-new ballad by Billy Strayhorn.

The brand-new ballad by Billy Strayhorn has the marvelous title "Ballade for Very Tired and Very Sad Lotus Eaters." Seasoned listeners to the Ellington orchestra will look at that title and know exactly what they are getting. But knowing what they are getting will not dull their anticipation; far from it. Instead, it will whet their appetites in anticipation of a hitherto unheard impressionistic dream-sequence in which Hodges's incomparably sensuous alto saxophone glides over Strayhorn's incomparably lush harmonies in a kind of late-night absinthe haze.

They will not be disappointed. "Ballade for Very Tired and Very Sad Lotus Eaters" is another showpiece in the uniquely Hodges-Strayhorn genre. It brings Hodges to the fore in a mood of quiet longing that unfolds over a backdrop of sustained chords by the ensemble. Although Strayhorn does not have the full orchestra to enrich his harmonies, he has many of its signature tones at his disposal (Ray Nance, Quentin Jackson, Jimmy Hamilton and Harry Carney as well as Hodges) and he knows how to make the most of the pared-down ensemble.

Frankly, in the context of the rest of the music on this album, "Lotus Eaters" sounds more than a little incongruous. It is a tropical island plunked down in a warehouse district, surrounded as it is by workmanlike finger-snapping jump tunes with simple structures. Its extravagant title makes the incongruity all the more obvious, stranded as it is among frivolities titled "Confab with Rab" (because "Rabbit" is Hodges's nickname) and "A-Oodie-Oobie." Never mind. Its incongruity may be a minor problem in the spur-of-the-moment context of *Duke's in Bed* but it is no problem at all, in fact it is a virtue, when it is seen in its proper place, alongside some 40 years worth of lotus-eating dream-like impressionistic ballads just like it (more or less).

Lotus Eaters, Genus and Species
Listening to the lotus-eating, dream-like music Johnny Hodges and

Billy Strayhorn made together for all those years, there can be no doubt that they were soul-mates. They shared a romantic strain that at its core evokes the French impressionists and, like the impressionists, verges at its edges on sentimentality. Their collaborations resonate with unity of feeling and shared compassion and easy soulfulness that is rare in music or any other art.

And it is belied by everything else we know. In the faces that the two men showed to the world there seemed to be nothing kindred, no hint of empathy or compassion or shared feeling.

Billy Strayhorn (1915-1967) was small, dapper and outwardly cheery. His nickname in the band was "Swee' Pea," after the cartoon baby in the Popeye comic strip, and the nickname was bestowed on him as much for his sweet temper as for his diminutive stature. As a schoolboy, Strayhorn dazzled his teachers and classmates with his musical talents at Westinghouse High School in Pittsburgh. At his graduation he played his own Concerto for Piano and Percussion and received a standing ovation. "Well Strayhorn – he was just like, you'd say, a genius," one of his classmates told his biographer David Hajdu, and all the other classmates nodded in agreement. But after he left high school Strayhorn's worldly ambitions faltered and he seemed content to rest on his high-school laurels. With fragile confidence and an abhorrence of competitiveness, he seemed destined, against the urging of everyone who knew him, to settle into mundane jobs in drug stores and confectionaries. He was gay and openly so, a rarity at the time, and his openness about it was not for declamatory purposes but because it was not in his temperament to pretend otherwise. He was attentive and observant and good company. He was a lifelong chain-smoker and in his final decades a benign and witty alcoholic.

In 1938, when he was 23 and looked younger, some well-placed friends arranged a backstage audition for him with Duke Ellington after a Pittsburgh concert, and Ellington did him the courtesy of listening as he played some of Ellington's compositions and then sang some his own songs. Ellington was immediately impressed by Strayhorn's ability as a lyricist and told him he might be able to use him. Strayhorn was flattered, of course, but after hearing no more as weeks and months went by he had pretty much put the moment behind him. Then months later, in 1939, Ellington called, and arranged for

Strayhorn to go to New York. He was put up at first in a YMCA, but when he met Ellington's son Mercer, just four years younger than him, he moved into the Harlem apartment of Ellington's sister Ruth, the same age as Strayhorn, where Mercer also lived. While Ellington was on tour with the orchestra, Mercer and Strayhorn busied themselves studying some of Ellington's band scores and working out the elements of his composing and arranging style.

They proved apt pupils. Both Strayhorn and Mercer Ellington would contribute original music to the orchestra within the year. Eventually, Strayhorn would augment the Ellingtonian elements with classical devices from his teenage studies. His first major success, however, showed none of that. He composed "Take the 'A' Train," named for the Manhattan subway line that had carried him to the Harlem apartment where his destiny lay. "Take the 'A' Train" is an exercise in big-band swing, rhythmically hot, eminently hummable and, in the spirit of the day, inviting for agile dancers. Ellington was so impressed that, from 1940 onwards, he used it as the band's theme, opening concerts and closing sets with it for the rest of his days. Ellington immediately recognized that Strayhorn had more to offer

Billy Strayhorn (1915-1967) in his high school yearbook 1934
(courtesy Heinz History Center)

than lyrics and gave him assignments as a composer and arranger. From then on, his salary would be boosted with royalties on his composer credits from Ellington's publishing wing, Tempo Music, which was administered by Ruth Ellington.

Within a few years the relationship between Ellington and Strayhorn grew from a loose master-apprentice arrangement to one of mutual dependency. Their bond proved durable, in fact indissoluble, though their orbits seldom intersected. While Ellington spent his days and nights in hotels and on stages all over the world, Strayhorn found his niche with the New York cabaret crowd, developing musical ideas for the orchestra at Ellington's beck and call by day while leading a vibrant life among the smart set by night. The antithetical work habits suited both men perfectly, and their bond was constant, whatever the distance between them. Their partnership lasted 28 years, ending only with Strayhorn's untimely death from cancer at 51. In his memoir, Ellington wrote, "Billy Strayhorn was my right arm, my left arm, all the eyes in the back of my head, my brain waves in his head, and his in mine."

Strayhorn was lovable. He was extraverted, an enthusiast, and a ready conversationalist on any topic. "Billy was very happy," said Aaron Bridgers, his partner. "That's the only reason he would drink. He was celebrating" (Hajdu, p. 210). Others were not so beguiled. The actor Paul Newman, who met him in Paris when he was working with Ellington on the soundtrack of *Paris Blues*, told Hajdu, "He seemed like quite a sad little man to me." If so, he covered it well. Most people were inclined to look no further than his ready smile, his even temper, and his self-deprecating wit. Ellington, in his moving elegy for him, said he "lived in what we consider the most important and moral of freedoms: freedom from hate, unconditionally; freedom from self-pity...; freedom from fear of possibly doing something that might help another more than it might himself."

Johnny Hodges (1907-1970), nine years older than Strayhorn, viewed the world through shifty eyes. He quit school at 14 and scuffled in the hard-knocks music world, joining the Ellington orchestra in 1928, when he was 22. On the bandstand, he fixed his gaze on his music stand or on the floor. When he soloed, he stood stock still, sometimes flicking a glance to the left or right but otherwise frozen in place. Bob Udkoff, a well-heeled tagalong in Ellington's entourage, said, "He had little or no personality.... Beautiful player, very soulful, but you couldn't have a conversation with him." Barry Ulanov, Ellington's first biographer, lists "the oldest members of the band... who freely put their memories and their scrapbooks at my disposal"; Johnny Hodges is conspicuously absent.

Though Hodges spent 38 years in Ellington's orchestra (from 1928 to 1951, and then from 1955 to his death in 1970), he had a thorny relationship with his boss. In November 1940 he quit playing the soprano saxophone forever to spite Ellington, according to rumor, because Ellington refused Hodges's demand to double his pay for playing soprano as well as the alto saxophone. In his last years he insisted on being paid nightly in cash because, he declared, "When I was pickin' cotton I used to get paid at the end of every day," leaving it to listeners to figure out where the cotton fields sat in relation to Cambridge and Boston, Massachusetts, where he was born and raised. Ellington, always one to avoid a dispute, went along with it, forcing Mercer Ellington, his road manager at the time, to carry a briefcase full of cash on road trips. It was all the more onerous because Hodges earned the highest salary in the band. Trumpeter Rolf Ericson, who played in the band in 1963-1964 and was one of the lowest paid, may have discovered his real motive for the cash payments. "Johnny Hodges had a habit of walking around in front of us counting rolls of hundred dollar bills," Ericson said. "He wanted to make us feel envious and he enjoyed it" (Westin interview). Hodges titled one of his riff tunes "sweet as bear meat," and the gamy irony of that title seemed an apt epithet for the image he projected.

Mercifully, the impression most people had of Johnny Hodges came from the music he made, and from that they were likely to envision a poetic figure, a spinner of melody, sometimes overly sensitive when the tempo was down but lyrical at all tempos. It was an impression very much at odds with the sullen figure they saw on the bandstand. The shifty-eyed stone face seemed like an impostor, and maybe he was. Edith Cue Hodges, his wife, said, "Everybody said Johnny was gruff. They thought he was cold. He was just afraid" (Hajdu, p. 178). At least that view reconciled the gap between the man and his music. What did it really matter, this gap between the

Young Johnny Hodges (1907-1970)

man and his music? To his bandmates, it meant nothing. "Nobody knows what Johnny Hodges feels inside when he walks out to the mike," trumpeter Shorty Baker told Stanley Dance. "He may look as though he's on his last walk to the gallows, but ... he thanks the audience with a million dollars worth of melody!"

We search in vain for the common ground that made Billy Strayhorn and Johnny Hodges such other-worldly, spectral collaborators. Maybe Wild Bill Davis, the organist and arranger who knew Hodges as well as anybody, said it best. "Neither one of them guys was really who they seemed," he opined. "Johnny was just as mushy inside as Strayhorn was froufrouy." Whatever that means, Ellington obviously understood it from the start. He recognized the potential for an alliance where many others would have simply looked away, and he orchestrated the alliance with all the ingenuity he showed in his musical compositions. It does not seem too far-fetched to say that the spectral alliance between Strayhorn and Hodges was one of Ellington's most exhilarating creations.

Penetrating Warm Valleys

The first step leading to the alliance came with Ellington's ballad "Warm Valley" in 1940. The title is a double entendre intended to evoke female physiology as well as geographic topography, and that neatly captures the mood of intimacy and quiet passion evoked by the sinuous, undulating melody. (Side B of the original 78 rpm release was "The Flaming Sword," sustaining the sexual imagery in its masculine side.) The quiet sensuality of "Warm Valley" has its roots in the dance hall convention of ending the evening with a quiet number that encourages the dancing couples to press close together and slowly make their way around the floor. It was a venerable tradition, of course, much older than "Warm Valley." Previously, Ellington had ended his dance dates with a quiet blues such as "Mood Indigo." "Warm Valley" is patently sexier, specifically designed for stimulating intimacy as the couples prepare to disappear into the night. Indeed, at Fargo, North Dakota in 1940, the most famous dance date ever recorded, Ellington calls "Warm Valley" twice, once leading up to the first intermission and again, at the end of the long evening, immediately before sending the dancers home for the night with "God Bless America."

Billy Strayhorn remembered the process of composing and arranging "Warm Valley" in considerable detail a couple of decades later even though, by then, his work with Ellington had evolved into a much closer, even intimate, collaboration. In 1940, in his first months with the band, Strayhorn was still absorbing lessons in jazz orchestration from his new boss. Those lessons were learned mainly by osmosis, through the practical experience of observing rehearsals and catching the reactions and responses of the musicians. What made "Warm Valley" especially memorable for Strayhorn was the rare deliberation and close contact as it unfolded. Strayhorn told Bill Coss, "You remember 'Warm Valley'? It was less than three minutes long. But we wrote reams and reams of music on that, and he [Ellington] threw it all out except what you hear. He didn't use any of mine. Now that's arranging. The tune was written, but we had to find the right way to present it."

Strayhorn's recollection is one of the few accounts he ever gave about what he had to put himself through in these early days at

Billy Strayhorn and Duke Ellington at work

Ellington's side. His schoolboy experience in Pittsburgh, however dazzling it may have seemed to the locals, was more than just a subway ride from the place he would occupy as Ellington's collaborator. Some of the leaps he needed to take are neatly conceptualized by Ethan Iverson, the pianist and educator. "Strayhorn needed to learn a lot about aesthetics from Ellington," Iverson points out. "Strayhorn wrote a corny piano concerto in high school; he knew more about musicals than jazz; in the first decade of writing for Duke he had a lot of meaningless decoration that Duke had to pare down in order to give it the right feel."

In the "reams of music" by Strayhorn that Ellington threw out in the making of the striking arrangement of "Warm Valley" it is not hard to imagine that much of it involved the paring down of what Iverson calls "meaningless decoration." Strayhorn's comment about finding "the right way to present it" is what Iverson calls giving it "the right feel." Undoubtedly Strayhorn had similar experiences working beside Ellington on numerous other arrangements in these apprentice years but none of the others stuck with him with the immediacy of this one. It appears that Ellington was grooming him to take on what became a kind of sub-genre for the orchestra. With "Warm Valley," Ellington seems to be nurturing Strayhorn's flair for the sub-genre. As he worked with the younger man at getting 'the right feel' in "Warm Valley," there was something larger at stake. Ellington was fostering what would become a new dimension for exploiting the strengths of his virtuoso band. Ellington would keep his hand in it for another year or two and after that he would sit back and watch as Billy Strayhorn and Johnny Hodges brought it to a bright polish.

Dreaming Day and Night
Strayhorn did not need a second invitation. In the next year, a busy one in which he took on all kinds of unfamiliar tasks for his boss, he composed two new compositions that came to stand as badges of the lotus eater's union. "Day Dream" was recorded on November 1940, just two months after "Warm Valley," and "Passion Flower" was recorded eight months after that, in July 1941. The very titles spin a story about the music – somnambulant, other-worldly, florid, exotic. Both "Day Dream" and "Passion Flower" were first recorded by small combos made up of the cream of the orchestra and marketed under the name "Johnny Hodges and His Orchestra." They were part of a spin-off enterprise in which Ellington's star players fronted small bands on the cut-rate Bluebird subsidiary as a supplement to the big band offerings on parent RCA Victor. One of the many duties Ellington assigned to Strayhorn was organizing the music and personnel for these dates. The small-band sessions were masterminded by Ellington but nominally led by either Hodges or Barney Bigard or Cootie Williams. Presumably Strayhorn arranged "Day Dream" and "Passion Flower" for the full orchestra and then pared them down for the septet because Ellington immediately started playing both numbers with the big band at concerts, broadcasts and dances.

"Day Dream" credits Ellington as co-composer, indicating that it went through an editing process in which Ellington again deleted some Strayhorn decorations. Strayhorn's beautiful melody hardly needs decoration, and the background of deep chordal harmonies is impeccably calculated to simultaneously enhance Hodges's recital of the melody and keep out of his way. The recording found an audience, and when Ellington announced the composition at his first Carnegie Hall concert (in January 1943) he could introduce it with some flair, saying, "And now comes All American number one saxophonist Johnny Hodges with another Strayhorn arrangement." Hodges plays the complete AABA melody once, and then repeats only the bridge and one chorus (BA) adding some grace notes including a dramatic glide at the bridge, but otherwise respecting Strayhorn's winsome melody all the way.

"Day Dream" remained a favorite of Johnny Hodges long after several other memorable pieces in the same sub-genre contended with it. It stayed in the orchestra's repertoire as long as Hodges was there to play it. As familiar as it was in the original small-band recording and in various concert recordings, it was several years later before "Day Dream" finally received its definitive big-band rendition. The occasion was an unexpected recording session made for Verve Records with Ellington nominally absent. The session came near the end of Ellington's recording contract with Columbia (December 1961). At the time, Ellington was unhappy with Columbia for denying him the budget to record an album of his symphonic works, and this surreptitious Verve session appears to have come about as a show of petulance. Hodges is credited as leader of the Ellington orchestra for the recording, with Ellington's normal roles taken by Jimmy Jones on piano and Strayhorn conducting as well as arranging all the numbers. The album, called *Johnny Hodges with Billy Strayhorn and the Orchestra* (Verve), otherwise includes the full Ellington orchestra intact. Beyond a doubt, Ellington is overseeing the whole affair.

The music glows, perhaps reflecting the aura of defiance that called it forth. Strayhorn's arrangement of "Day Dream," extended and updated especially for this occasion, sacrifices a touch of its serenity by raising the tempo slightly and giving the orchestra more notes (extending the arrangement to four minutes instead of the characteristic three of previous versions). But the orchestral nuances are sumptuous and they are richly preserved in Rudy Van Gelder's

Johnny Hodges and Billy Strayhorn in Rudy van Gelder's recording studio
(Verve Records)

famous recording studio in Englewood Cliffs, New Jersey. There is a kind of collective exhilaration that imbues every note. The musicians play as if they are intent on making a masterpiece. In its numerous surviving performances, "Day Dream" was never less than delightful but this performance, twenty years after the original airing, is its consummation.

The other absinthe ballad in the afterglow of "Warm Valley," "Passion Flower," recorded in July 1941 and again by the seven-piece spin-off known as Johnny Hodges and His Orchestra, gives composer credit solely to Strayhorn, tacit recognition that Ellington now believed Strayhorn could be trusted to edit himself. It is tempting to view this 14-month sequence from "Warm Valley" to "Day Dream" to "Passion Flower" as a report card charting Strayhorn's progress, from Ellington rejecting all his embellishments on "Warm Valley," and then tweaking his arrangement of "Day Dream" as co-composer, and finally accepting "Passion Flower" pretty much as Strayhorn presented it.

"Passion Flower" is darker, more somber. Hodges opens with 16 bars (two 8 bar AA sequences) in a gradual descending scale. The bridge presents a contrast with sustained ascension up the scale before descending again to the final iteration of the melancholy *A* melody. The long rise in the bridge, contrasted with the slow descent of the quiet *A* melody, gives the impression of a mournful sigh. The characteristically spare background here includes a prominent bass line by Jimmy Blanton (characteristic of numerous arrangements by Ellington in this period and clearly co-opted by Strayhorn here). One of the highlights is a stunning glissando when Hodges seemingly glides up the scale in a continuous run; the continuity is legerdemain, of course, as each note is made on a separate key on the alto saxophone and Hodges moves masterfully from one to the next in one sustained breath.

There is a kind of self-consciousness to "Passion Flower," perhaps artifice, that was not felt so clearly on "Day Dream," as if Strayhorn and Hodges had become self-conscious about their newfound roles as lotus eaters, and on this record were playing their roles to the hilt. Though the records found their audience, the novelty of the keening alto over resonant impressionist chords represents a refinement of sensibility that was uncommon in the Swing Era, and unknown in the jazz that went before. The delicacy of their collaboration did not go unnoticed, and it was not appreciated by some fans who liked their music hotter. In 1943, a young English critic wrote scornfully, "Mr. Strayhorn is an example of today's youth in jazz. He throws tradition overboard. He will have originality at the expense of beauty. ... [He has] an obsession for tone colour and voicing which excludes everything else that matters" (quoted by Hajdu). The English critic was Stanley Dance, who moved to the United States soon after publishing this cavil and ironically "slipped into Ellington's inner circle" (as Hajdu puts it), where among many other benisons he produced the record session that included the "Ballade for Very Tired and Very Sad Lotus Eaters." Dance obviously managed to reconcile his antipathy for Strayhorn's "originality at the expense of beauty," but his initial reaction aligned him with the jazz reactionaries longing for the imagined innocence of the jungle. Those reactionaries would soon be swamped by a generation of musicians and critics who recognized that Strayhorn set a new standard. Gerry Mulligan, 12 years younger than Strayhorn and a leading composer and arranger from the 1950s onward, told Hajdu, "When Strayhorn came on the scene, he just blew us away, because he was doing very complicated, sophisticated things, and they didn't sound complicated to the ear at all – they sounded completely natural and very emotional." Gil Evans, who raised the bar for jazz orchestration, put it more succinctly (and with characteristic modesty): "That's all I did – that's all I ever did – try to do what Billy Strayhorn did."

"Passion Flower" was not immediately brought into the orchestra's repertoire but once it found its way it was fairly frequently played. Like "Day Dream," "Passion Flower" got its consummate orchestral performance several years later, also in a revamped and extended arrangement and also under unusual circumstances. In 1956, Ellington and Strayhorn undertook a long-distance project with the singer Rosemary Clooney. Strayhorn prepared vocal arrangements of a selection of their songs and the orchestra recorded the instrumental parts in New York. Strayhorn then took the tapes to Hollywood and worked with Clooney in the studio dubbing in her vocal parts. Notwithstanding the continent-wide split between singer and orchestra, the resulting album, *Blue Rose* (Columbia 1956), is a great success, so much so that it gave rise to a widely-held quip that Rosemary Clooney is the best vocalist Ellington never had.

One of the further oddities of *Blue Rose* (and one of its treasures) is the inclusion of "Passion Flower": an oddity because Clooney does not sing on it. Probably Strayhorn and Ellington intended Clooney to add a wordless vocal to it, but if so it must have proved unsatisfactory. Or they may have meant it to stand alone from the start, because it constitutes a tacit celebration of the return of Johnny Hodges, who had rejoined the orchestra two months earlier after a five-year absence. "Passion Flower" on *Blue Rose* marks Hodges's first recorded solo after his return, and it is a glorious one, as might be expected, a grand reunion with Hodges's incisive tone framed sumptuously in Strayhorn's elaborate harmonies for the full orchestra.

This consummate recording of "Passion Flower," though largely unnoticed at the time, was the harbinger of a great period for Ellington. Hodges came back to a revitalized band and found himself pooling his gifts with the cohort of young musicians Ellington had gathered around him, including at least seven star soloists brought in while Hodges was absent. This aggregation would prove to be one of Ellington's most cohesive orchestras, a rival for the Blanton-Webster aggregation of 1940. Numerous triumphs would follow in the six years starting in 1956, including more masterpieces of the Strayhorn-Hodges alliance. It is tempting to see this recording of "Passion Flower" as the first fruit of a long sustained plateau for Ellington and his men.

"Romance is mush"
How did Duke Ellington know that young Billy Strayhorn had the sensibility that could unlock the deep, otherwise unarticulated romanticism of Johnny Hodges? Actually, from his first few minutes with Strayhorn he had ample evidence that he had discovered not only a creative young talent but also an irredeemable romantic. Backstage at that Pittsburgh theatre, the diminutive 23-year-old had sat down at the old upright piano and quietly explained that he would play variations on a couple of Ellington's compositions, first as Ellington would play them and then in his own style. His ornate playing attracted the attention of passing orchestra members, who shambled in to watch the audition (as vividly reconstructed by Strayhorn's biographer David Hajdu). At Ellington's urging, Strayhorn then sang some songs he had written, words and music, and he performed them with gusto in his chirping songwriter's tenor. One of the songs was "Something to Live For," destined to become a minor hit for Ellington and eventually to make its way into the standard repertoire of singers of serious-minded love songs. Another song, at the time untitled although Strayhorn said he had been working on it – refining it, reworking it – since his high school days, was the song now widely known and celebrated as "Lush Life." In the fullness of time it would be recognized as one of the jewels of the Great American Songbook, finding its place amidst the outpouring of pop creativity from 1900 to 1950 that emanated from the likes of Jerome Kern, Irving Berlin, George Gershwin, Cole Porter, Richard Rodgers, Harold Arlen, Frank Loesser and dozens of other tunesmiths and lyricists.

Strayhorn's "Lush Life" is a pained outpouring by a lovelorn suitor who seeks solace for his broken heart in "jazz and cocktails… in some small dive," along with other romantic consolations such as "a week in Paris." The lyric describes more or less the life that Strayhorn would lead as an adult in all those hours when he was not bent over manuscript paper writing music for Duke Ellington. It is ironic to think that he foresaw that sophisticated melancholy while still a teenager surrounded by iron smelters in Pittsburgh, years before he had any inkling of the high life he would lead under Ellington's umbrella. The lyric is a portrait of frustrated youth, unrequited and unraveling, driven by the cruel winds of fate to a life of long nights and dissolute pleasures. Its romantic despair is worthy of Childe Harold or young Werther, although blessedly shorter than anything by Lord Byron or Goethe, and happily besotted with Jazz Age predilections. In the canon of the Great American Songbook, its romantic melancholy is perhaps rivaled by Bob Hilliard's "In the Wee Small Hours of the Morning" ("…When the whole wide world is fast asleep/You lie awake and think about the girl/And never ever think of counting sheep"), and especially by Fran Landesman's "Ballad of the Sad Young Men" ("All the sad young men drifting through the town/Drinking up the night, trying not to drown") but even they seem mild or perhaps prosaic by comparison.

Billy Strayhorn's "Lush Life" took a long, meandering route before it found its rightful place in the Great American Songbook. One reason is that Duke Ellington did not see fit to incorporate it into his repertoire. Perhaps he saw it as too personal for general consumption. However, on at least two occasions, widely separated, he invited Strayhorn onto the stage to play it. The first occasion, indeed, proved to be the breakthrough it needed. On 13 November 1948, at Carnegie Hall, Strayhorn stepped out of the wings and accompanied the band vocalist Kay Davis in a five-minute rendition that was the public premiere of "Lush Life." Ellington, in an elaborate, minute-long homage to Strayhorn, introduces it as "a new tune of his," though it was by then more than ten years old, perhaps 15 if Strayhorn really wrote it while he was in high school (a claim that all his biographers accept). After hearing it in this august setting, the singer Nat King Cole recorded it, and within a year it became a minor hit record. From there, slowly but surely, it inched its way outward into the repertoires of dozens of singers and instrumentalists. It has been sung and played by literally hundreds of musicians from Ella Fitzgerald

Billy Strayhorn with score

(1957) and Johnny Hartman (accompanied by John Coltrane 1963) to Lady Gaga (2014) and Joey Alexander (2015, age 11). By the time Ellington next invited Strayhorn to the stage, 16 years later at a small band date at the New York club Basin Street East in 1964, this time to accompany himself as he sang his song in his workmanlike composer voice, the song was famous.

My personal favorite among the many brilliant renditions of "Lush Life" is Blossom Dearie's. Blossom Dearie has perfect pitch and is a masterly self-accompanist, two characteristics that do justice to the song's musical challenges. Pointedly, Dearie's soprano voice has an impish innocence that wrings out the dolor underlying the suave surface of Strayhorn's lyric. Dearie's performance is live, and she introduces the song to her audience by saying, "It's a very sad song, and it took me 11 years to learn. Very difficult to play, and even harder to sing. And on top of that it's sad." (Another measure of its "difficulty" – Frank Sinatra left behind several incomplete takes of the song at a 1958 recording session, none of which were released in his lifetime.)

Musically the difficulty of "Lush Life" lies in the fact that its harmonic underpinning after the first two verses is not based on a set of repeating chord changes. "The lyric," according to Walter van der Leur, "is set to a through-composed melodic line underscored by chromatic harmonies that spiral around the work's main key of D♭." Formally, it departs radically from songbook structure, though it begins deceptively with what appears to be the conventional AA structure, with the second verse sung to the same melody as the first:

> I used to visit all the very gay places
> Those come-what-may places
> Where one relaxes on the axis of the wheel of life
> To get the feel of life
> From jazz and cocktails
>
> The girls I knew had sad and sullen gray faces
> With distingué traces
> That used to be there you could see where they'd been washed away
> By too many through the day
> Twelve o'clock tales

The third verse appears to sustain the familiar songbook structure by introducing a new melody (as if it is *B*, the bridge) and with it the complicating sentiment that disrupts the situation introduced in the *A* verses:

> Then you came along with your siren song
> To tempt me to madness
> I thought for a while that your poignant smile
> Was tinged with the sadness
> Of a great love for me

At this point a song built on the conventional structure would return to the *A* melody and make some kind of resolution or denouement of the complication. Strayhorn presents a denouement, all right, but he abandons the melodies (*A* and *B*) he has introduced to this point.

In fact, the denouement constitutes four more stanzas of different lengths (2 lines, 4 lines, and two of 5 lines, each with its own or a variant melody). First comes a kind of operatic interjection directly addressing the illusion of the "great love" in the previous verse –

> Ah yes, I was wrong,
> Again, I was wrong

The next verse states the consequences of the lost love in what appears to be abject surrender to melancholy:

> Life is lonely again
> And only last year everything seemed so sure
> Now life is awful again
> A trough full of hearts could only be a bore

But then, more courageously, comes a new and brighter melody with the prospect of distraction and recovery:

> A week in Paris will ease the bite of it
> All I care is to smile in spite of it
> I'll forget you, I will,
> While yet you are still burning inside my brain

But in the end, despite the brave front, the damage proves irrevocable and the spurned lover faces life with jaded prospects and a cynical grin:

> Romance is mush
> Stifling those who strive
> I'll live a lush life in some small dive
> And there I'll be while I rot with the rest
> of those whose lives are lonely too

In any structural analysis of "Lush Life," the main question, it seems to me, is how the parts interact. The structure starts out more or less conventionally AAB and then erupts into CDE and F. There is no precedent for this structure, and no one, not even Strayhorn, tried it again. (The formal departure may explain why van de Leur identifies it as a *Lied* instead of a song.) The saving grace, of course, is that "Lush Life," however eccentric its structure, is perfectly coherent and cohesive. It not only hangs together, but it does so with wry and sly phraseology, and high sentiment. That surely explains the satisfaction of those singers who have sung it and, most of all, the listeners who have been moved by it. Strayhorn's taste for abject melancholy, his heart on his sleeve, is here put into words. That same taste comes through in the music he wrote for Johnny Hodges – with no less feeling and much more subtlety.

A Lovesome Lull Before the Lotus Blossoms

After "Passion Flower" in 1941, Strayhorn and Hodges, left to their own devices, appear to have momentarily exhausted their inspiration. Though they kept trying, their next attempts at absinthe ballads failed to find the integrity that made "Day Dream" and "Passion Flower" such paradigms. Maybe they mistook the success of those tunes for their superficial sentimentality, the bloated emotionality. An element of sentimentality was undeniably part of the genre, but it was not the crucial element. What was crucial was the underlying melancholy, the sense of loss and longing, that colored Strayhorn's music and Hodges's performance of it. It was the heartfelt depth of the blues, not the hangdog frown, that gave them their power. Strayhorn and Hodges would recover that depth in their last decade together, in three remarkable compositions that stand as masterpieces of their unique genre. Until then, however, "Day Dream" and "Passion Flower" would hold their places as perennial gems in Ellington's repertoire. The new attempts, and there were several, had their moments, but they lacked staying power.

First came "A Flower Is a Lovesome Thing," as blatantly sentimental as its lugubrious title suggests. Ellington tried it on radio audiences on his regularly scheduled Treasury Show broadcasts starting in June 1946, and then a month later recorded it non-commercially on a Capitol Transcription, a studio recording made for radio use only, always with Strayhorn replacing him at the piano (and, perhaps not accidentally, receiving sole credit for the piece). A small band with Hodges as nominal leader recorded it the next year, 1947, again with Strayhorn on piano, for a label called Sunrise Records that Ellington owned. The tune is pretty and danceable but somehow wispy. Ellington dropped it from the band's repertoire in 1947, soon after Hodges' recording. Years later he revived it in for an obscure 1960 small-band recording session released only in France, with himself at the piano and Harry Carney, not Hodges, as the soloist. Ellington was temperamentally averse to forthright acts; his treatment of "A Flower Is a Lovesome Thing" was as close as he was likely to come to outright rejection.

Strayhorn and Hodges apparently rated it higher. Strayhorn recorded "A Flower Is a Lovesome Thing" in 1961 with a string quartet and in 1965 with a lyric sung by Ozzie Bailey, thus giving it space on his only two turns as leader that were completely independent of Ellington. Hodges likewise recorded it in 1965 with a small band. None of these recordings overturned the maestro's implicit verdict.

Another Strayhorn-Hodges collaboration from the same time had a similar history. It was called, in keeping with Strayhorn's florid muse, "Violet Blue," thus invoking a slightly mellower shade than Ellington's famous "indigo" mood of 1930. "Violet Blue" also received its debut recording in a small-band session under Hodges's name for the short-lived Sunrise label. It is a little livelier in tempo than the other romantic ballads but it has an undulating vamp that might make for intimate dancing, and it shows off both principals, Strayhorn and Hodges, in very good form. Ellington dealt with it as he had "A Flower is A Lovesome Thing," introducing it first on radio broadcasts starting in 1945 (under the title "Ultra Violet") and recording it noncommercially as a Capitol Transcription in 1947 (as "Violet Blue"). It too was destined to be short-lived with Ellington and longer-lived with Strayhorn. In 1950, after it had been absent from Ellington's repertoire for a few years, Ellington brought it back at a few concerts with Kay Davis singing a new lyric that had been added by Strayhorn. After that, it was left to Strayhorn and he recorded it on both of his dates as a leader, as a piano feature in Paris in 1961 and as a vocal feature for Ozzie Bailey in New York in 1965, under yet another title "Multi-Colored Blue," thus giving it its third hue and a less distinctive one at that.

The third Strayhorn-Hodges collaboration from this period was more successful but not in the late-night ballad tradition. It made a brilliant small-band debut in 1947 under the title "Charlotte Russe," named not for a flower but for a French dessert (literally translated, a Russian *charlotte*), a cream-filled sponge cake with a cherry on top. Strayhorn's minor key melody has a haunting *noir* feeling, perfectly realized in the original recording in Hodges' sinuous tone, and made all the more haunting in Strayhorn's arrangement by Taft Jordan's muted trumpet fills. Here, surely, is a worthy new entry into the Strayhorn-Hodges canon of absinthe ballads. The recording caught the attention of other musicians, and Strayhorn immediately renamed it "Lotus Blossom," reverting to his floral theme. (The new title, of course, was the source of the "lotus eater" epithet that Strayhorn would play on in his 1956 *ballade*.)

"Lotus Blossom" is one of Strayhorn's most beautiful melodies (among many), but strangely Ellington never admitted it into his orchestral repertoire. He largely ignored it until 1961, when he recorded it as a feature for his piano playing with Aaron Bell on bass and Sam Woodyard on drums on *Piano in the Foreground*. From that moment on, Ellington played it frequently as a piano feature, sometimes accompanied by bass and drums but more often by bass only and sometimes as an unaccompanied piano solo. In 1967, his solo performance of "Lotus Blossom" at the recording session that was the memorial for Billy Strayhorn became the musical apogee of their kinship (as discussed in Chapter 5, "Panther Patter"). Thereafter, from October 1971 until his last performance in March 1974, Ellington played "Lotus Blossom" at every concert, usually as the encore, in a perpetual tribute to Strayhorn's memory. When asked about his choice of "Lotus Blossom," Ellington said, "This is what he most liked to hear me play" (Lambert, 309). "Lotus Blossom" is thus prominently represented in Ellington's repertoire but far removed from the form that Strayhorn and perhaps Hodges might have expected.

Strayhorn and Hodges had found their métier early with "Day Dream" and "Passion Flower," and with those compositions they set the bar high. Their next attempts gained momentary currency but never really rivaled the first two, which held their places tenaciously in Ellington's repertoire. Strayhorn was, in a sense, competing with himself, and he had set a very high standard. Luckily, this fallow period, if it really was fallow, would prove to be a momentary lull in the spectral alliance of Hodges and Strayhorn. That alliance was interrupted decisively by the period of estrangement when Hodges quit the band for almost five years to pursue his misadventure as leader. When he returned to the fold in 1955, the alliance would form anew, beginning with the unexpected definitive recording of "Passion Flower" inserted into Rosemary Clooney's vocal album, and from that moment it grew stronger than ever.

Back to his Natural Habitat
They were obviously happy to see each other, Strayhorn and Hodges. Not that they had been complete strangers. In the five years that Hodges had been gone, he recorded prolifically as a leader of small bands, thanks to the generosity of the impresario Norman Granz. Strayhorn was often among the cadre of Ellingtonians hired for the day to make records with him. The tunes were mainly simple riffs and easy blues by Hodges, devoid of sweat, as they were on *Duke's in Bed*, recorded the year after Hodges's return. The records Hodges made for Granz were pleasant, sometimes delightful, but no audience lined up to hear them, and fewer than half were issued in Hodges's lifetime.

After a few years without the cover of the Ellington orchestra where he had sat for 23 years, Johnny Hodges was scuffling. By 1955, Whitney Balliett wrote in the *New Yorker*, "Hodges had become an out-of-fashion bandleader of a small semi-rock-and-roll group."

If Hodges felt blessed by the opportunity of rejoining Ellington in October 1955, he did not betray his elation. On stage and off, he retained what Ellington's biographer Don George eloquently called "his old kiss-my-ass attitude." It was his playing, as always, that gave him away. His brilliant sound on the alto saxophone was now more assertive, more dramatic, freer than ever. Hodges knew it. In October 1958, arriving in England on tour with the orchestra, a reporter for *Melody Maker* asked him why he had returned to Ellington. "I had my own band and I had to scuffle, and when you scuffle you can't play what you like," Hodges explained, "but when you are famous and popular you can." His answer, a long one by his standards, is more revealing than most. In Ellington's orchestra, Hodges followed Ellington's agenda, traveled Ellington's itinerary, and played Ellington's music. To some onlookers it appeared that, far from playing what he liked, as he said, he was really in bondage to the Duke. That was nonsense, of course, and now Hodges knew it. He truly was playing what he liked, and the boss's agenda, itinerary and music were the annoyances he had to put up with to do it. Ellington's saxophone section, where Hodges would sit for 15 more years until his death in 1970, was his natural habitat.

Hodges's musical rejuvenation, first displayed in the definitive recording of "Passion Flower," went almost unnoticed as the lone instrumental on the recording of Rosemary Clooney vocals. Instead, his rejuvenation was very boldly proclaimed six months later at the Newport Jazz Festival on 7 July 1956, the breakthrough concert that brought about riotous dancing in the aisles. Though most of the musical discussion of that concert has centered on "Diminuendo in Blue and Crescendo in Blue" with Paul Gonsalves's rollicking 27-bar chorus that roused the rioters, the consummate musical moment actually belongs to Hodges with his keening, magisterial rendition of "Jeep's Blues," his blues wail riding the crest of the band in full shout and the roar of the audience rising in waves around them. Ellington and Hodges had played "Jeep's Blues" dozens of times since its debut record in 1938 and they would play it dozens more, but this Newport performance has no rival.

Hodges had been a master of his instrument long before his unhappy five-year hiatus. On his return, he brought a heightened dramatic sense to that mastery, a tolerance – perhaps even a receptiveness – for the occasion. It is surely no accident that the definitive performances of Billy Strayhorn's "Day Dream" and "Passion Flower," brilliant though they were in the 1940s when they were composed, came years later, in 1956 and 1961, when Hodges was temperamentally better disposed to rise to the occasion.

Masterpieces with the Bard, the Basmala and the Biopsy

The lotus-eaters thrived after their reunion. Johnny Hodges and Billy Strayhorn resumed their alliance with obvious relish. Among their absinthe-soaked love songs were three masterpieces that will take their place in any reckoning of Duke Ellington's finest moments. All three were written for specific contexts so that they were buoyed conceptually by impulses more concrete than the limp romanticism of "lovesome" flowers and cherry-topped *charlottes russes*. The new masterpieces show that the allies were prepared to make music that could inspire higher impulses than close dancing at the end of the night – though they could inspire that too if the need arose.

The Bard, William Shakespeare, provided the context for the first of the masterpieces. In 1956, in the heady glow of the Newport Festival triumph, Ellington and Strayhorn launched an ambitious project for a suite that would be "a tone parallel" to some of Shakespeare's memorable characters (discussed in detail in Chapter 6, "Bardland"). Among the characters chosen after Ellington and Strayhorn's fastidious review of the plays were two of Shakespeare's fabled romantic couples, either of which might have provided obvious opportunities for Strayhorn and Hodges. The plays *Antony and Cleopatra* and *Romeo and Juliet* probe intense love affairs that go tragically awry – ideal fodder for lotus-eaters. In the end, it was *Romeo and Juliet* that received their unbridled treatment. Instead, *Antony and Cleopatra* is represented by a winsome piece called "Half the Fun"; though written by Strayhorn[1] and featuring Hodges, its mood is one of charming frivolity, a far remove from the scent of lotus blossoms.

Romeo and Juliet provided the absinthe feature for Strayhorn and Hodges in the Shakespeare suite. "The Star-Crossed Lovers" is a triumph for the lotus-eaters' alliance, arguably its apogee. It is credited to Strayhorn alone as composer, but its final form was partly worked out in the recording studio, as can be heard in a nine-minute rehearsal take released under the working title "Pretty Girl" that was

---

[1] Composer credits for *Such Sweet Thunder* are confusing because Billy Strayhorn had recently lodged a complaint about his lack of credit and Ellington, with characteristic nonchalance, credited ten of the 12 movements jointly "(Ellington, Strayhorn)" with one to Strayhorn alone ("The Star-Crossed Lovers") and one to Ellington alone ("Half the Fun"). These credits are patently incorrect. Inspecting the MSS, Walter van de Leur (pp. 134-35) determined that Strayhorn was mainly responsible for both "The Star-Crossed Lovers" and "Half the Fun," and also "Up and Down, Up and Down." Van de Leur says, "Other than scoring a small section for Ellington's forceful opener of *Such Sweet Thunder*, Strayhorn apparently had little to do with the other nine movements."

recorded five months before the final version. Strayhorn's commentator, Walter van de Leur, documented the many changes from Strayhorn's original score to the definitive recorded version, including the omission of what he calls the "original majestic modulation and coda," replaced by a straightforward reiteration of the theme by the trombones. This stripping of ornament suggests the invisible hand of Ellington. Another change, a modulation from D^b to D, may have come about at Hodges's insistence, as it would have been, van de Leur says, "definitely uncomfortable for the alto." If so, it provides an example of the kind of change Strayhorn said he regularly made to accommodate Hodges: "If [Hodges] says, 'This is awkward here. This is an awkward position of notes,' then you say, 'Is it really? Is it impossible?' If he keeps trying it, and it is impossible, you say, 'Well, all right, I'll change it'" (quoted by van de Leur). The changes from Strayhorn's original score to the definitive recording, however they came about, definitely resulted in (in Ethan Iverson's phrase) "the right feel" – the right *everything*, one is tempted to say.

Even his band mates, who were used to playing Strayhorn's

The Bard, William Shakespeare (Oxford University Press)

melodies daily, agreed. At the recording session for "The Star-Crossed Lovers," clarinetist Jimmy Hamilton told Strayhorn, "Nobody going to forget this, man. This is the most beautiful thing you ever wrote" (quoted by Hajdu). Hamilton was remembering the tune from its earliest incarnation, two years earlier, when Strayhorn brought a sketch, then called "Pretty Little Girl," to a small-band session under Hodges's leadership. On that early version, the tempo is slightly brighter, the arrangement is rudimentary (little more than half the length of the definitive version, played by an octet), and Hodges shares the solo duties with Strayhorn, who plays a concerto-like piano interval. The original is a mere shadow of what it would become as "The Star-Crossed Lovers," but its gorgeous melody is intact, as Hamilton noticed. Hearing the small-band sketch alongside the definitive big-band version in *Such Sweet Thunder* provides an otherwise ineffable measure of the inspiration Shakespeare could bring to the music, for Ellington as well as Strayhorn. Subtle though the changes were, they turned a sketch into a masterpiece.

The melody of "The Star-Crossed Lovers" is unconventional, organized in melodic sequences AA'BC, in which *B* appears where the bridge normally occurs but then is superseded as the new *C* melody ascends from it as a dramatic *cri de coeur*, ramping up the drama from the mellow ballad flow that has gone before. That melodic sequence (AA'), Strayhorn's "most beautiful thing" (as Hamilton called it) captures the newfound, forbidden love of teen-aged Romeo and Juliet. The climactic *C* melody represents the portent of woe that would befall them. In Strayhorn's ingenious arrangement, the second repeat of the AA' melodies is played by the orchestra in low-key dissonances, leaving the dramatic BC statements for Hodges's controlled aggression in his climactic finale.

Admirers of the lotus eaters, reveling in "The Star-Crossed Lovers" at the time, might have quietly wondered if the sub-genre had reached its climax. Perhaps it had, but amazingly there would be other legitimate contenders still to come.

The Basmala, the ornate symbol of Islam, transfixed Duke Ellington in the autumn of 1963 when the State Department of the United States government sponsored him on a tour of the Middle East. From September until November, the orchestra played for large, appreciative audiences in Damascus, Amman, Jerusalem, Kabul, New Delhi, Dacca, Lahore, Ceylon, Tehran, Madras, Bombay, Baghdad and Ankara. (The musical sway on Ellington is discussed at length in Chapter 7, "Afro-Eurasian Eclipse.")

Though Ellington was by this time a seasoned traveler, he found the sights and sounds of the Mideast, with a relatively relaxed itinerary (by his hectic standards), endlessly fascinating. Always an interested and involved tourist, Ellington breathed in the new surroundings as never before. He published a detailed diary of the tour in *Music Is My Mistress* (pp. 301-330) celebrating "the smells of spices and garlic and exotic perfumes,... marvelous brocades, oriental rugs, glass and copper trays, inlaid and engraved,... [and] swarming masses of people everywhere."

"I hope much of this will go into music," Ellington said on his return. It took two more years for him to record what he called, with geographic license, the *Far East Suite*; eight of its nine movements pay homage in Ellington's unique terms to the Near East and the Middle East sites of his 1963 tour.

The gem in the 45-minute suite is the ballad "Isfahan," played with sinuous brilliance by Johnny Hodges. Named for the city in central Iran that was the capital of Persia in the eleventh century, Ellington remembered it in his diary (p. 325) as "a city of poetic beauty, where they give you poems instead of flowers." Strayhorn

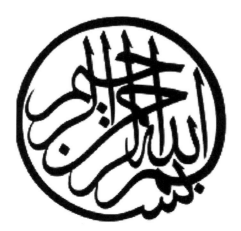

The Basmala (Wikipedia)

receives composer credit for "Isfahan," but as we have seen so many times Ellington's handiwork is unmistakable in the final take. "There were only two [complete] versions of the exquisite *Isfahan*," says Stanley Dance, who attended the recording session, "but they were born after much earnest discussion between Ellington and Johnny Hodges, particularly concerning those pauses during the performance that add so much significance to the picture of a city 'where everything is poetry'."

The "pauses" refer to the stunning compositional device whereby Hodges starts every melodic phrase a cappella and then carries the downward glide through what van de Leur calls the "unfolding major seventh chord in the alto" as the orchestra sidles in behind him with a subtle grace that is felt rather than heard. Van de Leur calls it "a cunning composition." It is formally unique, another monument to Billy Strayhorn's exploiting of form for captivating feeling. "Isfahan" became an immediate favorite among jazz saxophone players and it is a staple in the repertoire of many great players, but the performance by Johnny Hodges in the *Far East Suite* is probably unsurpassed.

On the occasion, the performance may have gained emotional depth because Strayhorn was conspicuously absent from the recording session. Early in 1966 he had been diagnosed with cancer of the esophagus and at the time of the recording session for "Isfahan" in December he was undergoing radiation therapy, as everyone in the band knew too well. Amazingly, "Isfahan" was not the last of his absinthe ballads. He would float one more to the world on the wings, so to speak, of his biopsy.

The Biopsy was a death sentence. The prognosis was fatal, but Strayhorn was determined to make his demise a creative one. Around the time that his esophagus was removed and Strayhorn was sustaining himself on a liquid diet ingested through a tube directly into his stomach (which included, to no one's surprise, dry martinis), he turned in a score at first called "Blue Cloud" but later re-named "Blood Count." At the moment he completed the score, Ellington and the orchestra were in the middle of a crowded European tour (24 January to 19 March 1967). On receiving the score, Ellington called a rehearsal in Milan, Italy, an uncommon occurrence when the band was playing nightly concerts. They polished Strayhorn's arrangement,

Billy Strayhorn (courtesy Free Social Encyclopedia)

and they then played it nightly for the remaining three weeks of the tour. Live performances are preserved in Stuttgart (where it is identified as "Freakish Lights") and a few other cities. The hallmarks of the lotus-eater genre are all in place in these performances – the keening alto saxophone of Hodges soaring over sepulchral muted horns. Obviously, it would take an extra-special performance before it could be mentioned alongside "Star-Crossed Lovers" and "Isfahan." And it would get it.

Billy Strayhorn died on 31 May 1967. Three months later, Ellington and his orchestra, still distraught, gathered in the RCA Victor Studio in New York to record 14 compositions by Strayhorn for an album that would be called ...*And His Mother Called Him Bill*. (Ellington's elegiac piano performance of "Lotus Blossom" on this recording is discussed in Chapter 5, "Panther Patter.")

"Blood Count" was one of the 14 compositions. It was not an obvious choice, having been introduced obscurely in European concerts just six months before and never recorded. It was, however,

Strayhorn's final composition, and its title carried a reminder to all of his band-mates of his fate. "He didn't write any more after 'Blood Count'," his great friend Marian Logan told David Hajdu (p. 253). "That was the last thing he had to say. And it wasn't 'Good-bye' or 'Thank you' or anything phony like that. It was 'This is how I feel,' and he felt like shit – 'Like it or leave it'."

The performance of "Blood Count" rose to the occasion. It is Billy Strayhorn's *memento mori*. The power of the performance was described by Robert Palmer in his notes for the album in words that convey its inspiration as well as it could be expressed by anyone:

> *Blood Count* has an immediate and devastating impact, speaking simultaneously of fear, longing, resignation, pride, doubt, faith and many more apparently conflicting emotions, all balanced on the knife's edge of a man's life, all vividly brought to life whenever the music is heard.

The core of the performance, its heart, as Palmer also notes, belongs to Strayhorn's longtime ally. Palmer writes

> This is one of Johnny Hodges's greatest performances. He is still *angry* that Strayhorn has been taken, and for once the familiar adjectives – serene, unruffled – cannot be applied to his playing. He sings, from deep inside, the certain knowledge that any moment can be a man's last moment, and his playing cuts right to the heart.

Amen to that. The aura surrounding Hodges with the airy, richly harmonized backgrounds is reverential but somehow, for the other fourteen musicians as for Hodges, there is also defiance shining through. It is a glittering monument to mark the final chord in the alliance of the lotus-eaters.

Last Gasp of the Lotus Eater

In 1951, when Johnny Hodges was eking out a living playing second-rate music on his own, he was asked why he had quit the Ellington orchestra. He grumbled, "We didn't like the tone poems much." A few years later, in a much better mood after he had returned to the band and reclaimed his rightful place in Ellington's cosmos, he recanted, so to speak, in a conversation with Stanley Dance. "*Warm Valley* is one of my favorite records. I like playing that kind of number – if it has the right backgrounds," he said. "*Day Dream* too. When I'm playing that, it's supposed to be very, very soft, and you're supposed to close your eyes and dream a while." It is reassuring to think that at least this one time, when he was for the moment not trying to bait his boss, Johnny Hodges was willing to acknowledge the summit to which his boss had led him.

Billy Strayhorn, of course, needed no second chances to express his gratification for the spectral alliance. He knew, as Johnny Hodges surely did too if only he would admit it, that Duke Ellington had made their dreams come true – had provided many kinds of settings for putting their singular gifts on display. Those settings included many musical forms from jump blues ("The Intimacy of the Blues") to svelte ornaments ("Half the Fun"), but most of all they included their late-night absinthe reveries. That handful of sensuous nocturnes is unique in all music, both one-of-a-kind and a genre unto themselves, momentary but somehow momentous.

If Strayhorn's and Hodges's entire expansive careers with Ellington were *charlottes russes* (to dip into Strayhorn's sucrose imagery), then their spectral alliance was the cherry on top.

References (page numbers to direct quotations are shown *in italics*)
Balliett, Whitney. 1962. *Dinosaurs in the Morning*. New York: Lippincott. *p. 124*
Berry, Bill. 1999. Liner note for *Such Sweet Thunder*. Columbia [CD stereo reissue]. *p. 16*
Chambers, Jack. 2001. "Sweet as Bear Meat: The Paradox of Johnny Hodges." *Coda* 298 (July/August). 16-20. Online <http://homes.chass.utoronto.ca/~chambers/hodges.html>
Coss, Bill. 1962. "Ellington & Strayhorn, Inc." *Down Beat*. Reprinted in *The Duke Ellington Reader*, ed. Mark Tucker. New York: Oxford University Press. 498-503. *p. 501.*
Dance, Stanley. 1970. *The World of Duke Ellington*. London: Macmillan. *p. 89, p. 18*
Dance, Stanley. 1995. Liner note to *The Far East Suite: Special Mix*. Bluebird CD.
Ellington, Duke. 1973. *Music is My Mistress*. New York: Doubleday. *p. 156,*

pp. 159-61, p. 301, p. 325

Ellington, Mercer, with Stanley Dance. 1978. *Duke Ellington in Person: An Intimate Memoir*. Houghton Mifflin. *pp. 105-06.*

George, Don. 1981. *Sweet Man: The Real Duke Ellington*. New York: Putnam's Sons. *p. 40*

Hajdu, David. 1996. *Lush Life: A Biography of Billy Strayhorn*. New York: Farrar Straus & Giroux. *p. 17, p. 210, p. 178, pp. 197-98, pp. 88-89. p. 160, p. 253*

Iverson, Ethan. 2017. Interview with Nicholas Payton. https://ethaniverson.com/interview-with-nicholas-payton/[accessed April 2017]

Lambert, Eddie. 1999. *A Listener's Guide to Duke Ellington*. Lanham, Maryland: Scarecrow Press. *p. 309*

Palmer, Robert. 1987. Liner note for ...*And His Mother Called Him Bill*. Bluebird CD.

Udkoff, Bob, interviewed by Stuart Nicholson. 1999. *A Portrait of Duke Ellington: Reminiscing in Tempo*. London: Pen Books. *p. 326.*

Ulanov, Barry. 1946. *Duke Ellington*. New York: Creative Age Press. *p. x.*

van de Leur, Walter. 2002. *Something to Live For: The Music of Billy Strayhorn*. Oxford, UK: Oxford University Press. *pp. 16-17, p. 150*

Westin, Martin, and Lars Westin. 2018. "Rolf Ericson Interview." *Duke Ellington Society of Sweden*, Bulletin 3. August 2018. 9-14. English translation from Swedish in *Orkester Journalen* (May 1994). *p. 11*

Playlist (recordings cited in order of appearance in the chapter)

"Ballade for Very Tired and Very Sad Lotus Eaters" (3:19) 1 September 1956. *Duke's in Bed* on CD1 of *Johnny Hodges and the Ellington Men 1956-1957*. 2-CD. Fresh Sound [2010].
Clark Terry flg, Ray Nance tp, Quentin Jackson tb, Hodges as, Jimmy Hamilton cl, Harry Carney bs, Billy Strayhorn p, comp, arr, Jimmy Woode b, Sam Woodyard d

"Warm Valley" (3:20) 17 October 1940. *Blanton-Webster Band*. RCA Victor CD-2 [1986].
Cootie Williams, Wallace Jones, Rex Stewart, tp; Joe Nanton, Lawrence Brown, Juan Tizol tb; Barney Bigard cl, Johnny Hodges as, Otto Hardwick as, Ben Webster ts, Harry Carney bs; Ellington p, comp, arr; Fred Guy g, Jimmy Blanton b, Sonny Greer d.
Solos: Ellington, Hodges, Rex Stewart (muted obbligato), Hodges again

"Day Dream" (2:56) 2 November 1940. Hodges, *Passion Flower*. Bluebird CD [1995].
Cootie Williams tp; Lawrence Brown tb; Hodges; Harry Carney bs; Duke

Ellington p; Jimmy Blanton b; Sonny Greer d

"Day Dream" (3:56) 12 December 1961. *Johnny Hodges with Billy Strayhorn and the Orchestra.* Verve CD [1999]. Cat Anderson, Shorty Baker, Bill Berry, Ed Mullens tp; Lawrence Brown, Quentin Jackson, Chuck Connors tb; Russell Procope, Jimmy Hamilton, Paul Gonsalves, Hodges, Harry Carney reeds; Jimmy Jones p; Aaron Bell b, Sam Woodyard d; Strayhorn arr, cond

"Passion Flower" (3:05) 3 July 1941. Hodges, *Passion Flower.* Bluebird CD [1995].
Ray Nance tp; Lawrence Brown tb; Hodges; Harry Carney bs; Duke Ellington p; Jimmy Blanton b; Sonny Greer d

"Passion Flower" (4:33) 23 January 1956. Rosemary Clooney and Duke Ellington, *Blue Rose.* Columbia CD [1999]. Cat Anderson, Willie Cook, Ray Nance, Clark Terry tp; Quentin Jackson, John Sanders, Britt Woodman tb; Hodges, Russell Procope, Jimmy Hamilton, Paul Gonsalves, Harry Carney reeds; Ellington p; Jimmy Woode b; Sam Woodyard d. (Clooney absent on this track.)

"Lush Life" (6:33) 13 November 1948. Duke Ellington, *Carnegie Hall November 1948* 2CD. Vintage Jazz Classics [1991]. Billy Strayhorn p, Kay Davis vocal. (Saxophones and bass are heard on the last chord.)

"Lush Life" (3:31) Basin Street East, NY, 14 January 1964. Billy Strayhorn, *Lush Life.* Red Baron CD [1992]. Cat Anderson, Cootie Williams, Rolf Ericson, Herbie Jones tp; Lawrence Brown, Buster Cooper, Chuck Connors tb; Russell Procope, Johnny Hodges, Jimmy Hamilton, Paul Gonsalves, Harry Carney reeds; Billy Strayhorn p and vocal; Ernie Shepard b, Sam Woodyard d

"Lush Life" (4:15) Reno Sweeny Ballroom, NY, 1978. Blossom Dearie, *Needlepoint Magic.* Daffodil Records. Blossom Dearie, piano and vocal

"A Flower is A Lovesome Thing" (3:22) Capitol Transcription, Hollywood, CA. 17 July 1946. *Jazz Legends Vol. 12,* Naxos [2006]. Taft Jordan, Shelton Hemphill, Cat Anderson, Francis Williams, Shorty Baker, Ray Nance tp; Lawrence Brown, Claude Jones, Wilbur DeParis, Tricky Sam Nanton tb; Jimmy Hamilton, Johnny Hodges, Russell Procope, Al Sears, Harry Carney reeds; Billy Strayhorn p; Fred Guy g; Oscar Pettiford b; Sonny Greer d

"A Flower is A Lovesome Thing" (2:44) New York. Autumn 1947. *The Johnny Hodges All Stars....* Prestige CD [1992]. Taft Jordan tp; Lawrence Brown tb; Johnny Hodges as; Al Sears ts; Billy Strayhorn p; Oscar Pettiford b; Wilbur de Paris d

"A Flower is A Lovesome Thing" (3:12) Hollywood, CA. 14 July 1960. *At the Bal Masque*. Originally Columbia, reissued Essential Jazz Classics CD [2006]. Ray Nance tp; Lawrence Brown tb; Johnny Hodges as; Harry Carney bs; Duke Ellington p; Aaron Bell b; Sam Woodyard d

"Violet Blue" (2:57) New York, June 1947. *The Johnny Hodges All Stars....* Prestige CD [1992]. Shorty Baker tp; Hodges; Al Sears ts; Harry Carney bs; Strayhorn p; Oscar Pettiford b; Sonny Greer dm.

"Charlotte Russe" (3:02) Autumn 1947, New York. Personnel, date and CD issue same as "A Flower is A Lovesome Thing" above.

"Half the Fun" (4:19), "Pretty Girl" (8:54 rehearsal) and "The Star-Crossed Lovers" (4:00). New York. 7 August 1956, 6 December 1956 and 3 May 1957. *Such Sweet Thunder.* Columbia CD [1999]. Cat Anderson, Willie Cook, Ray Nance, Clark Terry tp; Quentin Jackson, John Sanders, Britt Woodman tb; Harry Carney, Paul Gonsalves, Jimmy Hamilton, Johnny Hodges, Russell Procope reeds; Ellington p, Jimmy Woode b, Sam Woodyard d.

"Pretty Little Girl" (2:26) New York. 8 September 1955. Johnny Hodges, *Creamy* (originally Verve Records), CD2 on *Four Classic Albums*, Avid [2010]. Clark Terry tp, Lawrence Brown tb; Jimmy Hamiton ts, cl; Johnny Hodges as; Harry Carney bs; Billy Strayhorn p; Jimmy Woode b; Sonny Greer d.

"Isfahan" (4:02) and "Isfahan" alternate take (4:11) New York. 20 December 1966. *The Far East Suite: Special Mix*. Bluebird CD [1995]. Cat Anderson, Cootie Williams, Mercer Ellington, Herbie Jones tp; Lawrence Brown, Buster Cooper, Chuck Connors tb; Harry Carney, Paul Gonsalves, Jimmy Hamilton, Johnny Hodges, Russell Procope reeds; Ellington p, John Lamb b, Rufus Jones d.

"Freakish Lights" (4:15 = "Blood Count") Liederhalle, Stuttgart, Germany. 6 March 1967. *Big Bands Live.* Jazz Haus CD [Austria 2011]. Personnel as for "Isfahan" above.

"Blood Count" (4:17) Victor Studios, New York. 28 Aug. 1967. ... *And His Mother Called Him Bill.* (Bluebird CD [1987]). Cat Anderson, Mercer Ellington, Herbie Jones, Cootie Williams tp; Lawrence Brown, Buster Cooper, Chuck Connors, tb; Jimmy Hamilton, Russell Procope, Johnny Hodges, Paul Gonsalves, Harry Carney reeds; Ellington p; Aaron Bell b; Steve Little d

CHAPTER 5

Panther Patter

Duke Ellington at the Piano

"And now, the piano player moves in to steal the show!" Duke Ellington shouts near the beginning of a ragged version of "The Hawk Talks" at McElroy's Ballroom in Portland, Oregon, on the occasion of his 54th birthday. Of course the piano player, Ellington himself, did not really steal the show, though he did get off a rollicking chorus by way of introducing the drum feature that gave him a minor jukebox hit in 1951, two years earlier, when its composer, Louie Bellson, was his drummer.

Duke Ellington, the piano player, seldom stole the show. He was always overshadowed by Duke Ellington the composer, arranger, bandleader, songwriter and master of ceremonies. At the end of a concert or dance, fans who noticed his piano playing at all were most likely to remember him for using the piano like an outsize baton, cueing the band with it and playing filigrees for the singers and rallying his sidemen with a feverish version of "Kinda Dukish" as the preamble to "Rockin' in Rhythm."

And yet Ellington was proud of his piano playing, and not reluctant to show it off. Until his genius for composing and arranging blossomed at the Cotton Club in 1927, he must have assumed he would make his career as a piano player. His main ambition as a teenager, he once said, was to master the polydextrous fingering of James P. Johnson's "Carolina Shout," and to that end he spent countless hours studying the slowed-down piano roll. "And how I learned it!" he said in *Music Is My Mistress*. "I nursed it, rehearsed it. Yes, this was the most solid foundation for me.... It became my party piece." His first issued recording had him squarely in the role of accompanist for the singer Alberta Hunter (under the alias Alberta Prime).

His teenaged strutting morphed into 50 years of professional piano playing. Without consciously trying, in those 50 years Ellington recapitulated the entire history of jazz piano styles. He made the transition from style to style, apparently instinctively, simply to stay abreast of the currents that were moving his orchestral music and his own restless muse. In his last decade, he would occasionally interrupt his impressionist pianisms with a nostalgic foray into the ragtime style of his youth or the stride style of his first professional years, but they were offered (and received) as pieces of show-biz shtick rather than a boast about the stylistic miles he had covered. Among jazz historians, Mary Lou Williams is universally lauded as the piano player who stayed ahead of the stylistic curve for her leading role in swing piano and then bebop and then post-bop impressionism. But Ellington's starting point came a style or two before hers, and his finishing point, though seldom mentioned, rivaled stylists born 30 years after him.

Ellington and Harlem Stride

One of Ellington's first recordings after arriving in New York with the Washingtonians was a bravura piano solo called "Jig Walk" for Paramount Records in 1926. It is beyond a doubt one of the most bizarre entries in his voluminous discography. It was mainly intended to show off a percussion gimmick attached to the piano hammers so that the hammers play a ricky-ticky accompaniment to the sounded notes. Even with the advanced technology of the 21st century, "Jig

Duke Ellington in a barrelhouse pose (Bandcamp photo)

Walk" sounds awful. It is horrifying to think that, if the record had become a popular success, it might have launched the career of Barrelhouse Eddie Ellington on the vaudeville circuit. Luckily it failed, and a few months later the first of Ellington's great orchestral Brunswicks made their appearance with "East St. Louis Toodle-Oo" and "Birmingham Breakdown." At that point, it should have been clear to all observers that Ellington's destiny lay in composing and bandleading, but for a while longer he kept his piano ambitions active just in case.

In 1928 he recorded a pair of piano solos, "Black Beauty" and "Swampy River," in the dense Harlem stride style he admired in James P. Johnson, Willie the Lion Smith and Luckey Roberts (both on *Okeh Ellington*, listed in the Playlist at the end of the chapter). He played them with flash, showing off the genre-defining dexterity in the melodically complex right hand and the bumptious independence of the polyrhythmic left hand. There can be little doubt that he would have succeeded in the world of Harlem stride piano if it was his main chance, but the very same recording session that turned out the flashy piano solos also produced the orchestral recording "The Mooche," with Bubber Miley growling and Barney Bigard soaring in the ersatz uptown jungle. R.D. Darrell immediately declared "The Mooche" an "inimitable masterpiece" in *Phonograph Monthly*, a verdict universally held in all the decades since; the piano solos went largely unnoticed at the time, though "Black Beauty," a lovely melody dedicated to Florence Mills, a singer who had died tragically young the year before,

Young Duke Ellington – his accolades as a composer waylaid his amibitions as a piano soloist

would be played by Ellington throughout his career, especially in the last decades when he began playing piano features more often.

Ellington's gratification as a composer and bandleader apparently dampened his piano ambitions. For the next 12 years, Ellington allotted himself a lot of comping and an occasional solo as the band's piano player but no features. The irony of his dual role as bandleader and piano accompanist became part of his nightly routine. At some point on most evenings, he would sidle up to the microphone and announce, in his most unctuous tone, "And now, ladies and gentlemen, it is our pleasure to feature, for your listening and dancing pleasure, the piano player." He would then watch the audience turn to look at the empty piano bench, and he would laugh at them as they laughed at themselves upon realizing that the piano player was Ellington himself. Then he would take his turn just as Bigard had taken his turn on "Clarinet Lament" or Juan Tizol on "Pyramid" or Cootie Williams on "Echoes of Harlem."

One recorded piano feature from this relatively quiet period in Ellington's keyboard career is the dazzling "Lots o' Fingers" from a 1932 medley given a famous second life among audiophiles when record collector Brad Kay discovered two recordings made on microphones separated by a few metres, and synced the records to make accidental stereo 30 years before it became standard (*Stereo Reflections in Ellington*, Natasha NI-4106 [1993]). "Lots o' Fingers" occupies the middle part of a medley with orchestral pieces on either side, and it is excerpted (in mono) on *Solos, Duets and Trios* (listed with other full-length Ellington piano features in the appendix to this chapter "Piano in the Foreground"). Ellington's two-minute solo in the middle of the seven-minute medley represents what is surely his crowning achievement as a stride pianist. The interpolation of "Lots o' Fingers" between the orchestral features "East St. Louis Toodle-Oo" and "Black and Tan Fantasy," well-loved hits that were then a few years old, shows off Ellington's mastery of the keyboard in a dazzling display of technical prowess. Ellington never seemed to work on his piano technique, in this period or any other, though he doodled at the keyboard every day of his life, habitually in the hours from midnight to dawn, seeking voicings and harmonies for his arrangements. Apparently, that was enough. His piano technique never faltered.

Already in the 1930s there were portents of change in his interpretation. As the stride piano style was about to be supplanted by swing, Ellington was already altering his style too, using tenths infrequently in the bass clef and choosing instead richer chords with wider intervals. The next significant piano part he wrote for himself, almost three years later, had no trace of stride. It was the 32-bar piano concerto that ends Part 2 of "Reminiscing in Tempo" (1935), Ellington's brooding elegy to his mother. His mood in the elegy, needless to say, was far removed from the extraverted flourishes he indulged in his stride style though ornate in his early swing style, with showy runs.

As Ellington left behind the piano styles that had so beguiled him in his youth, he found a way of making fun – affectionate fun, to be sure – of his youthful dalliance. He would spin a tale about what he claimed to be the first piece of music he ever wrote, something called "Soda Fountain Rag," harking back to his days as a 15-year-old soda jerk in Washington. With feigned reluctance, he would embmark on a kind of stolid opening and gather enthusiasm as he accelerated, carrying the audience with him – and stop dead after about a minute, claiming that his memory had suddenly failed him. "Soda Fountain Rag" became an entertaining reminder of the changes he had worked through at the keyboard.

Homage to the Lion

Even as Ellington left behind his Harlem stride roots as a piano player, his debt to Willie the Lion Smith remained constant. In 1939, he composed "Portrait of the Lion," a big-band tribute to the piano player who was his first advocate when he arrived in New York. The piece is very much in the then-new swing groove, with bright, fairly intricate ensemble playing. Ellington's piano part in the composition mainly embroiders a baritone saxophone solo by Harry Carney and then an alto solo by Johnny Hodges. Except for four unaccompanied bars at the start, Ellington's piano pays little heed to the piano lessons he absorbed from the Lion. His homage to the Lion emanates instead from the loping rhythm, a happy infectious beat, a part of Ellington's debt that evidently he felt as deeply as any keyboard tutoring.

In Ellington's foreword to the Lion's memoir, *Music on My Mind*,

Ellington describes an uncanny sensation he felt as he and Sonny Greer walked down the stairs at the Capitol Palace in Harlem where Smith was the featured piano player and the genial host. It was 1923. Ellington was 24, unknown outside his old D.C. 'hood, penniless and scuffling away from home for the first time. What he felt is palpable in his description of it more than 40 years later: "My first impression of the Lion – even before I saw him – was the thing I felt as I walked down those steps. A strange thing…. [T]he tempo was the lope – actually everything and everybody seemed to be doing whatever they were doing in the tempo the Lion's group was laying down. The walls and furniture seemed to lean understandingly – one of the strangest and greatest sensations I ever had. The waiters served in that tempo; everybody who had to walk in, out, or around the place walked with a beat." Ellington's orchestral portrait tries to capture that lope.

Ellington obviously admired the Lion's piano playing as well as the lope. In that same foreword, amidst the words of praise, he singles

Willie The Lion Smith

out "his fire, his harmonic lavishness, his stride – what a luxury ... and of course I swam in it. Most of it still clings – agreeably." Ellington proved that it was still clinging many years later, in 1965, when he played a piano tribute, "The Second Portrait of the Lion," at the Jazz Piano Workshop, with the Lion himself looking on. (See *The Jazz Piano* in the annotated appendix "Piano in the Foreground.") It may have been the presence of the Lion, in fact, that called it forth. As I hear it in the live recording of the workshop, Ellington surprised the organizers (and maybe himself) with a spontaneous composition. Walking onstage for his turn among the assembled piano celebrities at the workshop, he casually announced, "Yeah, I tell you what I'd like to do, um, since I haven't warmed up my left hand today, I think I would like to do something called, um, my 'Second Portrait of the Lion.' You know who the Lion is? So if you hear some Lion in there, it rubbed off many years ago." He then played a four-minute romp with two distinct themes, the first fiery stride (to 1:34) and the second lavishly harmonic (2 minutes), and then he finishes by alternating the two themes, all of it played with Lion-like bravado and flourish. It is a tour de force, the more so if (as it seems to be) it is invented on the spot. Eddie Lambert calls it "a piece of considerable charm" that "certainly would be included in any short list of Ellington's best compositions for solo piano." Far removed though it is from the piano style Ellington was then displaying, this ode to the Lion seems at the very least a virtuoso exercise in nostalgia.

Ellington and Swing

Starting in 1940, Ellington began featuring his piano playing more frequently but it seems that he was spurred not by his own ambitions so much as by his ambitions for the extraordinary young bassist Jimmy Blanton, who joined his orchestra in September 1939. Blanton's resonating tone and paradoxically nimble touch gave the walking bass an uncommon presence in the ensemble. To appreciate Blanton's impact on Ellington and other musicians in 1939, modern listeners have to compare him to his swing contemporaries, who were generally stolid ensemble players whose presence was felt as much as heard. All Blanton's successors, knowingly or not, absorbed his style so thoroughly as to make it the hallmark of jazz bass playing. Blanton transformed bass playing in jazz ensembles so completely that we tend to hear him now as one more great player in the modern tradition without realizing that he is really the fountainhead of that tradition.

Ellington was awed by the 18-year-old's gifts and immediately elevated him into the solo pantheon in the band, alloting him solo choruses on "Ko-Ko," "Bojangles" and "Sepia Panorama," and showcasing him on the redoubtable "Jack the Bear," one of the first orchestrated features for the string bass (all 1940). As if to make sure no one would miss the point, Ellington also recorded duets with Blanton, thus giving him a prominence previously unknown for bass players. Exposing Blanton in this way fortuitously put Ellington's piano in the foreground as well. It may also have sped up Ellington's stylistic move into swing piano. If Ellington had any inclination to sustain the hyperactivity of his stride-style left hand, it would have

Jimmy Blanton (still photo from soundie 1940)

withered and died in these duets, where Blanton's bass conspicuously took charge of the chordal structure.

Ellington and Blanton recorded four titles on 1 October 1940, that are endlessly interesting (and survive hardily with alternate takes on *Solos, Duets and Trios* in the appendix). On two ballads, "Body and Soul" and "Sophisticated Lady," Ellington had Blanton state the melody arco, that is, on his bowed bass, at that time a sound almost unknown in jazz (though it would soon be well known through another up-and-coming bassist named Slam Stewart). The deep thrum of the bowed bass must have had the thrill of novelty at the time, and the preserved takes of these titles catch Blanton gathering confidence in his arco technique from one take to the next, but they do not exploit his most conspicuous strengths. Those strengths are showcased when he plays plucked bass, that is, pizzicato. On "Mr. J.B. Blues," which Ellington's title dedicates to him, his precocious talent shines as he and Ellington alternate the lead and modulate from major to minor keys with perfect empathy. Brilliant as "Mr. J.B. Blues" is, the treasure of the duets is "Pitter Panther Patter" based on an 8-bar figure that Ellington repeats with variations while Blanton plays counter-melodies, apparently improvised, and surges into the lead

Duke Ellington, Jimmy Blanton, *Blues Plucked Again* (rare European CBS LP)

whenever the piano rests. The nursery cadence of the "pitter patter" in the title expresses not only the syncopated lines of the melody but also the sense of pure joy that imbues this performance in spite of its daunting, untranscribable interplay. Although the piece was designed to show off Blanton, it is equally effective at showing off Ellington. Ellington's touch, no less than Blanton's, is panther-quick and aggressive, and the patter comes mainly from him, in the showy runs into the highest octaves that were elements of his style from the beginning.

Ellington expected that "Pitter Panther Patter" along with "Jack the Bear" and the other orchestral features would launch Blanton into a brilliant career as another stunning sonic hue in his orchestral palette. Instead, they proved to be his career peaks. Soon after these magnificent debut recordings, Blanton was afflicted with coughing fits and waning energy. Thirteen months later, he left the band debilitated by tuberculosis. He was barely 21 when he died in 1942.

Despite his tragically short career, Jimmy Blanton became a lasting inspiration to his boss. Ellington kept "Pitter Panther Patter" in the band book for six years after Blanton's death, first as a feature for Blanton's successor, Junior Raglin (1917-1955), and after that for Raglin's successor, the redoubtable Oscar Pettiford (1922-1960), one of Blanton's worthiest disciples. With Pettiford, Ellington also recorded a small-band elegy called "Blues for Blanton" in 1950 (on *Great Times!* in the appendix). Ellington included "Pitter Panther Patter" in the programs at the first two Carnegie Hall concerts in 1943 and 1944. All these performances accidentally showcased Ellington's piano while memorializing Blanton's accomplishment.

Ellington finally retired "Pitter Panther Patter" in 1946, and he did not record it again for 26 years, until 1972, when he found himself in a recording studio with one of Blanton's brightest latter-day descendants, Ray Brown (1926-2002). The recording, *This One's For Blanton* (see the appendix), would be Ellington's last bow to his doomed protégé. Ellington and Brown play "Pitter Panther Patter" reverently, in a straightforward three-minute recitation as close to the original as possible. Elsewhere on the disk, reverence gives way to ebullience, and Ellington's piano provides sparkling settings for Brown's full tone and supple time, much as he had 32 years earlier for Blanton.

Ellington Minimalist and Maximalist

The exposure Ellington accidentally gave himself as pianist in the Blanton duets undoubtedly played a role in the prominence he began giving to his piano from 1940 onward. He composed *New World A-Coming* as a 14-minute showcase for his keyboard versatility and premiered the big-band version of it at his second Carnegie Hall concert in December 1943 . He had never previously allotted himself the starring role in his orchestral compositions as he had done for Cootie Williams in "Concerto for Cootie," Johnny Hodges in "Jeep's Blues," and his other star soloists. Now, taking the starring role obviously suited him, at least once in a while. He took the title of *New World A-Coming* from a now-forgotten novel and he invested it with characteristically high-minded optimism. The New World that's coming, he declared in his commentary on the piece, is "a place in the future where there will be no war, no greed, no categorization, no non-believers, where love is unconditional, and no pronoun is good enough for God." Eventually he adapted *New World A-Coming* for settings both greater and smaller, from symphony orchestras to piano trios and unaccompanied solos. In 1966, he opened his concert at Coventry Cathedral with a nine-minute solo rendition while the orchestra and the audience sat in thrall. Among the many trio recordings, the one at Whitney Museum in 1972 finds him in good spirits as well as good form. At the other end of the spectrum, probably no other recording in Ellington's considerable discography reveals his keyboard mastery as fully as does his virtuoso soloing on *New World A-Coming* with the Cincinnati Symphony Orchestra (1970 MCA Classics 42318-CD), scored by Luther Henderson as a concerto grosso for piano and full orchestra. Ellington displays dexterity and discipline worthy of Oscar Levant, Arthur Rubinstein or the other contemporary virtuosi in whose company he was never really mentioned.

Other piano features slowly accumulated. In 1944, Ellington and Strayhorn wrote a raggy piano number called "Dancers in Love" as Ellington's contribution to a memorial concert at Carnegie Hall for Fats Waller, who had died in December 1943. Its jaunty humour – "a stomp for beginners," Ellington called it at the Whitney Museum recital – made it a crowd-pleaser. Thereafter Ellington slipped it into

Duke Ellington conducts from piano

his concerts as the third movement of the *Perfume Suite*, where it fit uneasily in the suite's coherence but served its purpose as both a respite for the orchestra and a showy feature for the piano player. In the same pianistic spirit, he revived "Reminiscing in Tempo," with its prominent piano role, for the Carnegie Hall concert in 1948.

Melancholia – A Softer, Gentler Duke

The next major advance for Ellington as pianist took place in the comparatively dismal years of 1952-1955 when he was under contract to Capitol Records. Beset by the shrinking big band circuit and bereft of Johnny Hodges. Lawrence Brown and Sonny Greer, who left him abruptly in 1950 to form their own band, he tried in vain to make pop hits in hopes of increasing the cash flow. He was in his fifties, and for perhaps the first and only time in his life he adjusted awkwardly, maybe even grudgingly, to the changes taking place around him. His biographer, John Edward Hasse, puts together the many changes that were making the world a harder place for an itinerant musician – the growth of suburbs and the death of nightclubs, the constant routine of one-night stands in arenas and gymnasiums separated by many miles, the competition from small bands in the diminishing venues that booked jazz. The depressing conditions show up graphically when Hasse notes that Ellington's orchestra was paid $5,000 for a week at the Blue Note in Chicago in 1954 – "about what he had been making 23 years earlier, when his band and staff were smaller and the cost of living was 43 percent less" (p. 309).

The changes were personal as well as cultural. From 1941 to 1950, Ellington's orchestra lost all but one of the musicians who had been with him in the formative years of the Washingtonians and the Cotton Club orchestra. Those men had been his running mates and peers. There had been camaraderie. The journalist Boyer had witnessed it first-hand while traveling with the band in the late thirties and early forties – with Ellington and his men mingling in the Pullman cars as they rattled across the country, sharing a bottle and playing jokes, and bantering in the post-performance rituals, for instance, with Ellington in his dressing room "playing a game of cassino with someone in his band" while "other members of the band keep walking in and out" (Boyer, p. 230). One by one those old running mates had dropped out, through death and dementia and defection. Now, out of economic necessity, the band traveled by bus rather than train, and Ellington, when distances permitted, rode separately, in a large Chrysler driven by Harry Carney, the one remaining old hand from the Cotton Club orchestra, a boy then but now grown, not coincidentally, into a taciturn, courteous, sober-sided gentleman. Those travel arrangements, as Hasse noticed, were the sign of a larger change:

> The reason he traveled by car was perhaps a desire to stay away from inquiries and squabbles about salaries; ...or a celebrity's superior stance; or a need to carry on a less hectic, inner conversation, to think in peace. ... 'Harry and I don't talk much,' Ellington would say to Nat Hentoff, 'so I can just dream and write.' Whatever the considerations, his switch to riding by himself was a sure sign that he was no longer one of the guys, but rather seemed to be growing increasingly aloof (Hasse, p. 307).

The dismal patch in the first years of the 1950s had a few consolations. Chief among them was Ellington's masterwork as a piano player. With the orchestra music faltering,[1] Ellington poured his heart and soul into a series of brilliant piano recordings in April and December 1953. Microgroove recordings raised the possibility of developing extended themes in a long-play (LP) format. Whether or not Ellington had this in mind is unclear. Most of the 15 piano tracks he recorded are short enough to be released as 78 rpm singles, and he may have hoped for a hit single with one or another. Instead they were collated on a new-look 12" record under the title *The Duke Plays Ellington* and later more aptly as *Piano Reflections* (in the appendix). By design or not, they make a striking collective statement. The sombreness of Ellington's mood at the time is reflected in the titles he gives to the brilliant new compositions "Retrospection," "Reflections in D," "Melancholia" and "December Blue." In this indigo setting, the extraverted "Dancers in Love" and "Kinda Dukish" seem intrusive on the same record; intrusive in mood, perhaps, but flawlessly played as are all the other titles. Harlem stride occurs as the barest hint in the bridge of "Who Knows?" a minor piece that Ellington may have pulled out of a bottom drawer in order to add a few minutes to the LP.

Stylistically, Ellington develops the moods of the new compositions patiently, staying close to the melodies and enveloping them in rich harmonies. Three of the tunes he chose to reinterpret pianistically from the band book had been features for his departed sidemen: "Prelude to a Kiss" and Billy Strayhorn's "Passion Flower" for Hodges, and "All Too Soon" for Brown. No less than the brand-new "Reflections in D" and "Melancholia," these older titles take on unfamiliar weight and gravity in Ellington's hands. It is not much of a stretch to imagine that Ellington's affectionate readings might have

---

1 Ironically, the first title recorded at Ellington's first recording session for Capitol (6 April 1953) was "Satin Doll," a minor hit as an instrumental and one that became Ellington's final contribution to the standard American songbook when it was outfitted with lyrics by Johnny Mercer a few years later. It became a source of welcome royalties when it was recorded by dozens of singers. From that start, Ellington might have anticipated high times to come, but it was not to be – not for another three years and for a different record label.

Duke Ellington, *Piano Reflections* (Capitol LP [1954])

been touched by old echoes of the departed sidemen.

This is a reformed (re-formed) Ellington at the keyboard, contemplative, moody, almost introverted. The pinnacle comes in the ruminations "Retrospection," "Melancholia" and "Reflections in D." Mark Tucker, an astute Ellington scholar who wrote the notes for the LP, calls "Retrospection" "a sober meditation with harmonies that echo the Victorian parlor songs and hymns of Ellington's youth." If so, it has none of the gaiety of those parlor songs or the holy-rolling of the sanctified church. It seems to be an improvisation on familiar harmonies, and that impression is reinforced by the sparse, almost unnoticed bowed accompaniment of bassist Wendell Marshall, which has the feel of a man looking for spaces to fill and not finding many. There is no melody, only a mood, and a quiet, brooding mood it is, far removed from Ellington's characteristic outgoing flair. Unlike the other two brooding originals, Ellington never played "Retrospection" again. Maybe it was too spontaneous for recreating, or too genuinely woebegone for the smiling bandleader.

Unlike "Retrospection," Ellington played "Melancholia" and "Reflections in D" on every occasion for the remaining twenty-odd years of his life when he found himself at a piano bench with no orchestra

Duke Ellington in a melancholy mood (Columbia Records photograph)

present. Mark Tucker, in his notes, says that "while they draw upon the harmonic vocabulary of jazz, their rythmic freedom and ethos belong to another world altogether: an idealized realm of memory, nostalgia and spirituality." Ellington's patience in sustaining the mood looks forward to the conservatory style of Don Shirley or Ran Blake, or – a decade later – Bill Evans's early intraverted ballads like "Peace Piece." (Ellington may never have heard these younger piano players, but they certainly heard him.) Again, he is accompanied unobtrusively by bowed bass. At a concert in 1964, he merged "Melancholia" and "Reflections in D" into a single composition for solo piano, not really a medley but an extended mood with two seamless themes.

Several years before, in 1935, composing "Reminiscing in Tempo" in the gloom that enveloped him after the death of his sainted mother, Ellington had stopped short of revealing the depth of his feelings; "Reminiscing in Tempo" presents a studied sorrow. Now, almost 20 years later, Ellington's emotion is less guarded, undeniably deeper, more palpable, spelled out in these brilliant pianistic compositions. Together, they make *Piano Reflections* the most striking of all Ellington's piano records.

Tripping into the Post-Bop Jungle

A diametrically different landmark in Ellington's piano legacy came nine years later in the controversial *Money Jungle* session with Charles Mingus on bass and Max Roach on drums. This recording came about as one of three all-star encounters instigated by Ellington in September 1962. His Columbia recording contract had expired and he was about to sign a contract with Reprise Records. Ellington took advantage of his momentary liberty by organizing two small-group recordings on Impulse! Records with tenor saxophone players as special guests, Coleman Hawkins (Impulse AS-9285) and John Coltrane (Impulse AD-39103), as well as Mingus and Roach (originally on United Artists, now Blue Note). Hawkins belonged to Ellington's generation, but the others were all about 25 years his junior. Presumably Ellington sought out the relatively youthful Coltrane, Mingus and Roach to prove that the rapid changes taking place in jazz in the early 1960s had not left him behind. In that regard, *Money Jungle* has to be counted a success.

The recording session featured several sideshows, as befits the yoking together of the benign maestro with the high-strung Mingus and the volatile Roach. Mingus had committed himself to Bellevue Asylum a few years before and was now making brash, spectacular protest music, and Roach had disrupted a Miles Davis concert at Carnegie Hall by sitting on the proscenium with a large placard reading *Freedom Now!*, the clarion call of civil rights protests that were happening all over the country, and the title of his most successful LP. Rumor persists that soon after the start of the recording session Mingus stomped out the studio, complaining that Ellington was embarrassing himself by "playing shit." Ellington reportedly sauntered up to him at the elevator and persuaded him to return. Some of the music they made gives credence to the rumor because several tunes have a frantic, edgy feeling, especially the title tune "Money Jungle," but also the drum feature called "A Little Max" and a rambunctious version of "Caravan," the old polyrythmic warhorse from Ellington's big band book. On these three tracks, Ellington punches out staccato dissonances against Mingus's repetitive bass drone and Roach's heavy-handed accents. The rambunctious combination is far removed from anything else in Ellington's works, and it aroused some critical ire. "That's ridiculous," Miles Davis complained when Leonard Feather played "Caravan" for him in a blindfold test. "It's a mismatch. They don't complement each other.... Duke can't play with them and they can't play with Duke."

Oddly enough, other tracks tend to dispel any hints of rancor in the studio. Four titles – "Very Special," "Wig Wise," a very straight, sensuous rendition of Ellington's old love song "Warm Valley," and the simple atmospheric "Fleurette Africaine" – all show a near-perfect balance of contrasts. The rapport among the three musicians is audible, and strong rapport was surely essential for a single recording session to yield an hour of complete takes, as this one did. Surprisingly all the compositions are Ellington's, though Mingus was (and is) admired as a composer. Ellington appears in control throughout. On the frantic tracks, his amusement at the goings-on is obvious; he sits back like the wry observer and punches away at the keyboard. On the balanced tracks, he plays inventive, romantic and ornamented lines, much more in his own metier than in Mingus's.

He may have been keeping an eye out for the bassist's famous temper, but the tension in the studio was clearly creative rather than threatening. "Do I think of Charles Mingus as a disciple?" Ellington once wondered aloud (in Stanley Dance's presence). "Well, that's

Ellington with drummer Max Roach and bassist Charles Mingus recording *Money Jungle* (photo United Artists)

what *he* says." Mingus was a disciple certainly, but by no means a fawning disciple. He is pushy with Ellington as he was with the benighted sidemen in his bands, and that push gave a unique spin to this singular recording session.

Even before *Money Jungle*, the new wave had made a shadowy appearance in Ellington's piano playing. A year and a half earlier, Ellington had recorded *Piano In the Foreground* for Columbia, a trio recording with his regular sidemen Aaron Bell on bass and Sam Woodyard on drums. The recording lacks the focus of *Piano Reflections* and it lacks the intensity of *Money Jungle*. It is dominated by foxtrots ("I Can't Get Started," "Body and Soul," "It's Bad to be Forgotten," "A Hundred Dreams Ago") and these tracks seem even more humdrum in the context because two other tracks provide striking contrasts. "Summertime" and "Springtime in Africa" are free-form, out-of-tempo experiments topped off (in "Summertime") with an elbow smash to the keyboard. It is a far cry from the reverance normally accorded Gershwin's "Summertime." At first you might suspect that Ellington is parodying the avant styles then emerging in the playing of Cecil Taylor and Sun Ra, among others, but there is no sign of irony in the unrelieved, rather grim seriousness of the performances. In hindsight, these two tracks served Ellington as warm-ups for the *Money Jungle* session and, though they are less convincing examples, they prove that Ellington did not need to be goaded by Mingus or anyone else into formal experimentation.

Ellington's post-bop venture is as fitting a place as any, I suppose, to draw attention to an extraordinarily prescient innovation that has so far gone unnoticed in Duke Ellington's well-scrutinized career. At the tail-end of Ellington's three-year contract with Capitol Records, on 19 May 1955, Ellington recorded a composition called "Once in a Blue Mood." It remained unreleased until compilations of the Capitol recordings came out decades later (first on Mosaic Records, and soon after on *The Capitol Sessions 1953-1955*, where the track under discussion is track 15 on the fourth disc of the 4-CD package). Although it is a contracted studio recording, "Once in a Blue Mood" has the undeniable *esprit* of a stockpile recording (as discussed more fully in Chapter 8 below) – it is a head arrangement with the band pared down to a sextet, in an exploratory but relaxed mood, and every solo sustains the easy mood. Russell Procope's opening solo, which may be the melody statement for the piece (if it has a melody), begins with a few bars of "St. James Infirmary Blues," the old New Orleans blues that has its roots in eighteenth century England. (Ellington recorded it in 1930 with a band that used the pseudonym the Ten Blackberries.) It is not uncommon to note that an Ellington recording has been unjustly neglected, a familiar lament when there is so much Ellington to hear, but "Once in a Blue Mood" has managed to escape notice altogether.

The reason for breaking the silence on it here is that Ellington plays an electric piano on "Once in a Blue Mood." (He also plays it on three forgettable vocal tracks recorded at the same session.) It is a jazz landmark despite its obscurity because we hear Ellington experimenting with an electric piano more than a full decade before the instrument came into widespread, highly fashionable use in the hot flash of jazz-rock fusion. The most auspicious practitioner, Herbie Hancock, first recorded on electric piano in December 1967 with Miles Davis (on "Water on the Pond," not issued until 1981). On that occasion, Davis surprised Hancock by bringing an electric piano into the studio, and Hancock had never touched one until then. Josef Zawinul was playing electric piano nightly with Cannonball Adderley's Quintet at the time, and that is what gave Davis the idea of using it in his band. Zawinul had perhaps been playing it for a year, since 1965 at the earliest. Hancock was in his twenties and Zawinul was in his thirties. They were in the forefront, the precedent setters for Chick Corea, George Duke, Lyle Mays, Lonnie Liston Smith, and others who took up the electric piano in their wake. But the jazz annals have to be revised because here we find the old master, Ellington, just turned 56, getting on it a whole decade before the young turks, when Herbie Hancock was still in high school. And, moreover, making it sound good. Ellington obviously knows that he has to rein in his characteristic flourishes and showy runs because of the reverb in the wired-up instrument. It is a rudimentary lesson that proved to be a hard one for many of the headhunters who took up the electric piano in the short-lived jazz-rock boom in the 1970s. Ellington's toned-down precedent, if it had been made available at the time, might have taught them a thing or two.

Piano Recitals

We now know that Ellington played his first piano recital on November 16, 1943, when he entertained air force personnel near Ottawa, Canada. The performance pushes back the accepted date of Ellington's debut as piano soloist by almost 20 years. Before that, all sources claimed that Ellington's first piano concert took place at New York's Museum of Modern Art on 4 January 1962 (for example, Hasse p. 347), but journalist Doug Fischer uncovered a note in the *Ottawa Citizen* on "a special solo piano performance Ellington gave for servicemen and their wives at the RCAF station at Uplands air base." At the time, this piano concert appears to be an isolated event in Ellington's itinerary, but it is clearly a sign of his growing involvement with the piano in the aftermath of his Blanton duets.

In his long career, Ellington presented only seven known piano recitals (itemized at the end of the appendix). The Uplands air force base concert in November 1943 is little more than a legend, known only from a one-inch note in a provincial Canadian newspaper. Another solo recital, almost thirty years later, is almost equally mysterious. It seems to have been the result of a meteorological accident, as unexpected for Ellington as it was for his sparse audience. On 22 February 1971, Ellington made his way to Baltimore, Maryland, expecting to play afternoon and evening concerts there with his orchestra. A sudden blizzard blanketed the Atlantic region, with the result that most of the band members were grounded in New York. That afternoon, Ellington entertained the ticket-holders who had braved the storm with a piano recital, joined for some or all of it by his bassist Joe Benjamin and drummer Rufus Jones. By the evening, the snowfall had apparently abated enough that both the band members and the audience had arrived, and the show went on as advertised.

A more casual recital, also accidental, came about when Ellington was honored with the inaugural honorary D. Mus. at Berklee College of Music, Boston, on 22 May 1971. After the ceremony, the dignitaries moved to the Charter Room for the reception. As luck would have it, there was a piano in the room, and Ellington needed little coaxing to sit down and play requests for 17 minutes.

The recital at the Museum of Modern Art (MOMA) in New York

in January 1962, hitherto considered Ellington's first, is slightly more real. A studio-qualty tape exists, and a cassette with four short titles (9 minutes) was distributed to participants at one of the annual Duke Ellington conferences in the 1980s but the rest of the recital remains unreleased. From the partial release, we know that Ellington played the first half alone and included three compositions from his bountiful *Piano Reflections* (Capitol), then nine years old. (Ellington's inclusion of "Melancholia," "Reflections in D" and "Janet" after so many years is good evidence that Ellington had special affection for these compositions.) In the second half of the recital he was joined by Aaron Bell and Sam Woodyard, his regular bassist and drummer. Strangely, they played chestnuts from the big-band repertoire ("Take the 'A' Train," "Satin Doll," "Caravan" and a medley of old hits, among others); they played nothing from the studio recording *Piano in the Foreground* (Columbia), which also included Bell and Woodyard with Ellington in the trio setting a few weeks before this concert at MOMA. *Piano in the Foreground*, judging by its timing, was assumed to be a warm-up for the imminent MOMA recital, but when the repertoire at MOMA came to light it turned out to be much more conservative in both style and content than the *Foreground* recording.

Ellington recital with John Lamb, bass, 1966 (photo St. Petersburg, FLA, *Catalyst*)

An unexpected gem, one of a kind, was preserved in July 1970 by French ORTF (*Office de radiodiffusion-télévision française*). The French national broadcast corporation invited Ellington to look into their cameras and discuss his concept of jazz. It is not the kind of topic that Ellington might have welcomed under other circumstances, but the producers sat him at a grand piano, with neither audience nor interviewer, and invited him to ruminate. As expected, Ellington obfuscates with characteristic elegance: "jazz is a never-ending discussion," "jazz is a tree," "it goes east west north south," it has "blue-black deep roots." He wisely interrupts his unscripted musings with improvisations on some of his most beautiful melodies. Among the 11 titles are a few uncommon ones for his solo piano excursions ("Warm Valley," "Black Beauty," "Come Sunday," and, with a clever nod to his surroundings, "Paris Blues"). The French producers surely did not expect such a generous outpouring, and Ellington may even have surprised himself. After 43 minutes of verbal whimsy and pianistic charm, Ellington blurts out a hasty thanks and farewell in French, and with a wave of his hand and a broad, self-conscious grin, sidles into the wings and out of the camera shot. Although at one point (27 minutes in) Ellington peeks at a note to remind himself of a name, the whole production has a wonderfully spontaneous air – an intimate 45 minutes with a man of elegance and wit, and more than half an hour of his piano playing.

The other two recitals, available in authorized recordings, crystallize Ellington's final piano style. One might be tempted to call it his *mature* style if it were not for the fact that he had reached maturity, pianistically and in every other way, years before. His final style is leagues removed from the ostentatious Harlem stride that beguiled him in his twenties, and considerably removed from the swing style that he had moved seamlessly into in his thirties and forties. It is, in the peak performances, reflective and romantic. Where the stride style prides itself on moving the hands faster than minds can fathom ("lots o' fingers," as Ellington titled his culmination of the style), his final style, the recital style, moves gracefully through hummable melodies, exalts harmony over rhythm, and gives the impression of a man searching for the perfect next note.

Ellington seemed fully aware of the transformation, though he was never likely to say so out loud. In an interview for a documentary called *The Duke* for the Canadian Broadcasting Corporation (broadcast 3 March 1965), Ellington had this exchange with the host, Byng Whittacker:

> *Q*: Where do you get your ideas from?
> *Ellington*: Ideas? Oh, man, I got a million dreams. That's all I do is dream – all the time
> *Q*: I thought you played piano.
> *Ellington*: No, no, this is not piano. [*He improvises a few quiet bars on the piano.*] This is dreaming.

Ellington, famously elusive as always in interviews, was not being merely flippant. For the last twenty years of his life, when he played piano for his own purposes rather than for the purpose of meeting orchestral demands or cajoling post-bop collaborators or filling other ulterior designs, he played with a dream-like romantic strain. That strain, that contemplative mood, seemed surprising, almost out of character, when it first came to light in *Piano Reflections* in 1953 but it flowed abundantly in recitals and other moments from then on, whenever Ellington's piano was in the foreground.

New York Concert captures a performance at Columbia University in May 1964, with cameo appearances by Billy Strayhorn and Ellington's old backroom tutor Willie The Lion Smith. Ellington had been invited for a piano concert by the New York chapter of the Duke Ellington Society, and it was probably the promise of a highly sympathetic audience that encouraged him to accept. He opens with tried and true numbers, easy for him and more than satisfactory for the audience ("Take the 'A' Train," "Satin Doll," "Caravan") but he grows more venturesome. He introduces a new composition, "Skillipoop," from the incidental music he had written a few months earlier for *Timon of Athens* at the Stratford Shakespearean Festival in Canada, and he takes obvious pleasure, as does his audience, in explaining its title: "One of its meanings is trying to make what you're doing look better than what you are really doing." He delights the audience by bringing on Willie the Lion Smith to play James P. Johnson's stride anthem "Carolina Shout," and then he brings on Billy Strayhorn to play four-handed with him on their party piece

Duke Ellington dreaming at the piano

"Tonk" (co-composed, and first recorded by them in 1946 [on *Solos, Duets and Trios* in the appendix]).

The real surprise, and the treat, comes in what apears to be the second half when Ellington comes on alone and plays "Melancholia/ Reflections in D" from *Piano Reflections* and a newer composition, "Little African Flower"(introduced two years before as "Fleurette Africaine" in the recording with Charles Mingus and Max Roach). He then swings into a very old and very rare piece, "Bird of Paradise," a composition he wrote in 1934 and published as sheet music as "a modern composition for piano"; the next year, 1935, the Jimmy Lunceford Orchestra recorded an orchestrated version of it along with another Ellington composition, "Rhapsody Junior," on its flip side (according to Lambert, p. 253). Oddly enough, Ellington completely ignored "Rhapsody Junior" and waited almost 40 years before he tried his hand at "Bird of Paradise." He never recorded it in any form until the transcript of his Columbia University recital was made public. He also plays "The Single Petal of a Rose," which we came to recognize as the piano gem among the orchestral gems of *The Queen's Suite* (1958), Ellington's private recording for Queen Elizabeth II that was made public only after his death. In these solo excursions,

Bird of Paradise sheet music (published 1934; recorded by Ellington 1964, photo courtesy DESUK)

Ellington reveals himself in what seems to be his most personal, deeply felt style. He uses the keyboard dynamically, alternating soft tones and rich sonorities, more dramatic than the younger piano players of the day and sometimes verging on the showy, but always respectful of melody and mindful of seeking the best notes.

The other recital released commercially, *Live at the Whitney*, is a priceless memento from the Whitney Museum, Manhattan, in April 1972. It too provides a relatively candid view of the usually guarded Ellington, with the spotlight on him alone, both musically and personally. At the Whitney Museum as at Columbia University, eight years earlier, Ellington relies more on intuition than on advance planning, and he buys time between tunes by bantering with the audience, reciting home-made doggerel: "Into each life some jazz must fall/With afterbeat gone kickin'/With jive alive, a ball for all/ Let not the beat be chicken." He solicits audience participation ("…we'd like to invite you to sing with us – even if you don't know the lyric"), and generally struts like the seasoned stage performer he was.

More important, these two issued recitals at Columbia University and the Whitney Museum emphasize the tremendously resourceful piano player he was. The repertoire is partly predictable ("Satin

Doll," "Caravan," "C-Jam Blues," the concerto from "New World A-Coming," the medley of old favourites) but it is also partly surprising and innovative. These recitals preserve the only extant piano versions of "Le Sucrier Velours," "Amour Amour" and "Soul Soothing Beach," the only live performances of "Melancholia" and "Reflections in D," and the only trio versions anywhere of "John Sanders' Blues" and "A Mural from Two Perspectives," as well as Ellington's only performance of "Bird of Paradise" at the Columbia recital.

Ellington's accompanists on bass and drums, Peck Morrison and Sam Woodyard at Columbia, Joe Benjamin and Rufus Jones at the Whitney, sometimes scramble trying to work out their parts on a moment's notice, and at the Whitney Museum performance Rufus Jones wisely sits silent most of the time.

But Ellington never scrambles. Of course not. He is ingratiating and charming and insouciant and endlessly inventive. At the Whitney Museum, where he was appearing as part of a prestigious subscription series called Composers Showcase, he starts off subdued. "I might as well warn you that you must be prepared for a totally unprepared program," he says, and after rambling for a while he announces, "I'm going to sit down and see if I'm in tune with the

Duke Ellington in concert (photo *Le Jazz Hot*)

piano." He sounds tired, and no wonder. He was about to turn 73, he had just finished a cross-country tour as far afield as California, he had premiered the Second Sacred Concert the night before at St. Peter's Lutheran Church, and he was slightly wheezy, probably from the lung cancer that would kill him almost exactly two years later. So he had lots of reasons for coasting through this superfluous Monday date in its upscale setting, and for the first few minutes he seems resigned to doing just that. But something overtakes him as he is noodling away at "Black and Tan Fantasy," the first number in the tried-and-true medley; his interest begins to quicken and by the time he reaches "Caravan" six minutes later he is in full swing. The rest of the hour is a brilliant multi-faceted performance, moving smoothly through shtick ("Dancers in Love"), anecdotal history ("Soda Fountain Rag"), nostalgia ("Mood Indigo," "Satin Doll"), technical adroitness ("New World A-Coming"), lyricism ("Lotus Blossom") and works in progress ("Meditation" and "The Night Shepherd" from the Second Sacred Concert the night before, "Amour Amour" and "Soul Soothing Beach" from *Togo Brava Suite*). The diffident beginning only makes the high points in the rest of the performance seem that much higher. *Live at the Whitney* might be the most comprehensive view of Ellington as a piano player. It is not the most profound or the most ambitious, but it is easily the most entertaining.

Ellington's obvious enjoyment at the Whitney recital may have inspired him to go into the recording studio on his own a few months later and develop solo versions of "Le Sucrier Velours," "Lotus Blossom," "Melancholia," "New World A-Comin'" and "A Mural from Two Perspectives," all of them among the most refreshing successes of his trio recitals. The solo recordings were finally released from the stockpile in 2017 as *An Intimate Piano Session* (in the appendix). Ellington's solitary turn in the studio is an anomaly in the scores of hours of private recordings he left behind, and it suggests that he was (however vaguely) thinking about ramping up his piano ambitions even further. Those ambitions had grown slowly for many years, and they seemed to bring him more gratification with each airing. All we really know is that they never came to fruition. Perhaps time ran out, or other ambitions took precedence. In the final analysis, the intimate piano solos stand as a kind of addendum to the recitals, and in their unhurried, unguarded intimacy, as a welcome extension of them.

A Choice One

Less entertaining, certainly, but emotionally deeper than the recitals are the pianistic originals on *Piano Reflections*. Come to that, if you had to choose *one* piano performance among the dozens that Ellington left us – so many, notwithstanding the slow start – you could hardly do better than "Lotus Blossom," the sumptuous Strayhorn melody that Ellington played at the end of an exhausting recording session. By a stroke of luck, an engineer captured it before shutting down the recording equipment for the day. Ellington and the orchestra had just wrapped up a session in August 1967 playing four Strayhorn compositions for the commemorative album that would celebrate Strayhorn's long, brilliant collaboration with the Ellington orchestra before he died of cancer three months earlier. The album is *...And His Mother Called Him Bill* (Bluebird). As the band members were packing up for the day, Ellington sat down at the piano and began picking out Strayhorn's "Lotus Blossom." You can hear the musicians chatting in the background and moving around. At one point (30 seconds in) Ellington stops for a moment – you might imagine him wiping away a tear – and then resumes with greater gusto. His performance cannot be separated from the elegiac occasion that called it forth. It is plain-spoken by Ellington's norms. It is heartfelt. It is heart-breaking.

And it did not end there. Two days later in the same studio, after the band had recorded three more Strayhorn compositions for the commemorative album, Ellington asked Harry Carney and Aaron Bell to stay behind. He began playing "Lotus Blossom" again, this time with Bell's sonorous bass bowing its accompaniment, and on the second chorus Carney's rich baritone saxophone is heard for the first time, easing into the foreground playing Strayhorn's melody while one of the greatest piano accompanists of all time spurs him along. There are no tears this time, just a heady mixture of sorrow and gratitude.

This alternate take was released 20 years after Ellington's solo version, and of course it does not strictly belong in a consideration

Duke Ellington and Billy Strayhorn (DeepRootsMag.org)

of Ellington's piano music. Fair enough. The piano version will more than suffice if you have to choose one performance. For the seven years that remained to Ellington after Strayhorn's death, Ellington played a solo version of "Lotus Blossom" in the encore of every concert in homage to his great collaborator.

Legacy

How good was Duke Ellington, the piano player? The question is meaningless, of course, because he was always so much more than a piano player. But if he had chosen to be a piano player or if destiny had chosen it for him, where would he stand? Mainly, he would stand apart. Ellington always talked about his closest contemporaries as if they were his elders. Stylistically they were. James P. Johnson (born 1894, five years before Ellington) is indisputably the greatest piano player of his generation, but compared to Ellington he seems locked into that time no less than Jimmy Yancey (also 1894) and Willie the Lion Smith (1897). Ellington's slightly younger contemporaries include Claude Hopkins (1903, three years younger than Ellington), Lil Hardin (1903), Fats Waller (1904) and Earl Hines (1905). Although Waller and Hines helped to define piano styles for their day, they were bound to the music of their formative years only slightly less than the others, and unlike Ellington. To find players with stylistic breadth comparable to Ellington's it is necessary to look ahead more than ten years, a whole generation in jazz evolution, to the likes of Art Tatum (1910), Mary Lou Williams (1910) and Teddy Wilson (1912). Maybe they could have played "Lots o' Fingers" without cramping, and *New World A-Coming* with the Cincinnati Symphony, and "Wig Wise" with Mingus and Roach, and "Dancers in Love" for a standing ovation at the Whitney Museum. Or maybe not. This much seems certain: few piano players, younger or older, are as audible in the piano music that came after them. Thelonious Monk, Herbie Nichols, Tommy Flanagan, Randy Weston, Cecil Taylor, Abdullah Ibrahim, Joanne Brackeen, Marcus Roberts, Ted Rosenthal – the list of piano players beholden to Duke Ellington goes on, and so does the piano playing of Duke Ellington, in this regard as in so many others, beyond category.

References (page numbers to direct quotations are shown *in italics*)
Boyer, Richard O. "The Hot Bach." *The New Yorker* (1944). Reprinted in *The Duke Ellington Reader*, ed. Mark, Tucker. Oxford University Press, 1995. 214-245. *p. 230*
Dance, Stanley. *The World of Duke Ellington*. London: Macmillan. 1970. *p. 259.*
Darrell, R.D. "Criticism in the Phonograph Monthly Review." In Mark Tucker (ed.) *The Duke Ellington Reader*. NY: Oxford University Press. 1993. *pp. 33-40.*
Ellington, Duke. *Music Is My Mistress*. Garden City, NY: Doubleday. 1973. *p. 93, p. 183.*
Feather, Leonard. "Blindfold test: Miles Davis." 1964. Reprinted in Bill, Kirchner, ed., *A Miles Davis Reader*. Washington: Smithsonian. *p. 131.*
Fischer, Doug. "The Duke of Jazz." *The Citizen's Weekly*, 11 April 1999. *p. C4.*
Hasse, John Edward. 1993. *Beyond Category: The Life and Genius of Duke Ellington*. NY: Simon & Schuster. *pp. 306-309, p. 347.*
Lambert, Eddie. 1999. *Duke Ellington: A Listener's Guide*. Lanham, Maryland: Scarecrow Press. *pp. 256, p. 253*
Smith, Willie the Lion, with George Hoefer. 1964. *Music on My Mind: The Memoirs of an American Pianist*. New York: Doubleday. Foreword by Duke Ellington, *p. x, p. xi.*
Tucker, Mark. 1954. Liner note to Duke Ellington, *Piano Reflections*. Capitol CD [1992].

Playlist (recordings cited in order of appearance in the chapter)

"The Hawk Talks." 29 April 1953. McElroy's Ballroom, Portland, Ore. *Happy Birthday Duke!* Laserlight, vol. 3 of 5-CD [1992]. Willie Cook, Cat Anderson, Clark Terry, Ray Nance tp; Britt Woodman, Quentin Jackson, Juan Tizol tb; Russell Procope, Rick Henderson, Paul Gonsalves, Jimmy Hamilton, Harry Carney reeds; Ellington p; Wendell Marshall b; Butch Ballard d.

Alberta Prime, "Parlor Social De Luxe" 3:09 NYC, November 1924. *Mrs Clinkscales to the Cotton Club* (JSP Records, UK4CD [2005]). Duke Ellington p, Sonny Greer perc, voc, Alberta Hunter aka Alberta Prime voc

James P. Johnson, ""Carolina Shout" 4:00 NYC, May 1921. QRS [piano roll]. *Carolina Shout*, Biograph Records [CD 1988]

"Jig Walk." 2:16 Probably June 1926. Paramount, NYC. *Masters of Jazz, Duke Ellington* Vol. 1 [France 1991]. Duke Ellington p.

"East St. Louis Toodle-Oo," "Birmingham Breakdown." 29 November 1926. Vocalion, NYC. *Early Ellington:Complete Brunswick and Vocalian 1926-1931* (Decca Jazz, GRP 3CD [1994]). Bubber Miley, Louis Metcalf tp; Joe Nanton tb; Otto Hardwick reeds; Ellington p; Fred Guy g; probably Mack Shaw tuba; Sonny Greer d.

"Black Beauty," "Swampy River." 1 October 1928. Okeh, NYC. *Okeh Ellington*, Columbia [1991]. Duke Ellington p.

"The Mooche." same session as "Black Beauty." Bubber Miley, Arthur Whetsol tp; Joe Nanton tb; Barney Bigard, Johnny Hodges, Harry Carney reeds; Ellington p; Fred Guy g; Wellman Braud b; Sonny Greer d.

"Lots o' Fingers" 2:00. NY, 9 Feb 1932 *Solos, Duets and Trios* (Bluebird CD [1990]). Duke Ellington p.

"Reminiscing in Tempo, Part 2." 3:09. 12 September 1935. Brunswick, NYC. *Classics 659*. Arthur Whetsol, Cootie Williams, Rex Stewart tp; Joe Nanton, Lawrence Brown, Juan Tizol tb; Barney Bigard, Johnny Hodges, Otto Hardwick, Harry Carney reeds; Ellington p; Fred Guy g; Hayes Alvis, Billy Taylor b; Sonny Greer d. Solos: Williams (muted), Hodges, Carney, Ellington (at 1:50, then solo 2:23-3:09)

"Soda Fountain Rag" 1:18. 10 April 1972 *Live at the Whitney* (Impulse!). Duke Ellington p.

"Portrait of the Lion." 21 March 1939. Brunswick, NYC. Cootie Williams, Wallace Jones, Rex Stewart tp; Joe Nanton, Lawrence Brown, Juan Tizol tb; Barney Bigard, Johnny Hodges, Otto Hardwick, Harry Carney reeds;

Ellington p; Fred Guy g; Billy Taylor b; Sonny Greer d.

"Second Portrait of the Lion" 0:30, 4:13. 20 June 1965, Pittsburgh Jazz Festival. Various Artists, *The Jazz Piano* (Mosaic Singles [2007]). Duke Ellington spoken introduction and piano solo. [Also on *Solos, Duets and Trios* (Bluebird)]

"Ko-Ko," "Bojangles," Sepia Panorama," "Jack the Bear." 6 March, 4 May, 24 July 1940. Chicago, Hollywood or NYC. *The Blanton-Webster Band*, Bluebird 3-CD [1986]. Wallace Jones, Cootie Williams, Rex Stewart tp; Joe Nanton, Lawrence Brown, Juan Tizol tb; Barney Bigard, Johnny Hodges, Otto Hardwick, Ben Webster, Harry Carney reeds; Ellington p; Fred Guy g; Jimmy Blanton b; Sonny Greer d.

"J. B. Blues" (3:02) and "Pitter Panther Patter" (3:01). Chicago, 1 October 1940. Ellington p, Jimmy Blanton b. *Solos, Duets and Trios* (Bluebird CD [1990])

"Pitter Panther Patter" 3:00. 5 December 1972, Las Vegas, Nevada. *This One's For Blanton*. Pablo 2310-721 (OJCCD [1987]). Ellington p, Ray Brown b.

"Blues for Blanton" 2:36 (comp Duke Ellington, Mercer Ellington) 13 September 1950, NYC. *Great Times!* Riverside Records (OJC CD [1984]) Duke Ellington p, Oscar Pettiford cello, Lloyd Trotman b, Jo Jones d.

New World A-Coming. 14:11. 11 December 1943. *Live at Carnegie Hall* (Storyville 2-CD [2001]). Ray Nance, Harold Baker, Taft Jordan, Wallace Jones, Rex Stewart tp; Lawrence Brown, Joe Nanton, Juan Tizol tb; Jimmy Hamilton, Johnny Hodges, Otto Hardwick, Skippy Williams, Harry Carney reeds; Ellington p; Fred Guy g; Alvin Raglin b; Sonny Greer d.

"New World A-Coming" 9:02. 10 April 1972. Whitney Museum of American Art, NY. *Live at the Whitney* (Impulse! [1995]). Duke Ellington p, Joe Benjamin b, Rufus Jones d.

"New World A-Coming" 9:13. 21 February 1966. Coventry Cathedral, England. *Duke Ellington in Coventry 1966* (Storyville [2018]). Duke Ellington piano solo.

New World A-Coming 11:14. 28 May 1970, Cincinnati, Ohio. *Duke Ellington Orchestral Works* (MCA Classics [1989]). Duke Ellington, piano with Cincinnati Symphony Orchestra conducted by Erich Kunzel.

"Retrospection" 3:53. "Melancholia" 3:17, "Refections in D" 3:32. Hollywood, CA. 13 and 14 April 1953. *Piano Reflections* (Capitol CD

[1992]). Duke Ellington p, Wendell Marshall b.

"Melancholia/Reflections in D" 4:08. Wollman Auditorium, Columbia University. 20 May 1964. *New York Concert* (MusicMasters CD [1995]). Duke Ellington p solo.

"December Blue" 3:32. 3 December 1953, NY. *Piano Reflections* (Capital CD [1992]). DE p, Wendell Marshall b, Dave Black d

"Fleurette Africaine" 3:33. New York, 17 September 1962. *Money Jungle* (United Artists [Blue Note CD]). Duke Ellington p. Charles Mingus b, Max Roach d. Other good ones are "Very Special" 4:23, "Wig Wise" 3:17, "Warm Valley" 3:31

"Springtime in Africa" 3:44, "Summertime" 3:50. Los Angeles, 2 March 1961. *Piano in the Foreground* (Columbia CD [2004]). DE p, Aaron Bell b, Sam Woodyard d

"Once in a Blue Mood." 19 May 1955. Chicago. *The Capitol Sessions 1953-1955*, Definitive Records 4-CD [2006]. Ray Nance tp, Quentin Jackson tb, Russell Procope cl, Ellington electric p, Jimmy Woode b, Dave Black d.

"Dancers in Love" 2:19. NYC, 30 May 1945. *Complete RCA Mid-Forties* 3-CD [2000] . Ellington p, Junior Raglin b. One of five movements of *The Perfume Suite*. 24 and 30 May 1945. Taft Jordan, Shelton Hemphill, Cat Anderson, Ray Nance tp; Claude Jones, Lawrence Brown, Joe Nanton tb; Jimmy Hamilton, Otto Hardwick, Johnny Hodges, Al Sears, Harry Carney reeds; Ellington p; Fred Guy g; Junior Raglin b; Sonny Greer d.

"Bird of Paradise" 4:00 Wollman Auditorium, Columbia University, 20 May 1964. *New York Concert* (Music Masters [1995]). Duke Ellington p.

"Lotus Blossom" 3:54. RCA Studios, NYC, 30 August 1967. ...*And His Mother Called Him Bill*, Bluebird [1987]. Duke Ellington p.

"Lotus Blossom." 4:58. Same studio, same release. 1 September 1967. Harry Carney, bs, Ellington p, Aaron Bell b.

Appendix A: Piano in the Foreground

Duke Ellington recorded dozens of piano features in concert halls and studios as part of his night's work with his orchestra, but once in a while he gave himself a longer turn. These are the full-length documents in chronological order. Tracks referred to in the chapter are listed specifically in the Playlist above. Piano recitals, issued and unissued, are itemized at the end.

Solos, Duets and Trios. Bluebird 2178-2-RB [1990]. Piano features from 1932, 1940, 1941, 1945, 1946, 1965 and 1967 from RCA Victor's vaults including nine takes of the monumental 1940 duets with Jimmy Blanton.

Great Times! Riverside OJCCD-108-2 [1984]. Duke Ellington and Billy Strayhorn duets, originally 1950 rarities on Mercer Records.

Piano Reflections. Capitol CDP 7 92863 [1989]. From 1953, 15 tracks with Wendell Marshall on bass and either Butch Ballard or Dave Black on drums.

Piano in the Foreground. French CBS (originally Columbia). Trio tracks with Aaron Bell, bass, and Sam Woodyard, drums, from 1961.

Unissued piano recital, Museum of Modern Art, New York, 4 January 1962. Ellington played the first half alone, and in the second half was accompanied by Aaron Bell, bass, and Sam Woodyard, drums. Four short titles from the first half were issued unofficially; 12 more titles were played. Itemized in **Piano Recitals** below.

The Piano Player. Storyville [2005]. Piano solos New York 1962, 1966, 1970, Tokyo 1964, Paris 1961, 1967, and trios New York 1971. The 1970 solos are the six sketches for movements of *The River*, discussed in Chapter 9 Three Steps into *The River*.

Money Jungle. Blue Note CDP 7 46398 [1987]. A 1962 post-bop outing with Charles Mingus and Max Roach.

Afro-Bossa Piano Summations 1 and 2. 8 January 1963. Unissued studio recordings with Ernie Shepard, bass, and Sam Woodyard, drums, of themes from *Afro-Bossa* (recorded for Reprise Records by the orchestra 29 November 1962, 4-5 January 1963); Ellington played 5 short pieces (7 minutes).

New York Concert. MusicMasters 1612-65122 [1995]. A trio performance at Wollman Auditorium, Columbia University in May 1964, with cameo appearances by Billy Strayhorn and Willie the Lion Smith. Peck Morrison plays bass and Sam Woodyard drums. Itemized in **Piano Recitals** below.

Various Artists, *The Jazz Piano.* Mosaic Singles [2007]. Jazz Piano Workshop at Pittsburgh Jazz Festival, 20 June 1965. Ellington plays two pieces and a duet with Earl Hines. Also features Charles Bell, Willie the Lion Smith, Billy Taylor, George Wein and Mary Lou Williams.

The Pianist. Carriere CA 98 561 (Fantasy USA). Two little-known trio sessions, one recorded in New York in 1966 and the other in Las Vegas in 1970.

Solo piano with commentaries. (44:41). French ORTF (TV), 2 July 1970. Ellington plays 11 compositions (two by Billy Strayhorn) and reminisces (with no audience or interviewer).

Jazz on the Tube (Australia Broadcast Co.) <https://jazzonthetube.com/video/solo-piano/?omhide=true> [accessed January 2018]. Itemized in **Piano Recitals** below.

Berklee College of Music, Boston, awarded Duke Ellington its first honorary Doctorate of Music on Monday, 22 May 1971. At the reception afterward, Ellington sat down at the piano and played a 17-minute impromptu recital. Itemized in **Piano Recitals** below.

Live at the Whitney. Impulse! IMPD-173 [1995]. A recital at the Whitney Museum, Manhattan, in April 1972 with Joe Benjamin, bass, and Rufus Jones, drums. Itemized in **Piano Recitals** below.

An Intimate Piano Session. Storyville [2017]. Relaxed studio versions in August 1972 of Ellington piano solos on 8 titles plus three alternative takes, and five more tracks accompanying singers Anita Moore and Tony Watkins

This One's For Blanton. Pablo 2310-721 [1987, now on OJC]. Ellington with Ray Brown in 1972 (not 1973, as the notes claim).

Duke's Big Four. Verve 2518-0703 [1988]. A 1973 all-star reunion with Louie Bellson plus Joe Pass and Ray Brown.

Appendix B: Piano Recitals annotated

Where the stride style seemingly prided itself on moving the hands faster than minds can fathom ("lots o' fingers," as Ellington titled his culmination of the style), his final style, **the recital style**, moved gracefully through hummable melodies, exalted harmony over rhythm, and gave the impression of a man searching for the perfect next note.

1943, Nov. 16, Uplands air base, Ottawa, entertained Royal Canadian Air Force personnel. Repertoire unknown.

1962, 4 January, at Museum of Modern Art, New York. Set 1 Duke Ellington solo: New York City Blues; Blue Belles of Harlem; The Clothed Woman; Melancholia; Janet; Reflections in D; Nobody Was Looking; New World A-Coming. Set 2 Ellington with Aaron Bell b, Sam Woodyard d: Take the A Train; Lotus Blossom (piano solo); Satin Doll; Single Petal of a Rose; Kinda Dukish; medley (Do Nothing Till You Hear From Me, Solitude, Don't Get Around Much Anymore, Mood Indigo, Asphalt Jungle Theme, I'm Beginning to See the Light, Sophisticated Lady);

Caravan, Dancers in Love.

1964, 20 May at Columbia University with cameo performances by Strayhorn and Willie the Lion (CD *New York Concert*), Duke Ellington p, Peck Morrison b, Sam Woodyard: Take the A Train (3:56); Satin Doll (4:01); Caravan (2:57); Skillipoop (6:04); Into Each Life Some Rain Must Fall (poem 0:33); Blues Medley (Happy-Go-Lucky Local, John Sanders' Blues, C Jam Blues 5:40); Tonk (duet with Billy Strayhorn 2:08); Things Ain't What They Used to Be (2:29); Melancholia/Reflections in D (4:08); Little African Flower (2:23); Bird of Paradise (4:00); The Single Petal of a Rose (3:04)

1970, 2 July recorded by French ORTF – intimate 45 minutes of musings in words and music. Duke Ellington, piano. plays Little African Flower, Take the A Train (Strayhorn), Warm Valley, Things Ain't What They Used to Be, Paris Blues, Come Sunday, In the Beginning God, Lotus Blossom (Strayhorn), Black Beauty, New World a-Comin', Satin Doll and Dancers in Love <https://jazzonthetube.com/video/solo-piano/?omhide=true> [accessed January 2018]

1971, 22 February, in Baltimore, Maryland. Blizzard interrupted arrival of musicians, so Ellington played afternoon concert on piano, with Joe Benjamin b, and Tony Watkins voc (four songs). Unissued. Discographies list Take the A Train, Lotus Blossom, Sophisticated Lady, Satin Doll, Dancers in Love, Mood Indigo, I'm Beginning to See the Light, Flamingo, Kinda Dukish, Jeep's Blues, Caravan, East St. Louis Toodle-Oo, Carolina Shout, Misty, and two unidentified titles.

1971, 22 May, at Charter Room, Berklee College of Music, Boston. After receiving honorary D. Mus., Ellington played requests for 17 minutes at the reception <http://tdwaw.ca> [accessed January 2018] Satin Doll; Take the A Train; Baby You Can't Miss (Ellington voc); Sophisticated Lady; Honeysuckle Rose; Love You Madly (Nell Brookshire voc); Come Sunday (Tony Watkins voc)

1972, 10 April, at Whitney Museum, NY (CD *Live at the Whitney*). Duke Ellington p, Joe Benjamin b, Rufus Jones b: Medley (Black and Tan Fantasy, Prelude to a Kiss, Do Nothing Till You Hear From Me, Caravan 6:51); Meditation (2:39); A Mural From Two Perspectives (2:56); Sophisticated Lady/Solitude (4:44); Soda Fountain Rag (1:18); New World A-Coming (9:02); Amour Amour (1:41); Soul Soothing Beach (2:51); Lotus Blossom (2:35); Flamingo (1:35); Le Sucrier Velours (1:44); The Night Shepherd (2:45); C Jam Blues (3:04); Mood Indigo (2:06); I'm Beginning to See the Light (1:23); Dancers in Love (2:13); Kixx (1:35); Satin Doll (3:07)

Chapter 6

BARDLAND

Shakespeare in Ellington's World

Photo montage © 1999 Jack Chambers

Duke Ellington's creative rebirth in 1956-1960 has all the trappings of an artistic pinnacle except for the one indisputable, certifiable, bona fide masterpiece that everyone can point to as its crystallization. Among several contenders, Ellington's Shakespeare suite is undoubtedly the critical favorite. No one has ever disputed the genuinely inspired writing in the suite Ellington called *Such Sweet Thunder* (Columbia/Legacy 65568 [CD 1999]). The twelve themes that Ellington and Billy Strayhorn composed, more than half an hour of music played almost flawlessly by one of Ellington's greatest orchestras, are rich in orchestral devices and full of feeling. Ellington's penchant for yoking together loosely connected pieces and calling them "suites" had more vindication here than in some others. His intention, he said, was to create a "tone parallel" to Shakespeare's works. Because those works are themselves among the most disparate, sprawling effusions of human creativity ever known, Ellington gave himself licence to create a disparate, sprawling effusion in response. In that he succeeded magnificently.

Orchestrating a Rebirth

Ellington had regained the easy self-confidence that for a few years had seemed more façade than mantle. He had known before any of his critics that the band he had assembled piecemeal in the early 1950s rivaled the great band of a decade earlier in talent and personality. The triumph at Newport in 1956 appeared accidental, but 'rehearsals' of Paul Gonsalves's show-stopping interval on the blues can actually be heard in obscure performances at Birdland in 1951 and Durham, North Carolina two months before Newport (Morton, p. 146). They were inspired by Gonsalves's performance on "The Happening," the only composition by Gonsalves that Ellington ever recorded, on Mercer Records in 1951. Stanley Dance, annotating that record years later (1992), identifies it "an early example of Paul Gonsalves's talent for stirring up excitement." Ellington knew exactly what he was doing when he unleashed Gonsalves on the pissed-up party-primed mob at the end of a long day at Newport.

Things had been going Ellington's way for a few years, and the Newport triumph was the coming-out party. *Time* magazine's cover story was already in the can, and Newport provided the hook that got it into print (20 August 1956). The new Columbia Records contract, with generous terms and artistic freedom, was under negotiation, and the inaugural LP *Live at Newport*, destined to be a top-seller, sealed the deal. Billy Strayhorn had briefly chafed at Ellington's cavalier attitude toward his composer credits, and though it pained him, he complained; Ellington, hitherto oblivious, capitulated instantly and set about making it right (Hajdu, pp. 153-54). It seemed to be a relief to both of them, and for the rest of their days they composed and arranged together with revitalized symbiosis.

The outpouring in the duration of the 1956-1961 Columbia contract included the notable entries *A Drum Is a Woman* (1956 soundtrack for a television fantasy by Ellington/Stayhorn), *Black Brown and Beige* (1958 adaptation featuring the gospel diva, Mahalia

Jackson, in a jazz context), *Anatomy of a Murder* (1959 movie soundtrack in an accidental suite of brilliant integrity), *The Queen's Suite* (1959, released posthumously as disussed in Chapter 8), and *Blues in Orbit* (1958-59 endlessly inventive small-band originals, among them "Sweet and Pungent," discussed in Chapter 2). These entries represent about one-fifth of Ellington's production in this five-year period and are limited to the ones that might find a critic somewhere who would advance a claim for them as masterpieces. By any standard, these entries mark an extraordinary creative plateau, and amidst these riches perhaps the piece with the most secure claim to masterpiece is the 1957 Shakespeare suite, *Such Sweet Thunder.*

Ellington's tone parallel to the works of Shakespeare is brilliantly conceived and impeccably realized. Each of its twelve movements boasts some or all of the Shakespearean attributes as entertaining and enticing and seductive and disquieting. Obvious though its strengths are, it does not proclaim its genius outright. There is something missing, and I think it is captured by the old saying that the whole is no more than the sum of its parts. When the parts are so splendid, they can blind even critical listeners to the overarching flaw – or at least that is how I rationalize my own blindness to it, which led me to overlook it for almost 50 years. From the time the music was released in 1957, when I was a teenager, the Shakespeare suite was probably the Ellington music I listened to most persistently, in whole or in part, year after year. It was only when I looked harder at it for purposes of talking about it publicly (to the Toronto Duke Ellington Society in 2004) that I noticed its lack of finish, the anti-climax that results from the succession of minor climaxes without a cumulative effect. And it took a little longer for me to realize that Ellington himself seems to have laid the groundwork for organizing the pieces into a coherent suite, with sub-themes and musical motifs, that might have given the suite the cumulative oomph that is missing. If so, he apparently ran out of time for implementing the grand scheme, as he so often did, speeding on to the next project or maybe merely to the next gig, and leaving the pieces of the Shakespeare suite in a heap, like so many glistening tiles forever awaiting the artist to make the immortal mosaic.

Ellington seems to have recognized its incompleteness, at least tacitly. After the premiere of the Shakespeare suite – actually a double premiere, as we will see – he never again performed it as an entity. From time to time, he picked out a few pieces and inserted them into his nighly concerts, but in spite of the inherent theatricality of the theme and his verbal flourishes by way of spoken introductions and his obvious gusto for the subject matter, he never again treated it as a single, coherent, performable piece of music, that is, as a suite.

Hark, the Duke's Trumpets

Ellington's inspiration for transliterating Shakespeare into jazz came from a chance encounter, as unexpected in its way as was his fixation on God in his final years. In July 1956, Ellington was booked to play two concerts at the Shakespearean Festival in Stratford, Ontario. It did not seem particularly remarkable at the time. From 1956 until 1958, while Louis Applebaum, a genteel composer turned administator, was its musical director, the Stratford Festival booked summer jazz and classical concerts as adjuncts to the dramatic offerings. Besides Ellington in 1956, Wilbur de Paris, Oscar Peterson, Dave Brubeck and the Modern Jazz Quartet also played evening concerts, spaced out in July and August. In the time-honoured tradition, the jazz musicians arrived in Stratford, played their one- or two-night stands and then hit the road for the next performance a day or two away.[1] Not Ellington. He played his two concerts, and then he carried with him for the rest of his days what he had seen and heard all around him in the quiet anglo-celtic market-town of 20,000 in southwestern Ontario.

Ellington played in an unimaginable number of settings in his day and in spite of their profusion he was often sensitive to their idiosyncrasies and their charms. He arrived in Stratford from a resort ballroom in the town of Bala, in the lake district about 150 miles to the north, played non-consecutive nights on Wednesday and Friday, the 18th and 20th, 1956, with concerts on the alternate Thursday and

---

[1] It was not always that ephemeral. Oscar Peterson's performance that year resulted in a Verve recording that captured the head-banging competitiveness of his original Trio as no other record had until then: *Oscar Peterson at the Stratford Shakespearean Festival* (Verve CD [1993]).

Saturday nights at the Brant Inn in Burlington, 70 miles to the east. (The Wednesday performance at Stratford is preserved *Live at the 1957* [sic] *Stratford Festival*, Music & Arts CD-616 [1989], details in Playlist below.) Tom Patterson, the soft-spoken newspaperman whose persistence had persuaded the town council to risk a top-flight professional Shakespeare festival based solely on the coincidence of the colonial namesake (not only Stratford itself, named for Shakespeare's birthplace in Warwickshire, England, but also the River Avon running through it, replete with swans), met Ellington and Harry Carney on their arrival. Patterson was flattered when the Duke asked him to show him around. Ellington stayed in Stratford three days, commuting to the Brant Inn in between, and it is worth speculating that he might have altered his lifelong routine by hauling himself out of bed for mid-afternoon matinee performances of *Henry V* and *Merry Wives of Windsor* on the festival's main stage.

The Shakespeare Festival was (and is) a highbrow spectacle in the bourgeois heartland, and none if it was lost on Ellington. Stratford's thrust stage, modeled on the Elizabethan Globe Theatre where Shakespeare's plays were first performed, was new not only to Stratford but

Festival Theatre, Stratford, Ontario, pencil sketch (Stratford Festival Archives)

Festival Theatre thrust stage, Stratford (Stratford Festival Archives)

to the theatre world at large. The proximity of actors and audience added to the excitement of the whole heady venture. Shakespeare had seldom been treated so well. His plays were directed by Sir Tyrone Guthrie and Michael Langham, costumed resplendently by Tanya Moiseiwitsch and acted by a brilliant young company that included Lloyd Bochner, Martha Henry, Christopher Plummer and William Shatner – all of them destined to become iconic figures in the theatre world.

Ellington loved what he saw, so much so that he began angling to be part of it. He opened his Stratford concerts with a new composition he introduced as "Hark the Duke's Trumpets." The Shakespearean resonance of the title is Ellingtonian licence; it is a fanfare played by trombones, not trumpets. No matter. His title paid homage, as his audience was pleased to note, to the medieval trumpets that called playgoers into the theatre for the start of the play, a festival specialty then and now. Ellington's trombones play a handsome fanfare-like cadence, thus making it an ingenious adaptation to the Stratford setting. The trombones provide the smooth underscore for a mobile solo by the bass player (and when the composition was finally recorded it was called "Bassment," its actual title). By opening his concerts with a salutation to the Stratford setting, however oblique, Ellington clearly signaled his delight in being there.

His delight proved to be more than a one-night stand. Ellington told everyone he met in Stratford and everywhere he went in the months that followed that he and Billy Strayhorn were preparing a jazz suite based on Shakespeare that he would premiere at the festival the next summer.

Sweet Thunder Indeed
The premiere happened, but not the way Ellington envisioned it. When the Stratford program for 1957 was announced, Ellington was not listed. He then had to persuade the program committee to bring him in as a late addition. As he explained in a CBC radio interview with Harry Rasky, "The Stratford Festival are not repeating any of the jazz artists this year that they had last year. But I've already informed Mr. Patterson that there's one hazard in allowing us to do the Shakespearean suite, which is called *Such Sweet Thunder*, and that is that we are liable to get publicity on it, which will sort of throw them into the position of having to be more or less graceful and inviting us back this year."

The Stratford organizers capitulated and brought Ellington to town for the premiere late in the season, but by then Ellington had already premiered *Such Sweet Thunder* at Town Hall in New York, with considerable fanfare, on 28 April 1957, the day before Ellington's 58th birthday and, as it happened, two days after what would have been Shakespeare's 393rd birthday. (Shakespeare and Ellington were both born under the zodiac sign of Taurus.) When Rasky interviewed him, Ellington, was taking advantage of a two week engagement at Birdland in Manhattan (18 April-1 May) by rehearsing two movements of the suite that had been written months earlier in the flush of his Stratford visit and for working out nine new movements on the bandstand. "We started recording some of them before we finished writing others," he told Rasky. "You know, the eleventh tune was finished the day of the performance," and when Rasky pressed him for details he named both "Sonnet for Hank Cinq" and "The Telecasters" as last-minute additions. In the end, there was a twelfth movement, a finale called "Circle of Fourths," that was not even ready in time for the Town Hall premiere. It was recorded in the studio with four other movements a week later (3 May) and included as the finale with the seven parts already recorded on the 35-minute, 12-track LP called *Such Sweet Thunder,* subtitled (in parentheses) *Dedicated to the Shakespearean Festival, Stratford, Ontario.*

The Stratford premiere took place at an afternoon concert on 5 September 1957, more than four months after the Town Hall premiere. Apparently neither the Town Hall premiere nor the Stratford premiere was recorded. There are later live recordings that preserve Ellington playing a few of his favourite movements (the

Such Sweet Thunder (Dedicated to the Shakespearean Festival, Stratford, Ontario), original LP cover (Columbia CL 1033, 1957)

opener "Such Sweet Thunder," the strikingly romantic Hodges specialty "The Star-Crossed Lovers" and a couple of others) but the only extant performance of the complete suite remains the original studio recording. All twelve movements were recorded in three studio sessions during a four-week period in April and May. With unusual efficiency, five movements came in the May session alone, attesting to the concentrated work in the nightly Birdland 'rehearsals'. This compact chronology no doubt accounts for the wonderful cohesion of the playing throughout. The compositions are consistently ingenious and the performances are uniformly brilliant, a reflection undoubtedly of the genuinely inspired aura in which they were conceived. From the first release, listeners recognized the parts as glorious efflorescences of Ellingtonia. Literate listeners also recognized them as worthily Shakespearean in the variety of ensemble voicings and infallible casting of instrumental voices in character roles. Those were always Ellington's strengths, whether Shakespeare was involved or not, but they were seldom found in such sustained profusion.

"A truly Shakespearean universality"

The stars were aligned for an Ellington masterpiece in 1957. "I was born on July the 7th 1956 at Newport, Rhode Island," Duke Ellington liked to tell reporters in the 18 good years that came after it (and ironically ignoring the thirty-odd years that had come before it). It was just two weeks after the Newport triumph that Ellington swaggered into Stratford. By then he had already sat for the impending *Time* cover profile and he had broken new ground by signing a CBS-TV contract for his jazz fantasy *A Drum is a Woman* (music recorded September 1956, televised May 1957). "Ellington's second wind has been felt in the music business for months, and the major record companies have been bidding for his remarkable signature," the *Time* profile announced. "This week he plans to sign (with Columbia Records) a contract designed to give him the broadest possible scope. He will have time to write more big works, both instrumental and dramatic." Little wonder, then, when Ellington bumped into William Shakespeare at Stratford, he embraced him as a kindred spirit.

Across the gap of more than 350 years that separated them, Shakespeare and Ellington shared an uncommon creative space. An

"Hark the Duke's Trumpets" (photo Don Hunstein, courtesy SONY Canada)

English reviewer of Ellington's London Palladium concert way back in 1933 had been the first to note the parallel. "His music has a truly Shakespearean universality," said the reviewer, "and as he sounded the gamut, girls wept and young chaps sank to their knees."

Both men raised what were thought to be "low" entertainments into high art. William Shakespeare (1564-1616) had sidled into the bawdy domain of groundling skitcraft and had given it scope and depth hitherto unimaginable. Ellington (1899-1974) had done something similar with nightclub kicklines and lowdown blues. Both men had been pushed into leading their troupes by dint of personal charisma, Shakespeare starting as an actor and becoming a dramatist, Ellington as a piano player and becoming a composer. Both broke the seal on their creative juices out of a desperate need to keep their troupes working. Once those juices started flowing they proved to be ground-breaking and unbridled, overflowing across sub-genres and styles. Shakespeare loved music as much as Ellington loved theatricality. The interpolations of music into Shakespeare's plays and his occasional comments enrich the dramas. In *Merchant of Venice*, Lorenzo, the lover of Shylock's daughter, counsels her (V, i):

> The man that hath no music in himself,
> Nor is not mov'd with concord of sweet sounds,
> Is fit for treasons, stratagems, and spoils;....
> Let no such man be trusted.

It is a sentiment that Ellington would certainly endorse. And both Shakespeare and Ellington relied inordinately on their native instinct and personal taste, which led some of their their highbrow critics to conclude that they were unschooled in the finer points of their craft, a claim that shadows Shakespeare to this day, and Ellington too – never more so than when he took Shakespeare into his own world.

Ellington felt the kinship with Shakespeare. In his program notes for the Stratford premiere, he wrote, "Somehow, I suspect that if Shakespeare were alive today, he might be a jazz fan himself – he'd appreciate the combination of team spirit and informality, of academic knowledge and humor, of all the elements that go into a jazz performance. And I am sure he would agree with the simple and axiomatic statement that is so important to all of us – when it sounds good, it *is* good."

The compact recording schedule for the Shakespeare suite may have helped to promote the notion that the suite was a quick affair, as Ellington's Columbia producer suggested in his notes on the recording, an error that Ellington made no effort to correct. On the contrary, Ellington's preparations were more fastidious than ever. He made a preliminary recording of one of the twelve movements only three weeks after playing at Stratford that first summer, in the afterglow. It was "Half the Fun," a sensuous glide featuring the saxophone sound of Johnny Hodges over a *faux* Middle Eastern rhythm that conjured up Cleopatra sapping the vital juices of her imperial Roman lovers. In the studio ledger, the piece was called "Lately," and the suspicion lingers that Ellington did not design it for the suite but merely plucked it from his canned stockpile to add weight to his new pet project.

Similar suspicion surrounds the second composition recorded soon after the Stratford experience. "The Star-Crossed Lovers" was recorded as "Pretty Girl" in December 1956 and then re-recorded the next May with its new title and the same arrangement with an

Cleopatra costume for Maggie Smith in *Antony and Cleopatra*, 1976, designed by Daphne Dare (Stratford Festival Archives)

added piano cadenza. (Listeners get a rare look at the orchestra working out the arrangement in a nine-minute sequence on the 1999 CD reissue that includes two rehearsal takes, two false starts and a final complete take.) It too is a feature for Hodges, and one of the most unforgettable movements framed as Juliet's lament for her dead lover (also discussed in Chapter 4, "Lotus Eaters Unite!").

Both pieces came into existence outside the neatly compressed timeline that Ellington and Strayhorn recounted for the writing of the suite. "We're very happy that we had a deadline, a short deadline on it, because… you could spend a whole lifetime preparing an unfinished work as far as trying to do something with Shakespeare," Ellington told Rasky. "We had a deadline and we knew that we had to do little things and we had to do them quickly. So we spent two months talking about it and then we spent three weeks actually writing it." Strayhorn said much the same thing five years later, in a CBC radio interview with Bob Smith in Vancouver. "When we were doing, for instance, the Shakespearean suite, well, the talk on that went on for weeks," he said. "We read all of Shakespeare, and, uh, [had] great discussions at midnight over various and sundry cups of coffee and tea and what-not. ...And the actual writing, of course, took no time. The actual writing took no time."

Their deadline was short but their preparations were fastidious. On the occasion of the Stratford premiere, Ellington and Strayhorn spent several days mingling with the performers and scholars, and they made a great impression. The Festival founder, Tom Patterson, told Strayhorn's biographer, "Frankly I wasn't prepared for the depth of [Strayhorn's] knowledge. We were literally with the top Shakespeare scholars in the world, and Strayhorn didn't have anything to apologize for. His knowledge was very deep" (Hajdu, p. 163).

While Ellington and the orchestra were stationed in New York for more than six weeks from 8 April to 22 May 1957, a rare occurrence, they devoted the first three of those weeks to the suite, as Ellington reported, recording the parts almost as soon as they were written at Columbia's Manhattan studio on 15 April, 24 April and 3 May. But the two movements written and recorded beforehand, "Half the Fun" and "The Star-Crossed Lovers," are no less integral in the conceptual framework of the suite than are the others. "Half the Fun" virtually requires the Shakespearean context to vindicate its slithering sensual excesses. "The Star-Crossed Lovers" has its excesses too, although they are not as alien in jazz because they flow from the old swing tradition when dancers snuggled at the end of the evening, akin in its sensuality to "Warm Valley" (1940) or "Day Dream" (1943), also specialities for Johnny Hodges (as discussed at length in Chapter 4). Played out of context in a concert hall or jazz club, "Half the Fun" and "The Star-Crossed Lovers" might seem odd. Contextualized by Cleopatra and by Juliet, they are gorgeous. They were composed soon after the Shakespeare suite was conceptualized, in the afterglow, as we said, of Ellington's infatuation with the Stratford Festival. If they really did find their way into the suite by accident, as some critics opine, there was a powerful serendipity at work to make them fit so perfectly.

Scenes and Sonnets

Knowing Shakespeare is hardly necessary for appreciating these or any of the other parts, but it definitely adds a dimension to the music. As composer, Ellington always took his inspiration from the outside world, and hearing his music often evokes an extramusical setting of some kind. Listeners don't have to know what railway train he was on when he wrote "Daybreak Express" (1933) or "Happy-Go-Lucky Local" (1946), but it would be hard to get full value from them without imagining passenger trains rushing across the landscape. It isn't possible to know Harlem as it was when Ellington sketched it musically in "Harlem Air Shaft" (1940) and "A Tone Parallel to Harlem" (1952), but it is surely impossible to hear those compositions without imagining tenement smells and street-corner signifying and church-going families in their Sunday-best. Bill Berry, a trumpeter, discovered Ellington's real-world orientation his first day in the band. Ellington invited him to take a solo on "Lullaby of Birdland," a jazz standard he knew well. While he was playing it, he said, "it occurred to me that Duke's arrangement was quite unusual. It was slow-medium in tempo and used very strange background figures. When we had finished, Duke called me over and said, 'That was very pretty, Bill, however, it shouldn't be approached that way. This arrangement depicts the club itself: traffic sounds, night club sounds – a picture of the club.' After Duke's explanation, the arrangement, the tempo – everything was right."

For Ellington, music was grounded in the world. Instead of self-referential titles like "C-Minor Prelude," he chose "Prelude to a Kiss"; not "Concerto for Cello and Orchestra" but "Concerto for Cootie"; not "Cantata No. 140" but "Canteen Bounce." His songs were sonic correlates for real experiences or, in the term he preferred, tone parallels to the sensory world.

In the Shakespeare suite, the inspiration for the content was obviously literary, and for four of the movements the form was also literary. For the four pieces called sonnets, Ellington literally lifted the musical structure from literature, and his sonnets are unlike anything in jazz or any other musical genre. For the other eight movements, Ellington relied on the conventional 32-bar form from American popular song that jazz has used as its staple since about 1928 or on the 12-bar blues form from the dawn of folk music. The four sonnets occupy their own space, set apart from the other eight movements, which I will call 'scenes', to convey their common purpose as dramatic portrayals of mood and character. I discuss the structurally unique sonnets on their own in a later section.

Shakespearean words and phrases
The months of discussion that preceded the actual writing were consumed with finding a tactic for transliterating Shakespearean scenes and characters in music. "You have to adjust your perspective as to just what you're going to do and what you're to say and what you're going to say it about and how much of it you're supposed to be covering," Ellington said in the interview with Bob Smith. "Actually, in one album you're not going to parallel anything of Shakespeare. What do you need? A thousand writers and a thousand years to do it, you know, to cover Shakespeare. So we said we'll just devote one number to one Shakespearean word or one Shakespearean phrase."

Taken literally, it sounds simplistic to make melodies based on a word or phrase, but in fact what Ellington did in practice was to pick out keywords and key-phrases that allowed him to crystallize dramatic action into three-to-four-minute sonic capsules. When he sticks to it, the result is brilliantly concise, a perfect realization of his goals.

Four of the eight scenes actually take their titles from Shakespeare's words and phrases. Three of them match the mood and music brilliantly.
- "The Star-Crossed Lovers," a phrase from the Prologue to *Romeo and Juliet*, captures the romantic tragedy of the double suicides of the young lovers, children of feuding families. It is Juliet's lament, conveyed with heart-rending sorrow in Billy Strayhorn's arrangement, which perfectly sets off alto saxophonist Johnny Hodges's keening cry.
- "Madness in Great Ones" characterizes Prince Hamlet in the words of his uncle Claudius, who, as Hamlet's father's murderer and his mother's lover, is the obvious cause of Hamlet's madness. Ellington chooses to dramatize not the corruption in the Danish court (Claudius's line, the source of Ellington's title, in its entirety says,

Oberon in *A Midsummer Night's Dream*, 1960, designed by Brian Jackson
(Stratford Festival Archives)

"Madness in great ones must not unwatch'd go"). Instead, he fixes on Hamlet's jangled psyche. It is a discordant composition, with the brass interrupting the playful swing of the reeds with jarring staccato riffs on the off-beat; Cat Anderson's climactic cadenza on trumpet, which sounds like he is trying to blow his brains out, was never put to more strategic use. This brilliant orchestration makes a perfect analogue for Shakespeare's words (though spoken by Richard II, not Hamlet):

> How sour sweet music is
> When time is broke and no proportion kept!
> So is it in the music of men's lives.

- At the opposite pole, "Up and Down, Up and Down (I Will Lead Them Up and Down)," based on Puck's promise that he will make fools of the coupling humans in *A Midsummer Night's Dream,* is airy, and every bit as ingenious in ensemble writing. The humans are mainly represented by a nursery-like motif for unison violin and clarinet (Ray Nance and Jimmy Hamilton). As the hobgoblin, Clark Terry on flugelhorn bobs across the simple surface with great good humor in what is the second longest solo turn in the suite after Hodges on "The Star-Crossed Lovers."

- The fourth scene with a Shakespearean title is "Such Sweet Thunder," also a phrase from *A Midsummer Night's Dream* (Queen Hippolyta: "I never heard/ So musical a discord, such sweet thunder"). Ellington chose it as the title of the entire suite as well as for the introductory movement of the suite. It is wonderfully apt as the title for the movement but less so for the whole suite (and probably for that reason the whole is usually referred to as the Shakespeare suite rather than *Such Sweet Thunder*). The music of "Such Sweet Thunder" is indeed thunderous, a 12-bar blues based on a cracking drum cadence on the strong beats and a primitive vamp by the low horns. It is hotly declarative, almost a burlesque bump-and-grind, and, as such, an explosive opening for the suite. Unlike the other scenes, however, it is only tangentially Shakespearean. It has no connection to its source play. Originally titled "Cleo," it might have been intended as an evocation of Cleopatra's sexuality, which certainly works, but instead Ellington always introduced it as (at Juan les Pins in 1966) "the sweet swinging line of talk that Othello gave to Desdemona which swayed her into his direction." That does not work. "Such Sweet Thunder" is not pillow talk, by any criterion.

  The title perfectly matches the music, however, and the music works perfectly as the overture, a rousing opener for the delights that follow. Its dramatic use as an opener is further enhanced because, as Bill Berry says in his annotations for the 1999 reissue, "The final note of the piece is the lowered 7th tone of the major scale creating a feeling of ambivalence, asking a question instead of providing a resolution." What's next, it seems to ask. Bring it on.

Ellington words and phrases

One of the victims of the short deadline, apparently, was the scheme for linking music to drama through Shakespearean keywords. The other four scenes have Ellingtonian titles, and the titles (though not the music) show signs of haste.

"Half the Fun" celebrates Cleopatra's sensuality with a sly, winkiing subtlety, but the title is oddly flippant, and anachronistic to boot. (The word "fun" was coined a century after Shakespeare.) Despite its genealogy, the title suits the music, and the mood of the music is simply perfect. Ellington described the setting of the piece (to trumpeter Bill Berry), "Imagine this great golden barge floating down the Nile, with beautiful dancing girls, mounds of food and drink, elephants, ostrich feather fans, a hundred slaves rowing the barge and Cleopatra lying on a satin bed." They are all here – Cleopatra lolling on her barge with fawning attendants, driving the muscle-bound Roman consul to distraction. Shakespeare has her say

> Give me some music – music, moody food
> Of us that trade in love.

Ellington and Strayhorn oblige her royally with "Half the Fun."

"The Telecasters," as a title, is an obvious anachronism. The music, however, is a glorious feature for the low horns – the trombone trio (Britt Woodman, Quentin Jackson, John Sanders) and baritone saxophone (Harry Carney). "We took the liberty of combining characters from two plays," Ellington said. "It seems that the three witches [from *Macbeth*] and Iago [from *Othello*] had something in common in that they all had something to say, so we call them the Telecasters." That is a lame rationalization for the title, and no better for trying to link three malevolent hags and a psychopathic villain to the legato mood of the music. However, with music so fetching, it is easy to ignore the title. Best of all, spare a smile for Ellington's winsome attempt to vindicate its title. Simply love the music; it is eminently lovable.

"Circle of Fourths" is a wailing vehicle for Paul Gonsalves, the hero of Newport, designed as a flag-waving closer with little regard to the theme of the suite, but it is certainly resonant. The title, according to producer Irving Townsend in his notes for the original album, "is inspired by Shakespeare himself and the four major parts of his artistic contribution: tragedy, comedy, history and the sonnets."

Musically, the circle of fourths denotes the movement through the 12 tones of the chromatic scale ascending by perfect fourths from any pitch. "There is no beginning or ending," says Bill Berry in his notes on this composition. The suite ought to end with an exclamation point. "Circle of Fourths" gives it an exclamation point.

The remaining scene, "Lady Mac," makes a useful caveat for anyone who might underestimate Ellington's involvement in the subject matter of the suite and the depth of his understanding of Shakespeare's characters. The breezy title suits Clark Terry's extraverted portrayal of Lady Macbeth, but the whole conception might at first seem an odd portrayal of the woman who goaded her husband into murdering a king and then went insane with guilt. But Ellington fully intended the paradox. "We portrayed some of her by using a jazz waltz," Ellington told Harry Rasky, when Rasky questioned the fit, "and in so doing we say that she was a lady of noble birth but we suspect that she had a little ragtime in her soul." Ellington's producer, Irving Townsend, looking back a few years later (1960), said, "Duke likes Lady Macbeth, whether you're supposed to like her or not, and he treats her right." In fact, instead of portraying Lady Macbeth in madness and decline, as she is at the end of the play, Ellington chooses to portray her as she appears before her breakdown, as the temptress and socialite. The music is a charming merger of nobility and ragtime, as intended. But Ellington leaves no doubt that he knows her fate. He ends "Lady Mac" with a thick, melodramatic chord that spells impending disaster. It is a jarring note, and with one deft stroke it completes the portrait.

Ellington's Shakespeare

Ellington made it easy for critics to underestimate his grasp of his subject and his sincerity in taking it on. The flippant titles were only the beginning. Throughout his professional life, he found it hard to keep a straight face when he was asked to explain his art and esthetics. Audiences might be forgiven for failing to realize that his comment about "Lady Mac" having "a little ragtime in her soul" was a conclusion he had come to after careful reflection. Equally, they may be forgiven for misreading his pronouncement on CBC radio: "We feel that Shakespeare was not only sage, and has a tremendous appeal right now to the intellectual, but as the jive boys say, Shakespeare was down, which means that he is dug by the craziest of cats." That comment came after Rasky questioned Ellington about ignoring Elizabethan musical devices in his homage to Shakespeare. To that, Ellington replied, with justifiable indignation, "We think that Shakespeare is just a little beyond chronology." Generations of playgoers would agree with that, of course, Harry Rasky among them. But Ellington was not one to hold the high ground for long. He immediately covered up his indignation by restating his case in "jive boy" terms, which says much the same thing but with such flippancy that it is easily discounted.

Ellington was much better versed on Shakespeare than his critics gave him credit for, or, for that matter, some of his admirers, including his producer Irving Townsend. Don George, Ellington's occasional lyricist and one of the few outsiders admitted to Ellington's Sugar Hill apartment, raved about Ellington's well-stocked library, which conspicuously included "everything by Shakespeare, in many different versions." George added, "In all his copies of the Shakespearean plays, he had underlined parts that appealed to him, not only to be set to music but to be performed by him.... Passage after passage in his books is underlined, indicating that there were far more ambitions in this man than the average human being could appreciate by just seeing the orchestra leader and composer."

Ellington's admiration for Shakespeare was no passing fancy. It is impossible to know when he started reading and annotating Shakespeare, but a good guess would be that it started, as did his other literary interests, with Miss Boston, his English teacher at Garrison Junior High School in 1913-1914 in Washington, D.C., whom he credited for many lessons. "I think she spent as much time in preaching race pride as she did in teaching English, which, ironically and very strangely, improved your English," he recalled 55 years later (quoted by Tucker 1991). Actors fascinated Ellington all his life, especially Shakespearean actors. One of the more exotic artifacts in the Duke Ellington Music Society archive is a three-minute tape made in Ellington's dressing room in Milan in 1966 as the actor Vittorio Gassman recites Hamlet's soliloquy in Italian ("Essere, non essere...") while Ellington plays a delicate version of

"Such Sweet Thunder" in accompaniment. Richard Burton, the greatest Shakespearean actor of his day before he succumbed to Hollywood stardom, told Don George, "I actually appeared on stage with the Duke once in the Rainbow Grill [in Rockefeller Center, Manhattan]. I was sitting in the audience with my daughter when the Duke called me up onto the stage. I said, 'What do you want me to do?' He said, 'You talk and I'll play.' I spoke Shakespeare, I spoke iambic pentameter and iambic hexameter, while Duke's fabulously infatuated brown fingers stroked the keys. It was a thrilling and extraordinary experience, one of the greatest theatrical experiences that I've ever had."

When Ellington pulled into Stratford on that fateful day in July 1956, the sight of Shakespeare being treated as a contemporary hero inspired him to make a jazz analogue. The minute the inspiration hit, Ellington phoned Billy Strayhorn in New York with very specific instructions. "We read all of Shakespeare!" Strayhorn told Stanley Dance. "We had to interpret what he said, just as we had to interpret what Tchaikovsky was saying [for the jazz version of *Nutcracker Suite* in 1960]. The only difference with Shakespeare was that we had to interpret his *words*. It took about the same amount of time too – about six months. We had all these books we used to carry around, and all these people all over the U.S. we used to see and talk to." Ellington also talked about "consultations with two or three Shakespearean actors and authorities." "We'd sit down and discuss for hours, you know, so forth and so on," he told Bob Smith. Haste came at the end, in the wrap-up, but the preparation Ellington and Strayhorn put themselves through was fastidious. And the result shines through.

"A Curious Mixture"
At the moment when the final touches of the suite were being workshopped at Birdland, Harry Rasky asked Ellington how he thought "Shakespeare purists or even jazz purists will take to this curious mixture of the Bard and jazz." There was more than a sniff of disdain in Rasky's question, and perhaps it was his tone that led Ellington to defend his goals and, incidentally, reveal how carefully he had worked them out. Ellington replied, "We sometimes lean a little bit toward caricature, but other people I think have gone about the business of

actually changing Shakespeare, which I think is a much more hazardous thing than what we've done. All we did is just little thumbnail sketches, you know, of very short periods, never at any time trying to parallel an entire play or an entire act or an entire character throughout, but just some little short space of time during a character's performance." Ellington's triumph in composing the scenes stems precisely from his ability to make three-dimensional portraits with a few deft musical strokes.

Neither Ellington's lifelong infatuation with the Bard nor the preparations he and Strayhorn had undertaken were mentioned in any publicity about the suite or in critical commentaries afterward. Ellington's reviewers often showed embarrassing ignorance. Leonard Feather, in his review in *Down Beat*, the most influential jazz journal at the time, wrote, "I've been searching in vain for 14-bar themes or 14-note phrases in the sonnets, all of which allegedly are scored to coincide with regular sonnet form, but who cares?" In this, Feather shows an abysmal depth of ignorance. Ellington's sonnets, as we shall see, are in fact meticulous transpositions of the 14-line (not "14-bar" or "14-note") literary sonnets by Shakespeare. They are masterful evidence of Ellington's brilliance as a composer and evidence of the depth of his knowledge of Shakespeare. "Who cares?" says Feather. Any self-respecting music critic assigned the task of reviewing *Such Sweet Thunder* should indeed care.

For many years, the main medium for public relations on jazz projects, for better or worse, was the liner note on the sleeve of the recordings. Irving Townsend, Ellington's producer at Columbia Records, assigned himself the task of annotating *Such Sweet Thunder*. Townsend was a Princeton graduate who joined Columbia Records as an advertising copywriter, and then charmed his way into the sound booth after a spate of raids on the production staff. A facile writer, he made the notes on *Such Sweet Thunder* into a breezy sketch with anecdotes about haste and eccentricity. He obviously took Ellington's jive talk literally, and he enlivened his own superficial descriptions with quotations from Ellington that added nothing of substance.

Townsend's proximity to Ellington as his Columbia producer obviously gave him no special insights when it came to the Shakespeare suite. In both his liner notes and his later comments, Townsend appears to have had no idea of the preparations that went into it and little appreciation of what was accomplished. Looking back a few years later on the projects he produced for Ellington, Townsend dismissed the Shakespeare suite with lofty, Ivy-League disdain. "Ellington gathered together a series of short pieces descriptive of various impressions he had received from his quick course in the Bard, and we recorded them under such temporary titles as 'Cleo,' 'Puck,' and 'Hamlet'," he recalled. "We all searched later for the final titles, and I found 'Such Sweet Thunder' in Bartlett's Quotations." So the Shakespeare project, according to Townsend's recollections three years after recording it, was accidental (a compilation), superficial (the result of a cram course), arbitrary (titled after the fact), and ersatz (Bartlett as a scholarly short-cut).

Important as he was in revitalizing Ellington's career, Townsend might better have been left off the Shakespeare project not only as liner-note writer but also, dare one say it, as producer. The grossest discrepancy between Shakespearean title and Ellingtonian parallel, as noted above, comes in the movement called "Such Sweet Thunder"; it appears that Townsend, not Ellington or Strayhorn, was responsible for it. But the production flaws went deeper than that. The order of the movements on the original recording has no thematic or developmental basis, and that also appears to be Townsend's doing. At the Stratford premiere, the only live performance of the entire suite, Ellington used an entirely different order (also, it must be admitted, with no thematic basis). The order of the movements on the LP is not just arbitrary, it actually detracts; and nowhere is that more evident than in the placement of the sonnets.

Suspended Animation
The four sonnets are clearly labeled in their titles – "Sonnet for Caesar," "Sonnet for Hank Cinq," "Sonnet for Sister Kate," "Sonnet in Search of a Moor." Even if they were not labeled, their formal peculiarities would set them apart. They are through-composed and last exactly 28 bars. The melodies (so-called) are recited in their entirety by one instrumentalist. They are exacting and somewhat stiff, like technical exercises, but they are also soulful. In all four sonnets,

every even-numbered bar ends with a tied note, and the last eight bars are played over stop-time rhythm and sustained chords. The melodies are played once only and last a little more than a minute, though the recorded versions vary from 1:24 to 3:00 depending upon their orchestral settings. They do not swing.

In the context of the whole suite, they feel like interludes, or four moments of suspended animation. Programming them close to one another in the sequence of the suite as they are on the original recording (tracks 2, 3, 5 and 8) is simply egregious. It both breaks up the flow – an interlude followed by another interlude – and dilutes the singularity of each one by clustering their singularities. They need to be spaced out, at the very least, and spacing them judiciously might have put them to use as prefaces for thematically compatible movements, as I show below.

Ellington's sonnets are, literally, Shakespearean sonnets transliterated into music. Ellington was obviously fascinated by the sonnets. In his rationale for the title "Circle of Fourths," he identified what he called the four major parts of Shakespeare's works as tragedy, comedy, history and the sonnets. But Shakespeare scholars conventionally divide his plays into tragedy, comedy, history and romance (the latter group consisting of *The Winter's Tale*, *Measure for Measure* and two or three others, depending upon whether *Romeo and Juliet* belongs here or with the tragedies). The sonnets belong, obviously, with the poems, not the plays. Among the poems, they occupy formidable space. There are 154 of them, and Shakespeare was almost as masterful at sonnets as he was at drama. They are love poems, sometimes sexual ("The expense of spirit in a waste of shame/Is lust in action"), and often extravagantly flattering ("Shall I compare thee to a summer's day?/Thou art more lovely and more temperate"). The hottest ones are addressed to a woman known as the Dark Lady ("I will swear beauty herself is black/And all they [are] foul that thy complexion lack"). Ellington must have found them appealing on all these grounds.

As literary forms, sonnets are challenging. They are structurally rigid, and lesser poets than Shakespeare have found them stifling. Though Duke Ellington usually had little patience with formalism, he seems to have relished the formal rigidities of the sonnet form. In that respect, again, he was just like Shakespeare, who readily bent literary conventions in his plays but in the sonnets conformed strictly to conventions, doing so with obvious relish. Shakespeare took no liberties with the sonnet form, and neither did Ellington.

As far as the form goes, if you have seen one Shakespearean sonnet you have seen them all. Shakespearean sonnets are made up of 14 lines divided into three quatrains and a final couplet. The lines must be iambic pentameter (five sequences of alternating weak and strong stresses), and they must rhyme alternately until the final couplet, which rhymes successively. I have marked these features in Sonnet CXXVIII below in the alternating end-rhymes of the quatrains (*a b a b* in the first, etc.) and the final couplet (*g g*), the punch line. Each of the 14 lines has ten syllables, paired into five feet (pentameter, where 'penta' is Greek for five) of alternating weak and strong stress, known as iambs (also Greek).

CXXVIII

How oft when thou, my music, music play'st,	a
Upon that blessèd wood whose motion sounds	b
With thy sweet fingers, when thou gently sway'st	a
The wiry concord that my ear confounds,	b
Do I envy those jacks[1] that nimble leap	c [1]hammers
To kiss the tender inward of thy hand,	d
Whilst my poor lips, which should that harvest reap,	c
At the wood's boldness by thee blushing stand!	d
To be so tickled, they[2] would change their state	e [2]his lips
And situation with those dancing chips,[3]	f [3]keys
O'er whom thy fingers walk with gentle gait,	e
Making dead wood more bless'd than living lips.	f
Since saucy jacks so happy are in this,	g
Give them thy fingers, me thy lips to kiss.	g

Sonnet CXXVIII is less well known than many others but it has the attraction, in this context, of a musical theme. Shakespeare's main image in the poem involves an Elizabethan keyboard instrument, a primitive harpsichord. When his lover (whom he calls "my music," a pun on 'my muse') presses the keys ("chips"), she then has to use her other hand to keep the hammers ("jacks") aligned after they pluck the strings. (The sound must have been primitive too, and the sonneteer cannot resist letting his readers know that the "wiry concord" of the instrument sounds god-awful to his ears.) The gist of the poem is that Shakespeare wishes his lover would offer her palm ("the tender inward of thy hand") for him to kiss as readily as she offers it to the "jacks" (a pun as the word also means men or, really, guys). The last two lines, the rhyming couplet, are supposed to supply a surprise ending, and Shakespeare here comes up with the bright idea that instead of bothering with her palm he would kiss her lips instead.

Making Music in Iambic Pentameter

Ellington and his co-composer Billy Strayhorn take this rigid literary form and render it into a rigid musical form that matches it point for point. They vary the mood of the four sonnets, but mood is indicated mainly by the orchestral accompaniment rather than by the sonnet soloists, who obviously have enough to contend with making sure the accents fall on 2 and 4 (the strong iambic syllables), sustaining notes at the end of every second bar (equivalent to the rhyme-words) and raising the range over stop-time and/or suspended chords in the last four bars (bars 25-28), the counterpart of the rhyming couplet.

Playing the music under all these constraints is a challenge even for Ellington's virtuoso soloists, and the tension is clearly audible in all four sonnets. It accounts for a large part of the esthetic delight. The sonnets as Ellington conceives them are small marvels of technical brilliance, atmospheric and eccentric, fresh and somehow unexpected even after numerous listenings. They have delighted generations of listeners whether or not they knew (or cared) about the precision with which Ellington and Strayhorn had transliterated the literary form. Townsend, in his liner note, simply says that "they are scored to coincide with the fourteen-line sonnet form," and lets it go at that. Rightly so. But it surely adds another source of admiraton, an unexpected one, to see how masterfully they succeeded in transposing one art form to another.

"Sonnet in Search of a Moor" features Jimmy Woode on bass playing the melody (trascribed in the illustration below). The bass in the foreground resonates in contrast to the accompaniment made up of upper-register trills from piano and three clarinets (harmoniously played by Jimmy Hamilton, Russell Procope and Harry Carney). The contrast between the plodding bass melody and the trilling background is striking, and the drama increases as the bass line increases its range from quatrain to quatrain. It starts mellow and ends up straining. The complexity of mood was fully intended by Ellington,

Sonnet In Search of a Moor

by Duke Ellington

"Sonnet in Search of a Moor" by Duke Ellington (transcribed by Martin Loomer) with Sonnet cxxviii by William Shakespeare

and he signaled it cleverly in the title (though the ambiguity went unnoticed in Townsend's program notes). As Ellington explained it to Bob Smith, "The sonnet to a Moor was a triple entendre, because you had to decide whether we were talking about Othello [the Moor of Venice], or whether we were talking about love [*amour*], or we were talking about the moors where the three witches were." And the melody carries the "search" motif, starting playfully and darkening as it goes on, an uneasy alternation, not unlike the plays known as 'romances' with their mix of comedy and tragedy.

The perfect concurrence of musical and literary form becomes obvious in a Shakespeare sing-along. In the illustration, "Sonnet in Search of a Moor" transcribes the sonnet melody as played by bassist Jimmy Woode. I have laid Sonnet CXXVIII into the transcription, as if it were the lyric. All of the coincident ingenuities are graphically evident – rhymes and tied notes, full notes (when they occur at all) on two and four, the complexity of the last four bars. Yet, for all its complexities, singing the words of the sonnet while listening to the music is a rote exercise, because the musical transliteration is letter-perfect. In fact, any of Shakespeare's 154 sonnets would fit as lyrics for any of Ellington's four melodies.

I chose "Sonnet in Search of a Moor" for the illustration because would-be 'singers' can sort of place the words of the sonnet on Jimmy Woode's pizzicato notes without getting distracted by melodic leaps. Not that it is easy. Coordinating the rigidities of the literary form to the rigidities of the musical form is a challenge. A truly successful peformance requires memorizing the words and assimilating the music to the point where coordinating them comes naturally. It is, you might think, best left to the professionals.

Happily, there exist authentic professional renditions. The brilliant, smoky-voiced English contralto Cleo Laine and bandleader/arranger Johnny Dankworth put together a program of jazz and pop-influenced renditions of Shakespeare's music, with folksy pieces such as "O Mistress Mine" from *Twelfth Night*, and they included among them two of the Ellington/Strayhorn sonnets mated to Shakespeare sonnets. It is an act of courage by the British musicians, and they succeed in making them into fascinating adjuncts of the Shakespeare suite.

Cleo Laine featuring John Dankworth, *Shakespeare and All That Jazz*
(Fontana CD [1990])

Jazz musicians and musically-literate singers develop a feel for four-bar and eight-bar structures, and for multiples that add up to 12 bars and 32 bars. Ellington's sonnets, as 28-bar constructions organized in two-bar segments, demand a different feel. Ellington assigned the challenge of playing the sonnets to the most astute technicians in his band. "Sonnet to Hank Cinq," its title a glib reference to *Henry V*, the warrior-king who led the British troops against the French army led by Joan of Arc at Orléans, features trombonist Britt Woodman in an astounding performance that requires octave leaps and sudden transitions. "The changes of tempo," Ellington says, "have to do with the changes of pace and the map as a result of wars" (quoted in Townsend's liner notes). It is a performance that other trombone players marvel at and all listeners find startling.

Cleo Laine takes on the challenge of Britt Woodman's virtuoso performance by singing Sonnet XL "Take All My Loves" to his melody. The sonnet is a mournful lament about unrequited love that ends with the mock-hopeful couplet –

> Lascivious grace, in whom all ill will shows,
> Kills me with spite, yet we must not be foes

Laine is up to the challenge. Her performance is as admirable in its way as Woodman's.

At the other extreme, "Sonnet for Caesar" features clarinetist Jimmy Hamilton in an almost motionless line that might be the musical equivalent to a marble bust of the Roman emperor for whom it is named; the drama is supplied by ominous drumbeats (played with open hand by drummer Sam Woodyard) and solemn chords behind Hamilton's decorous line, symbolizing the unrest among the Roman senators leading to assassination while Caesar was oblivious.

The stately melody of "Sonnet for Caesar" poses fewer challenges for Cleo Laine. She sings Sonnet CXLVII "My Love Is As a Fever" to it, which rides on the conceit of unrequited love (again!) as a cause of madness –

> My reason, the physician to my love,
> Angry that his prescriptions are not kept,
> Hath left me....

The lovesick complaint seems ill-suited to the gracious, sober melody, notwithstanding the thud of the drum, perhaps too subtle to be truly ominous. The mismatch of words and music grows more pronounced at the end where the ryhming couplet spews loathing and abhorrence –

> For I have sworn thee fair, and thought thee bright,
> Who art as black as hell, and dark as night.

Cleo Laine, like Caesar, seems oblivious as she sweetly intones this harsh message in her richly modulated voice. Technically, the scansion of Shakespeare's lines melds perfectly with the pulse of Ellington's notes, as promised, notwithstanding their mismatched moods.

Ellington and Strayhorn's fourth sonnet, "Sonnet for Sister Kate," features Quentin Jackson on plunger-muted trombone. It is an appropriately humorous portrait of Katharina, the shrew of *The Taming of the Shrew* (nicknamed "Kate" in the play and in Ellington's title, and also by Cole Porter in his musical comedy *Kiss Me, Kate*). The recording is mildly flawed by a wooden reading of the opening

Caesar in *Julius Caesar*, 1978, costume design by Susan Benson
(Stratford Festival Archives)

lines, in which Jackson is almost audibly counting the beats, and by a minor disruption of the strict metre when he slips in some glisses between beats, probably from force of habit. Brilliant as it is, it deserved another take. Ellington may have recognized that, given the technical challenges of the sonnet form while Jackson was manipulating the slide with his right hand and the plunger with his left, even this masterful trombonist was not likely to make it flawless.

The Parts and the Whole
The thematic gamut of the four sonnets again raises questions about the way they were used in the suite as a whole – or, more to the point, not used. There is one sonnet for each of Shakespeare's four subjects in the plays: history ("Sonnet for Hank Cinq"), tragedy ("Sonnet for Caesar"), comedy ("Sonnet for Sister Kate") and (with a small stretch) romance ("Sonnet in Search of a Moor"). So they could have been deployed, as I said earlier, as interludes for intro-

ducing the musical scenes that emanate from the same subjects. Ellington may have intended them to be used that way and simply lost sight of the grand plan in his haste to finish this project and get onto the next (that being the telecast of *A Drum Is a Woman*, whose importance he grossly overvalued). As it turned out, the sonnets have no structural role in the suite as a whole, and the fact that they cover each of the sub-genres of Shakespeare's plays appears to be merely an accident. While they are good enough on their own to entrance listeners, they could have been used to shape the suite into a more cohesive whole.

Apart from the first and last movements, the declamatory "Such Sweet Thunder" and the synoptic "Circle of Fourths," Ellington did not leave any hints about an order for the parts, and even those two movements were played out of order at the Stratford premiere, the only full performance other than the original LP. In the listing, the order of the movements on the original LP and their order at Stratford is shown beside the titles. There is, obviously, no schema governing it. The left column replaces the anarchic diarray of the original LP and the Stratford premiere by organizing the titles thematically, with one of the sonnets preceding scenes from the same subject, thus imposing a kind of implicit order on the suite, for which they seem so perfectly suited.

thematic order	*original LP order*	*Stratford 1957 order*
OVERTURE		
1. Such Sweet Thunder	1	7
HISTORY		
2. Sonnet for Hank Cinq	3	2
3. Half the Fun	11	unlisted
4. The Telecasters	6	3
COMEDY		
5. Sonnet for Sister Kate	8	8
6. Up and Down, Up and Down	7	9
ROMANCE		
7. Sonnet in Search of a Moor	5	6
8. The Star-Crossed Lovers	9	10

TRAGEDY
9. Sonnet for Caesar	2	1
10. Lady Mac	4	4
11. Madness in Great Ones	10	11

FINALE
12. Circle of Fourths	12	5

In the thematic order, "Sonnet for Hank Cinq" follows the overture and prefaces the history scenes; then "Sonnet for Sister Kate" re-sets the stage, in a sense, for comedy, and so on through romance and tragedy to the finale. In a stage presentation, the linked themes would benefit from spoken transitions. It is easy to imagine Ellington, the most verbal of bandleaders, delivering those with panache. In notes and interviews and the few scattered performances, he devised a patter for many of the parts – about the ragtime in Lady Mac's soul, Othello's "sweet and swinging story," Hamlet's craziness ("in those days crazy didn't mean the same thing it does now"), and so on – that might be cobbled together into an accompanying text that is essentially Ellingtonian.

Incidental Music, Sort of

After the premiere of *Such Sweet Thunder*, Ellington would return to Stratford three more times. The last two, in 1966 and 1968, were performances by the orchestra that were merely stops in their familiar routine of one-night stands. A more auspicious sojourn took place in 1963, five years after the Shakespeare suite, when Ellington was invited to spend some weeks there as composer-in-residence for the purpose of writing incidental music for *Timon of Athens*. It was a gratifying acknowledgement of the special feeling for Ellington that had developed in the gifted Stratford troupe. Though Ellington's score for *Timon of Athens* is minor compared to the sustained brilliance of the suite, it was a small triumph for Ellington and certainly another landmark in the kinship of the Bard and the Bandleader.

As incidental music, it defers appropriately to the onstage action. Billy Strayhorn, Ellington's associate composer on *Timon* as on the Shakespeare suite, said, "*Timon* was different, because Duke didn't have the burden of explaining it musically. He was only accompany-

Duke Ellington at Stratford, 1966, entertaining actors Rosalind Ann Knapp and Martha Henry (Stratford Festival Archives)

ing the action. In *Such Sweet Thunder* we were doing the whole job, but in *Timon* you heard the actors and saw the action" (quoted by Dance). For at least some of the pieces in *Timon*, Ellington developed complete arrangements (as he also did for his Hollywood soundtracks), making stand-alone concert numbers out of the fragmented underscore or, more likely, deriving the fragments from more fully developed pieces. Ellington never recorded *Timon* as an entity, and so the score has to be cobbled together from the best extant performances from various sources. The complete score was belatedly recorded by the Stratford Festival Orchestra when it was revived in a 1993 performance, on the 30th anniversary of its composition (and almost 20 years after Ellington's death).[2] Ellington himself recorded

---

[2] There is also an impressionistic version derived from the Stratford Festival recording released as *Timon of Athens Suite*, by the Lydian Sound Orchestra, arranged and conducted by Riccardo Brazzale (Flex Records CD [1995] Italy).

two pieces with Arthur Fiedler and the Boston Pops Orchestra at Tanglewood in 1965, and three others, in much livelier versions, with his orchestra in a private recording made in New York in 1965 (a stockpile recording, released posthumously).

Timon of Athens is an awkward play, early in the canon and written in collaboration with another young playwright, Thomas Middleton. It is almost episodic, dominated by set pieces (banquets with dancing girls, marching armies, static characters with a lot of posturing, which Ellington, in an inspired stroke, called "skillipoop," as defined below). Director Michael Langham (1919-2011) hoped that Ellington's music would add pizzazz to the play. As with most of Langham's initiatives, it succeeded brilliantly. After its Stratford debut in 1963, Langham took the play with its incidental music to the Chichester Festival in England for a three-week run in 1964. Subsequent performances of *Timon of Athens* at Stratford have usually revived Ellington's incidental music, as in the 1993 revival that resulted in the Festival recording.

Because of the episodic nature of the play, Ellington's titles are largely self-explanatory:

- "Timon of Athens March" marks the triumphal entrance of the millionaire Timon at a banquet at which he will bestow overly generous gifts on all his acquaintances. The grand entrance provides an easy setting for Ellington, though not a jazzy one. He recorded this piece with Arthur Fielder and the Boston Pops Orchestra. In the play, the march returns at the very end when an exiled Athenian marches on Athens and informs the crowd that Timon has died in exile. The narrative distance between these two iterations of the march is vast and defies any sensible attempt at plot summary.
- "Banquet Scene" accompanies the mellow action as Timon's acquaintans, basking in his generosity, flatter him in hopes of stimulating his generosity further. Ellington's score has the feeling of serendipity, which he naturally assigned to his alto saxophonist Johnny Hodges in the studio recording. The various pit bands that later played the score, in Statford and elsewhere, faced the challenge of not only playing Ellington's score but also approximating Hodges's sound and feeling.
- "Love Scene," as played with the Boston Pops orchestra with

Ellington as piano soloist, accompanies the masque and dance after the banquet. As the soundtrack for a love affair, it is uncommonly sprightly, dominated by an ebullient showing from Ellington on piano and his bassist John Lamb and celebrity drummer Louie Bellson. (Ellington also recorded "Love Scene" with his own orchestra along with "Banquet Scene" and Skillipoop" in a fairly standard dance band version with solos by Ray Nance, Lawrence Brown and Johnny Hodges that pays little heed to the *Timon* connection.)

- "Skillipoop" is probably the most successful Ellington composition in the score, certainly linguistically if not musically. "Skillipoop," Ellington delighted in telling his audiences, "is the art of making what you're doing look better than you are supposed to be doing." The music has a sheen to it, a chaleur, a self-conscious elegance. It is bright and restless, borne along by a steady walking bass line that is broken by a drum solo and finally, after a pregnant pause, a blaring discord by the entire band.
- Ellington obviously enjoyed himself in keying music to the onstage action. He was not shy about introducing tried-and-true themes into it. His score includes "Overture: Black and Tan Fantasy," "Dance: Skillipoop/The Mooche," "Compulsive Giving: Creole Love Call," and "Alcibiades' Camp: Ring Dem Bells," invoking melodies that he composed in 1929, 1928, 1927 and 1930. For attentive listeners, slotting in old favorites adds the thrill of recognition to the sometimes puzzling plot twists of Shakespeare and Middleton's play.

With *Timon of Athens*, the Stratford Festival gave Ellington an opportunity to collaborate in a sense with Shakespeare on this early play. The incidental music was a different kind of enterprise, as Strayhorn had noted. Where Ellington had conveyed the drama for *Hamlet* in "Madness in Great Ones" and for *Midsummer Night's Dream* in "Up and Down Up and Down," here he was charged with underlining the narrative thrust in his own genre. The play itself is structurally odd, said by some critics to be "experimental" and by others, perhaps more realistically, to be "unfinished." Ellington's incidental music, neither unfinished nor experimental, definitely gives playgoers another dimension for their enjoyment.

Suite Fragments in the Afterglow

As luck would have it, the Stratford Shakespearean Festival abandoned the music business soon after Ellington premiered the suite there in 1957. The drama business, always their priority, attracted international accolades and soon demanded all the administrative attention. But Ellington's affection for the Stratford Festival was requited. He remained a favorite. After his stint as composer-in-residence, he was invited to Stratford twice more. Three years after *Timon*, in May 1966, Ellington and the orchestra played a concert there. No program survives, but it seems likely that he revived four of the Shakespearean scenes for this concert because they show up in his repertoire when he toured France immediately after. Two years after that, Ellington made his last appearance at Stratford, on 7 July 1968, a Sunday, when he staged a Sacred Concert there.

Either of these concert performances might have provided a glorious opportunity for reviving the Shakespeare suite in its entirety. Apparently Ellington did not see it that way. At Stratford and everywhere else, the Shakespeare suite went unperformed except for isolated pieces that caught Ellington's fancy, if only momentarily. Of the four sonnets, only "Sonnet to Hank Cinq" was ever played in performance after the debut performances in 1957. It remained in the book as a *pièce de résistance* for trombonist Britt Woodman until

Promotion for Ellington's 1968 Stratford concert (and also Van Cliburn's) from a brochure celebrating the history (Stratford Festival Archives)

1960, when he left the band. The other sonnets were ignored, perhaps because they were difficult or perhaps because their lack of swing fit uneasily into the expected fare at one-nighters. Ellington did compose one more sonnet some years later, simply called "Sonnet," for the 1968 *Degas Suite,* Ellington's soundtrack for a documentary that was never completed; trumpeter Willie Cook is the soloist, the music fades after one minute, and it too was never played again.

The scenes fared slightly better. "The Star-Crossed Lovers" was played frequently, and it stayed in the book until 1970, when Johnny Hodges died. "Such Sweet Thunder," with its bumptious rock rhythm, was played regularly until 1960. In the summer of 1966, Ellington revived "Such Sweet Thunder," "Madness in Great Ones" and "Half the Fun" and played them as a sequence with "The Star-Crossed Lovers" for a month or two on a French tour (captured on record, for instance, at Juan les Pins, listed in the Playlist). Though Ellington told his French audiences that he was playing them in response to their requests, the timing makes it likely that they were prepared for Ellington's Statford one-nighter, which took place just before the orchestra left for France.

When he did interpolate one piece or two, at most four, of the 12 movements into his nightly fare, they were not presented as movements at all but isolated numbers, resplendent in their own right and much appreciated by knowledgeable fans, but merely tunes on the playlist for that night. Without context, there was no reason to think of them as a suite.

So the Shakespeare suite, as a suite, did not outlive its Stratford premiere in 1957. All told, it provided Ellington with two concerts – two one-night stands, albeit auspicious ones, one at Town Hall in New York and the other at Ontario's Stratford Shakespearean Festival. And that's all. Of course, looking at it as concert fare unfairly limits its actual life-span. As listening fare, the recorded version has proven to be one of Ellington's most successful recordings, admired by reviewers, popular with listeners beyond the jazz core, and continuously in print since its first release in 1957, over sixty years ago. Its success is not surprising, looking back at the circumstances. It was conceived in a buoyant moment when both the composer and his orchestra were riding a wave of popular and artistic success. The link to Shakespeare gave Ellington lofty themes and rich characters to work with. Clearly, Ellington relished being associated with Shakespeare. We delight in their association too, but in the end we have to wonder if it could have amounted to more. Each piece of the Shakespeare suite is self-fulfilling, brilliantly so. And that, as it stands, is all there is. There is an unfinished air to it. The parts are great but the whole is not greater. Listeners find themselves supplying rationales and themes long after Ellington has snapped his fingers and moved on.

References (page numbers to direct quotations are shown *in italics*)
Berry, Bill. 1999. Notes to *Such Sweet Thunder*. Columbia Legacy [stereo CD reissue]. *p. 16*.
Dance, Stanley. 1970. *The World of Duke Ellington*. London: Macmillan. *p. 28*.
Dance, Stanley. 1992. Liner notes on *The Johnny Hodges All-Stars with the Duke Ellington All-Stars and the Billy Strayhorn All-Stars*. Prestige CD [1992].
George, Don. 1981. *Sweet Man: The Real Duke Ellington*. New York: Putnam's Sons. *p. 136, p. 256*.
Hajdu, David. 1996. *Lush Life: A Biography of Billy Strayhorn*. New York: Farrar Straus Giroux. *pp. 153-154, p. 163*.
Morton, John Fass. 2008. *Backstory in Blue: Ellington at Newport '56*. New Brunswick, NJ, and London: Rutgers University Press. *p. 146*
Rasky, Harry interview, ca. 29 April 1957, New York City. Broadcast CBC radio 15 May 1957.
Smith, Bob interview, Georgian Towers Hotel, Vancouver. Broadcast on "Hot Air," CBC radio (Vancouver), 1 November 1962.
Townsend, Irving. 1960. "When Duke records." Reprinted in Mark Tucker, ed., *The Duke Ellington Reader*. New York: Oxford University Press. *p. 320, p. 321*.
Townsend, Irving. 1957. Notes to *Such Sweet Thunder*. Columbia Records. Reprinted in Columbia Legacy CD [1999]
Tucker, Mark. 1991. *Ellington: The Early Years*. Oxford: Bayou Press. *p. 25*.
Unsigned [Carter Harman and others]. "Mood Indigo & Beyond." *Time* [cover story]. 20 August 1956. Reproduced in *Annual Review of Jazz Studies* 6 (1993): 54-64. *p. 64*.

Playlist (in order of appearance in the chapter)

"The Happening" 2:38 (comp Paul Gonsalves) NYC, 19 June 1951. *The Johnny Hodges All-Stars with the Duke Ellington All-Stars and the Billy Strayhorn All-Stars*. Prestige CD [1992].
Juan Tizol tb, Willie Smith as, Jimmy Hamilton cl, Duke Ellington p, Wendell Marshall b, Louie Bellson d.

"Diminuendo in Blue and Crescendo in Blue" 14:20. Freebody Park, Newport, R.I. 7-8 July 1956. *Ellington at Newport Complete* (Columbia Records 2 CD [1999]).
Cat Anderson, Willie Cook, Ray Nance, Clark Terry tp; Quentin Jackson, Britt Woodman, John Sanders tb; Harry Carney, Paul Gonsalves, Jimmy Hamilton, Johnny Hodges, Russell Procope reeds; Duke Ellington p, Jimmy Woode b, Sam Woodyard d.

"Hark, the Duke's Trumpets" 3:03 (Ellington) *Live at the 1957* [sic] *Stratford Festival* (Music & Arts CD-616) 18 July 1956.
Cat Anderson, Willie Cook, Ray Nance, Clark Terry tp; Quentin Jackson, John Sanders, Britt Woodman tb; Jimmy Hamilton cl, ts, Paul Gonsalves ts, Johnny Hodges as, Russell Procope cl, as, Harry Carney cl, bs; Duke Ellington p, Jimmy Woode b, Sam Woodyard d.
Solos: Jimmy Woode

"Lately" 4:08 (= "Half the Fun," alternative take, Ellington/Strayhorn) *Such Sweet Thunder* (Columbia Legacy CD [1999]) Columbia 30th Street Studios, 7 August 1956.
Cat Anderson, Willie Cook, Ray Nance, Clark Terry tp; Quentin Jackson, John Sanders, Britt Woodman tb; Jimmy Hamilton cl, ts, Paul Gonsalves ts, Johnny Hodges as, Russell Procope cl, as, Harry Carney cl, bs; Duke Ellington p, Jimmy Woode b, Sam Woodyard d.
Solo: Johnny Hodges

"Pretty Girl" 8:54 (= "The Star-Crossed Lovers" rehearsal, Strayhorn) Same as "Lately" except 6 December 1956. Solo: Johnny Hodges

"The Star-Crossed Lovers" 4:00 (Strayhorn) Same as "Lately" except 3 May 1957. Solo: Johnny Hodges

"Madness in Great Ones" 3:26 (Ellington/Strayhorn) Same as "The Star-Crossed Lovers." Solo: Cat Anderson

"Up and Down Up and Down (I Will Lead Them Up and Down)" 3:09 (Ellington/Strayhorn). Same as "The Star-Crossed Lovers" except 24 April 1957. Solos: Clark Terry, Jimmy Hamilton cl/Ray Nance violin

"Such Sweet Thunder" 3:22 (Ellington) Same as "Up and Down Up and Down." Solo: Ray Nance tp

"Half the Fun" 4:19 (Ellington/Strayhorn). Same as "Lately."
Solo: Johnny Hodges

"The Telecasters" 3:05 (Ellington/Strayhorn). Same as "Madness in Great Ones." Solos: Harry Carney, and trombone section

"Circle of Fourths" 1:45 (Ellington/Strayhorn). Same as "Madness in Great Ones." Solo: Paul Gonsalves

"Lady Mac" 3:41 (Ellington/Strayhorn) Same as "Up and Down Up and Down"). Solos: Duke Ellington. Russell Procope as, Clark Terry

Hamlet's soliloquy ("To be or not to be"/"Essere non essere") 3:05 (Shakespeare). Vittorio Gassman, recitation in Italian translation except last lines, with piano variations on "Such Sweet Thunder" by Duke Ellington. Backstage in Milan, 30 January 1966. DEMS souvenir tape 1987, compiled by Sjef Hoefsmit. <https://www.linkiesta.it/it/blog-post/2012/04/06/quando-gassman-duettava-in-tv-con-duke-ellington/5378/

"Sonnet in Search of a Moor" 2:22 (Ellington/Strayhorn) *Such Sweet Thunder* (Columbia Legacy CD [1999]) Columbia 30th Street Studios, 15 April 1957.
Cat Anderson, Willie Cook, Ray Nance, Clark Terry tp; Quentin Jackson, John Sanders, Britt Woodman tb; Jimmy Hamilton cl, ts, Paul Gonsalves ts, Johnny Hodges as, Russell Procope cl, as, Harry Carney cl, bs; Duke Ellington p, Jimmy Woode b, Sam Woodyard d.
Solo: Jimmy Woode

"Sonnet for Hank Cinq" 1:24 Same as "Sonnet in Search of a Moor" except 3 May 1957. Solo: Britt Woodman

"Take All My Loves" Sonnet XL. 1:20 (Ellington/Strayhorn, Shakespeare, arr Dankworth) Cleo Laine featuring John Dankworth, *Shakespeare and All That Jazz* (Fontana CD [1990]) London, March 1964
Ken Wheeler horn, John Dankworth cl, Alan Branscombe p,
Ray Dempsey gtr, Alan Ganley d, Cleo Laine voc
Solo: Cleo Laine

"Sonnet for Caesar" 3:00 Same as "Sonnet in Search of a Moor."
Solo: Jimmy Hamilton

"My Love Is As a Fever" Sonnet CXLVII. 2:23 (Ellington/Strayhorn, Shakespeare, arr Dankworth) Cleo Laine featuring John Dankworth, *Shakespeare and All That Jazz* (Fontana CD [1990]) London, March 1964. Ken Wheeler, Leon Calvert tp; Tony Russell tb; Ron Snyder tuba; John Dankworth cl, Al Newman fl, cl, bs, Vic Ash cl, ts, Alan Branscombe

as, cl, vibes; Maria Kochinska harp, Ken Napper b, Johnny Butts d, Cleo Laine voc
Solo: Cleo Laine

"Sonnet for Sister Kate" 2:24 Same as "Sonnet in Search of a Moor."
Solo: Quentin Jackson

"Timon of Athens March" 3:09 (Ellington). CD2 of *Live and Rare*, Bluebird [3 CD, 2002]. Tanglewood Music Center, Lenox, Massachusetts, 28 July 1965.
Duke Ellington p, John Lamb b, Louie Bellson d, with Arthur Fielder and the Boston Pops Orchestra. Richard Hayman, arr.

"Banquet Scene" 2:20 (Ellington) *Private Collection*, Vol. 8 (WEA 55924 [1989]). New York, 17 March 1965. Private Collection, Vol. 8.
Howard McGhee, Cat Anderson, Herbie Jones, Ray Nance tp; Lawrence Brown, Buster Cooper, Chuck Connors tb; Johnny Hodges as, Russell Procope as, cl, Jimmy Hamilton cl, ts, Paul Gonsalves ts, Harry Carney cl, bass cl, bs; Duke Ellington p, John Lamb b, Sam Woodyard d
Solo: Johnny Hodges.

"Love Scene" 2:24 (Ellington-Strayhorn). Same as "Timon of Athens March" above.

"Skillipoop" 2:00 (Ellington). Same as "Banquet Scene" above.
Solos: John Lamb/Jimmy Hamilton, Sam Woodyard

"Overture: Black and Tan Fantasy" 2:58, "Dance: Skillipoop/ The Mooche" 3:27, "Compulsive Giving: Creole Love Call" 3:40, and "Alcibiades' Camp: Ring Dem Bells" 1:01. *Duke Ellington's Timon of Athens*, Musicians of the Stratford Festival (Varèse Saraband CD, 1993), Waxworks Studio, St. Jacobs, Ontario, Canada. James Ford tp; Jerry Johnson tb; Derek Conrod, Heather Wootton Fr horn; Ian Harper fl, cl, as, ts; Gary Kidd cl, bass cl, ts; Donna-Claire Chiasson oboe, English horn; Christopher Chiasson vln; Patricia Mullen cello; Arthur Lang b; Laura Burton p, synthesizer; Terry McKenna g, banjo; Michael Wood perc; adapted and conducted by Stanley Silverman .

"Sonnet" 1:08 (Ellington) Degas Suite, on *The Suites: Private Collection*, Vol. 5 (WEA 55402 [1987]). New York, 6 November 1968.
Willie Cook tp, Chuck Connors tb. Johnny Hodges as, Russell Procope as, cl, Paul Gonsalves ts, Harold Ashby ts, Duke Ellington p, Jeff Castleman b, Rufus Jones d
Solo: Willie Cook

"Such Sweet Thunder" 3:58, "Half the Fun" 5:03, "Madness in Great Ones" 6:00, and "The Star-Crossed Lovers" 4:46. *Passion Flower*

(Moon 074 CD [1995]) Juan les Pins, France, 27 July 1966. Cootie Williams, Cat Anderson, Herbie Jones, Mercer Ellington tp; Lawrence Brown, Buster Cooper, Chuck Connors tb; Johnny Hodges as, Russell Procope as, cl, Jimmy Hamilton cl, ts, Paul Gonsalves ts, Harry Carney cl, bass cl, bs; Duke Ellington p, John Lamb b, Sam Woodyard d

Sweet Thunder

CHAPTER 7

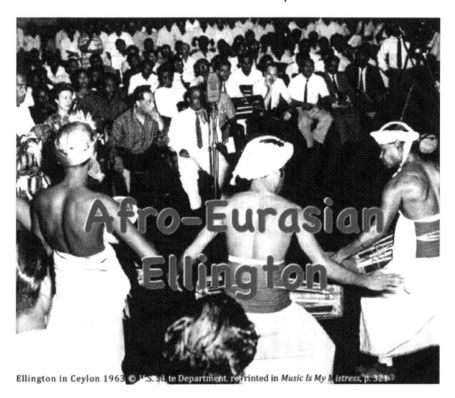

Afro-Eurasian Ellington

Ellington in Ceylon 1963 © U.S. State Department, reprinted in *Music Is My Mistress*, p. 321

Duke Ellington relished change. In 1967, decades after his first hits, he told a reporter for *Time* magazine, "We could've gone on for 50 years playing the old things and saying, 'This is our noise, baby.' But it's a form of condescension, the worst of all artistic offences" (quoted by Cohen, p. 511). He was then 68, and great changes were happening all around him. He had always been, as Barry Ulanov put it, "a teller of tales, three minutes or thirty. He has never failed to take compass points, wherever he has been, in a new city, a new country, a redecorated nightclub, to make his own observations and to translate these… into fanciful narratives." That was true when his world comprised Harlem and Hollywood and points between. Now, in his sixties, his far-flung travels exposed him to unfamiliar worlds that dazzled him. The most exotic sights came to him in a 10-week tour of the Near and Middle East sponsored by the U.S. State Department in the autumn of 1963, The tour took him to Amman (Jordan), Kabul (Afghanistan), New Delhi (India), Colombo (Ceylon, now Sri Lanka), Tehran (Iran), Madras (now Chennai, India), Bombay (now Mumbai, India), Baghdad (Iraq), and Ankara (Turkey). (Concerts in five more cities were canceled when the orchestra was abruptly flown home after the assassination of President John F. Kennedy in Dallas, Texas.) Ellington's state-sponsored tour, like the state-sponsored tours of Louis Armstrong and other jazz musicians in the early 1960s, was a blatant attempt by the U.S. government to counteract Soviet charges of American persecution of their African-American citizens.[1] Ellington, characteristically, blinked at the political overtones and luxuriated in the first-class treatment of his musicians, the regimen of playing three or four concerts a week instead of seven or eight, and the lavish hospitality in the embassies, in theaters great and small, and on the streets.

"The tour was a great adventure for us on what is indeed the other side of the world," Ellington wrote on his return. "Sometimes I felt it was this world upside down. The look of the natural country is so unlike ours and the very contours of the earth seem to be different. The smell, the vastness, the birds, and the exotic beauty of all these countries make a great impression" (Ellington, "Orientations"). Ellington's sensations naturally found their way into his music, starting with the *Far East Suite* (1966) and persisting as an Afro-Eurasian thematic thread in his music from then on.

Seeping Impressions of the East

Inspiring as the indigenous music was for him, Ellington had no interest in imitating the music that he heard in the Middle East or importing their musical devices. "The minute you become academic about it you are going to fall into the trap of copying many other people who have tried to give a reflection of the music," he said. Instead, he would conceptualize the music in his own terms, and his

---

[1] In "Orientations," Ellington wrote, "At the press conferences... I always told them that the Negro has a tremendous investment in *our* country. We have helped to build it, and we have invested blood in every war the country has fought." Without denying the issue, he denied its propaganda value. "It must be remembered," he told the foreign press, "that this is not an international issue but a national one."

rationale for doing so stands as a succinct statement of the esthetic principle that stood him in good stead throughout his career. About the exotic rhythms and the scales, he said, "It's more valuable to have absorbed them while there. You let it roll around, undergo a chemical change, and then seep out on paper in the form that will suit the musicians who are going to play it." The gestation period for Ellington and Billy Strayhorn, his co-composer of the *Far East Suite*, took more than three years, until December 1966, when they recorded the music as a suite of nine movements.

The second movement, "Bluebird of Delhi (Mynah)," makes a simple illustration of the way Ellington and Strayhorn transmuted their eastern experience. The trumpeter Rolf Ericson said, "Ellington and Strayhorn were very observant with what was going on around them. I remember once when we were sitting at a café in Hyderabad in India and a bird was twittering in a bush. Strayhorn said to Duke, 'Hey, you hear that?' The bird was twittering something and they pulled out a piece of paper and wrote it down. That became the idea to the *Far East Suite*" (Westin interview). "Bluebird of Delhi (Mynah)" is built around a two-bar trill played on clarinet by Jimmy Hamilton. Out of context, this short melodic figure seems a bit effete – a staccato run up and down the scale. The trill, Ellington tells us, imitates "the pretty lick" sung by a mynah bird. Tellingly, not *any* mynah bird but a particular mynah bird. "He sang [the pretty lick] all the time Billy Strayhorn was in his room," Ellington says, and in fact it "was the only answer the bird ever made to Strayhorn's repeated efforts at conversation throughout his stay" (Dance liner). From this germ of melody, a modest starting point by any standard, the mynah's repeated call becomes the decorative foreground for the busy, bustling orchestration that surrounds it and gives it substance. Like the teeming city that surrounded the elegant mynah bird and was its habitat, the orchestration is dense but somehow supple, weighty but sprightly, indeed toe-tapping.

Another movement, the unpronounceable (and unexplained) "Depk," brings the busy, bustling background of "Bluebird of Delhi" into the foreground. It was inspired, Ellington said, by "a wonderful dance by six boys and six girls" at one of the stops along the way. Not that the music resembles the dance in any way. By the time he got

Duke Ellington and Harry Carney study a young sitar player in India, 1963
(U.S. State Department, reprinted in *Music Is My Mistress*, p. 313)

around to writing it, Ellington says, "All I could remember afterwards was the kick on the sixth beat" (Dance liner). That kick on the sixth beat is what Ellington "absorbed" of the dance, and "Depk" is the tune that seeped out onto Ellington and Strayhorn's manuscript. Notwithstanding its putative origin as a dance, "Depk" would pose a real challenge for any choreographer. It proves well suited, however, as a platform for inspired solos by Jimmy Hamilton on clarinet and Harry Carney on baritone saxophone. The East inspired it, but it is the East with Ellington and his men in the middle of it.

The Truly *Far* East

When the *Far East Suite* was released, reviewers could hardly resist commenting that most of the music (and all but one of the locales of the tour that called it forth) belonged not to the Far East but to the Middle East and Near East. The one exception in the music was a long, suite-like concoction called "Ad Lib on Nippon." Nippon, the name that the Japanese call their country, is the only movement out of nine that is truly set in the Far East. (Regardless of the geography, it is hard to imagine Ellington choosing "near" East or "middle" East as his title; they somehow diminish the exotic impression, whereas the "far" in Far East conjures up something more to Ellington's taste, that is, something far-fetched, a far cry, far out.) Ellington and the orchestra had visited Japan for the first time in 1964, the year after the Middle East tour.

"Ad Lib on Nippon" is a kind of pastiche. Its unusual length (over 11 minutes) comes from its merger of four distinct parts, and its strength comes from their seamless merging, a credit not only to Ellington as orchestrator but to his virtuoso musicians who negotiate the transitions with uncanny ease. Three of the four parts focus on Ellington's piano and the last, the climactic part, on Jimmy Hamilton's clarinet –

> *Part 1* (to 2:54) piano, bass and drums playing a melody Ellington wrote for an American Airlines commercial
> *Part 2* (2:26 in length, 2:54 to 5:20 sometimes called "Igoo") double tempo, piano trio and then orchestra
> *Part 3* (2:14 in length, 5:20 to 7:34) piano solo with arco bass
> *Part 4* (4:00 in length, 7:34 to the end, sometimes called "Tokyo") Hamilton clarinet, then orchestra, then Hamilton with rhythm section, and orchestrated finale from 10:10 to 11:34

Knowing that three of the four parts were prefabricated (the American Airlines jingle and the themes known independently as "Igoo" and "Tokyo") might lead one to think that "Ad Lib on Nippon" came into being as an addendum to give the *Far East Suite* suitable length for the long-play record on which it was first issued; indeed, circumstantial evidence makes that inference eminently credible. Even so, it is a coup for Ellington because it coheres as a piece of music. Both on the record and in its many live performances, critics and audiences relished its rousing spirit. And as we credit Ellington for making it coherent, we must also recognize the role of Jimmy Hamilton. Though Ellington is given sole composer credit, Jimmy Hamilton later reported that he was the composer and orchestrator of Part 4, which he titled "Tokyo." In 1991, 25 years after the recording of "Ad Lib on Nippon," Hamilton told a Smithsonian archivist, "I wrote it, I composed it, I arranged it, and Duke collaborated by adding to it."

Ellington's additions, to be fair, including the orchestrated finale as well as the piano sections, trebled its length, and almost certainly include his tweaking of Hamilton's original orchestrations. A few years after his Smithsonian interview, with his memory less firm, Hamilton was ready to take credit for the whole composition and not just the "Tokyo" segment. "That 'Ad Lib on Nippon', that's mine," he told the interviewer. "I composed that, and I did the arrangement for the band.... It was a matter of me writing me a solo, some melody to play and then showcasing it with an arrangement so that I would stand out. It went over good. It went over quite good. But he never give me credit for it."

By the time Hamilton staked his claim, Ellington was not available to respond one way or the other. He almost certainly would have said nothing anyway. Ellington famously made many of his compositions from a glimmering of melody played by his musicians. He enveloped those hints into compositions, and he expected the musicians to add nuances and fills in their performances. From the start, the collective process raised questions about authorship and accreditation. Many of Ellington's works do indeed list one of his musicians as co-composer, and many more do not. Ellington walked a fine line, though it must be said he walked it with great self-assurance. He said little about it, certainly nothing more revealing than the wonderful line in the Ellington esthetic quoted above: "You let it roll around, undergo a chemical change, and then seep out on paper in the form that will suit the musicians who are going to play it." It fell to Billy Strayhorn to address the issue more specifically. "Something like a solo, perhaps only a few notes, is hardly a composition," Strayhorn told Bill Coss. "So this guy [who played those notes]... thinks he wrote it. He thinks you just put it down on paper. But what you did was put it down on paper, harmonized it, straightened out the bad phrases, and added things to it, so you could hear the finished product. Now, really, who wrote it?... The proof is that these people don't go somewhere else and write beautiful music. You don't hear anything else from them. You do from Ellington."

The Global Village
As Ellington's travels became global, he became acutely conscious of

the shrinking of the planet. People in exotic places like Senegal, where he performed at the Negro Arts Festival in 1966, when he got to meet them face-to-face, melded into a common humanity. "After writing African music for thirty-five years, here I am at last in Africa!" he said, upon discovering that his music evoked a response in Dakar no different from the response in, say, Detroit or Davenport. "We get the usual diplomatic applause from the diplomatic corps down front, but the cats in the bleachers really dig it.... It gives us a once-in-a-lifetime feeling of having truly broken through to our brothers."

Ellington's encounters with the shrinking planet coincided perfectly with the thinking of a momentarily fashionable professor of English literature, Marshall McLuhan, whose musings on mass media and telecommunications in *Understanding Media* (1964) and other books were a revelation at the time. McLuhan had an epigrammatic bent, spinning out maxims such as "the medium is the message," and "art is anything you can get away with," and "there are no passengers on planet earth, we are all crew." The maxims were mostly inscrutable but in their moment of currency they traveled very well. In the hip 1960s they resonated as smartly anarchic. (With guile worthy of Ellington himself, McLuhan frequently told interviewers, "I don't necessarily agree with everything I say.") McLuhan presented a conception of the world as a "global village," and in that concept Duke Ellington recognized a kindred spirit.

McLuhan inspired the title of Ellington's *Afro-Eurasian Eclipse*, a 1971 suite in eight movements. It opens with a long composition called "Chinoiserie," a perfect title for Ellington's slant on the Orient. The French loanword *chinoiserie*, literally 'Chinese-like', came into being as the name for the westernized adaptation of Chinese decoration, and Ellington's conception, as the word implies, is predictably as much Ellington as Orient. Ellington concocted a wry spoken introduction to the suite that took up a minute-and-a half at performances. In his most studious tone, he explained the inspiration for the title:

> "This is really the chinoiserie. Last year about this time we premiered a new suite entitled *Afro-Eurasian Eclipse*. And of course the title was inspired by a statement made by Mr. Marshall McLuhan of the

University of Toronto. Mr. McLuhan says that the whole world is going oriental, and that no one will be able to retain his or her identity, not even the orientals. And of course we travel around the world a lot, and in the last five or six years we, too, have noticed this thing to be true. So as a result, we have done a sort of thing, a parallel or something, and we'd like to play a little piece of it for you.

"In this particular segment, ladies and gentlemen, we have adjusted our perspective to that of the kangaroo and the didjeridoo. This automatically throws us either Down Under and/or Out Back. And from that point of view it's most improbable that anyone will ever know exactly who is enjoying the shadow of whom.

"Harold Ashby has been inducted into the responsibility and the obligation of possibly scraping off a tiny bit of the charisma off the chinoiserie, immediately after our piano player has completed his rikki-tikki."

As promised, Ellington's piano opens the piece in a style well described by his phrase "rikki-tikki," for less than a minute (0:45, from

Rolf Ericson, the Swedish trumpet player in Ellington's orchestra for the Middle East tour, with a didjeridoo

(courtesy Lars Westin, *Orkester Journalen*, and Duke Ellington Society of Sweden)

1:39 to 2:24 following the spoken introduction). It is followed by a ravishing alto saxophone duet played by Russell Procope and Johnny Hodges, a 30-second masterpiece (2:24 to 2:54) that is one of those sonic marvels that only Ellington could write; attentive listeners will wish that it were much longer. Then comes the orchestra, dense and brooding, and then the promised soloist (at 3:24 for four-and-a-half minutes), tenor saxophonist Harold Ashby, "scraping a bit of the charisma off the chinoiserie," as Ellington puts it, in his most faithful replication of his mentor Ben Webster. In both the spoken introduction and the music, "Chinoiserie" provides a rousing opening for the suite.

Strangely, in his spoken introduction Ellington intermingles comments about the second movement of the *Afro-Eurasian Eclipse* as wellas about the opener "Chinoiserie." Ellington's middle paragraph (above), with its references to Down Under and the Outback, obviously points to Australia, the world of "the kangaroo and the didjeridoo." In fact, the second movement of *Afro-Eurasian Eclipse* is called "Didjeridoo," named for the long, tubular horn played by Aborigines that Ellington was serenaded with on his tour of Australia in 1972 (his second-last stop on a Pacific tour of Japan, Taiwan, Philippines, Hong Kong, Thailand, Myanmar [then known as Burma], Malaysia, Indonesia, Singapore, New Zealand, Australia and Hawaii; in Hong Kong, all the junks were "motor-powered," Ellington says, "which confirms the views of Marshall McLuhan"). The basso profundo tone of the didjeridoo inspired Ellington to compose a feature for Harry Carney's baritone saxophone, played austerely in its lowest reaches throughout. Ellington strives to convey the aboriginal feel with a boogaloo beat and insistent rhythmic splashes by the piano and horns. Carney's low grumble underpins the whole composition until he finally emerges from the didjeridoo depths with a final cadenza that shows off his unequalled elegance on the big saxophone.

An African Stamp of Approval
Ellington's Afro-Eurasian impulse was further quickened in 1967 when he was honored with a postage stamp by the Togolese Republic, the small West African state sandwiched between Ghana and Benin.

Ellington's stamp was one of four commemorating composers, and he found himself in good company with Bach, Beethoven and Debussy. Soon after, he began performing new compositions that he introduced as parts of his *Togo Brava Suite*. He told audiences, "Our humble suite is just a token of gratitude and appreciation." In concerts, he performed the suite in four parts but posthumous releases from the stockpile (discussed in the next chapter) contain three other movements making seven in all (released in 2001 by Storyville Records). The uncertainty surrounding *Togo Brava Suite* is one more casualty of Ellington's hectic schedule in these last years. Self-imposed though the schedule was, the convergence of sacred concerts, commissions of all kinds, incessant travel for fly-by-night concerts and much more meant that several worthy projects were left in varying states of near completion (as we will see in Chapter 9).

When the seven parts of *Togo Brava Suite* were finally collated, listeners discovered that Ellington had imbued the suite with a kind of serenity that was distinctly different from his more energetic, typically restless, bottom-heavy approaches to his other African dedications, and indeed to most of the other Afro-Eurasian outposts that caught his musical fancy. He never visited Togo, and his impressions of it were formed by hearsay from dignitaries and travelers and undoubtedly from travel writers. The serenity of the suite had a straightforward interpretation in the opening movement, which is called "Soul-Soothing Beach," a reference to what tourist guidebooks

Togo postage stamp commemorating Duke Ellington, 1967. Other stamps in the same issue commemorated Bach, Beethoven and Debussy

such as *The Lonely Planet* call "palm-fringed beaches along the Atlantic coastline," one of Togo's main attractions.

Ellington's "Soul-Soothing Beach" does indeed soothe the soul, notably by assigning harmonic prominence to the trombone section. Over the lush background blend of the three trombones, Ellington solos on piano with unhurried flourishes and then turns over the foreground to Norris Turney on flute. Until this moment, the sound of the flute was unfamiliar in Ellington's music, but it is suddenly elevated as the principal solo instrument in *Togo Brava Suite*. Norris Turney joined the orchestra primarily as an alto saxophone player. He was versatile, and in addition to alto saxophone his horn selection included clarinet, as expected, tenor saxophone, and also, for the first time in Ellington's sound scheme, flute. Ellington's newly-discovered affection for Norris Turney's deft intonation on the elegant transverse horn may be the root cause of the delicacy of so many of the movements.

That delicacy is dramatically illustrated in a movement of the *Togo Brava Suite* known as "Toto." As it happens, "Toto" recycles the theme of the composition called "Afrique" from the *Afro-Eurasian Eclipse*. Listening to the two thematically-related compositions in succession illustrates the contrast between these two Afro-Eurasian suites with stunning directness. The contrast, I admit, is exacerbated by choosing perhaps the most bullish recording of "Afrique" among the many that Ellington recorded. This one was recorded in Cologne, Germany, in a private session with an ambitious, young engineer named Conny Plank, who would go on to make his name in something called "1980s synthpop" (the term used by annotator Henrik von Holtum in the German release of "Afrique"). Ellington, finding himself in Cologne with an infrequent off-day for the band, booked a small studio for the day. Conny Plank, the sound engineer, was just getting started in the profession, but he certainly shows his craftsmanship in this impromptu one-time encounter with the Ellington orchestra. "Afrique" is a complex, roiling big-band shout, and in the Cologne studio the sound is perfectly balanced, a notable achievement that the young engineer credits to Ellington's inspiration. "Conny was fascinated by how great the difference in tone was between his prior studio work and these takes," the annotator says.

"The Ellington big band was delivering something totally different."

The crowning achievement is the third complete take of "Afrique" made on that day, and it uniquely integrates the ornamental soprano voice of Lena Junoff into the ensembles, adding further panache to the performance.[2] The heady orchestration is wafted along from start to finish by Rufus Jones's energetic drum work.

Admittedly, almost any other performance might come out sounding quiescent after one hears this rendition of "Afrique." The value in considering "Toto (Afrique)" from *Togo Brava Suite* alongside "Afrique" from *Afro-Eurasian Eclipse* is not to expose "Toto" as a pallid reflection of "Afrique" but to demonstrate how Ellington can manipulate the same melodic content to create an entirely different mood. "Toto," like "Soul-Soothing Beach," is relatively relaxed. Though still exotic, its movement is sinuous rather than driving. The orchestral textures are relatively spare, dance-like. Instead of the drums providing the rock-steady undertow as in "Afrique," they assume the more familiar accompanying role, supporting Ellington's piano, Joe Benjamin's bass and, once again, Norris Turney's flute.

Eddie Lambert, the most comprehensive reviewer of Ellington's music, sees his latter-day Afro-Eurasian impulse as a kind of throwback to his beginnings. Ellington, he says, is "re-asserting an aspect of his musical character which had been dormant for much of the time he worked with Strayhorn. The music of … *The Afro-Eurasian Eclipse* relates to the menacing music of Ellington's first period such as *Black and Tan Fantasy* and *The Mooche*. Had Ellington been a time traveler," says Lambert, "*Afrique* would have been a wholly acceptable substitute for *Jungle Nights in Harlem* as a background for a Cotton Club dance routine."

Presumably he would not have made the same claim for

---

2 Ellington added Lena Junoff to his entourage on the 1970 European tour and she remained with him on their return to the United States. She recorded with Ellington at the Rainbow Grill, New York City, in August. According to a website (http://monolover.blogspot.ca/2014/06/johnny-bodebordellmammas-dotter-plp-102.html): "She was a rising Swedish star in the sixties – a pretty girl with an amazing voice, reaching over five octaves. … [She was] spotted by Duke Ellington who brought her to America as vocalist for his band. For some reason it didn't work out and she left after just a few months. I've seen theories it failed either because of her reputedly hot temper, drug abuse or the fact that she participated in porn movies."

"Afrique"'s fraternal twin sister "Toto," or for *Togo Brava Suite* in general (which unfortunately he never got to hear in full). Afro-Eurasian Ellington runs the gamut from "menacing" (Lambert's term) to "soul-soothing" (Ellington's term).

Soul Flute – An Intimate Interlude

Norris Turney, the main solo voice on *Togo Brava Suite*, joined Duke Ellington's orchestra in May 1969, when he was 48, as a temporary replacement for Johnny Hodges who was having health problems. Before that, Turney had shuttled back and forth between his native Ohio and New York City, an itinerant musician finding work with various bands. Surprisingly, when Hodges returned, Ellington kept Turney in the band. Under ordinary circumstances, that would have overloaded the alto saxophone allotment with the veterans Russell Procope and Hodges already there, but Turney was a master of the tenor saxophone as well. Indeed, Turney's versatility led to a real oddity in the annals of the Ellington orchestra (or any other): after he became the extra man in the band the trombone player Booty Wood injured his hand and could not play; Turney sat in the trombone section playing trombone parts on his tenor saxophone. Then when Johnny Hodges died in May 1970, Turney naturally moved into the saxophone section and took over his alto saxophone parts. His role included occasional ensemble turns on clarinet, as it had for Hodges, but with Turney there was another nuance. For the first and only time, Ellington had three tenor saxophone players. At almost every concert he asked Turney to pick up his tenor saxophone, warm up the reed, and step onto the proscenium and perform in a trio alongside the other tenor saxophonists Paul Gonsalves and Harold Ashby (as discussed in Chapter 2, "The Fifth Reed"). The music they made was energetic at best but they provided a visual spectacle that audiences took home with them.

At some point in Turney's first year in the band, Ellington discovered that he was also adept on the flute. How this happened is hard to guess because there were absolutely no flute parts in any music ever written by Ellington before 1969. As Stanley Dance said (in his note to the *Third Sacred Concert*), "Ellington, with his strong likes and dislikes where tone color was concerned, long resisted the use of flute in his orchestra." Elsewhere, Dance claimed that Turney's "expertise on flute had partly overcome Ellington's preference for the clarinet." His arrival in the band, by luck or design, came soon after the retirement of clarinet soloist Jimmy Hamilton.

Ellington's infatuation with Turney's flute from 1970 onward was akin to his enthusiasm for the tenor saxophone from 1940 onward after resisting it for so many years (as discussed in Chapter 2). In any case, by the time Ellington was composing *Togo Brava Suite* in 1971, Turney's flute had risen in his esteem to the point at which it became the principal solo instrument. In keeping with his Afro-Eurasian zeal, Ellington may have regarded the flute as the conservatory descendant of all kinds of Afro-Eurasian pipes and kazoos and whistles. In any event, its rise coincides with the ascendance of the Afro-Eurasian theme in Ellington's music. But Ellington soon found himself exploiting it in contexts that went beyond the Afro-Eurasian theme.

Among the flute specialties that came to light posthumously (including the full *Togo Brava Suite*) are a few minor delights. "Soul Flute" was a showcase for Turney that was played regularly in live performances. At a concert in Bristol, England (not coincidentally, a concert that featured four parts of the nascent *Togo Brava Suite* as well) Ellington entrusted six solo choruses to Turney on "Soul Flute," the kind of homage that in days of yore he reserved for such stalwarts as Johnny Hodges and Cootie Williams. The composition itself is a simple blues with a rock rhythm, and Turney is given plenty of freedom to show off his prowess.

Ellington's growing feeling for the flute also shows in a studio recording in which he reduces the band to a quintet in order to highlight the magnificently contrasting timbres of Turney's soaring flute and Harry Carney's bass clarinet. The minimalist arrangement, called "Intimate Interlude," is an unhurried lope characteristic of the music Ellington liked to play at the end of recording sessions. It may have originated as a kind of trial run so that Ellington could gauge the mettle of his soloist on the new instrument that he was absorbing into his musical palette.

Sad to say, this late-career kinship between the Maestro and his flutist ended on a sour note. According to Mercer Ellington, Turney went to Ellington sometime in 1972 when he had been in the band for three years, and told him he thought Ellington was setting the tempo too fast on one of his features. Ellington returned a blank stare. Turney, obviously unknowingly, had crossed a line. In Ellington's view, Turney was, Ellington's son says, "defying his authority." From that day on, Ellington deliberately increased the tempo every time he called the number. For a while, Turney simply put up with it rather than offering an apology or otherwise backing down. After several months, in the middle of the feature at the Persian Room in the Marco Polo Hotel in Miami Beach on 1 February 1973, Turney quietly packed up his horns and walked off the bandstand for good. Ellington had invited this ending. His feeling for the flute did not disappear with the flutist. After Turney left, Ellington turned over the flute parts to Harold "Geezil" Minerve, an alto saxophonist who had joined the band in 1971. As for Turney, it turned out well enough. He found himself in some demand after he left, playing regularly in good company and making his first recordings as a leader. (He died in 2001 at 80.) After laboring in relative obscurity for more than two decades, he had bloomed in his four years under Ellington's tutelage. He brought a unique sound to Ellington's palette, and as a result he felt the glow of the Ellington spotlight as well as, blessedly, its afterglow. It is, in the scheme of things, Turney's legacy.

Afro-Eurasian Ellington is still Ellington
Afro-Eurasian Ellington came as a surprise after 40-odd years of music-making. It is actually just one more surprise from a composer who never stood still for long. The epitome of Afro-Eurasian Ellington, for me at least, is his composition "Blue Pepper (Far East of the Blues)." Though it is placed near the middle of *The Far East Suite*, it is hardly unobtrusive. The pushy rhythms and brassy repetitious riffs in "Blue Pepper" could accompany belly-dancers in Beirut or sabre-jugglers in Senegal or any number of exotic, mind-boggling rites in some upside-down world. And then, when the orchestra softens momentarily and Johnny Hodges takes center stage with a glimmering alto saxophone solo, it suddenly becomes clear that what we are hearing is the blues. For all its rhythmic trappings "Blue Pepper (Far East of the Blues)" is a blues, and as such it is clearly related to all the blues we have heard so many times before. As for those pushy

Paul Gonsalves and Duke Ellington sampling exotic wares in Ctesiphon, Iraq, 1963 (U.S. State Department, reprinted in Music Is My Mistress, p. 326)

rhythms and brassy riffs, they are not so exotic after all. They could equally accompany a pole dancer in Atlantic City or a kick-line at the Cotton Club.

"Blue Pepper (Far East of the Blues)" may be prototypically Afro-Eurasian Ellington, but it is still Ellington. "The audiences that come to see us want to hear us, so they don't expect anything but us, and they don't get anything but us," Ellington told a critic at a press conference in Calcutta. Mozart might have said something similar 200 years earlier when he faced his critics in the farthest reaches of the world *he* lived in, that is, London to the west and Prague to the east.

Duke Ellington saw more of the world in the last decade of his life than he could have imagined. That much he had in common with everyone else born at the turn of the twentieth century. The greatest social changes in his formative years manifested themselves in mobility – social and occupational mobility and above all geographical mobility. Born into a world where steam engines were a source of wonderment, glimpsed at state fairs by the lucky few, and telephones, radios, motor-cars and airplanes were still science fiction, the chances of an ordinary American visiting Rome or Athens or Cairo in one's lifetime were almost nil. Europe was remote, and India, China and Japan were beyond imagining. In the 1960s, which were also Ellington's sixties, he visited them all. He became an annual fixture in London, Paris, Stockholm, Rome, Tokyo and other great cities. He traveled to Singapore, Sydney, Auckland, Dakar, Monaco, Zurich, Vienna, Venice, Warsaw, Ljubljana and points between.

For Ellington, it came at a cost. Visiting them meant stifling the aviophobia, his dread of flying, and the germaphobia that was nurtured by his hypochondria. He was not a particularly brave man in many ways, but he sucked in his breath, closed his eyes and kept the phobias at bay. The whole world was suddenly accessible, and it was the price he knew he had to pay to see it.

As a tourist, Ellington was most of all a sensualist. He left no recollections about museums or palaces or battlegrounds. Instead, he talked about the sounds and smells and sights wherever he went. About the birds and the snake-charmers and the bustle in the bazaars. His reaction to Damascus in 1963 was the same as his reaction to Harlem in 1923. Both piqued his creative juices. Where Harlem had raised him into the ranks of the most interesting composers of his time, the Levantine cities rejuvenated those instincts for a final spirited flourish.

The stimuli came from the clatter that surrounded him – the smells in a Harlem air-shaft and the trill of a mynah bird, the amble of a family in their Sunday-best on the way to church and the kick on the sixth beat by children dancing for him at a state banquet. The sensations of the world around him seeped in and stayed. The inner urge, unique and personal, was a mystery even to him. In Harlem, he learned from his elders but he never borrowed from them. In faraway lands, he heard the rhythms and the harmonies but he never replicated them. He had no interest in becoming adept at generic stride piano or at world music. The real value in being there, as he said, is soaking in the rhythms and the harmonies along with the sights and smells. Nobody put it better: "You let it roll around, undergo a chemical change, and then seep out on paper in the form that will suit the musicians who are going to play it." A whole esthetic theory in fewer than thirty words.

Afro-Eurasian Ellington is still Ellington.

References (page numbers to direct quotations are shown *in italics*)

Author unknown. The Johnny Bode Story. [biographical sketch of Lena Junoff] http://monolover.blogspot.ca/2014/06/johnny-bodebordellmammas-dotter-plp-102.html [accessed July 2015]

Cohen, Harvey G. 2010. *Duke Ellington's America*. Chicago: University of Chicago Press. *p. 511*

Coss, Bill. 1962. "Ellington & Strayhorn, Inc." *Down Beat* (June 1962). Reprinted in *The Duke Ellington Reader*, ed. Mark Tucker. 1993. New York: Oxford University Press. 498-503. *pp. 502-503.*

Dance, Stanley. 1967, 1995. Liner note to Duke Ellington, *The Far East Suite*. Bluebird CD [1995].

Dance, Stanley. 1975. Liner note to *Duke Ellington's Third Sacred Concert*. Westminster Abbey, 24 October 1973. BMG CD [1996].

Hamilton, Jimmy. 1991. Interview in Duke Ellington Archive, Smithsonian Institution. March 1991.

Holtum, Henrik von. 2015. Liner note to *The Conny Plank Session, Duke Ellington & His Orchestra*. Grönland CD [2015].

Ellington, Duke. 1964. "Orientations." *Musical Journal* (March 1964). "Press Conference in Calcutta 1963." Reprinted in Stanley Dance, *The World of Duke Ellington*. 1971. London: Macmillan. 14-22. *p. 14, pp. 17-18 (fn), p. 19.*

Ellington, Duke. 1973. *Music Is My Mistress*. New York: Doubleday. "Dakar, Journal 1966," pp. 337-338. "Pacific Journal 1972," 381-389. *p. 383.*

Ellington, Mercer, with Stanley Dance. 1978. *Duke Ellington in Person*. Boston: Houghton Mifflin. *p. 161*

Lambert, Eddie. 1998. *Duke Ellington: A Listener's Guide*. New York: Scarecrow Press. *pp. 298-299*

McLuhan, Marshall. 1964. *Understanding Media: The Extensions of Man*: Cambridge, Mass: MIT Press.

Ulanov, Barry. 1960. "The Ellington programme." In *This Is Jazz*, ed. Ken Williamson. London: Newnes Press. *p. 168.*

Westin, Martin, and Lars Westin. 2018. "Rolf Ericson Interview." *Duke Ellington Society of Sweden*, Bulletin 3. August 2018. 9-14. English translation from Swedish in *Orkester Journalen* (May 1994). *p. 11*

Playlist (in order of appearance in the chapter)

"Bluebird of Delhi (Mynah)" 3:18. (Ellington/Strayhorn) *The Far East Suite* (Bluebird CD [1995]). 21 December 1966, RCA Victor Studio, New York. Cootie Williams, Cat Anderson, Mercer Ellington, Herbie Jones tp; Lawrence Brown, Buster Cooper, Chuck Connors tb; Russell Procope as, cl; Jimmy Hamilton cl; Johnny Hodges as; Paul Gonsalves ts, Harry Carney bs; John Lamb b; Rufus Jones d. Duke Ellington conducts; there is no piano.

"Depk" 2:38. Same as "Bluebird of Delhi" but add Duke Ellington, p.

"Ad Lib on Nippon" 11:34 (Ellington [Hamilton]) *The Far East Suite* (Bluebird CD
[1995]). 20 December 1966. Personnel same as "Depk.".

"Chinoiserie" (Ellington) 8:13. *The Afro-Eurasian Eclipse* (Fantasy 1975, OJCCD 1991). New York, 17 February 1971. Cootie Williams, Money Johnson, Mercer Ellington, Eddie Preston tp; Booty Wood, Malcolm Taylor, Chuck Connors tb; Russell Procope as, cl; Norris Turney as, cl; Paul Gonsalves, Harold Ashby ts; Harry Carney bs; Ellington p; Joe Benjamin b; Rufus Jones d.
Solos: Ellington spoken introduction (to 1:35), Ellington piano (1:39-2:24), alto saxophone duet (to 2:54), Harold Ashby enters at 3:24 over dense orchestration (to 8:09)

"Didjeridoo" 3:37. Same as "Chinoiserie"
Solos: Ellington, Harry Carney (beneath ensemble) cadenza at 3:00

"Soul-Soothing Beach" ("Mkis") 3:34. *Togo Brava Suite* (Storyville CD [2001]). New York, 28 June 1971.
Cootie Williams, Money Johnson, Mercer Ellington, Richard Williams tp; Booty Wood, Malcolm Taylor, Chuck Connors tb; Russell Procope as, cl; Buddy Pearson, Norris Turney fl; Paul Gonsalves, Harold Ashby ts; Harry Carney bs; Ellington p; Joe Benjamin b; Rufus Jones d
Solos: Ellington, Turney

"Afrique" (take 3, vocal version) 5:25 *The Conny Plank Session, Duke Ellington & His Orchestra* (Grönland CD 2015). Rhenus Studio, Cologne, Germany, 9 July 1970
Cat Anderson, Cootie Williams, Mercer Ellington, Fred Stone, Nelson Williams tp; Chuck Connors, Malcolm Taylor, Booty Wood tb; Russell Procope, Norris Turney, Harold Ashby, Paul Gonsalves, Harry Carney reeds; Duke Ellington p; Wild Bill Davis org; Joe Benjamin b; Rufus Jones d; Lena Junoff soprano vocalese
Solo: Rufus Jones

"Toto (Afrique)" 2:58 (same as "Soul-Soothing Beach" except 29 June 1971)
Solos: Ellington, Benjamin, Turney

"Soul Flute" 3:05 *Togo Brava Suite* (Blue Note CD [1994]) Odeon Theatre, Bristol, England 22 October 1971.
Cootie Williams, Johnny Coles, Mercer Ellington, Eddie Preston, Harold Johnson tp; Chuck Connors, Malcolm Taylor, Booty Wood tb; Russell Procope, Harold Minerve, Norris Turney, Paul Gonsalves, Harold Ashby, Harry Carney reeds; Duke Ellington p; Joe Benjamin b; Rufus Jones d
Solo: Turney fl plays six choruses

"Intimate Interlude" 5:01 *The Intimate Ellington* (Pablo 1977 [CD 1992]) New York, 2 Feb. 1971. Norris Turney fl; Harry Carney bass cl; Ellington p; Joe Benjamin b; Rufus Jones d

"Blue Pepper (Far East of the Blues)" 3:00 *The Far East Suite* (same as "Bluebird of Delhi (Mynah)")
Solos: Johnny Hodges, Cat Anderson

Chapter 8

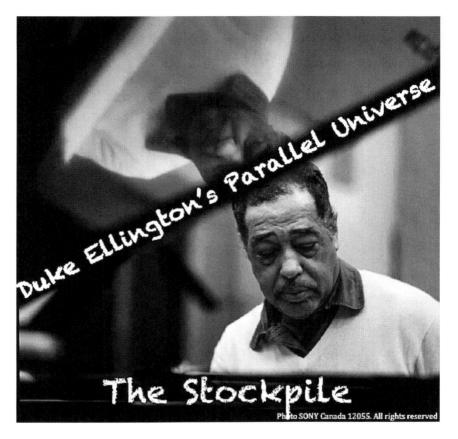
Duke Ellington's Parallel Universe
The Stockpile

When Duke Ellington died in 1974, the rumor circulated that several hundred reels of professional recordings had been found among his possessions. All were supposedly produced by Ellington himself, sometimes with his son Mercer Ellington, and recorded in the best recording facilities he could find in his travels. Some were live performances but most were made in studios. They had never been played publicly after the recording date.

The rumor had some credibility because from time to time Ellington had vaguely mentioned something he called his "stockpile." It took ten more years after his death for the rumor to gain full credence. In 1984, newspapers announced that Mercer Ellington had sold a huge hoard of materials to Radio Denmark. Eight months after that, in May 1985, Dr Erik Wiedemann whetted global appetites by playing a few excerpts from Mercer's trove at the third annual Duke Ellington conference, held that year in Oldham, Lancashire. Wiedemann introduced himself as a professor of Danish literature and a jazz discographer who had volunteered his services to Radio Denmark for the monumental task of sorting out the donation. It was too soon, he said, for him to know precisely what was in the stockpile, but he did mention that it took him a week just to move the reels from their cartons onto shelves.

Final Reckoning
The reality actually measured up to the rumor. The reckoning finally came in 1992, when the Danish society hosted the Ellington conference in Copenhagen. Bjarne Busk, a lawyer and civil servant who had been sorting out the stockpile from the beginning with the help of Wiedemann and many others, presented a sober accounting of what they discovered. There were 781 tapes, but many were duplicates (back-up reels, stereo and mono versions of the same music, cassette copies of studio sessions for Ellington's personal use). Some of the materials were marginal with respect to Ellington's music. Thirty-six tapes came from studio sessions produced by Ellington that featured musicians outside the band. These included the sessions by singer Bea Benjamin, pianists Abdullah Ibrahim (then known as Dollar Brand) and Bud Powell, and the violin summit of Svend Asmussen, Stéphane Grappelli and Ray Nance, all of whom Ellington had recorded in Paris in 1963 for Reprise Records, his label at the time. There were also 53 tapes of Ellington interviews from radio and television. And, least important, there were 52 tapes dubbed from commercial records by various musicians, of interest as indications of what Ellington might have been listening to but more likely things that other people gave him in hopes he might listen to them.

More important are recordings of 35 public performances, including eleven complete concerts, on 69 tapes. The performance tapes probably amount to thirty or forty hours of live music, and they will inevitably reveal some novelties, but probably not many. Ellington tended to stick with the same concert program for whole seasons, and in the last two decades of his life – the period covered by the stockpile recordings – his concerts are already well documented.

The gold dust is what remains, and even after culling out all these other things, it comes in almost unimaginable profusion. There are 400-odd tapes, capturing 128 studio dates, and on these, embedded in the false starts and the muffled conversations and shouted corrections, there might be as many as forty hours of polished, new music. Forty hours, to put it in perspective, is more than the complete recorded output of many jazz greats, including Fats Waller, Artie Shaw, Django Reinhardt, Lester Young, Charlie Parker, and dozens of others. (For another kind of perspective, the Beatles, the most popular of all pop groups, recorded a total of ten hours and 28 minutes in studios.) For Ellington, these forty or so hours are merely the add-ons, the gobsmacking bonus to the 200 or more hours of Ellington's music on record in his lifetime, in what is possibly the most profuse recorded documentation of any musician in history.

More than thirty hours of the music in the stockpile has been released. We have heard enough to know that it is a passport to a parallel universe. Listening to it is like following Ellington through the looking glass into a carnival where unexpected combos assemble and great actors try on unfamiliar roles and spontaneous ambitions get kindled, and the whole world is somehow looser and more congenial. In the table appended to this chapter ("The Stockpile So Far"), I make an attempt at listing the original CD releases of all known or suspected stockpile music so far, a partly hopeless task (as we shall see) but one that has to start somewhere.

Romance of the Posthumous

Posthumous artworks have special resonance. One of our cultural archetypes is the artist who starves in his or her garret perfecting an oracular vision in works that will come to light only after death. There are two sub-types, one tragic (and rare) and the other pathetic. The tragic one is symbolized by Vincent van Gogh (1853-1890), who sold one painting in his lifetime and had been dead for decades by the time the public caught up with the profundity underlying his turbulent vision.

The pathetic version, much more common, is the shrinking violet, convinced that his or her view is unworthy of an audience and too frightened to try it out. It is symbolized by a pair of Franzs: Franz Kafka (1883-1924) and Franz Schubert (1797-1828). Kafka's literary reputation rests on his posthumous works more than on anything he published in his lifetime, notably the novels *The Trial* and *The Castle*, salvaged from the wastebasket by his literary executor. Schubert's chamber music, piano concertos and symphonies, almost everything he had written apart from some Lieder, were found wedged into crannies in his apartment after his death at 31.

Duke Ellington, despite his voluminous posthumous legacy, has nothing in common with the archetype in either guise. Unlike van Gogh, Ellington refused to settle for indifference, and when the audience failed to grasp what he was trying to do, as in his earliest concert-length extended works, he just kept coming back at them with more until they finally got it. Unlike Kafka and Schubert, whose posthumous works trebled their life work, Ellington was out there testing his mettle on audiences daily. His posthumous works, as we have seen, may ultimately amount to a fifth of his prodigious life work at most.

Ellington believed, as Schubert and Kafka obviously did not, that finding an audience is as crucial for an artist as is finding the truth, and not unrelated. He was convinced, as van Gogh apparently was not, that audiences could be educated – or nurtured, or cajoled, or even, somewhat pathetically, indulged. In his lifetime Ellington registered literally thousands of compositions, played Carnegie Hall eleven times, performed on every continent except Antarctica, and received more honorary degrees than Stravinsky (1882-1971), the only composer among his contemporaries who even comes close.

Ellington's stockpile came into being not from the repression of his creative urge but from its overflow. His muse was hyperactive, and the stockpile is its yardstick. That muse flowed more profusely than any commercial distributor could afford to distribute or any audience could keep pace with. Releasing works from the stockpile over almost fifty years since Ellington died, and still counting, has given an unprecedented artistic afterlife to a man who dreaded death for the awful waste of music he would not get a chance to write.

"A Treasure House"
Hints about the stockpile in Ellington's lifetime were scarce, and so

casual as to be easily overlooked. In 1970, the Toronto broadcaster Ted O'Reilly asked Ellington if record companies could keep up with his musical output. "Not really," Ellington replied. "Not if I do my own thing. ... You write every day, and you just accumulate too much. It's just like they can't absolutely consume everything that we *perform* – so many things that have been performed. That's the reason I started recording them myself because you can't expect record companies to take everything, to take that much volume." Ellington's comment was vague; it was possible to think that he meant simply that he was recording the orchestra's live performances, as many jazz musicians routinely do.

That same year, Stanley Dance mentioned the stockpile in print, and he was more specific. "Ellington likes to hear his music performed as soon as possible after it has been composed, and when this does not coincide with the policies of record companies, he goes ahead and records it at his own expense," Dance wrote in the preface to *The World of Duke Ellington*, and then he added the fillip that gave the first clue about its contents: "A treasure house of experimental music and spontaneous, small-group improvisations awaits posterity – or the attention of a record company as much concerned with music as with money."

Ellington himself had expressed his desire – really, his need – to hear his compositions played immediately many years before he started taking his band into recording studios at his own expense. "I'm something like a farmer, a farmer that grows things," he told Richard Boyer in a *New Yorker* profile in 1944. "He plants his seed and I plant mine. He has to wait until spring until his comes up, but I can see mine right after I plant it. That night. I don't have to wait. That's the payoff for me." A few years later, in 1948, as recording technology became more user-friendly, Ellington took his indulgence a step further and began recording new compositions and much more in studios.

Radio Denmark became the beneficiary through several happy accidents. Soon after his father's death in 1974, Mercer Ellington began considering options for an institutional home for the stockpile. "I felt that the archives should be placed somewhere where there was an absolute and definite musical intelligence and also a sincere effort

Mercer Ellington (IAJRC photo)

to preserve these things and use them to the best [advantage], to more or less give them exposure," he said in an interview broadcast on Radio Denmark in 1984. There was undoubtedly pressure to place them in the Smithsonian Institution in Washington, D.C., where Ellington's papers are stored, or in the Library of Congress, where Jerry Valburn's voluminous collection of Ellingtonia is housed.

Around the time he was settling his father's estate, Mercer had started a second family with a Danish woman, and on one of his visits to Copenhagen he was guest at the annual conference of the Ben Webster Foundation, a memorial trust for Ellington's first tenor saxophone star, who had emigrated to Europe in 1964 and died in Copenhagen in 1973. Mercer quickly recognized the advantages of making Radio Denmark the repository of the stockpile. "This has always been a true area for the appreciation of the Old Man," he told the Danish interviewer. "I find, I think, the most avid group of jazz people gathered here in Denmark, if not possibly Sweden, anywhere," he said. "We can look across Europe, Japan, wherever, [at] the musicians who have gathered in this particular area [meaning Webster, Oscar Pettiford, Dexter Gordon, Kenny Drew, and other American expatriates], ... they came here because the music was always on such a high plane." Mercer insisted that the stockpile should not only be preserved but that it should be played, and he did not believe any American institution could find an audience for it, or would even try. "In essence the reason the tapes are rested here," he said, "is because we have the audience which is much more equipped to appreciate what's on the tapes."

Mercer Ellington died in Copenhagen in 1996. By then, most of his hopes for the archive had been realized. The stockpile had been transferred onto fresh tape, and Radio Denmark had produced 59 hour-long broadcasts of stockpile materials from 1984 on. He would not live to see the exemplary CD releases of stockpile material from Storyville Records, Radio Denmark's designated distributor, that started in 2001 and thus far amount to more than eight hours of fresh music on seven CDs (listed in the appendix).

Times and Places
Ellington's practice of recording his musicians at his own expense had its roots in a commercial venture called Mercer Records, a label owned by his son and Leonard Feather. The label existed as a public entity for only a couple of years starting in 1950, and after that it had a shadow existence as a tax haven for Ellington. Its earliest holdings were destroyed by fire. The earliest recording that survives was made in 1952, and it is one of the most famous, though the generations of listeners who have admired it have no idea that it originated in the stockpile. It survived only because it was lifted from the stockpile for commercial release on a Columbia record called *Ellington Uptown* (now Columbia CD 87066 [2004]). It is the famous recording of "Skin Deep," composed by drummer Louie Bellson as a showcase for his tumultuous drum work. George Avakian produced all the other tracks on *Ellington Uptown* in Columbia's 30th Street studios, and it was Avakian who alerted me to the unusual provenance of "Skin Deep." In the 2004 reissue, its stockpile origins are obvious because Duke Ellington and Mercer Ellington are identified as producers rather than Avakian, and the recording site is identified as the Rainbow Ballroom in Fresno, California.

Soon after Bellson joined Ellington's band in 1951, Ellington recognized the mass appeal of "Skin Deep," which was bringing audiences to their feet night after night. It is a brassy blast of big-band pyrotechnics that encases a tumultuous drum break by Bellson, a brilliant technical drummer as well as a gifted composer and orchestrator. Bellson famously used two bass drums, making him the only two-footed (ambipedal?) drummer to attain fame. "Skin Deep" was his spectacle. At the climax, his hair matted and his arms flailing, audiences were amazed to see that his pantlegs had ridden up around his knees. Ellington realized that replicating Bellson's performance in a studio would be difficult, if not impossible. So for the first and perhaps only time in his life he dipped into the stockpile, and offered Columbia Records the studio-quality live performance from Fresno.

His instinct proved infallible. "Skin Deep" became Ellington's first sizable hit in several years, albeit by a circuitous route. *Ellington Uptown*, Avakian told me, was picked up by a high-fidelity electronics company so that they could use "Skin Deep" as a promotional demo for showing off the dynamic range of their speakers. From there, it caught the wave as a cult record for the new breed of music-mongers who became known as audiophiles. They were one post-World War

Louie Bellson (IAJRC photo)

II phenomenon among many. In the American suburbs that were springing up everywhere in the early 1950s, men in grey flannel suits and boys in white bucks filled their rec rooms with pricey "high fidelity" sound systems. To show off their tweeters and woofers, they bought *Ellington Uptown* and hiked up the volume on Bellson's thundering drums. Columbia quickly caught on to the merchandising advantage and re-packaged the LP with the title *Hi-Fi Ellington Uptown*.

By the time the stockpile came into the hands of the Danish beneficiaries, nothing as early as "Skin Deep" existed. The earliest music so far premiered on Radio Denmark originated in 1956. There exist performance tapes from 1953 that may have been removed from the stockpile if they ever were part of it (as shown in the end-table of stockpile releases). But nothing earlier is there, not even the rest of the 1952 Fresno concert that "Skin Deep" came from. The theoretical end-date for the stockpile is 1974, the year of Ellington's death, but the actual end may come a year or two earlier. The last studio sessions played on Radio Denmark or released on CD are from 1972.

The Unhappy History of Mercer Records

As owner of Mercer Records, Mercer Ellington was not only trustee of the stockpile after his father's death but also its legal owner. In 1950, Mercer and Leonard Feather, then working as Ellington's publicist, started the new record label (named for Mercer at Feather's insistence). The seed money came from Ellington enterprises. and its original goal was to generate records that would get radio-play and stimulate cash flow for the business, which already included music publishing. But by 1950 that goal was already doomed, because the popularity of dance bands was not merely in a slump but had actually ended, and even the newfound pop wave of crooners and thrushes with big-band backing was destined to be short-lived with rock 'n' roll around the corner.

Mercer Records lasted two years as a commercial label. Its output was small, and commercial distribution proved impossible. Its failure was hardly remarkable in the industry at the time. For Mercer, there may have been some grudging consolation in knowing that his father had failed with an almost identical enterprise called Sunrise Records in 1948. In fact, one of the functions of the new company was to pick up the pieces of the old one, so to speak, as Mercer Records fell heir to the Sunrise catalogue.

Years later, when some aficionados approached Mercer Ellington about compiling some of the Sunrise and Mercer records on LPs, they discovered that the master tapes no longer existed. They had been in storage at a place called Apex Studios in Manhattan, which according to Mercer was run by thugs. "They had begun to have problems there," Mercer said, "a mysterious fire started, and everything was totally destroyed. The Mercer Records backlog that might have been sold to another company was gone."

Vestiges of Sunrise and Mercer
Paradoxically, it was the commercial failure of Mercer Records that ensured its posterity. While Mercer Records existed, as with Sunrise before it, Duke Ellington grew accustomed to assembling his musicians in recording studios whenever he felt like it. Not only did Ellington need to hear his music played as soon as it was written, as Stanley Dance said, but he also needed to hear his musicians in various roles in order to tap their individual strengths in the uniquely Ellington mode of composition. He made no secret of the fact that his compositions sometimes used melodic fragments that came spontaneously from his star soloists, and those fragments were more likely to come when he placed the musicians in unfamiliar settings. He was inclined to take his band members, most of whom were salaried, into studios more often than his record contract stipulated, and he was thus producing more music than the company could market. Trying out novel combinations and hearing the music instantly became indispensable adjuncts to his creative regimen, and when Mercer Records died as a public venture Ellington kept it alive as a ghost corporation for registering recordings and writing off his out-of-pocket expenses.

The stockpile legally belonged to Mercer Records but Ellington had no intention of issuing records on the label, at least not in his lifetime. For most of his career he was under contract to other companies. His continuous production of private recordings alongside contracted recordings smacks of the kind of conflict of interest that would undoubtedly lead to legal hassles in the present-day corporate climate of the music industry, but at the time it seems to have aroused little concern. In his years with Columbia, Ellington's bosses knew about his private recordings for the defunct Mercer label and tolerated them in an "unspoken agreement," Avakian told me, that was "not spelled out in his Columbia contracts." Presumably the same terms held for his dual activities during his subsequent affiliations with Reprise, Atlantic, Verve and the other companies he recorded for. Ellington's part in the unspoken agreement apparently precluded his releasing music from the stockpile, and that condition made the music in the stockpile all the more intriguing and novel when it finally became accessible.

The only vestiges of the brief commercial existence of either Sunrise or Mercer Records came about, as so often happens in the annals of jazz, because a couple of independent producers recognized how crucial it is for a performance art to preserve as many performances as possible. Orrin Keepnews of Riverside Records licensed piano duets by Duke Ellington and Billy Strayhorn and cello performances by Oscar Pettiford that had been recorded as 78 rpm singles in 1950 by Mercer Records. Keepnews brought them back into print in 1984 by transferring them from the best-preserved 78 rpm records he could find and compiling them for an LP collection. Around the same time, Leonard Feather prevailed upon Prestige Records to take the time and trouble of transferring tracks made by small-band off-shoots of the Ellington orchestra in 1947 for Sunrise Records and in 1950 and 1951 for Mercer Records, bringing them back into print in the 1980s.

Having made it onto vinyl, both compilations got digitized onto compact discs in the anything-goes boom of the early 1990s. The piano duets and Pettiford's cello tracks are on *Great Times!* (Original Jazz Classics 108 [ca. 1991]), unconscionably short at 35 minutes but full of fun. The various small bands are on Prestige with the ungainly title *The Johnny Hodges All Stars With the Duke Ellington All Stars and the Billy Strayhorn All Stars* (CD 24103 [1992]).

The all-star sessions are invaluable as evidence of Ellington's rationale for the stockpile. The 1950-1951 small-group sessions all include Juan Tizol on trombone, Willie Smith on alto saxophone and

Louie Bellson on drums, the three men whom Ellington had wooed from Harry James's band as replacements for Lawrence Brown, Johnny Hodges and Sonny Greer. In four different recording sessions, Tizol, Smith and Bellson are surrounded by combos that include some veteran Ellingtonians (Cat Anderson, Quentin Jackson, Jimmy Hamilton and Wendell Marshall, with either Ellington or Strayhorn on piano) and a couple of relative newcomers (Paul Gonsalves and Britt Woodman). Ellington is clearly using the sessions to acclimatize the newcomers to his style and, at least as clearly, to discover where their special gifts might lie so that he and Strayhorn could build new arrangements around them. Willie Smith gets a lot of play – Ellington had played with Bellson once and with Tizol for years, so that Smith was the only real outsider. As Hodges's replacement, Smith was also the man who had the biggest hole to fill.

Like the best of the later music in the stockpile, this small-band music that actually got released on Mercer Records has a certain comfort level. It is mainly made up of blues with minimal ensembles and lots of solos, but also, like the best of the stockpile music, it is at the same time exploratory, probing and prophetic. A 1950 track called "The Happening" lets young Paul Gonsalves loose on a booting blues, a harbinger beyond a doubt of his famous wailing interval at Newport six years later. A 1951 Strayhorn piece, "Swamp Drum," harmonizes the three trombones (Tizol, Jackson, Woodman) in a sustained underscore, precursor to the trombone choir that would become one of the joyful innovations of the Brown-free trombone section of the next ten years.

Ellington's autonomy with Sunrise and Mercer Records became an indispensable indulgence for him for the rest of his days. Because the recordings were private, Ellington did not have to pay any heed to market forces or any kind of outside pressures in deciding what he should play. The result is a hoard of music of exquisite diversity, often playful and capricious, sometimes experimental and daring, and, at its best, all those things at once.

Anatomy of a Stockpile Session

In truth, we should be amazed that so much survived. The recording sessions that produced all this music were often impromptu, chaotic, spur-of-the-moment affairs. The scattershot circumstances no doubt account for the mystery about the very existence of the stockpile in Ellington's lifetime. They also account for the confusion about some of the recording details.

I started making inquiries into a particular stockpile recording that took place in Toronto in 1972. At the time, I was trying to solve some mysteries surrounding Ellington's latter-day masterpiece, the ballet called *The River* (the subject of the next chapter). Ron Collier, the Toronto-based composer and bandleader, was Ellington's collaborator on *The River* and several other projects, in effect serving part-time in one of the roles that Billy Strayhorn had filled full-time until his death in 1967. It was Ron Collier who hastily organized this stockpile session. Ellington and the orchestra were coming to Toronto to perform at the O'Keefe Centre on 23 June. They were arriving the day before, and Ellington decided to fill what would otherwise have been a free evening for the musicians. "Ellington's sister Ruth called [from New York], 'Book a studio and bring some charts,'" Collier recalled in a presentation at the 1996 Duke Ellington conference in Toronto. Collier then apparently called Phil Sheridan, the leading jazz producer in the city, at Thunder Sound Studio, and Sheridan in turn called the technician George Simkiw. The next step was then recounted by Simkiw in an interview with the pianist and promoter Bill King. Forty-five years after the fact, Simkiw remained awe-struck at the evening's proceedings:

> **Bill King:** ...you did a recording with Duke Ellington.
> **George Simkiw:** The Duke Ellington thing was like a crime mystery. I get a call during the day. ... I get a call saying, listen we need to do a session at 7 o'clock this evening. Can you be there? He said, set up for about 25 pieces. I said give me a rough idea. He says, four trumpets – I say just give me a rough sketch, so I did a rough set-up for them. Around a quarter to seven, musicians crept in. I didn't recognize any of them. I usually know every musician in town. Then Duke Ellington walks in. They are doing this secret session. I remember Ron Rully was there. He was part of that whole thing; the jazz drummer. There were some heavyweight people there and my jaw dropped. I actually went out and talked to the Duke as he was having some problems with his music stand. I helped adjust it for him. He thanked me, broke another pencil [because he] never used

the same pencil twice. It was like surreal.
BK: What was the session all about?
GS: I never heard anything more about it.
BK: Did it sound good?
GS: I thought it did. I think the music was something Ron Rully wrote, or a local guy wrote.

The "local guy" who wrote the music, of course, was Ron Collier. Ron Rully was Collier's drummer in his regular quintet and in other bands, including studio work. It is not surprising that he was there that evening, undoubtedly at Collier's invitation, or that Simkiw recognized him, because (as he said) "I usually know every musician in town" – though apparently not Collier or, for that matter, Cootie Williams, Harry Carney and the other Ellingtonians, other than Ellington himself.

Ellington liked company in recording studios and on other public occasions. It was hardly a "secret session," as Simkiw called it. Among the other guests were Ted O'Reilly, jazz broadcaster on the Toronto radio station CJRT-FM, and Bill Smith, co-editor and photographer of *Coda* magazine. They appear to be the only survivors of that long-ago session, and luckily when I started trying to figure out what had gone on based on Simkiw's recollections, they came forward with corrections and further details.

It turns out that there were two stockpile sessions in Toronto that June, though only one has ever been listed in discographies. (The tapes from both sessions were apparently merged, as if it had been one.) The second session took place in the same studio on Tuesday, 27 June, five days after the one on 22 June, a Thursday. In between, Ellington and the orchestra covered hundreds of miles as part of their normal grueling routine (scrupulously documented, as always, by Klaus Stratemann). After the Friday concert at O'Keefe Centre (23 June), the day after the first session, they played concerts at Seekonk, Massachusetts (24), Endicott, New York (25), and Latham, New York (26). Their second turn in the Toronto studio would otherwise have been an off-day for the band, but they returned to the city because it made a convenient stop en route to their next one-nighter at a lakeside town west of the city. Ellington was not one to encourage idleness.

There were numerous contingencies in the two studio sessions, and they no doubt account for some of the confusion about the music that resulted. (The confusion may also sound a cautionary note for the numerous other "secret sessions" about which we know much less.) Arnie Chycoski (1936-2008), the preferred lead trumpet player in Toronto bands at the time including the Boss Brass, played on several of the charts that evening but his presence has never been acknowledged. Ted O'Reilly says, "Mercer Ellington was the band's lead trumpet, [but he] had insufficient chops – that day, anyway – to cut the book and Arnie Chycoski arrived about half an hour in to play it, on at least the Collier things." Discographies mistakenly list Fred Stone, the Toronto flugelhorn player who played with Ellington for a few months in 1970, apparently mistaking Chycoski for him. Chycoski may have escaped notice because his name never appeared on the payroll. O'Reilly says, "I recall him turning down a couple of hundred cash from Mercer, saying something like, 'No thanks, it's my honor to have played for Duke'."

Tyree Glenn had returned to the band as lead trombone temporarily replacing Booty Wood, who had injured his hand. O'Reilly says, "The [first] Thunder Sound session is missing Tyree Glenn in the trombone section. He just didn't show up." Ellington made an unusual contingency plan in Glenn's absence. O'Reilly says, "Norris Turney played Glenn's trombone parts on tenor sax, sitting beside [the trombonists Vince] Prudente and [Chuck] Connors. I recall remarking to someone that it was a real talent to be able to transpose on sight."

Glenn must have caught up with the band in the next few days, perhaps when they were playing in New York state, because he was definitely present at the second session. Amazingly, so was a reporter from the *New York Times*, Tom Buckley, who followed the band in order to file a story in time for their performance at the Newport Jazz Festival at Carnegie Hall on 8 July. He documented Glenn's presence in a memorable exchange with Ellington that appeared in the *Times* six days later (3 July 1972):

> Duke Ellington sat cater-cornered on a folded plaid blanket on the piano bench. "Lemme hear it now," he said. With his left hand he cued the brass section for the biting attack he wanted on the riff

theme of "New York, New York."

It is the newest of the countless hundreds of compositions he has written since he began his career with "Soda Fountain Rag" in 1915, and he and his band will probably play it during their concert appearance at the Newport Jazz Festival here this week.

After a few measures the Duke signaled a halt. "Ooh, no, no, no," he said.

"You want the same B-flat as in the first bar?" asked Tyree Glenn, the lead trombonist. "Bah, bah, beyow?"

The Duke shook his head.

"What do you want?" asked the trombonist, a large, dark pudding of a man with a graying goatee.

"I want it together, mainly," the Duke replied with a laugh. "Play it ... play it with a drawl and an accent."

He illustrated his conception by bending the word "drawl" with a full southern intonation and tightening his mouth around "accent" so that it came out as pure Mayfair.

"Tyree, keep it that way," he said, after the band had played the figure again.

"I don't know what I did," the trombonist replied, and the 15 musicians in the recording studio in Toronto last week laughed appreciatively.

The issued take of the piece they were rehearsing, "New York New York," was not this one. It came three months later, in September, from a different stockpile session made by a small group with vocalist Anita Moore (the title track on *New York New York*, Storyville 1018402 [2008] in the appendix). By then, Glenn had left the band. The Toronto rehearsal with the full band has never been issued, or even listed.

Buckley noticed, as Smith and O'Reilly had also noticed, that Ellington was dressed casually. "Once a fashion plate, the Duke now seldom dresses up except when he is performing," Buckley wrote. "On this night he wore a loose long sleeved woolen polo shirt, a pair of bright blue narrow legged trousers, long out of fashion, that sagged below a noticeable paunch, and unpolished loafers. On the massive Ellington head was perched, incongruously, a fuzzy, narrow-brimmed blue fedora, punched out into derby shape." Ellington's careless attire accidentally increased the 'secrecy' of the event. Bill Smith had his camera around his neck, as always, but, he says, "I was asked not to

Duke Ellington in rehearsal (photo IAJRC files)

take photographs of Duke as he was too scruffy." O'Reilly also recalls "the unshaven and disheveled Ellington saying to Smith, 'No pictures – Duke doesn't feel pretty today', so he put his camera down." Otherwise Smith would have documented the session in *Coda* magazine.

What about Ron Collier's charts, the centerpieces of the secret session? He brought two with him into the studio. One, titled "Vancouver Lights," was a feature for Cootie Williams. It ended with a mild rebuff. After Collier worked through the piece with the band, Cootie quietly said, "That's a take." When Collier started tweaking some ensemble changes for a second take, Collier recalled, "Duke gets up from the piano and he comes over, puts his arm around me, says, 'Ron, when Cootie says that's a take that means he's not gonna play it any more.' So that was it for that piece." In hindsight, maybe another take was necessary. "Vancouver Lights" has never been issued.

Collier's other chart on the day, "Relaxin'," fared somewhat better. It is a blues built around an astute sonic contrast between Russell Procope's Albert-style clarinet and Harry Carney's velvety baritone saxophone. By this time, Ron Collier was a familiar figure in the Ellington camp, admired for his talent and well liked. "That Collier is all right," Harry Carney told Tom Buckley. "You know those arrangements we were playing last night. On my part, he wrote 'Harry-tone' instead of baritone. No one ever came up with that one before."

"Relaxin'" was released with other stockpile material from Toronto and Chicago on a 1992 CD called *Cool Rock* (Laserlight 15782 in the appendix). Twenty years after the fact, Ron Collier was gratified, but not overjoyed. "Relaxin'" appears on the CD with the title "Vancouver Lights." Whoops! When Collier asked the CD producer, Stanley Dance, about the mistake, Dance shrugged and said, "When we got the boxes, it was rather confusing."

We can only hope that it was less confusing for the other 500-odd tapes capturing 200 stockpile sessions (128 in Radio Denmark's trove and 83 released before the bequest). These Toronto sessions were witnessed by a radio broadcaster, a jazz magazine editor/photographer and a *New York Times* feature writer. Somehow, they managed to remain (as the technician said) "a mystery."

Stalking the Stockpile

In 1970, when Ted O'Reilly asked Duke Ellington how much unreleased material he had, Ellington said, "I don't know how deep that

Oscar Pettiford (1922-1960) played bass in the orchestra 1945-48, and recorded on cello for Mercer Records, 1950.

thing is." He added, "It's wonderful. It's beginning to be very valuable because it goes way back, you know, it goes way back to [Al] Hibbler, Ben Webster, Ray Nance, Clark Terry, all those great cats who were in the band." Apparently no one had informed Ellington about the warehouse fire that had wiped out the earliest recordings. Hibbler was indeed recorded by Mercer Records, but if Webster was ever in the stockpile it must have been at the very beginning because there is no trace of him in what survives. Hibbler, though, had given the label "a big hit," in Mercer Ellington's recollection, with his recording of "White Christmas." Feather remembers it differently. According to him, Oscar Pettiford's cello recording of "Perdido" gave them their "solitary near-best-seller." Pettiford's records survive on *Great Times!* transfered from the original 78s, and Hibbler's records could also eventually be transferred from the original 78s if there is a revival of interest in the wobbly old baritone, but contrary to Ellington's claim, no master tapes for Hibbler or Webster (or, for that matter, Pettiford) exist today.

    For better or worse, the stockpile took on a life of its own before it came into the possession of Radio Denmark. Ten years had gone by since Ellington's death until the bequest was made. In those ten years, Mercer Ellington and Ellington's amanuensis Stanley Dance made concerted efforts to get the music into the hands of listeners through commercial releases, and they had fair success. They did it, in a sense, by skimming off some of the treasures for Norman Granz (Pablo Records), Ahmet Ertegun (Atlantic), Bob Thiele (Doctor Jazz) and other producers, but they apparently required them to take some lesser sessions along with the undisputed gems (as indicated in the list of issued material at the end). The first public notice of this skimming was made in 1986, two years after the bequest, when the Bulletin of the Duke Ellington Music Society (DEMS) reported, "Many major record companies, such as Reprise, Atlantic, Fantasy, Pablo, etc., bought or leased material from the stockpile recordings, one of the latest being Doctor Jazz." For archivists interested in keeping track of Ellington's music, the commercial dissemination of so much of the stockpile poses two large problems. First, it means that there is no convenient, one-place repository for the complete stockpile, because materials bought by record companies appear to have been removed from the cartons that were turned over to Radio Denmark. The tally is large: records released in the ten years before the bequest come from 83 additional stockpile sessions. In other words, Radio Denmark's holdings, voluminous as they are, do not hold the entire stockpile. Second, it means that several hours of Ellington's music, whether leased or bought, exists independently of any kind of firm control, since its publication makes it accessible for repackaging by other companies, whether licensed or bootlegged.

Repackaging began early, and led to this indignant statement in the DEMS Bulletin (2000): "A few years after Mercer Ellington sold a huge collection of tapes from Duke's so-called stockpile to the Danish Radio, we were surprised with two sets of 5 CDs titled 'The Private Collection'. ... More recently, we saw quite a number of releases on the market with recordings copied from the original CDs." (In the table of stockpile releases at the end of this chapter, the ten Private Collection CDs are listed for the SAJA/Atlantic label but they have appeared on at least two other labels since then.) Keeping track of what is new and what is recycled involves more than simply watching for old music turning up in new packages. Neither Mercer Ellington nor anyone else seems to have kept an accounting of what had been sold or leased, and as a result the complete holdings that belonged to the stockpile may never be entirely known.

Concert performances are the most elusive. Dozens of concerts have been issued on CDs since the late 1980s but few appear to come directly from the stockpile or to be replicated in it. Many are easy to distinguish. Norman Granz is producer on several, derived from European tours he sponsored for Ellington in the 1960s, including almost eight hours of Ella Fitzgerald and Duke Ellington on the Cote d'Azur (Verve [1998], with Fitzgerald absent for about six of those hours). Some are harder to distinguish. Three notable concert performances appeared for the first time on Music Masters (Chicago 1946 [1995], London 1963 and 1964 [1993] and New York 1964 [1994]), a label that had already released at least one stockpile recording (see the table). But these concert performances apparently come from Library of Congress transcriptions that were donated by Jerry Valburn (though the credit line on the CDs says, "Produced by Mercer Ellington"). Though their provenance is not the stockpile, they are posthumous gems that shine welcome light on Ellington's versatile genius.

More insidious, and more worthy of DEMS indignation, is the appearance of CDs that pretend to be stockpile music but are not. Most conspicuous offenders are a paired set called *Duke Ellington Vol. 1 Live*, and *Duke Ellington Vol. 2 Private Collection* (J.Bird 80298 and 80299 [1999]). The producers thank Paul Ellington, Mercer's son, "for providing the original master tapes and family photos." In the notes for Vol. 1, Paul Ellington is quoted as saying, "I know that each time we uncover music that has not been released previously, I get very anxious to see what else he [Duke Ellington] is trying to relay to people because, although you may have heard the song before, you never hear a performance in the same manner twice." Vol. 2 repeats the claim: "These recordings with Duke and his Orchestra represent some of Duke's favorite selections, now made available for the first time." But in fact the music has all been released before, and it consists of second-rate performances transferred from old bootlegs. Details about the music, personnel and sources are not included in the CDs, but a little searching shows that Vol. 1 comes from McElroy's Ballroom in Portland, Oregon, from 1953 originally on an old Soundcraft LP (and now expanded multifold in a 5-CD set leased by Laserlight Records), and Vol. 2 has selections from the Civic Opera House from 1946 released in its entirety on a Prima (French) double-LP. As fraud goes, this one is petty, and the music is mediocre at best. It is only worth mentioning as an example of the shenanigans that bedevil the job of stalking the stockpile.

Unmentioned by DEMS but surely implicated in Danish Radio's indignation is the skimming, which deprives the Danish custodians and their chosen distributor, Storyville Records, of Ellington classics such as *The Queen's Suite* and the studio version of *Black Brown and Beige* (discussed in the next section). Galling as that may be, Storyville must be consoled that the stockpile is deep enough to give them masterworks of their own. Their seven CDs since 2001, meticulously assembled, strike a fine balance between historical significance and musical adventure. The intervals between their releases are becoming longer, a sign we hope of painstaking production values rather than waning enthusiasm.

High Points from the Parallel Universe
The wealth of new music from Ellington's career beyond the grave offers powerful new testimony to his irrepressible muse. But the music comes from recording sessions so diverse that by now it may appear to be a random jumble. In all the profusion, it is possible to pick out certain themes, such as the six discussed below, that give it the semblance of structure.

The Apotheosis of Paul Gonsalves. One of the themes worth pursuing in the stockpile is the showcasing of Paul Gonsalves. The tenor saxophone player was featured in Ellington's orchestra from 1950 until his death in 1974 (as discussed in Chapter 3, "The Fifth Reed"). He was by no means undervalued in his nightly performances with the orchestra, but his role was narrowly defined, especially after his riotous escapades at the Newport Jazz Festival in 1956, as he mainly played uptempo numbers. Ellington obviously thought Gonsalves had a lot more to give, but he seldom put him on display in public. Ellington could not give Gonsalves more latitude in concert performances without incurring the wrath of his more demanding stars. Away from the spotlight in several stockpile sessions, Ellington made Gonsalves the featured soloist on specialties that by night belonged to Hodges and other members of the band.

Gonsalves, we now know, can only be fully appreciated with the posthumous evidence. On at least three occasions, once in 1958 and twice in 1962, Ellington went into the studio and gave Gonsalves all the solos. Those sessions are now available on three CDs on three different labels: *Happy Reunion* (Zillion, 16 minutes of Gonsalves with rhythm trio), *Featuring Paul Gonsalves* (Fantasy, 39 minutes with full orchestra), and *Private Collection Vol. 3* (SAJA, 27 minutes with nonet and septet). Reviewing the Fantasy album when it first came out on LP in 1984, Gary Giddins said, "Gonsalves's quicksilver improvisations resonate with passion and wit, and though he hesitates momentarily, he never loses his footing – a remarkable feat considering that he probably didn't have a clue what would happen when he walked into the studio." His eight tracks on the *Private Collection, Vol. 3*, show him off at least as cogently, coming as they do a few months later with smaller bands tailored more closely to Gonsalves's

Paul Gonsalves and Duke Ellington in full flight

strengths. "He had good musical education, has great solo taste, and plays with profound authority," Ellington wrote of him in *Music is My Mistress*. "But he is shy, hates microphones, and loves *au naturel*. ...He wants to be liked by everybody, and doesn't want anything from anybody except a kind word and a water chaser." In these three releases from the stockpile, Gonsalves's "profound authority," removed for once from all shyness, shines through, even overflows.

Strayhorn in the Foreground. Billy Strayhorn, Ellington's backstage collaborator from 1939 when he was 24 until his death in 1967, finally takes center stage as both leader and piano player in a glorious compilation of stockpile recordings called *Lush Life* (Red Baron), bringing together two late-night features recorded at Basin Street East in 1964, and three studio sessions in 1965. Best of all are five quintet tracks with Clark Terry on flugelhorn and Bob Wilbur, unlikely as it seems, on clarinet and soprano saxophone. There are also four moody piano solos, and Strayhorn sings his romantic anthem "Lush Life" in a shyly memorable reading. In the notes accompanying the CD, Stanley Dance writes, "Almost every aspect of Strayhorn's creativity is to be found in this set – the lyricist, the singer, the composer, the arranger, the piano player (as soloist and accompanist) – all are here." For Strayhorn, this recording is simply indispensable.

Billy Strayhorn at the piano

For Dancers Only (or Especially). Four full CDs from the stockpile present dance dates. *All Star Road Band* (Signature), two volumes of the *Private Collection*, 2 and 6 (SAJA), and *Hot Summer Dance* (Red Baron) find the orchestra playing for dancers in 1957, 1958 and 1960, three of them at military bases. Though the context seems like a throwback to the Swing Era, there is more than nostalgia on display. "Countless live recordings have appeared," Whitney Balliett once pointed out, "[but] few have been done at dances, which jazz musicians love, because they can see their music reflected in the bodies of the dancers: the better the music the better the dancing, and the better the dancing the better the music." While none of the stockpile dances measures up to the one Balliett was reviewing at the time – the incomparable 1940 Fargo, North Dakota, dance date (*Ellington at Fargo*, Storyville 2CD) – they have their niche. Bob Thiele, proprietor of both the Signature and Red Baron labels, points out that Ellington's dance music has special charms. "At a dance like this," he says in the liner notes of *Hot Summer Dance*, "everybody would be, surprisingly often, happy, relaxed and full of enthusiasm." Those virtues are here in profusion for listeners who value them.

Black, Brown and Beige (Complete). There are masterpieces in the stockpile, known and unknown. *Black, Brown and Beige,* despite its auspicious debut at Carnegie Hall in 1943, never got the fully elaborated studio recording it cried out for. The original Carnegie Hall performance has been preserved warts and all (on Prestige 2PCD-34004), and the later pared-down version re-tooled for gospel diva Mahalia Jackson (Columbia 1958) is masterly but not really the suite. It was widely believed that Ellington was so stung by its critical reception in 1943 that he ignored it ever after. As Whitney Balliett put it, "The New York newspapers gave it poor marks, and Ellington, dismayed, never played the piece again." Not so, as it turned out. Ellington filled the obvious lacuna by recording the complete *Black, Brown and Beige* in stockpile studio sessions in March and May 1965. Who knew? The suite is intact on *The Private Collection, Vol. 10* (SAJA). His 1965 orchestra could not measure up to the original 1943 aggregation or, for that matter, to the band a few years earlier at the end of the 1950s, but here is Ellington's most ambitious extended composition conducted by him under studio conditions. There is no substitute.

Unique Suites in theStockpile. Also indispensable are two volumes of suites uniquely found in stockpile recordings, and another one complete only in the stockpile.

Togo Brava Suite was Ellington's homage to the African Republic of Togo, where he had been honored on a postage stamp in 1967 (along with Bach, Beethoven and Debussy). The suite had originally been known from 1971 performances as a four-part, 7-minute concert piece (as performed in Bristol, for example, on *Togo Brava Suite,* Blue Note CDP 30082 [1994]). But in the stockpile, it was preserved in much fuller form, as a seven-part 29-minute, studio recording, issued in its entirety on Storyville's first stockpile release (2001; *Togo Brava Suite* is discussed further in Chapter 7, "Afro-Eurasian Ellington"). The playing is crisp and spirited, with striking contributions from Norris Turney on flute, Harold Ashby on tenor and Ellington himself on piano. As a bonus, the suite is presented there with more than 40 minutes of other material from 1971, the year Ellington turned 72, showing beyond a doubt Ellington's unflagging vitality in writing, playing and leading his orchestra.

The year before he wrote *Togo Brava Suite*, Ellington composed *The River* for a ballet commissioned by the American Ballet Theatre, which also commissioned Alvin Ailey as its choreographer. The ballet has been known mainly from the symphonic score orchestrated by Ron Collier and played by the Detroit Symphony (on Chandos Records) and others. The stockpile supplies two alternate forms, both of them much more intimate reflections of Ellington himself. One is a series of solo piano sketches that Ellington recorded and then turned over to Ron Collier for elaborating and orchestrating as the symphony score. The piano sketches are now issued by Storyville on *The Piano Player* (2005).

The other alternate version of *The River* are Ellington's 1970 arrangements for his own orchestra, some with added percussion, released on the *Private Collection, Vol. 5* (SAJA). These big-band arrangements were totally unexpected until their release from the stockpile. They were apparently written because Ailey pleaded for fleshed-out versions for his choreography. They were never performed in concerts but they are wonderful expressions of the sonic possibilities that Ellington could wrest out of his music. The orchestrations are whimsical and impressionistic, and replete with ingenious instrumental couplings (flute and bass clarinet on "The Run," tenor saxophone and tympani on "The Falls," among others). This glorious amalgam of variations on several themes – piano trios, big band renditions and the final, definitive orchestral score – is the subject of the next chapter (Chapter 9, "Three Steps into *The River*").

The jazz-band version of *The River* is perfectly mated on the *Private Collection* CD with *The Degas Suite*, a soundtrack Ellington wrote in 1968 for a documentary on Degas's racetrack paintings that never got filmed (through no fault of Ellington's). Degas's paintings obviously inspired him, and it appears that Degas's impressionism seeped into Ellington's composing. Impressionism remained firmly fixed in his palette when it came time to compose *The River* two years later, making *Private Collection, Vol. 5* an indispensable showcase for Ellington's latter-day large-scale compositional style.

A Suite Fit for a Queen. The first selection ever commercially released from the stockpile was *The Queen's Suite* (Pablo [1990, originally a 1976 LP]), long anticipated by Ellington fans even before they knew there was any other music in the stockpile. Ellington composed the suite in homage to Queen Elizabeth II of England, to whom he had been presented at a command performance in 1958. Enraptured by the royal presence, he composed six tone-poems or, more aptly, pastorals, for her, music inspired by personal experiences of natural beauty. He called them "Sunset and the Mocking Bird," "Lightning Bugs and Frogs," "Northern Lights," "Le Sucrier Velours" (a mythic French bird), "Apes and Peacocks," and, as a closing homage an exquisitely romantic piano solo, "Single Petal of a Rose."

Ellington had his contractor, Columbia Records, press one vinyl record of the suite. He annotated the jacket with descriptions of his inspiration for each movement – about "Apes and Peacocks," he wrote, in part, "Besides all that wealth of gold, silver and ivory [among the Queen of Sheba's gifts to Solomon], there were apes and peacocks. To us, apes and peacocks seemed like the splendor of all time." (He included his descriptions in *Music Is My Mistress*, pp. 111-113, recounting scenes he had witnessed while traveling from place to

The rare LP label for *The Queen's Suite* (1959), presented by Duke Ellington to Her Majesty Queen Elizabeth II, and publicly released posthumously in 1976

place in Harry Carney's car; they are repeated in Stanley Dance's notes in the 1976 LP release along with Ellington's impressions of the command performance.)

Ellington then had the unique pressing delivered to the Queen. At concerts afterwards, he occasionally played "Single Petal of a Rose," and he made a point of dedicating it to the Queen of England. The only other movement he ever played at concerts was "Le Sucrier Velours," and he prefaced it by telling the audience about his composing of *The Queen's Suite* and his resolve to keep it private. With characteristic Ellingtonian finesse, he would then tell the audience that it was their own graciousness that inspired him to give them this taste of the Queen's suite. But he stuck to his word, as if it had been a sacred trust from the Queen herself. He never played the other movements in public, and he flatly refused all offers to make the music available to a wider audience in his lifetime. Its existence tantalized his admirers, and it is a measure of the brilliance of the suite that its release, when it finally came, beguiled even the most critical listeners.

The public release of *The Queen's Suite* two years after Ellington's death coupled it with two later suites, the *Goutelas Suite* from 1971, his recollection of a stately occasion when he had been invited to dedicate the *salle de musique* in a restored medieval chateau in the north of France, and *UWIS Suite* from 1972, when he had conducted master classes at the University of Wisconsin. *The Queen's Suite* thus finds itself in good company, and in comparison to that good company it stands out all the more brilliantly as a masterwork.

A Surfeit, and (We Hope) More to Come

The stockpile has been a source of wonder and delight for decades now, and the Radio Denmark custodians surely have a great deal more to show us, though they appear to be slowing down. They have been fastidious about releasing only relatively polished works. Besides these, they hold many hours of rehearsals, breakdowns, spontaneous re-arrangements, and other studio happenings that have been heard on the Radio Denmark broadcasts and offer a candid view of the creative process leading up to the final takes. These too may someday find an audience among musicologists and scholars, akin perhaps to the scholars who pore over James Joyce's page proofs and Leonardo's sketchbooks.

Searching for parallels in Joyce and Leonardo and anywhere else in the art world truly brings home the magnitude of the stockpile. In sheer size it dwarfs any comparable output by any artist, and it also has the incalculable advantage of its kinetic medium, so that even the least valuable moments in an esthetic sense come wrapped in the dynamism of human interplay and technical fallibility and interactive tensions. The least valuable moments, that is, show Ellington's delight in the process of music-making, what his son Mercer in his memoir called "his pleasure with the imperfect." The most valuable moments, of course, show how close he came time after time to a kind of perfection.

The stockpile is all the more interesting for being, in a sense, accidental. In many of his public activities, Ellington was driven by the urge to please, and that urge sometimes led him along paths that ended in the maudlin, the cloying and the ephemeral. But the stockpile represented a private indulgence, and Ellington could indulge himself without regard for public approval, at least not directly, and so it gives a glimpse of the private man. For someone as guarded as Ellington about what he was willing to reveal about himself, the stockpile gives him a third dimension, or perhaps a fourth.

References (page numbers to direct quotations are shown *in italics*)

Balliett, Whitney. 1988. "Jimmy Knepper, Peggy and the Duke." Originally *New Yorker*. In *Collected Works: A Journal of Jazz 1954-2001*. 2002. New York: St. Martin's Griffin. 716-719. *p. 718.*

Balliett, Whitney. 1981. *Night Creature: A Journal of Jazz 1975-1980*. New York: Oxford University Press. *p. 192.*

Boyer, Richard O. 1944. "The Hot Bach." *The New Yorker*. 24 June -1, 8 July. Reprinted in *The Duke Ellington Reader*, ed. Mark Tucker. 1995. New York and Oxford: Oxford University Press. 214-245. *p. 229*

Buckley, Tom. 1972. "Duke: His Creative Impulse – All That Jazz – Throbs On." *New York Times*, 3 July, p. 19. https://www.nytimes.com/1972/07/03/archives/duke-his-creative-impulse-all-that-jazz-throbs-on-duke-his.html [accessed 12 July 2018]

Chambers, Jack. 2000. "What really happened at Newport? The dimming of a masterpiece." *Coda* 291 (May/June): 39. [Author note: Some quotations from George Avakian in the text come from this article but most are unpublished; I am grateful to Mr. Avakian for allowing me to interview him.]

Dance, Stanley. 1970. *The World of Duke Ellington*. London and New York: Macmillan. *p. xv.*

Dance, Stanley. 1992. Liner note for Billy Strayhorn, *Lush Life* (Red Baron CD).

Dance, Stanley. 1976. Liner note for The Ellington Suites. (Pablo Records, reprinted 1990 in OJCCD.)

Ellington, Duke. 1973. *Music Is My Mistress*. New York: Doubleday. *p. 221, pp. 111-113.*

Ellington, Mercer, with Stanley Dance. 1978. *Duke Ellington in Person*. Boston: Houghton Mifflin. *pp. 102-103, p. 170.*

Feather, Leonard. ca. 1985. Liner note for *The Johnny Hodges All Stars With the Duke Ellington All Stars and the Billy Strayhorn All Stars*. Prestige CD 24103 [1992].

Giddins, Gary. 1998. *Visions of Jazz: The First Century*. New York: Oxford University Press. *p. 498.*

O'Reilly, Ted. 1970. Interview with Duke Ellington. CJRT-FM (Toronto) broadcast 17 March.

Appendix: The Stockpile So Far

Record companies are shown in bold. Each CD is listed with (1) recording year, (2) title, catalogue number and year of CD release [in brackets], and (3) place, date and instrumentation. Recording dates were confirmed by Sjef Hoefsmit and Benny Aasland in DEMS Bulletins and may differ from dates listed on CDs. Items in {curly braces} are mnemonics and not part of the original title.

Year	CD Issue *Title* (catalogue [release date])	Discography Place, date, instrumentation
SAJA Records (distributed by Atlantic)		
1956 1957	The Private Collection, Vol. 1 (91041 [1987])	Chicago. March 1956 and Jan. 1957 Orchestra
1958	The Private Collection, Vol. 2 (910422 [1987]). Dance Concerts, California	California. Travis Air Force Base, 4 March 1958. Orchestra
1962	The Private Collection, Vol. 3 (255400 [1987]) {feat. Paul Gonsalves}	New York. 25 July and 12-13 Sept 1962. Nonet, septet, and orchestra
1963	The Private Collection, Vol. 4 (255401 [1987])	New York. 17 April, 15 May and 18 July 1963. Nonet, orchestra
1968 1970	The Private Collection, Vol. 5 (255402 [1987]) The Suites	New York. Degas Suite: 6 Nov, 3 Dec 1968. Chicago. The River: 25 May 1970 New York. 3, 8 and 15 June 1970 Orchestra
1958	The Private Collection, Vol. 6 (255922 [1989]). Dance Dates, California	California. Travis Air Force Base and Mather Air Force Base, 4 and 5 March 1958. Orchestra
1957 1962 1963	The Private Collection, Vol. 7 (255923 [1989]) {Sonny Greer's last stand}	Chicago. 17 and 29 Jan, Feb 1957. Quartet (+ vocal group), quintet, sextet, septet, orchestra. New York. 29 March and 6 June 1962, 20 May 1963. Octet, orchestra
1965 1966 1967	The Private Collection, Vol. 8 (255924 [1989])	San Francisco. 30 Aug. 1965. New York. 17 Mar, 14 Apr and 23 Sept 1965, 30 Aug and 29 Dec 1966, 11 July 1967. Orchestra
1968	The Private Collection, Vol. 9 (255925 [1989])	New York. 23 and 29 Nov, 3 and 4 Dec 1968. Orchestra
1965 1971	The Private Collection, Vol. 10 (255926 [1989]) {Black Brown and Beige}	New York. 4 March, 18 Aug 1965. Chicago. 31 March, 18 May 1965, 6 May 1971. Orchestra

Black Lion

1962	The Feeling of Jazz (Black Lion BLCD 760123 [n.d.])	New York. 24, 25 May and 6 June 1962. Orchestra

Fantasy (Original Jazz Classics CD)

1962	Featuring Paul Gonsalves (OJCCD 623 [1991], Fantasy LP 1984)	New York. 1 May 1962. Orchestra
1966 1970	The Pianist (OJCCD 561 [1991?], Fantasy LP 1974)	New York. 18 July 1966. Las Vegas. 7 Jan 1970. Trios
1967 1970	DE Small Bands, The Intimacy of the Blues (OJCCD 642 [1991], Fantasy LP 1986)	New York. 15 March 1967, 15 June 1970. Las Vegas. 7 Jan. 1970. Octets, septet, sextet, quintets

Laserlight

1965 1972	Cool Rock (15 782 [1992])	Chicago. 20 May 1965. Toronto. 22 June 1972 or 27 June 1972. Orchestra
1953	Happy Birthday, Duke! (15 783-4-5-6-7 [1992] 5 CD)	Portland, Oregon. McElroy's Ballroom, 29-30 April 1953. Orchestra

Moon

1966	Passion Flower (074 [1995])	Juan les Pins, France. 26-27 July 1966. Orchestra
1967	Live at the Rainbow Grill (049 [1993])	New York. Rainbow Grill, 17 August 1967. Octet

Music Masters

1965 1966 1969 1970 1971 1972	DE and His Orchestra 1965-1972 (5041 [1991])	Chicago. 31 March 1965. San Francisco. 30 Aug 1965. New York. 18 Aug 1966, 10 Sept 1969, 9 and 11 Dec 1970, 13 May 1971, 2 Aug 1972 Los Angeles. 23 June 1967 Milan. 23 July 1970 Piano + vocal (1 title), tentet (1 title), orchestra (6 titles), plus Wild Bill Davis organ (8 titles)

Pablo (Original Jazz Classics CD)

1959	The Ellington Suites	New York. The Queen's Suite:
1971	(OJCCD 446 [[1990]	25 Feb, 1 and 14 April 1959.
1972	Pablo LP 1976)	The Goutelas Suite: 27 April 1971.
		The UWIS Suite, 5 Oct. 1972

1969	The Intimate Ellington	New York. 25 April, 14 July, 29 Aug 1969.
1970	(OJCCD 730 [1992],	15 June, 9 Dec 1970. 1 and 2 Feb, 6 May,
1971	Pablo LP 1977)	29 June 1971. Orchestra (6 titles), solo
		(Ellington piano + vocal), trio (2 titles),
		tentet (3 titles)

1969	Up in Duke's Workshop	New York. 25 April, 20 June 1969,
1970	(OJCCD 633 [1991]	15 June, 19 Dec 1970, 1 and 3 Feb,
1971	Pablo LP 1979)	29 June 1971, 12 June 1972. Orchestra
1972		(8 titles + organ on 5), tentet (1)

Red Baron (distributed by SONY Music)

1960	Hot Summer Dance	California. Mather Air Force Base,
	(AK 48631 [1991])	22 July 1960. Orchestra

1964	Billy Strayhorn, Lush Life	New York. 14 Jan 1964, 30 June, 2 July,
1965	(AK 52760 [1992])	14 Aug 1965. Piano solo (+ vocal) and
		orchestra at Basin Street East (1964),
		quintet, trio, piano solos (+ vocal)

Signature (CBS Special Products)

1957	All Star Road Band, Vol. II	Carrolltown, Penn. (dance) June 1957.
	(AGK 39137 [1989],	Orchestra
	originally LP 1983)	

Zillion (distributed by SONY Music)

1962	New Mood Indigo	Japan. June 1964 (one title).
1964	(2610682 [1989], original	New York. 3 July 1962, 5 Jan. 1966,
1966	Doctor Jazz LP 1986)	29 March 1966. Orchestra (7), septet (4)

1956	Happy Reunion	Chicago. 19 March 1956, septet
1957	(2610642 [1991], original	[not 1957 as stated]. 24 June 1958,
	Doctor Jazz LP 1985)	quartet feat. Paul Gonsalves (3 titles)

Grönland

1970	The Conny Plank Session	Rhenus Studio, Cologne, Germany,
	(Grönland CD [2015])	9 July 1970 CD is named for the recording
		engineer. Orchestra plays three takes of
		"Alerado" (comp Wild Bill Davis, who
		plays organ on session) and three takes
		of "Afrique" (comp Ellington from *Afro-Eurasian Eclipse*). Alternate take 3 of
		"Afrique" has soprano vocalese by Lena
		Junoff. Master takes of "Alerado" (take 3)
		and "Afrique" (take 2) are on *New York New York* (Storyville [2008]) listed below

Storyville

1971	Togo Brava Suite (STCD 8323 [2001])	New York. 3 and 23 Feb., 28 March, 13 May, 28 and 29 June 1971. Orchestra
1958	The Duke in Munich (STCD 8324 [2003])	Munich. Deutsches Museum concert, 14 Nov 1958 Orchestra
1966 1967	The Jaywalker (STCD 8390 [2004])	New York. 29 March, 18 Aug 1966, 23 March, 4 April 1967. Los Angeles. 23 June 1967. Orchestra
1961 1962 1964 1967 1971	The Piano Player (STCD 8399 [2005])	Paris. March 1961. New York. TV show, 14 Dec 1962. Tokyo. 1 July 1964 Paris. 10 March 1967. New York. 11 May 1971. Solo piano. New York. 11 and 23 Feb 1971. Quartet with Wild Bill Davis organ.
1970 1971 1972	New York New York (STCD 8402 [2008])	New York. 27 April, 8 and 15 June 1970 Cologne. 9 July 1970 Milan. 23 July 1970 New York. 9 and 11 Dec 1970, 3 and 11 Feb, 5 May 1971; 12 June 1972. Orchestra. 5 Sept. 1972. Tentet (1 track).
1963	My People: The Complete Show (STCD 8430 [2012])	Chicago. 20, 21 and 27 August 1963 16-piece orchestra cond. Jimmy Jones, with vocalists Irving Bunton Singers, Joya Sherrill, Jimmy Grissom, Lil Greenwood and Jimmy McPhail.
1972	An Intimate Piano Session (STCD [2017])	New York, August 1972 Relaxed studio versions of Ellington piano solos on 8 titles plus three alternate takes, and five more tracks accompanying singers Anita Moore and Tony Watkins

CHAPTER 9

"Everything flows and nothing stays. You cannot step twice into the same river." Heraclitus's famous dictum (reported by Plato in *Cratylus*) was obviously not something that Duke Ellington subscribed to. One of the masterpieces of Ellington's final period, the years 1970-1974, perhaps the one indisputable masterpiece of these years, is his ballet suite *The River*, and as we shall see he stepped into it (metaphorically) three times. These final four years of his life were colored by the irreplaceable losses of Billy Strayhorn and Johnny Hodges (Strayhorn died in 1967, and Hodges in 1970). Halfway through this period, early in 1972, Ellington was diagnosed with the lung cancer that would kill him exactly two years later, though he and his doctor and beloved friend, Arthur Logan, conspired to keep the diagnosis secret even from his family members (according to Cohen, p. 562). Through it all, Ellington sustained a manic globe-trotting regimen, remarkable even by his nomadic standards, covering more miles and performing (usually, repeating) concerts almost daily. Ellington had overcome his aviophobia, acute fear of flying, beginning with a short trial flight in 1958 (according to Dan Morgenstern), a sheer act of will by a man who realized that the only way to maximize the audiences he craved was to cover more miles, and, it followed, the only way to cover more miles was by air. Even before the fatal diagnosis Ellington seemed perpetually on the move, as if aware that his time was rationed. He accomplished a great deal, and he did it by accepting every commission and every invitation that came his way. Amazingly, the legacy of these hectic years included, amidst so much more, three versions of the suite called *The River*, in three different musical genres with three distinctive sonic palettes and three overlapping but distinct re-imaginings. He stepped into *The River* not twice but thrice but, *pace* Heraclitus, it remains a fair question as to whether it is really the same river.

All three versions of *The River* are incomplete, reflecting the frantic pace of these years. More than that, they are all incomplete in different ways, reflecting Ellington's fragmented attention as he seemed intent on spending his waning resources in too many directions.

A Rich and Ambitious Conception

The River came into being through a commission from Lucia Chase, director of the American Ballet Theatre, as part of the festivities celebrating their 30th anniversary. Chase conceived the commission as an all-star package, with Alvin Ailey providing the choreography for Ellington's score. Ailey, a tall athletic African American dancer, had risen out of what he called "a rambling, rural" childhood in Texas to Broadway chorus lines. He founded the Alvin Ailey American Dance Theatre in 1958, when he was 27 years old. The agile grace of his productions became touchstones of modern dance, broadening the audience and influencing classical dance companies. Ailey's crowning achievement, *Revelations*, came early, in 1960, a celebration of gospel music and down-home spirituality conveyed with supple

Alvin Ailey first worked with Ellington on *My People* in 1963

motion and striking elegance. It has become a mainstay of the modern dance repertoire. Although Ellington was 32 years older than Ailey, Lucia Chase sensed that bringing together these icons of American music and American dance held great promise for an innovative meeting of minds.

Ailey had worked with Ellington seven years earlier on the production of Ellington's *My People*, an oratorio Ellington composed as a celebration of African American achievement for the Century of Negro Progress Exposition in Chicago in 1963. The show received a lukewarm reception and was never staged again. (The complete soundtrack was finally released by Storyville Records in 2012, listed in the appendix to Chapter 8.) Ailey's role was minor, but he came away mightily impressed. "Duke Ellington *really* is a genius – what an incredible man!" he wrote to a friend in New York (Denning, p. 175). "He never seems to sleep & new music pours out of him like a tap – not only was he constantly rewriting the show music but other things for the band to record here – and the most gracious, tactful, charming human being I've ever met." Ailey, needless to say, eagerly accepted the commission from the American Ballet Theatre.

The River, Mercer Ellington points out (1978, 172-173), was a concept that had been mooted for some time by Ellington's inner circle –

> The idea for *The River* had been kicking around for several years, ever since Stanley Dance had suggested an extended work depicting the natural course of a river. He had the Mississippi in mind... and he wrote out a description of it from source to sea. Billy Strayhorn liked it and there was often talk of doing it, but it was not until the American Ballet Theater accepted the proposal that Pop went to work on it.

The ballet commission not only revived it in Ellington's mind but inspired an ambitious re-conception – *overly* ambitious, as we shall see. Stanley Dance, the jazz biographer and "aide-de-camp" (Whitney Balliett's term) on both Ellington's *Music Is My Mistress* (1973) and Mercer Ellington's *Duke Ellington in Person* (1978), told Stanley Slome about his fairly modest original idea. "I had no thought of a symphonic treatment," he said, "but suggested it as an idea for an LP theme, thinking in terms of the band and a climactic affair like Ravel's *Bolero*." With the commission in hand, Ellington reconceived it as a gargantuan 12-movement ballet score that would enact in music and dance the river's movement from the trickle of "The Spring" through waterfalls and lakes and whirlpools to its mouth where it flows into "Her Majesty the Sea." In his initial enthusiasm, Ellington fashioned a long, quasi-poetic narrative describing the river's circuitous course as it would be covered in the musical movements. The narrative is preserved in its entirety in *Music Is My Mistress* and also in an apparently impromptu vernacular version that he recited for Whitney Balliett (2002). I quote from both versions in my discussion of the movements below.

Ellington saw the twelfth movement as a reprise of the first movement, "The Spring," following its flow into the sea. As he says in his narrative, "The river... romps into the mother – her majesty the sea – and of course is no longer a river. This is the climax," he wrote, "the heavenly anticipation of rebirth, for the sea will be drawn up into the sky for rain and down into wells and into springs and become the river again." Mercer Ellington later explained Ellington's purpose in plain terms: "By 1970 Ellington's mind was much more on spiritual

Stanley Dance (right) suggested *The River* as an LP theme; Ellington re-conceived it as a ballet suite (photo Stephen Somerstein, courtesy Hot Club de France)

values, so he turned the whole thing into a kind of religious allegory that dealt with the cycle of birth and rebirth." The "spiritual values" showed themselves most blatantly in Ellington's Sacred Concerts, the gospel-influenced biblical-themed productions that he presented first at Grace Cathedral in San Francisco (September 1965) and last at Westminster Abbey in London (October 1973), and at many other auspicious venues in between. Although *The River* is secular in its theme and theatrical in the occasion that called it forth, it undoubtedly gains its power and spirituality from the plain-spoken faith that Ellington professed so openly in these final years. It is no stretch, it seems to me, to hear in the two rhapsodic movements of *The River*, "The Lake" and "Village of the Virgins," a more profound musical expression of Ellington's spirituality than anything in the Sacred Concerts, for all their sentimental pleasantries.

Conception and Realization

Now, a half-century after the debut of *The River*, we realize that no performance of the ballet or of its score has ever reprised "The Spring" as the cyclical start-and-end point. Notwithstanding Ellington's good intentions, it was probably not esthetically justifiable. For one thing, "The Spring" is a legato movement; as such, it makes an appropriate beginning as a kind of awakening, but it would be an anticlimactic note to end on. For another, its symbolism would surely be lost after the hour of music and motion that would have come between its original appearance and its reprisal in Ellington's original conception. We are better off, perhaps, with what we ended up with than with Ellington's conceptualization of it.

Paradoxically, that seems to be true of *The River* in all its details. Between the conception and its realization there is a considerable abyss. In its realization, *The River* has seven movements (later eight), not the 12 that Ellington conceived. Performance time is around 30 minutes, about half the length that Ellington envisaged. The movements are orchestrated and arranged not by Ellington but by Ron Collier, a Canadian composer hired by Ellington for that purpose. Collier, as we shall see, constructed the symphonic movements from themes Ellington first picked out on his portable Wurlitzer keyboard and then from arrangements he wrote for his jazz band as he traveled the world on his endless round of live performances. When *The River* had its well-publicized debut at the anniversary gala of the American Ballet Theatre at Lincoln Centre in New York on 25 June 1970, Ellington was 1100 km (700 m) away in Chicago. What business kept Ellington away? He was playing yet another one-nighter in yet another venue, this one at the Grant Park Music Shell in the Chicago Loop. It is a sobering indication of Ellington's priorities that he chose to spend that evening beaming at the small crowd on the grass around the band shell while his band played "Take the A Train" for the six-thousandth time (literally, at least 200 times a year for 30 years) rather than, tuxedoed at Lincoln Centre, graciously accepting the bouquet of roses after the triumphal premiere of his brand-new ballet. In fact, in the three healthful years that remained to him, Ellington never saw the ballet performed, and he probably never heard the symphonic score played in its entirety.

This should not imply that Ellington withheld his creative juices. Notwithstanding his benign neglect, *The River* was a huge success in its debut performance, and it continues to be widely lauded whenever ballet companies and symphony orchestras dare to take it on. It has the most solid claim, as I said at the start, to the status of masterwork of any piece of Ellington's in his hyperactive final four years.

As remote as Ellington was from the actual woodshedding of

the ballet, his fingerprints are definitely on the work. His conception, though pared down, is intact. His sound reverberates in the score. And it is because of Ellington's physical distance from the place where *The River* was being workshopped that we have the three versions of the music in three genres shown in the Table. First, chronologically, came a set of piano sketches, played by Ellington in a recording studio and delivered to orchestrator Ron Collier and choreographer Alvin Ailey with the hopes that they could develop the score and fashion the choreography from them; the piano sketches are listed in the left column of the accompanying Table along with some discographical details. When the piano sketches proved too sparse to serve as guides for the choreographer, Ellington wrote out band arrangements and took his orchestra into local studios to record them; the band sketches are listed in the middle column. Finally, the symphonic movements that Collier built out of the piano and big-band sketches are listed in the right column.

TABLE – Three Trips Down *The River* with their dates and original CD sources

Piano sketches	Big Band sketches	Symphonic score
The Piano Player. Storyville [2005] • recorded 11 May 1970, NYC	Private Collection Vol. 5 [1987] • recorded 25 May 1970, Chi (1-5), 8 June 1970 (6), 3 June (7-10), 15 June (11), NYC	Suite from *The River* orchestrated by Ron Collier • Detroit Symphony Orchestra, Neeme Järvi cond. Oct. 1992 Chandos Records 9154
The Spring (3:20)	The Spring (2:26)	Spring (3:00)
The Run (2:46)	The Run (2:34)	
The Meander (2:36)	The Meander (5:08)	Meander (3:57)
Grap [Giggling Rapids] (2:48)	The Giggling Rapids (4:19)	Giggling Rapids (2:55)
The Lake (3:36)	The Lake (6:53)	Lake (6:51)
	The Falls (2:59)	[Falls (3:14)]*
	The Whirlpool (3:23)	Vortex (2:13)
	The River (3:55)	Riba (3:18)
Stud [The Neo-Hip-Hot Cool Kiddies Community] (2:25)	New Hip-Hop [Stud] (1:46)	
	Village of the Virgins (5:09)	Village Virgins (4:21)
	Her Majesty the Sea (2:35)	

*"Falls" was not included in premiere performance or on some symphonic recordings including the Detroit Symphony recording, but it was added in subsequent performances of the ballet and on some recordings

In the Table, I have cited the symphonic score from a 1992 recording by the Detroit Symphony Orchestra with the addition of "Falls," the movement inserted after the premiere performance (and omitted from the Detroit Symphony performance, as it sometimes is in subsequent symphonic performances). Strictly speaking, the definitive symphonic performance should be the one conducted by Ron Collier, the orchestrator and arranger of the music, in April 1974, at a Toronto concert on the occasion of Duke Ellington's 75th birthday. However, the extant recordings of Collier's performance are homemade tapings taken from the radio broadcast (for instance, in the archives of DEMS, the Duke Ellington Music Society). I have a studio-quality version of this music designated "for academic use only," and therefore publicly inaccessible. As long as it remains inaccessible, the Detroit Symphony recording makes a reasonable substitute because Collier himself gave it his imprimatur in a talk at the Duke Ellington conference in Toronto in 1998 when he cited it as a "really a beautiful recording." All seven movements in the Detroit Symphony rendition, though played slightly faster than Collier conducted them in his own concert performance, are delivered with estimable musicianship and considerable flair.

"Only God knows what time that is"
The orderly tabulation of the three iterations shown in the Table masks a creative frenzy that seems to have driven everyone except Duke Ellington to near-madness. Collier got around to reminiscing about his experience only after 26 years had passed, and by then he could say, with considerable aplomb, "I had to orchestrate from the band charts. For most of the pieces he [Ellington] would write them out because the choreographer needed pieces of music so that he could work with the dancers; and instead of Duke writing out a piano piece, he would write out a chart for the band, send [the recording] on to Alvin Ailey and that's what they would use to work with." One can only guess at the challenges Collier faced in transforming sketches whether by piano or jazz band into full symphonic scores with the composer largely incommunicado.

Alvin Ailey was not so benign. A glance at the recording dates of the big-band recordings in the middle column of the Table shows why there was panic in the rehearsal hall. Ellington recorded piano sketches of six of the 11 movements on 11 May, about six weeks before the premiere on 25 June. When they proved too 'sketchy', literally, for Ailey to metamorphose into ballet, Ellington prepared big-band sketches. The magnitude of Ellington's task, writing the scores and herding the orchestra into studios while maintaining a constant round of travel and nightly performances, brought inevitable delays. Ellington's big-band sketches of the first five movements arrived a month before they were due to be performed by a full orchestra and *corps de ballet* at Lincoln Centre. Even if they were delivered a day or two later (in the pre-internet era), that seems perilously close to the limit for orchestration, choreography and rehearsal time. After that, it gets really tense. Four other movements were recorded with three weeks to spare, and another, "The Falls," five days after that. "Her Majesty the Sea" arrived ten days before its scheduled performance. That timeline explains how Ellington's master plan was reduced by almost a half.

Getting any music at all from Ellington required pursuing him on his seemingly endless rounds. After Lucia Chase had the two icons under contract for her project, she sent Ailey to Vancouver where Ellington and his orchestra were playing in a hotel ballroom for several nights so that Ailey and Ellington could work out preliminary details of their collaboration. Ailey discovered that Ellington's workdays had an unyielding, idiosyncratic shape. "My workday begins the minute I wake up, and ends the minute my head hits the pillow – only God knows what time that is," Ellington once told a reporter for *Jet* magazine. Ailey found out that Ellington really meant it. In Vancouver, the band finished playing at 1:30 a.m. Ellington received visitors backstage and then more visitors in his hotel room after the show. When the room finally cleared, Ailey got his moment. "I told him that I wanted to do a kind of rhapsodic ballet," Ailey said, "but Duke had another idea." Ellington talked about his conception for *The River* and illustrated the movements on the electric piano at the foot of his bed. In his autobiography, Ailey recalled: "At five o'clock in the morning I was sitting in Duke Ellington's apartment bathed in beautiful music. I said, 'Let's do it. Let's do *The River*'." They shook hands and Ellington abruptly left for a flight to Los Angeles for his next performance. Ailey was mesmerized, though he came away from their meeting with no music in hand.

"After we agreed to a collaboration, he was gone all of the time," Ailey said in his autobiography.

Weeks later, Ailey caught up with the band in a Toronto jazz club. Ellington's routine now had a familiar ring to Ailey. "At eight his room would be full of 60-year-old ladies, probably Canadian, whom he called girls," Ailey said. "They just adored him. The shows were at nine and eleven, and during the interval between shows he would party with the ladies." Finally alone together in the wee hours of the morning, Ellington proudly showed Ailey a collection of water themes he had acquired in his travels – recordings of Handel's *Water Music*, Debussy's "La Mer," and other classics. He told Ailey, "I've been listening to this to see what other people have done with water music." These explorations by Ellington were reminiscent of the study sessions on Shakespeare that Ellington and Strayhorn had undertaken 14 years earlier when they were preparing the Shakespeare suite. The water classics are not discernible in the music that Ellington eventually composed, but Ailey was willing to believe that Ellington's interest in them, amidst all his distractions, meant that the music for *The River* was palpably in progress. "He liked to work from 4:30 until 7 o'clock in the morning," Ailey said. "Then he would go to bed and sleep until 3 or 4 in the afternoon." Ailey recounts answering the phone in his hotel room at 4 a.m. It was Ellington. "Did I wake you, Alvin?" "I'd say, 'No, Duke', and he'd say, laughing, 'Come on over, I've got something for you to hear'."

Ailey, exhausted, returned to New York with a few scraps of music. "The music was just beautiful, but it was driving me out of my mind," Ailey said. "I talked to people who worked with him. They said, 'Well, that's the way he works. You're just going to have to learn how to work with him like that. He'll take 16 bars into a studio, eight bars of this and two bars of that, and come out four hours later with eight fantastic pieces. That's just the nature of the way he works.' He wrote with the orchestra – the orchestra was his instrument. He composed in the recording studio; his band was his Stradivarius" (reported by Henken 2007).

Jennifer Dunning, Ailey's biographer, says, "The rest of the

Alvin Ailey with dancers

score... arrived in pieces, sometimes brought to the sixth floor studios at City Center by Ellington himself to the delight of the dancers and a nervously watchful Chase, who was growing worried that *The River* would never be completed. 'Ah, we have a few more bars here,' Alvin would slyly announce to the dancers after such a visit. 'Let's go on'."

Finally, with the performances only days away, Ailey reached his breaking point. Don George, one of Ellington's occasional lyricists and his most spirited biographer, describes the climactic events:

> Three days before the [dress] rehearsals were to start, Ailey still hadn't received the written music. He had occasionally received bits and pieces in the mail, a few bars now and then that didn't seem to match up. One day he got a tape with four pieces, and he was trying to choreograph those. He finally threw up his hands. All the Ballet Theatre people were in the rehearsal studio and Ailey was hot to go, but he was completely frustrated because he didn't have the music. He flipped. He went clean out of his mind. He hurled the whole thing – notebooks, tapes and all – up against the mirror and yelled, 'Fuck it, I can't work like this.'
>
> At that precise moment the door opened and in walked Duke in his white cashmere coat surrounded by his entourage. The whole room stopped. In fact, it fell to its knees. Ailey told me later that what he wanted to scream was, 'Where's the music?' Instead they went outside and sat and talked. Ailey told Duke he couldn't work without

the whole score. Duke said to Alvin, 'Listen, if you'd stop worrying about this music and do more choreography, we'd be a whole lot better off.'

The show, needless to say, did go on. The program for the Lincoln Centre premiere billed the ballet as "Seven Dances from a Work in Progress Entitled *The River*." With one exception, the movements that were not performed were the ones that arrived too late: "The Falls," recorded by the big band only 17 days before the premiere without the benefit of a piano 'preview' on which Ailey might have based preliminary choreography; "The Neo-Hip-Hot Cool Kiddies Community," a mere sketch (less than two minutes) recorded by the big band the same day as "The Falls"; and "Her Majesty the Sea," recorded just ten days before the premiere. There remains one anomaly: the movement called "The Run" was available on time in both the piano sketch and the big band sketch (as the Table shows); its omission may represent an esthetic choice by Ailey because its peculiar (though winsome) march rhythm offers less balletic scope (as discussed below).

There can be no doubt that it was Ailey's choreography chores that were the sticking point. Collier orchestrated "The Falls" in time for the premiere, but Ailey could not choreograph it in time for the premiere performance. He later integrated it into subsequent performances of the ballet. According to John Franceschina, the movement called "Riba" (pronounced "ribba," a dialect rendering of "river") had to be improvised by solo dancer Denis Nahat at the premiere because there was no time for choreographing it; eventually, it was elaborately choreographed in what DeFrantz (2004, p. 152) describes as "a jokey parody of Cotton Club routines… suggested by Ellington's hard-swinging, twelve-bar blues." There may have been more orchestrations that were omitted for lack of choreography. Looking back years later, Collier said, "I don't know how many [movements] were written," that is, orchestrated. However many there were, only "The Falls" survived, and was added in later performances.

"A cohesive, elegant work of art"

Maybe it was the backstage tension that Ellington provoked that gave

The River its creative glow. It was recognized as a singular achievement at its opening and has been taken on in the repertoire of ballet companies ever since. Ailey's choreography is brilliantly described and discussed by Thomas DeFrantz (2004, 149-155), an aspect that will necessarily be underplayed here but is highly recommended for listeners who want a fuller appreciation.

The critical reception at the premiere is well documented by John Franceschina (2001, pp. 162-164), the foremost writer on Ellington's theatre music. Harriet Johnson in the *New York Post* praised its "fluid, cumulative structure and vivid suggestive power." Hubert Saal, in *Newsweek*, called it "a tone poem...like a river, constantly flowing, changing speed and shape, instantly accessible melodically." Clive Barnes, in the *New York Times*, praised its "blend of classical ballet, modern dance and jazz movement, a most rewarding hybrid." Barnes noted, "The piece is not finished. But it is a delight. It is the most considerable piece from Mr. Ellington since his *Black, Brown and Beige Suite*; it is quite lovely. And Mr. Ailey has never previously created with such power and force for a classic troupe.... At the moment we have only seven dances from a prologue, an epilogue and 11 sections [but] it is already a major work, complete in itself." Saal also felt the need to recognize it as incomplete, but more reluctantly: "the fact that the work looked and sounded incomplete and fragmented only served to suggest how coherent the finished work would be." He added, "The separate parts could not be shifted around or omitted. At the same time, what there was provided its own satisfactions," a point that will certainly strike home for those listeners (myself among them) who came to *The River* innocent of its backstory, hearing it simply as a completed suite of music.

Franceschina (164) summed up its theatrical reception as "an immediate popular and critical success, ... in which Alvin Ailey [bridged] the gap between modern dance and classical ballet," and he points out that it "became a staple of the American Ballet Theatre's repertoire." When the critics' raves came in, Ailey's frustrations quickly dissipated. He acknowledged the power of his collaboration with Ellington by performing *The River* frequently in the next decade and twice revising his choreography. Ailey's most astute critic, Thomas DeFrantz, compared it favorably to Ailey's masterpiece: "In terms of length and ambition, the work rivaled *Revelations* with its tiers of casting and as a sustained suite that gathered power cumulatively." Ailey died in 1989, age 59, but his choreography for *The River* lives on as a feature for many dance companies. Indeed, Ailey occasionally choreographed other Ellington compositions for the rest of his professional life. He danced to Ellington's "Reflections in D," a piano trio recorded in 1953. A television tribute called *Ailey Celebrates Ellington* on CBS Festival of Lively Arts for Young People in November 1974, six months after Ellington's death, included his dances set to Ellington's "The Mooche," a 1928 composition, and a "shimmering" *Night Creature*, a 1963 symphony.

Night Creature is "one of Alvin's wittiest and most ravishingly pretty dances," according to his biographer Jennifer Dunning, and it is still regularly performed by the Alvin Ailey American Dance Theatre. These collaborations were obviously less stressful for Ailey because he started with the music safely in hand.

Ellington's music for *The River* also has taken on a life of its own apart from the ballet. Of Duke Ellington's three distinct instrumental takes on *The River*, the symphonic version was the last written and

Alvin Ailey's stunning choreography for Ellington's *Night Creature*, 1974
(photo © Gert Krautbauer)

the first made public. Both the piano sketches and the big-band sketches were released posthumously, among the treasures of the stockpile, the vast cache of private recordings that Ellington amassed in the 1950s and 1960s. The piano sketches, his first outlines of the movements in May 1970, were finally made public in 2005 on the Danish Storyville label as part of a compilation of Ellington piano solos called *The Piano Player*. As the Table above shows, they cover six of the projected 11 movements, including two that never made it into the ballet score. The big-band sketches were released in 1987 on a CD called *The Suites, Private Collection*, Vol. 5 (originally on a label called Saba but since reissued on a bewildering number of imprints). They include all 11 movements and thus give a full account, albeit in sketchbook form, of Ellington's original conception.

Ellington's symphonic score, in Ron Collier's orchestration, has been recorded by several orchestras. I list five here that are either historically interesting or fairly accessible (but not usually both):

- 1974 CJRT Symphony Orchestra, cond. Ron Collier
  [7 mvts, 30:34]
- 1977 Warsaw Symphony Orchestra, cond. Mercer Ellington.
  [8 mvts, 27:00]
- 1983 Louisville Orchestra, cond. Akira Endo. First Edition Records. [8 mvts, 27:00]
- 1993 Detroit Symphony Orchestra, cond. Neeme Järvi. Chandos Records. [7 mvts, 26:50]
- 2012 Buffalo Philharmonic Orchestra, cond. JoAnn Falletta. Naxos American Classic. [5 mvts, 21:04]

Some of the confusion surrounding the premiere apparently still clings to the cataloguing of *The River*. The publisher of the symphonic score, G. Schirmer, lists the seven movements in the order shown in the Table above, which is also their order at the premiere performance at Lincoln Centre in 1970, the definitive performance conducted by Collier in 1974, and in the 1993 recording by the Detroit Symphony. However, the manuscript of the score, as displayed on the Schirmer website (listed in References), prepared by Tempo Music Inc., Ellington's publishing company that his son, Mercer Ellington, sold to Schirmer after Ellington died, lists eight movements, adding "Falls" (actually "Fals," a typo); it also reverses the order of the last two movements so that "Riba" follows "Village of the Virgins." These revisions show the meddlesome hand of Mercer Ellington, who recorded the score with both of these revisions – the insertion of "Falls" and the inverted order of the last two movements – with the Warsaw Symphony Orchestra in Poland in 1977. After Ellington's death, Mercer occasionally traveled with a nostalgia band that he called the Duke Ellington Orchestra, and on one of their European tours, three years after Duke Ellington's death, he arranged for a recording of *The River* and other Ellington symphonies in Warsaw. Mercer added some of his big-band musicians to the symphony players. He plays all the movements relatively fast, and he inserts jazz solos into "Village of the Virgins" and "Riba." Mercer had a special feeling for "Riba," because it originated in a melody he wrote (as discussed in the next section), and he quite blatantly beefs it up by making it the climactic end. Mercer's recording with the Warsaw Symphony is out of print, and (in my experience) impervious to searches of any kind. It appears to be one of the cultural artifacts that got buried after the Iron Curtain fell in the 1990s. We can hope that it will be rediscovered some day and brought back into circulation.

At any rate, the movement called "The Falls" is available in the symphonic manuscript published by Schirmer. The 1983 recording by the Louisville Symphony restores it to the score but most renditions do not. Some symphonic versions are even more selective in the movements they play, no doubt representing a trend by cultural institutions in the internet age to keep the music short and to the point in hopes of holding the attention of their audiences. The 2012 recording by the Buffalo Philharmonic pares down the suite to five movements, leaving out "The Vortex" and (inexplicably, in my view) "Village of the Virgins" as well as "The Falls." The Los Angeles Philharmonic, in their 2007 season, also selected five movements. Still, the integrity of the original seven movements, accidental though it may have been, appears to hold sway; Symphony Silicon Valley, a California orchestra, played the original seven movements in their 2014-2015 season, as do most others.

The River has considerable currency in concert halls. The Schirmer website lists 31 leases in the decade from 2005 to 2015 by orchestras in Australia, Austria, Canada, Croatia, England, France,

Ron Collier's title page (detail) of MS "Giggling Rapids (GRAP)," third movement of *The River*. The three-minute movement fills 22 manuscript pages. <issuu.com/scoresondemand/docs/giggling_rapids_27665>

Germany, Switzerland, and 14 states of the United States from Washington and Wyoming to Massachusetts and North Carolina. Ellington's ballet suite is now almost 50 years old, and so its currency is no mere passing fancy. In their program, Symphony Silicon Valley note that "Duke Ellington's music demonstrated that the divergent idioms of jazz and classical music could merge into a cohesive, elegant work of art."

Amen to that.

"Eight bars of this and two bars of that, and four hours later ... eight fantastic pieces"

While the symphonic suite has carved out a space for itself in various parts of the world, scrutinized by conductors and musicologists in matters of tempo and voicing, Ellington's piano sketches and his big-band sketches have received no attention from musicians (and almost none from critics), even though they flow directly out of what the whole world recognizes as his natural idiom. No single title has ever been played by any jazz piano player or by any jazz orchestra. Both the piano sketches and the big-band sketches rest in their separate digital nooks, admired by listeners who come upon them, almost exclusively Ellington admirers (or scholars), but otherwise ignored.

One reason is their belated appearance. The band sketches came out of the stockpile 13 years after Ellington's death, and the piano sketches a whopping 31 years after. They were virtually unknown, even to aficionados, unlike *The Queen's Suite* and a few other items in the stockpile. The ballet suite *The River* received less attention in its symphonic version than it deserved at the moment of its conception, from Ellington and from everyone else, and the process of its composition, which the sketches embody, are a further step removed and easy to ignore. Mercer Ellington tried to provide a corrective, but to no avail. "It contains some beautiful themes," he wrote in his memoir, "and the music deserves more attention independent of the dance, although together they have always been very well received." True enough, and better late than never.

Listeners who knew the background might have assumed that the sketches were fragments, some kind of shorthand or musical palimpsests, unworthy of consideration in their own right. Strangely, Ron Collier seemed to espouse this view. In his 1998 talk, he launched into an impromptu complaint about the release of the big-band sketches. Talking about the movement called "The Lake," Collier abruptly brought up the CD release of the sketches. "I got a beef here," he said. "Mercer released this. I'm sure if Duke were alive he wouldn't have allowed them to be released. They were really very rough. That was just to be a guide track for the choreographer, not written to be band pieces or for a symphony orchestra." Collier is right, of course, about the casual circumstances in which the band sketches came into being, but he undervalues the facility with which Ellington in 1970 prepared material for the orchestra and the depth that his virtuoso sidemen brought to his arrangements on the bandstand and in the studio. These were talents that Collier had seen at first hand in other circumstances and admired fervently. But the best clue that Collier's complaints on this matter are hastily put together and born of flawed memory comes when he talks about the big-band sketch of "The Lake."

"I'm embarrassed when I hear this 'Lake'," he says, "because it

Ron Collier rehearsing the orchestra

was a rough job, no resemblance to what I did with the symphony orchestra." In fact, "The Lake" was the one big-band sketch that Collier himself wrote, not Ellington, as I will point out when I discuss the movements individually below, and hence the one that most closely matches the symphonic score. It was the one Collier should have had no beef about.

More pointedly, neither Collier nor anyone else has a legitimate beef about their release. Stanley Dance, who saw to the release of the big-band sketches together with Mercer Ellington, wrote in the liner note accompanying the CD, "None of these were intended for release, but today they are the equivalent of a great artist's sketchbooks, and as such are presented here." It is a rare privilege, perhaps unprecedented, to have two or sometimes three renditions of a composition and see it unfurl from a piano solo to a 14-piece band to a symphony orchestra. And it is a stroke of luck beyond imagining that each rendition is listenable in its own right and brings its own distinct pleasures.

The River from spring to sea

For each movement in the following descriptions, I cite Ellington's often rhapsodic prose description from his exposition in *Music Is My Mistress* (pp. 201-202), sometimes supplementing it with the colloquial version he recited for Whitney Balliett. Ellington may have intended his description as a program note for the premiere or perhaps as a narration for a concert version, but it was never used. It is useful because it provides another clue to Ellington's original conception. For each movement, I then consider Ellington's music in whatever renditions he has left us.

The Spring. Ellington says, "*The River* starts as THE SPRING, which is like a newborn baby. He's in his cradle...spouting, spinning, wiggling, gurgling, making faces, reaching for his nipple or bottle, turning, tossing, and tinkling all over the place."

In Ellington's conception, the spring is no artesian gush but a minimal, almost invisible trickle of water. "The Spring" opens the ballet almost in silence. Ron Collier describes Ellington's piano sketch, his first draft of the movement, as "noodling," and Ellington's use of the word "tinkling" in his description suits it as well, applied to the piano. In his conference talk, Collier noodled several bars on an out-of-tune upright and said, "There's a lot of spontaneity in that.... It's almost like a little bit of noodling but he never wrote it out." According to Collier, Ellington gave a tape of his piano noodling to organist Wild Bill Davis and asked him to transcribe it. Davis was traveling with the orchestra at the time and playing organ in the ensemble as well as contributing a few charts (his arrangement of "April in Paris" had been a hit for Count Basie four years before, in 1966). Writing out Ellington's piano sketch was obviously not to Wild Bill's taste because what Collier received, he said, was "just melodies, no chords, no bar lines." He also received the tape, and Collier re-copied it, putting in the bar lines, and then sending it to the rehearsal pianist at the American Ballet Theatre. The sparse melody may explain why Ellington's second sketch of the movement was not played by the band, as all the others were, but by piano with bass accompaniment. Moreover, it is brief (more than a minute shorter than either the piano sketch or the symphonic score). Ellington was apparently working

The American Ballet Theatre with William Carter in *The River*, 1970
(photo Martha Swope, courtesy American Ballet Theatre)

from Davis's transcription but Ailey and Collier were working from Collier's fuller version. As a result, in this case the piano/bass sketch, lyrical though it is, is an impoverished reflection of the other two versions.

Collier's orchestration rightly begins with noodling but it is noodling of a different order, as he has contextualized it strikingly. Collier said, wryly, "I can't start off with bassoon because Stravinsky did that in *Rite of Spring*, so I start off with French horn." And the French horn, somber and mysterious, almost motionless at first, adds color to the tinkling opening and then carries the music into the accelerando as the spring stirs and gathers momentum. The quiescent opening makes a clever adaptation of Ellington's conception of the spring as birth, and it is easy for listeners to imagine the slow stirring of the dancers with the slow stirring of the music in the first half of the three-minute movement, until it comes fully alive with a beautiful melody and recedes gracefully.

***The Run**,* intended in Ellington's conception as the second movement, was pulled from the ballet. Circumstantial evidence suggests that it was an esthetic decision rather than a logistical problem because both the piano sketch and the big-band sketch were prepared in time for the ballet score; they were ready at the same time as four other movements that did make it in. "The Run" is an affecting piece of music written in march time and, in the big-band sketch, buoyed by interesting syncopations by the reed instruments and ingenious interchanges between flute by Norris Turney and bass clarinet by Harry Carney.

Perhaps it was Ellington who noticed that its staccato rhythm interrupted the riverine flow or maybe it was Ailey who noticed that it disrupted the danceable rhythms that came before and after. We will never know for sure. Collier did not prepare an orchestral score for it, indicating that its exclusion must have been decided soon after Ailey received the music. "The Run," as it happened, had a previous history. Ellington had written it two years earlier for the soundtrack of a documentary on Edgar Degas's racetrack paintings; the documentary was never produced (through no fault of Ellington's) and

Nat Orr, April Berry and Carl Bailey in *The River*, 1981 (photo Bill Hinton)

the soundtrack, called *Degas Suite*, had been lying idle for two years when *The River* was in the works. In *Degas Suite*, "The Run" is called "Marcia Regina" (Latin for the queen's march) and ironically its 1968 recording in *Degas Suite* was released on the same CD as the 1970 big-band sketch for *The River*. Ellington was right in thinking it was far too good a piece of music to waste, but it fits much more happily in *Degas Suite,* as intended, than in *The River.*

The Meander, the movement that came second, was characterized by Ellington as "rolling around from one side to the other..., up and down, back and forth." The rest of Ellington's description mixes metaphors and empurples the prose, but these few phrases capture fairly the indecisive motion of meandering.

The music of "The Meander" meanders capriciously from a swaying motion at the start to a lonely flute solo, and then it resounds momentarily with rich jazz-like chords, before quieting with woodwinds, lonely again at the faded ending. Its caprices were undoubtedly intended to provide Ailey with shape-shifting choreographic possibilities but, according to Dunning (p.256), "this quick-darting *Meander*" ended as an "unemotional, almost abstract... dance." For listeners, the music of this movement is the least defined – or perhaps, put positively, the most meandering. Ellington's big-band sketch (5:08) doubles the length of the piano sketch (2:26) without noticeably adding color or spice to it. Collier's orchestration, wisely, reins it in (3:57), but judging by Dunning's critique of Ailey's choreography, even that was perhaps too long.

Giggling Rapids, also known as **Grap** (following an unexplained practice in which Ellington gave four-letter nicknames to many of his compositions starting in the 1960s). The meandering river comes to a rough, rocky expanse that, Ellington says, "races and runs and dances and skips and trips... until exhausted."

The tempo rises, and stays up for this lively, fetching movement. Ellington's piano version is a delight in its own right, a jazz waltz that he plays with great panache. The big-band version is played with similar gusto, opening with Ellington's piano accompanied by bass, and then gaining depth as the band enters playing rich counter-melodies around the piano/bass motif. The arrangement is intricate and deft (and deserves to be played by other bands). Collier's symphonic score retains the constant bass motif but assigns Ellington's piano melody mainly to the woodwinds with counter-melodies played by brass and other instrumental groupings. The latter half of Collier's score has the feel of a bouncy Broadway arrangement, eminently danceable but perhaps less Ellingtonian than it might have been. All three versions are lively and vivacious. All three giggle in their own ways.

The Lake, Ellington says, "is beautiful and serene. It is all horizontal lines that offer up unrippled reflections. There it is, in all its beauty, God-made and untouched, until people come – people who are God-made and terribly touched by the beauty of the lake. They, in their admiration for it, begin to discover new facets of compatibility in each other, and as a romantic viewpoint develops, they indulge themselves."

This movement glows with the romantic impetus that Ellington's words express, with long melodic lines and languid sensuality. It is the centerpiece of the ballet, as the fourth of seven movements. It is also the longest movement, and the most lyrical. Ironically, it came into being at the point at which Ellington appears to have been losing interest in the ballet. We can infer this from the production gap that follows this movement, as Ellington takes ever longer to produce the music so urgently needed by the others.

Ellington's waning interest can be inferred from Collier's recollection of the way this movement came into being. "He gave me one piece, it was called 'Lake', and it was up in his room," Collier said. "I had dinner at his place. [He handed me] just a little piece of sheet music, single-line chord changes, and he said, 'This is a *pas de deux*, two dancers.' I said, 'What would you like me to do with it?' He says, 'Well, you know what to do with it'." Collier was dumbfounded. Collier said, "You know, it's almost seven minutes long on the tape but that's all the instructions: 'You know what to do with it.' So I went home and it sat on the brief case." A few days later, Collier got a call from Ellington telling him that the band would be recording "Lake" the next day. Collier stayed up all night writing the arrangement, "doing it for a small orchestra," with the help of Joe Benjamin, Ellington's bass player who also served as his copyist.

Judging by the three versions, Collier must have had the symphonic score of "The Lake" underway when he carried out the rush job on the band arrangement. Both the big-band arrangement and the symphony score double the length of Ellington's piano solo. They are rich expansions of the piano sketch, and the ballet music mirrors the big-band arrangement more faithfully than any of the other sketches. Ellington obviously knew exactly what would happen when he told Collier that he knew what to do with it. Collier's expansion of Ellington's piano sketch perfectly sustains its lush romanticism, and indeed elaborates it to make this sumptuous, breath-taking centerpiece.

DeFrantz calls "The Lake" "a rich adagio," and he describes how Ailey's choreography of the *pas de deux* complements the music (149-150): "Ellington's score... develops a two-part melodic theme set in alternating minor and major modes. Ailey's choreography develops this binary as a tension between romantic partners. A shirtless man

Sally Wilson and Keith Lee in *The River*, 1970
(photo Martha Swope, courtesy American Ballet Theatre)

enters suddenly from the side of the stage. The woman becomes wary, discarding her lyrical freedom to move with sharpened precision, retreating from his pursuit. He reaches her and manipulates her into a series of awkward, sharply angled positions. Eventually she surrenders to his advances to dance with, rather than against, him. Her acquiescence is timed to a melodic swell and release into a major mode articulation of the musical theme."

Ellington's music is heartfelt and moving, as is the dance it inspired from Ailey. If Ellington's enthusiasm for *The River* was waning at this point, as seems evident, he should have been gratified to see that Collier's was not. "The Lake" forms an expansive, show-stopping still-point at the heart of the ballet.

The Falls, Ellington writes, "always looks [*sic*] the same at the top and always sounds the same at the bottom. You can always hear the voice of the spirit that has gone over the falls and into the whirlpool, yelling and reaching back up the falls to regain the place of serenity that is the lake."

The calm of the lake spills into a bombastic waterfall. Ellington did not compose this movement on the piano, presumably because he would have needed at least three hands to create its dissonances. He augmented his band for it by adding a fifth trumpet and a battery of percussionists (tympani, glockenspiel, and xylophone/marimba). Whitney Balliett, jazz critic of the *New Yorker*, witnessed its recording in the studio, "which," he says, "like most of the places Ellington goes, was crowded with relatives, friends and hangers-on." Balliett, in his special way, provides an evocative account of "The Falls." It "turned out to be unlike anything I had heard Ellington do. But then," he says, "nothing new of his is quite like anything he has done before. The section passages... are brief but dense and booting, there are solo parts by Paul Gonsalves, and there are heavy, dissonant full-band chords. All of this is done against the furious *rat-a-tat* of the snare, the glockenspiel, and the tympani. It is exciting, tight crescendo music, and it reminded me of early Stravinsky, except that it was unmistakably a jazz composition." It is, like so many of the band sketches, music that stands up to repeated hearings and it surely merits a niche in the repertoire of adventurous contemporary jazz

The corps de ballet in motion

bands.

The symphonic movement, the late-comer to the ballet, retains the percussive undertow of snare and tympani. It transfers the raunchy tenor saxophone to wind ensembles, and the effect is much more dulcet, and surely a letdown to anyone who knows Ellington's big-band sketch. In the ballet setting, Collier's relatively civil transposition undoubtedly sounds bombastic enough.

Vortex, also known as **The Whirlpool**, captures the precipitous motion that Ellington describes, simply, "Then he goes over the falls and down into the whirlpool, the vortex of violence" (quoted by Balliett).

One of the drawbacks for people listening to the score instead of watching the ballet is that "The Falls" and "Vortex," coming side by side, place the two most sonically similar movements together in a single stretch. Rhythm dominates in "Vortex," as it does in "The Falls." For both, Ellington bolstered his rhythm section by adding percussionists (and, for both, he did not attempt a piano sketch).

Ailey's "virtuosic" choreography in "Vortex"

Ailey apparently saw their similarity as a potential problem as well. It was not an issue for him at the premiere because "The Falls" was not yet prepared. (Ellington's band arrangement of "The Falls" was recorded five days after "Vortex," the margin of difference, apparently, between the inclusion of "Vortex" and the exclusion of "The Falls.") In subsequent performances when "The Falls" was added, Ailey made them distinctive by assigning the dances to different sexes. De Frantz (p. 151) describes them in this way: "Ellington's spare *Vortex* features percussive outbursts against an incessant snare drum roll. Ailey's choreography matches the angular oscillations of the score with a virtuosic woman's solo designed to test the balance and rhythmic ability of its dancer.... The virtuosic demands of *Falls* offer the male counterpart to *Vortex* in a pure dance variation for four men.... [I]t is explicitly concerned with the technical rendering of densely ordered virtuosic feats." The dense percussion of both movements required extraordinary athleticism from the dancers (leading De-Frantz to use the word "virtuosic" three times in his description).

Listening to the score without the advantage of Ailey's visual contrasts in the sex of the dancers, ensemble size, costumes, lighting and motion confronts one with the aural similarity. Undoubtedly, that similarity is the reason that many symphonic performances omit "The Falls."

Riba, also known as **The River** and **Mainstream**. Ellington writes: "From the whirlpool we get into the main train of ...the river, which gallops sprightly and, as it passes several inlets, broadens and loses some of its adolescence. Becoming ever more mature, even noble, it establishes a majestic wave of monumental cool as it moves on with rhythmic authority."

"Riba" is the most obviously jazz-rooted piece in the suite, and indeed it has a mainstream jazz pedigree. It is based on a simple riff-based blues number by Mercer Ellington called "Taffy Twist." In his autobiography Mercer wrote (p. 173): "I take some credit for the section known as 'Mainstream,' or 'Riba,' which was borrowed directly from one of my compositions. All in the family, you might say!" If he had not said so, it might have escaped notice. "Taffy Twist" was obscurely recorded by Ellington's orchestra in 1962 and obscurely released a quarter of a century later in England on a compilation of stockpile recordings on the Black Lion label in 1988. Ellington adapted the undulating riff of "Taffy Twist," which drew on a repetitive dance rhythm that was a late 1950s craze called "the twist." The bumptious rhythm becomes the musical counterpart of the free-flowing current of the rumbling river. Mercer's original jazz version is mainly a peg for hanging improvised solos onto (by Ray Nance on cornet and Jimmy Hamilton on tenor saxophone). Ellington's big-band arrangement for *The River* preserves the swing of the repeated riff and enriches it with shifting layers of harmony. His big band "Riba" is a textured, greatly enriched "Taffy Twist."

For Collier, arranging the textures of "Riba" with the resources available in the large orchestra must have been a joyful exercise, and it comes through in the music. For Ailey, choreographing this movement – one of the longest at almost four minutes – proved impossible in the ten days he had after delivery of the music. Presumably it was the inherent appeal of the jazzy score that led him to keep it in the ballet at the premiere by the extraordinary measure of sending the principal dancer and budding choreographer Denis Nahat onto the stage to improvise a solo. For Nahat, not surprisingly, it was a harrow-

"Riba" was staged as an improvised solo at
the premiere and choreographed afterwards

ing experience, but his performance, Dunning says, was enthusiastically received and drew a laugh when at the last note he made a gesture of resignation and hurried off the stage. Ailey's choreography, when he got around to it a few days after the premiere, also played heavily on the comic. "*Riba (Mainstream)* demands that the dancers 'play black' in a jokey parody of Cotton Club routines," DeFrantz says. "Mining a tradition of derisive dance as parody, *Riba* signifies on stereotypical modes of public black performance suggested by Ellington's hard-swinging twelve-bar blues."

Village of the Virgins, the last movement of *The River*, is sometimes erroneously titled "Two Cities" because of confusion about Ellington's conception and its realization. Ellington's conception envisioned two cities at the mouth of the river. He wrote: "At the delta, there are two cities, one on each side, and there is always something on one side of the river that you cannot get on the other. Sometimes it's bootleg booze, or hot automobiles, or many other things."

The **Neo-Hip-Hop Kiddies Community** (also called "Stud"),

Ellington's city with booze and fast cars, was laid out in his piano sketch as a bright, happy melody not nearly as rock 'n' roll as might have been expected. The band sketch, recorded at a marathon session along with three other movements, is, uh, sketchy to a fault, less than two minutes of hasty music. For all his nonchalance, Ellington apparently was willing to stretch himself under the pressure of the deadline. His pseudo-arrangement of "The Neo-Hip-Hop Kiddies Community" is not so much a game try as a lame excuse, and he must have known at some level that it was destined for the cutting room.

The other city is "Village of the Virgins," which became the final movement of the ballet suite, and will be discussed in its appropriate place. In Ellington's original conception, he intended the final movement to be **Her Majesty the Sea**, and the progress, as he described it, "The river passes between [the two cities] and romps into the MOTHER – Her Majesty the Sea." It exists in a band arrangement hurriedly put together ten days before the premiere performance, presumably as Collier was preparing and rehearsing the orchestral versions of "Riba" and "Village of the Virgins" and Ailey was choreographing the five movements that he already had in hand and anxiously awaiting Collier's delivery of the other two. But "Her Majesty the Sea" came far too late. It was apparently never orchestrated, and it was never integrated into the ballet.

In the big-band arrangement of "Her Majesty the Sea," Ellington uses long lush romantic chords to convey the vastness of the ocean. The river, he says, "has passed its point of disembarkation and here we realize the validity of religion which is the HEAVENLY ANTICIPATION OF REBIRTH. The mother, in her beautiful romantic exchange with the sun, gives up to the sky that which is to come back as rain, snow, or fog on the mountains and plains." At this point, Ellington intended the music and the dancers to segue back to "The Spring."

For Ellington, the absence of "Her Majesty the Sea" may have stung, given his investment in its rebirth theme. Its deletion may go some distance in explaining his disinterest in *The River* from that day forward. For the rest of us, the audience, knowing only what *The River* includes and neither knowing nor caring about what might have been, we can only rejoice that the de facto ending, "Village of the Virgins," makes a graceful, rhapsodic and altogether inspiring finale.

Village of the Virgins is the city "on the opposite bank," Ellington says, and he adds obscurely (even by his norms), "whose riparian rights are most carefully preserved." If his verbal synopsis slights the city in its curtness, he more than makes up for it in his composition, which is a graceful, hymn-like rhapsody that rises into a soaring crescendo.

Ellington opens the big-band sketch playing the 12-bar hymn austerely on piano with bass accompaniment, and then he repeats the hymn in a stately succession of 12-bar sequences by varied ensembles. The melody is played three times in rich and varied orchestral textures, each more graceful than the last. After 48 bars, the orchestra plays a rising 4-bar crescendo, and the melody then returns in still more varied textures. The melody is at once stately and spiritual, worthy of comparison to "Come Sunday" from *Black Brown and Beige*, and the arrangement embellishes it with sumptuous variations.

Following Ellington's lead, Ron Collier's orchestration pays homage to the hymn-like melody, varying the orchestral textures in its reiterations and replacing the third repeat with a variation that in Ellington's big-band sketch (as I hear it) originates as one of the lyrical improvisations on the melody, so that the orchestral structure

American Ballet Theatre (photo New York Times)

is AAB leading into the 4-bar crescendo. Appropriately for the end-point of the ballet, the orchestra swells on its final iteration and ends in a climactic cadenza that palpably cues the audience to rise to its feet in homage to the audio-visual feast provided by Ellington and Ailey. It is a glorious, uplifting finale – life-affirming and in its own dignified way perhaps "a heavenly anticipation of rebirth."

What remains
When we listen to *The River*, in any of its forms or (better yet) in all of them, the faintly harrowing back-story counts for nothing. Duke Ellington's hyper-active schedule, as if he was trying to slow the relentless turning of the earth, his taunting of the people he so depended on, giving a token to one and saying, "you know what to do with it," handing scraps to another and saying, "we'd be better off if you would do more choreography" – if these incidents count for anything, it is to increase our wonder in what is accomplished. What appear to us to be Duke Ellington's distractions, his bizarre priorities, his impossible daily regimen, his sensitivities and his insensitivities – well, they were not that different in his seventieth year, when *The River* came into being, than at any other time in his long creative life. What we are left with, when all is said and done, is a glorious sequence of music, rich in texture and mood and especially in movement.

We should be thankful for the "little feeling of insecurity" that brought it into being, for the imperfections that made it fall short of the original epic conception. Mercer Ellington, as I have noted earlier, wondered at his father's "pleasure with the imperfect." The poet/songwriter Leonard Cohen elevated that pleasure with the imperfect into an esthetic principle. "There is a crack in everything," he tells us in his beautiful quatrain –

> Ring the bells that still can ring.
> Forget your perfect offering.
> There is a crack in everything –
> That's how the light gets in.

The River, cracks and all, is one more cause for celebration, among many.

ACKNOWLEDGEMENTS. Ted O'Reilly, producer of Duke Ellington's 75th Birthday Concert on 29 April 1974, graciously made *The River*, conducted by Ron Collier, available to me. John Hornsby, archivist and fan, graciously gave me access to rarities such as Mercer Ellington's Warsaw recording and Ron Collier's talk at the 1996 Ellington conference.

References (page numbers to direct quotations are shown *in italics*)
Ailey, Alvin, with A. Peter Bailey. 1995. *Revelations: The Autobiography of Alvin Ailey*. New York: Birch Lane Press. *pp. 114-116*.
Balliett, Whitney. 2002 *Collected Works*, New York: St. Martin's Griffin. *p. 521, p. 334*
Cohen, Harvey G. 2010. *Duke Ellington's America*. Chicago, London: University of Chicago Press. *p. 562*
Collier, Ron. 1996. [Working with Duke Ellington.] Presentation at Ellington '96 [conference]. Park Plaza Hotel, Toronto.
Dance, Stanley. 1987. Liner note to *The Suites, Private Collection* Vol. 5. SAJA Records 255402.
DeFrantz, Thomas F. 2004. *Dancing Revelations: Alvin Ailey's Embodiment of African American Culture*. New York: Oxford University Press. *pp. 149-155*.
Dunning, Jennifer. 1996. *Alvin Ailey: A Life in Dance*. Reading, MA: Addison-Wesley. *p. 175*
Ellington, Edward Kennedy. 1973. *Music Is My Mistress*. New York: Doubleday. *pp. 201-202*
Ellington, Edward Kennedy. 1974. "Words of the Week." *Jet Magazine* (13 June 1974). *p. 26*. <https://books.google.ca/books?id=DaYDAAAAMBAJ&pg=PA16&dq=Ellington%27s+doctor+Logan > [accessed 27 September 2016]
Ellington, Mercer, with Stanley Dance. 1978. *Duke Ellington in Person: An Intimate Memoir*. Boston: Houghton Mifflin. *p. 173, p. 172*
Franceschina, John. 2001. *Duke Ellington's Music for the Theatre*. Jefferson, NC: McFarland & Co. *p. 162*
George, Don (1981) *Sweet Man: The Real Duke Ellington*. New York: George Putnam's Sons. *p. 133, pp. 195-196*
Henken, John. 2007. "About the piece 'Suite from The River.'" Los Angeles Philharmonic Association. <http://www.laphil.com/philpedia/music/suite-from-river-duke-ellington> [accessed May 2015]
Morgenstern, Dan. 2014. "Ellington in the 1960s and 1970s: triumph and tragedy." In *Cambridge Companion to Duke Ellington*, ed. Edward Green. Cambridge University Press. *p. 154*
Schirmer Music Sales Classical, "Edward K. (Duke) Ellington, The River

(1970). <http://www.musicsalesclassical.com/composer/work/27671> [accessed 29 September 2016]

Slome, Stanley. n.d. "The River." Newsletter of the Duke Ellington Society, Southern California chapter. <http://ellingtonweb.ca/Slome-River.htm> [accessed 13 April 2013]

Symphony Silicon Valley. 2014. Program notes on "Orchestral Suite from the ballet *The River*." <https://www.symphonysiliconvalley.org/con certs.php?pagecontID=56&showID=57> [accessed September 2016]

Playlist (recordings cited in order of appearance in the chapter)

Duke Ellington's My People, the Complete Show. Chicago, 20, 21, 27 August 1963. Storyville CD [2012].

"The Spring" 3:20 New York, 11 May 1970. *The Piano Player* (Storyville CD [2005]). Duke Ellington solo piano

"The Spring" 2:26 Chicago, 25 May 1970. *The Private Collection: The Suites*, Vol. 5. (SAJA Records [1987]). Duke Ellington p with overdubbed grace notes in middle section, Joe Benjamin b

"The Spring" 3:32 Toronto, 29 April 1974. Unissued. CJRT Orchestra conducted by Ron Collier. ISSUED "Spring" 3:00. Detroit, 3 October 1992. Detroit Symphony Orchestra conducted by Neeme Järvi. Chandos American Series (Chandos Digital 1993)

"The Run" 2:46 New York, 11 May 1970. *The Piano Player* (Storyville CD [2005]). Duke Ellington solo piano

"The Run" 2:34 Chicago, 25 May 1970. *The Private Collection: The Suites*, Vol. 5. (SAJA Records [1987]). Cat Anderson, Cootie Williams, Mercer Ellington, Fred Stone tp; Chuck Connors, Booty Wood, Julian Priester tb; Russell Procope as, cl; Norris Turney fl; Harold Ashby ts, cl; Paul Gonsalves ts; Harry Carney bs, cl; Duke Ellington p, Wild Bill Davis org, Joe Benjamin b, Rufus Jones d

"Marcia Regina" (= "The Run," also called "Promenade" in studio file) 1:24 New York, 6 November 1968. *The Degas Suite. The Private Collection: The Suites*, Vol. 5. (SAJA Records [1987]). Willie Cook tp, Chuck Connors tb, Russell Procope as, cl, Johnny Hodges as, Paul Gonsalves ts, Harold Ashby ts, cl, Harry Carney bs, Duke Ellington p, Jeff Castleman b, Rufus Jones d

"The Run" was not included in *The River* and is not orchestrated

"The Meander" 2:36 New York, 11 May 1970. *The Piano Player* (Storyville CD [2005]). Duke Ellington solo piano

"The Meander" 5:08 Chicago, 25 May 1970. *The Private Collection: The Suites*, Vol. 5. (SAJA Records [1987]). Band personnel as for "The Run" above

"The Meander" 4:01 Toronto, 29 April 1974. Unissued. CJRT Orchestra conducted by Ron Collier. ISSUED "Meander" 3:57. Detroit, 3 October 1992. Detroit Symphony Orchestra conducted by Neeme Järvi. Chandos American Series (Chandos Digital 1993)

"Grap" (= "The Giggling Rapids") 2:48. 11 May 1970. *The Piano Player* (Storyville CD [2005]). Duke Ellington solo piano

"The Giggling Rapids" 4:19 Chicago, 25 May 1970. *The Private Collection: The Suites*, Vol. 5. (SAJA Records [1987]). Band personnel as for "The Run" above

"Grap" (= "The Giggling Rapids") 3:11 New York, 28 April 1971. *Togo Brava Suite* (Storyville CD [[2001]).
Cootie Williams, Eddie Preston, Mercer Ellington, Money Johnson tp; Chuck Connors, Booty Wood, Malcolm Taylor tb; Norris Turney as, fl; Harold Ashby ts, cl; Paul Gonsalves ts; Harry Carney bs, cl; Duke Ellington p, Joe Benjamin b, Rufus Jones d

"The Giggling Rapids" 3:17 Toronto, 29 April 1974. Unissued. CJRT Orchestra conducted by Ron Collier. ISSUED "Giggling Rapids" 2:55. Detroit, 3 October 1992. Detroit Symphony Orchestra conducted by Neeme Järvi. Chandos American Series (Chandos Digital 1993)

"The Lake" 3:36 New York, 11 May 1970. *The Piano Player* (Storyville CD [2005]). Duke Ellington solo piano

"The Lake" 6:53 Chicago, 25 May 1970. *The Private Collection: The Suites*, Vol. 5. (SAJA Records [1987]). Band personnel as for "The Run" above

"The Lake" 7:58 Toronto, 29 April 1974. Unissued. CJRT Orchestra conducted by Ron Collier. ISSUED "Lake" 6:51. Detroit, 3 October 1992. Detroit Symphony Orchestra conducted by Neeme Järvi. Chandos American Series (Chandos Digital 1993)

"The Falls" 2:59 New York, 8 June 1970. *The Private Collection: The Suites*, Vol. 5. (SAJA Records [1987]).
Dave Burns, Cat Anderson, Cootie Williams, Al Rubin, Fred Stone tp; Chuck Connors, Booty Wood, Cliff Heathers tb; Russell Procope as, cl; Norris Turney fl; Harold Ashby ts, cl; Paul Gonsalves ts; Harry Carney bs, cl; Duke Ellington p, Wild Bill Davis org, Joe Benjamin b, Rufus Jones d, Elaine Jones tympani, Walter Rosenberger glockenspiel,

David Fitz marimba and xylophone

"The Falls" not included in Toronto (1974) or Detroit (1993). Issued "Falls" 3:14 Louisville, Kentucky 1983. *Suite from The River* (First Edition Records 1983). The Louisville Orchestra conducted by Akira Endo.

"The Whirlpool" (= "Vortex") 3:23 New York, 3 June 1970.
The Private Collection: The Suites, Vol. 5. (SAJA Records [1987]).
Cat Anderson, Cootie Williams, Al Rubin, Fred Stone tp; Chuck Connors, Booty Wood, Julian Priester tb; Russell Procope as, cl; Norris Turney fl; Harold Ashby ts, cl; Paul Gonsalves ts; Harry Carney bs, cl;
Duke Ellington p, Wild Bill Davis org, Joe Benjamin b, Rufus Jones d, Elaine Jones tympani, Walter Rosenberger glockenspiel,
David Fitz marimba and xylophone

"Vortex" 2:27 Toronto, 29 April 1974. Unissued. CJRT Orchestra conducted by Ron Collier. ISSUED "Vortex" 2:13. Detroit, 3 October 1992. Detroit Symphony Orchestra conducted by Neeme Järvi. Chandos American Series (Chandos Digital 1993)

"Taffy Twist" 5:49 (Mercer Ellington) New York, 6 June 1962. *The Feeling of Jazz* Black Lion CD [1988]).
Cat Anderson, Bill Berry, Harold Baker, Ray Nance tp; Lawrence Brown, Chuck Connors, Leon Cox tb; Jimmy Hamilton cl, ts, Russell Procope as, Johnny Hodges as, Paul Gonsalves ts, Harry Carney cl, bs;
Duke Ellington p, Aaron Bell b, Sam Woodyard d
Solos: Ray Nance, Jimmy Hamilton ts

"The River" (= "Riba" or "Mainstream") 3:55 New York, 3 June 1970.
The Private Collection: The Suites, Vol. 5. (SAJA Records [1987]).
Cat Anderson, Cootie Williams, Al Rubin, Fred Stone tp; Chuck Connors, Booty Wood, Julian Priester tb; Russell Procope as, cl; Norris Turney fl; Harold Ashby ts, cl; Paul Gonsalves ts; Harry Carney bs, cl;
Duke Ellington p, Wild Bill Davis org, Joe Benjamin b, Rufus Jones d

"Riba" (= "The River") 3:50 Toronto, 29 April 1974. Unissued. CJRT Orchestra conducted by Ron Collier. ISSUED "Riba" 3:18. Detroit, 3 October 1992. Detroit Symphony Orchestra conducted by Neeme Järvi. Chandos American Series (Chandos Digital 1993)

"Stud" (= "The Neo-Hip-Hop Cool Kiddies Community") 2:25
New York, 11 May 1970. *The Piano Player* (Storyville CD [2005]).
Duke Ellington solo piano

"The Neo-Hip-Hop Cool Kiddies Community" (= "Stud") 1:46
New York, 3 June 1970. *The Private Collection: The Suites*, Vol. 5.
(SAJA Records [1987]). Band personnel as for "The River" above

"The Neo-Hip-Hop Cool Kiddies Community" was not included in *The River* and is not orchestrated

"Her Majesty the Sea" 2:35 (also called "The Mother Her Majesty the Sea") New York, 15 June 1970. *The Private Collection: The Suites*, Vol. 5. (SAJA Records [1987]). Cat Anderson, Cootie Williams, Mercer Ellington, Fred Stone tp; Chuck Connors, Booty Wood, Julian Priester tb; Russell Procope as, cl; Norris Turney fl; Harold Ashby ts, cl; Paul Gonsalves ts; Harry Carney bs, cl; Duke Ellington p, Wild Bill Davis org, Joe Benjamin b, Rufus Jones d

"Her Majesty the Sea" was not included in *The River* and is not orchestrated

"Village of the Virgins" 5:09 New York, 15 June 1970. *The Private Collection: The Suites*, Vol. 5. (SAJA Records [1987]). Band personnel as for "Her Majesty the Sea"

"Village of the Virgins" 5:38 Toronto, 29 April 1974. Unissued. CJRT Orchestra conducted by Ron Collier. ISSUED "Village Virgins" 4:21. Detroit, 3 October 1992. Detroit Symphony Orchestra conducted by Neeme Järvi. Chandos American Series (Chandos Digital 1993)

Index of People and Places

Aas land, Benny 295
Abdullah Ibrahim 194, 266
Adderley, Julian "Cannonball" 183
Addison, Bernard 122
Afghanistan 246
Africa 39, 182, 197, 251
African-American 12, 17, 35, 38, 62, 120, 246, 300, 301, 332
African Republic of Togo 253, 289
Afro-Eurasian 7, 82, 117, 245-247, 249, 253-259, 260, 261, 289
Ailey, Alvin 290, 300-301, 305, 306-310, 311-312, 319, 320, 321, 323-324, 326, 327-328, 331, 332
Alexander, Joey 143
Alexandria 77
Allen, Henry "Red" 121
Alsop, Marin 22, 40
Alvis, Hayes 42, 122, 195
Amarillo 91, 92
American Airlines 249
American Ballet Theatre 290, 300, 301, 302, 304, 311, 318, 319, 323, 330
American Dance Theatre (Alvin Ailey) 300, 312
Amman 154, 246
Amsterdam 106, 119
Anderson, Ivie 84, 89, 121, 122
Anderson, Marian 12
Angier, Daryl 9
Ankara 154, 246
Annual Review of Jazz Studies 239
Antarctica 268
Antibes 119
Apex Studios 274
Applebaum, Louis 204
Arlen, Harold 84, 121, 141
Armstrong, Louis 24, 25, 28, 41, 67, 85, 87, 246
Ashby, Harold 80, 102, 116, 118, 124, 125, 242, 252, 253, 257, 263, 264, 289, 333-336
Asmussen, Svend 266
Atlantic City 260
Atlantic Records 117
Auckland 261
Auld, Georgie 90
Australia 253, 314
Australia Broadcast Co. 199
Austria 123, 161, 314
Avakian, George 271, 272, 275, 294
Avid Jazz Records 124

Bach, Johann Sebastian 2, 4, 6, 39, 194, 254, 289, 294
Baghdad 154, 246
Bagley, Don 125
Bailey, A. Peter 332

Bailey, Buster 121
Bailey, Ozzie 147
Baker, Harold "Shorty" 43, 78, 79, 123, 124, 125, 133, 160, 161, 196, 335
Bala, Ontario 204
Ballard, Butch 123, 195, 198
Balliett, Whitney 15, 39, 96, 120, 149, 158, 288, 289, 294, 302, 318, 324, 325, 332
Baltimore 184, 200
Barcelona, Danny 41
Barefield, Eddie 79
Barnes, Clive 311
Baron, Art 48, 71, 72, 74-76, 80
Barron's Club 13
Barton, Bruce 8
Irene Barton 8
Bascomb, Dud 78
Basie, William "Count" 67, 68, 79, 90, 93, 106, 111, 318
Basin Street East 143, 160, 287, 297
Battersea Bridge 102
Bearden, Romare 12
Beatles, The 267
Beethoven, Ludwig van 2, 254, 289
Beirut 259
Bell, Aaron 80, 148, 160, 161, 182, 185, 192, 197-199, 335
Bell, Charles 198
Bellevue Asylum 180
Bellson, Louie 43, 115, 124, 163, 199, 236, 240, 242, 271-273, 276
Beneke, Tex 90
Ben Webster Foundation 270
Benin 253
Benjamin, Joe 80, 124, 184, 190, 196, 199, 200, 256, 263, 264, 323, 333-336
Benjamin, Sathima Bea 266
Benson, Susan 231
Bergen 74
Berigan, Bunny 90
Berklee College of Music 74, 184, 199, 200
Berlin, Irving 141
Bernotas, Bob 76
Berry, April 320
Berry, Bill 158, 160, 214, 217-219, 239, 335
Berry, Chu 90
Berry, Emmett 124
Bert, Eddie 49
Bethlehem Records 78
Big Band Era, The 72, 79
Bigard, Barney 17, 18, 23, 24, 34, 41-43, 67, 78, 81, 82, 84-86, 88, 89, 92, 96, 114, 121, 122, 136, 159, 166, 167, 195, 196
Biograph Records 40, 195
Birch Lane Press 332

Birdland 109, 202, 208, 209, 214, 221
Black, Dave 79, 123, 124, 197, 198
Black Lion Records 296, 327, 335
Blake, Eubie 12
Blake, Ran 179
Blanton, Jimmy 32, 43, 59, 78, 91, 94, 95, 101, 122, 123, 139, 159, 160, 170-174, 184, 196, 198, 199
Blanton-Webster Band 32, 33, 43, 78, 94, 95, 122, 159, 196
Bloom, Rube 89
Bluebird Records 78, 122, 136, 158-161, 192, 195-198, 242, 247, 262-264
Blue Light DESUK journal 6, 7, 9
Blue Note Records 125, 176, 180, 197, 198, 264, 289
Bochner, Lloyd 206
Bombay 154, 246
Boss Brass, The 279
Boston 39, 74, 132, 184, 199, 200, 220, 262, 294, 332
Boston Pops Orchestra 235, 242
Botchinsky, Allan 126
Boyer, Richard O. 5, 33, 39, 194, 269, 294
Brackeen, Joanne 194
Brackley, Jim 8
Bradley, Ian 9
Branscombe, Alan 241
Brant Inn, The 205
Braud, Wellman 41, 42, 77, 78, 121, 195
Bricktop (= Ada Beatrice Louise Virginia Smith) 12, 13
Bridgers, Aaron 131
Bristol 258, 264, 289
Brookshire, Nell 200
Broomer, Stuart 9
Brown, Les 85
Brown, Ray 173, 196, 199
Brown, Scott 22, 39
Brubeck, Dave 204
Brunswick Records 17, 55, 120, 165, 195, 239
Buffalo Philharmonic 313, 314
Buckley, Tom 279, 281, 294
Burma 253
Burns, Dave 123, 334
Burrowes, Ray 42, 79
Burton, Laura 242
Burton, Richard 221
Busk, Bjarne 266
Byas, Don 104, 106-110, 113, 123

Caesar, Julius 230, 231
Cairo 260
Calcutta 260, 262
California 70, 191, 271, 295, 297, 314, 333
Calloway, Cab 61, 65, 72, 90, 91, 93
Calvert, Leon 241
Camden 78
Canada 123, 184, 187, 210, 242, 314
Canadian Broadcasting Corporation (CBC) 10, 187, 207, 212, 219, 239
Capitol Palace, The 13, 169
Capitol Records 66, 124, 175, 182, 194, 196, 197
Capitol Transcription 146, 147, 160

Capp, Frank 125
Carman, Ray 36
Carmichael, Hoagy 101
Carnegie Hall 23, 39, 43, 58, 63, 77, 103-106, 113, 119, 123, 137, 142, 160, 173-175, 180, 268, 279, 289
Carney, Harry 26, 27, 29, 37, 41-43, 58, 63, 77-80, 85, 92, 95, 98, 121-125, 128, 147, 159-161, 168, 176, 192, 195-197, 205, 218, 227, 240-243, 248, 253, 258, 263, 264, 278, 281, 292, 320, 333-336
Carter, Benny 26, 61, 98
Carter, William 319
Castleman, Jeff 242, 333
Cavanaugh, Inez 52, 54, 76
Cavett, Dick 46
Ceylon 154, 246
Chamberlain, Dorothy 77
Chamblee, Eddie 79
Chandos Records 290, 305, 313
Chase, Lucia 300, 301, 307
Chennai 246
Chiasson, Christopher 242
Chiasson, Donna-Claire 242
Chicago 39, 78, 79, 86, 87, 122, 124, 176, 196, 197, 262, 282, 284, 295-298, 301, 304, 332-334
Chichester Festival 235
China 24, 261
Chopin, Frederic 55
Christian, Charlie 106
Chycoski, Arnie 279
Cincinnati Symphony Orchestra 43, 174, 194, 196
CJRT-FM (Toronto) 10, 278, 294
CJRT Symphony Orchestra, 313, 333-336
Clarke, Kenny 106
Clooney, Rosemary 140, 149, 150, 160
Cobbs, Alfred 79
Cohen, Harvey G. 39, 262, 332
Cohen, Leonard 331
Connors, Chuck 42, 79, 80, 125, 160, 161, 242, 243, 263, 264, 279, 333-336
Cooke, Mervyn 76
Cooper, Buster 42, 79, 160, 161, 242, 243, 263
Cole, June 121
Cole, Nat "King" 142
Coles, Johnny 80, 264
Collier, Ron 277, 278, 281, 282, 290, 304-306, 313, 315-318, 330, 332-336
Cologne 255, 263, 297, 298
Coltrane, John 67, 83, 143, 180
Columbia Records 105, 113, 158, 160, 161, 179, 197, 201, 202, 208, 209, 222, 239, 240, 241, 271, 272, 291
Cook, Willie 43, 78, 79, 109, 123, 124, 160, 161, 195, 238, 240-242, 333
Corea, Chick 183
Cornell University 114, 119, 120, 124
Cotton Club, The 13, 15-18, 23, 26, 29, 30, 34, 40, 42, 56, 87, 93, 164, 176, 195, 256, 260, 310, 328
Coss, Bill 134, 158, 250, 262
Coventry Cathedral 174, 196
Cox, Leon 335

INDEX OF PEOPLE AND PLACES

Craig, James 79
Cranshaw, Bob 42
Creamer, Henry 12
Croatia 314
Crosby, Bob 90
Cullen, Countee 12
Cullen, Jack 49, 76
Cummings,. E.E. 3

Da Capo Press 5, 40, 77
Daffodil Records 160
Dakar 251, 261, 262
Dallas 246
Damascus 154, 261
Dance, Stanley 39, 48, 61, 63, 71, 72, 77, 92, 94, 96, 109, 114, 120, 133, 139, 155, 158, 159, 181, 194, 202, 221, 234, 239, 247, 248, 257-258, 262, 269, 274, 282, 283, 287, 292, 294, 302-303, 317, 332
Dankworth, Johnny 228, 229, 241
Dare, Daphne 212
Darrell, R.D. 2, 3, 7, 166, 194
Davis, Kay 142, 147, 160
Davis, Miles 2, 105, 180, 181, 183, 194
Davis, Richard 125, 126
Davis, Wild Bill 125, 133, 263, 296-298, 318, 333-336
Dearie, Blossom 143, 160
Debussy, Claude 254, 289, 308
DeFrantz, Thomas F. 310, 311, 323, 326, 328, 332
Degas, Edgar 290, 320. Also see *Degas Suite*
Dempsey, Ray 241
Denmark (Radio Denmark) 265, 266, 269-271, 273, 282-284, 292
de Paris, Wilbur 160, 204
Desdemona 217
Dessertine, Jordan 8
Detroit Symphony Orchestra 290, 305, 306, 313, 333-336
Diamond, Jack "Legs" 23
Dietrich, Kurt 54, 77
Dixon, Charlie 121
Dollar Brand 266
Douglas, Aaron 12
Down Beat 70, 158, 222, 262
Drew, Kenny 270
DuBois, W. E. B. 12
Duke Ellington Music Society (DEMS) 7, 9, 10, 93, 95, 120, 241, 283-285, 295, 306
Duke Ellington Society of Sweden (DESS) 9, 46, 159, 252, 262
Duke Ellington Society New York (DESNY) 10, 36
Duke Ellington Society United Kingdom (DESUK) 9, 10, 189
Duke, George 183
Dunn, Johnny 54
Dunning, Jennifer 308, 312, 332
Duvivier, George 125

Edinburgh 25
Ellington, Edward Kennedy "Duke" is cited on every page. Here are a few themes that recur:

"aristocrat of Harlem" 13-16, 26, 27, 40
Barrelhouse Eddie Ellington 19-20, 164, 165, 168
Billy Strayhorn disciple and peer 12-13, 101-102, 131, 134-138, 141, 157-158. 192-193, 202, 212-213, 221, 287
composing, methods and styles 2, 18, 27-28, 31, 45-46, 48-49, 51, 58-60, 74, 78, 87, 97-98, 114, 177-178, 214, 246-247, 249-250, 261, 269, 276, 279-280
daily regimen 8, 205, 254, 300, 304, 306-310, 331
mother presence and influence 15, 56, 91-92, 179
Music Is My Mistress 10, 36, 39, 120, 154, 158, 164, 194, 248, 260, 262, 287, 291, 294, 302, 318, 332
rebirth at Newport 1956 45, 60, 113, 150, 202, 286
Sacred Concerts 191, 237, 254, 257, 262, 303
travel by taxi, bus, luxury liner, rail, air and Chrysler 24, 36, 70, 176, 184, 214, 260-260-261, 291-292, 300
Ellington, Mercer 25, 39, 75, 80, 109, 119, 124, 125, 130, 132, 159, 161, 198, 202, 243, 258-259, 262-264, 265-266, 269-271, 273-276, 279, 282-285, 293, 294, 301, 302, 313, 314, 316, 317, 327, 331, 332-334, 336
As composer 96, 125, 196, 314, 327, 335
Also see Mercer Records
Ellington, Paul 285
Ellington, Ruth 131
Elliott, Lu 108, 123
Elliott, Tim 8
Endo, Akira 313, 335
England 26, 89, 117, 125, 149, 183, 196, 205, 235, 258, 264, 291, 292, 314, 327
Englewood Cliffs 138
Ericson, Rolf 80, 125, 132, 159, 160, 247, 252, 262
Ertegun, Ahmet 283
Evans, Bill 179
Evans, Gil 140
Evans, Herschel 90

Fairweather, Digby 103, 120
Falletta, JoAnn 313
Fargo, North Dakota 101, 121, 122, 134, 288
Farrar Straus Giroux 40, 159, 239
Fass, John 120, 239
Feather, Leonard 39, 43, 181, 194, 218, 222, 271, 273, 275, 283, 294
Fiedler, Arthur 235. 242
Fields, Dorothy 16, 40, 41
Fifty-Second Street 103, 105
Fischer, Doug 184, 194
Fitz, David 335
Fitzgerald, Ella 63, 125, 142, 284
Flanagan, Tommy 194
Ford, Fats (aka Andres Merenguito) 79
Ford, James 242
Forrest, Jimmy 108, 109, 113, 123
France 10, 36, 60, 119, 147, 195, 237, 238, 243, 292, 296, 303, 314

339

Franceschina, John   310, 311, 332
Frazier, George F.   38, 39
Free Trade Hall   125
Freebody Park   240
Fresh Sound Records   125, 159
Fresno   271-273

Ganley, Alan   241
Garland, Joe   84-86, 89, 121
Garrison Junior High School   220
Garvey, Marcus   12
Gaskin, Victor   125
Gassman, Vittorio   220, 241
Gee, Matthew   77
Gene Coy's Aces   91
Gershwin, George   97, 141, 182
Giddins, Gary   286, 294
Gillespie, John Birks "Dizzy"   99, 105, 106
Gioia, Ted   105, 120
Glenn, Tyree   60-65, 78, 79, 114, 123, 124, 279, 280
Goldberg, Joe   112, 120
Gonsalves, Paul   42, 43, 77-79, 102, 109-111, 113-115, 117, 118, 120, 123-125, 150, 160, 161, 195, 202, 218, 240-243, 257, 260, 263, 264, 276, 286, 287, 295-297, 324, 333-336
Goodman, Benny   31, 82, 88, 90, 95
Gordon, Dexter   270
Grant Park Music Shell   304
Granz, Norman   119, 149, 283, 284
Grappelli, Stephane   266
Green, Edward   332
Greenwood, Lil   298
Greer, Sonny   17, 18, 40-43, 49, 50, 70, 77-79, 121-124, 159-161, 169, 175, 195-197, 276, 295
Grieg, Edvard   73
Grissom, Jimmy   298
Gross, Walter   43
Guy, Fred   40-43, 50, 56, 77, 78, 121-124, 159, 160, 195-197

Hajdu, David   35, 40, 129, 131, 132, 139, 141, 153, 157, 159, 202, 213, 239
Hall, Barry Lee   80
Hamilton, Jimmy   42, 43, 59, 61, 67, 69, 74, 77-82, 111, 114-117, 123-125, 128, 153, 159-161, 195-197, 217, 227, 230, 240-243, 247-250, 258, 262, 263, 276, 327, 335
Hampton, Lionel   49
Hancock, Herbie   183
Handy, W. C.   75
Hardin, Lil   193
Hardwick, Otto   15, 17, 29, 40-43, 49, 50, 52, 55, 77, 78, 85, 92, 121-123, 159, 195-197
Harlem Renaissance, The   27, 34
Harman, Carter   239
Harper, Ian   242
Harris, Little Benny   110
Harrison, Bailey   121
Harrison, Jimmy   121
Hartman, Johnny   143
Hasse, John Edward   5, 35, 38, 40, 49, 77, 93, 95, 120, 175, 176, 184, 194
Haughton, Chauncey   43, 82

Hawkins, Coleman   26, 67, 83, 87-90, 96, 105, 106, 121, 122, 180
Hayman, Richard   242
Heathers, Cliff   334
Heinz History Center   130
Hemphill, Shelton   78, 123, 124, 160, 197
Henderson, Fletcher   68, 79, 87-89, 91, 106, 121
Henderson, Horace   122
Henderson, Luther   174
Henderson, Rick   79, 123, 124, 195
Henry, Martha   206, 234
Hentoff, Nat   40, 77, 176
Heraclitus   299, 300
Herbert, Mort   41
Hibbler, Al   283
Hilliard, Bob   142
Hines, Earl   193, 198
Hinton, Bill   320
Hinton, Milt   125
Hodeir, André   59, 60, 63, 77
Hodges, Edith Cue   132
Hodges, Johnny   6, 27, 41-43, 55-56, 61, 70, 77-79, 90, 92, 96, 100, 102, 111, 112-113, 114fn, 115, 117, 121-125, 127-133, 136-141, 146-157, 157-161, 168, 174, 175, 177, 195-197, 209, 211-212, 213, 215, 217, 235, 236, 238, 239-243, 253, 257, 258, 259, 263-264, 275, 276, 286, 294, 299, 333, 335
Hoefer, George   77, 194
Hoefsmit, Sjef   9, 241, 295
Holiday, Billie   91
Hollywood   23, 78, 79, 122, 140, 160, 161, 196, 221, 234, 245
Hong Kong, 253
Hopkins, Claude   193
Horn, David   76
Hornsby, John   8, 332
Howard University   51
Hughes, Langston   12
Hughes, Patrick Cairns "Spike"   26, 40
Hunstein, Don   210
Hunter, Alberta (alias Alberta Prime)   164, 195
Hurston, Zora Neale   12
Hyderabad   247

IAJRC (International Association of Record Collectors)   6, 7, 9, 10, 270, 272, 281
Ibsen, Henrik   73
Impulse! Records   22, 83, 125, 126, 180, 195, 196, 199, 253, 256, 294
India   246-248, 261
Irvis, Charlie   49-54, 68
Iverson, Ethan   135, 152, 159
Iran   154, 246
Iraq   246, 260
Irving Bunton Singers   298

Jackson, Brian   216
Jackson, Mahalia   202-203, 289
Jackson, Milt   68
Jackson, Rudy   41, 77, 82
Jackson, Quentin "Butter"   43, 46, 59-61, 65, 66, 68-70, 78, 79, 109, 123-125, 128, 159-161, 195, 197, 218, 230, 240-242, 276

Index of People and Places

James, Harry 276
Japan 249, 253, 261, 270, 297
Järvi, Neeme 305, 313, 334, 335, 336
Jazz Piano Workshop 170, 198
Jean, George 123, 124
Jefferson, Hilton 122
Jenkins, Freddie 18, 27, 41, 42, 78, 84, 121
Johnson, Agnes 91
Johnson, Budd 91
Johnson, Harold 264
Johnson, Harriet 311
Johnson, Jack 12
Johnson, James P. 12, 19-21, 39, 40, 164, 165, 187, 193, 195
Johnson, Jerry 242
Johnson, J.J. 49
Johnson, Money 80, 124, 263, 334
Johnson, Osie 126
Johnson, Walter 122
Jones, Claude 78, 123, 160, 197
Jones, Elaine 334, 335
Jones, Herbie 160, 161, 242, 243, 263
Jones, Jimmy 125, 137, 160, 298
Jones, Jo 196
Jones, Philly Joe 125
Jones, Rufus 124, 125, 161, 184, 190, 196, 199, 200, 242, 256, 263, 264, 333-336
Jones, Thad 68, 79, 93
Jones, Wallace 42, 43, 58, 78, 122, 159, 195, 196
Jordan, Taft 123, 148, 160, 196, 197
Joyce, James 293
Junoff, Lena 256, 262, 263, 297

Kabul 154, 246
Kafka, Franz 268
Kansas City 91, 93, 116
Kay, Brad 167
Keepnews, Orrin 275
Kellaway, Roger 125
Kelly, Ted 123
Kennedy, President John F. 246
Kenny, Nick 23, 41
Kentucky Club 15, 40, 50, 52, 87
Kern, Jerome 141
Kessel, Barney 125
Kidd, Gary 242
Killian, Al 78, 123, 124
King, Bill 277
Kirby, John 122
Kirchner, Bill 194
Kirk, Andy 90
Knapp, Rosalind Ann 234
Knepper, Jimmy 294
Kochinska, Maria 242
Koehler, Ted 84, 89, 121
Krautbauer, Gert 312
Kunzel, Erich 196

Lady Gaga 143
Lahore 154
Laine, Cleo 228-230, 241, 242
Lamb, John 161, 185, 236, 242, 243, 263
Lambert, Eddie 86, 88, 90, 117, 120, 148, 159, 170, 188, 194, 256, 257, 262

Lanauze, Yvonne 64, 79
Lang, Arthur 242
Langham, Michael 206, 235
Landesman, Fran 142
Lazare, Gerry 8
Le Jazz Hot 190
Leonardo da Vinci 293
Levant, Oscar 174
Lewis, Mel 68
Lincoln, Abraham 12
Lincoln Centre for the Performing Arts 304, 307, 310, 313
Liston, Melba 49
Little, Steve 161
Ljubljana 261
Loesser, Frank 141
Logan, Arthur 300
Logan, Marian 157
London Palladium 210
Loomer, Martin 8, 227
Los Angeles Philharmonic 314, 332
Louisville Symphony Orchestra 313, 314, 335
Lovett, Leroy 124
Lunceford, Jimmy 90, 188
Lydian Sound Orchestra 234

Madras 154, 246
Malaysia 253
Manchester 117, 125
Manhattan 12, 26, 50, 130, 189, 199, 208, 213, 221, 274
Manley, Mel 8
Marion, Percy 80
Mather Air Force Base 295, 297
Marshall, Kaiser 121
Marshall, Wendell 43, 79, 123, 124, 178, 195, 197, 198, 240, 276
Mays, Lyle 183
McCain, Alva Beau 106, 113, 123
McElroy's Ballroom 163, 195, 285, 296
McEvilly, Chris 8
McGhee, Howard 242
McHugh, Jimmy 16, 40, 41
McLuhan, Marshall 251-253, 262
McPhail, Jimmy 298
Melody Maker 26, 40, 149
Melvin, Charles 30
Mercer, Johnny 177
Mercer Records 124, 198, 202, 271, 273-276, 282, 283
Merenguito, Andres (aka Fats Ford) 79
Metcalfe, Louis 17, 40, 41, 77, 121, 195
Meyers, Arnold 25
Middleton, Thomas 235
Milan 155, 220, 241, 296, 298
Miley, Bubber 27, 28, 40, 41, 47, 50-55, 67, 121, 166, 195
Miller, Eddie 90
Miller, Glenn 85, 90
Miller, Mark 8
Millinder, Lucky 85
Mills Blue Rhythm Band 85
Mills, Ernie 8
Mills, Florence 166

Mills, Irving 56
Minerve, Harold "Geezil" 80, 259, 264
Mingus, Charles 67, 68, 180-182, 188, 194, 197, 198
Miss Boston 220
Modern Jazz Quartet 204
Moiseiwitsch, Tanya 206
Mondragon, Joe 125
Monk, Thelonious 2, 31, 106, 108, 194
Moore, Anita 199, 280, 298
Morgenstern, Dan 300, 332
Morrison, Peck 190, 198, 200
Morton, Benny 121
Morton, Jelly Roll 88, 121
Moten, Benny 91
Mrs Clinkscales 195
Mullen, Patricia 242
Mullens, Ed 160
Mulligan, Gerry 139
Museum of Modern Art (MOMA) 184, 185, 198, 199
Musso, Vido 90

Nahat, Denis 310, 327
Nance, Ray 37, 42, 43, 63, 67, 77-79, 95, 112, 122-124, 128, 159-161, 195-197, 217, 236, 240-242, 266, 283, 327, 335
Nanton, Joe "Tricky Sam" 16, 17-18, 27, 28, 34, 40-43, 53-60, 61, 66, 70, 75, 76, 77, 78, 89, 90, 121, 122, 123, 159, 160, 195-197
Napper, Ken 242
National Association for the Advancement of Colored People (NAACP) 10, 35, 36, 38
NBC Symphony 36
Nelson, Oliver 68
Newman, Al 241
Newman, Paul 131
Newport Jazz Festival 45, 60, 110, 113, 114, 124, 150, 151, 240, 279, 280, 286
New Zealand 253
Nichols, Herbie 194
Nicholson, Stuart 5, 11, 40, 109, 120, 159
Norris, John 9
Northover, Jim 8
Norway 74

O'Keefe Centre 277, 278
Okeh Records 17, 41, 55, 77, 121, 165, 195
Oldham, Lancashire 266
O'Reilly, Ted 8, 269, 278-282, 294, 332
Orkester Journalen 159, 252, 262

Palmer, Robert 157, 159
Paris 25, 26, 31, 32, 42, 43, 131, 142, 145, 147, 160, 186, 198, 200, 204, 261, 266, 298, 318
Parker, Charlie 105, 110, 267
Pass, Joe 199
Pastor, Tony 90
Patterson, Tom 205, 213
Payton, Nicholas 159
Pearson, Buddy 263
Peress, Maurice 94, 120
Perkins, Walter 125
Persson, Ake 75, 80

Persson, Jan 30
Peterson, Oscar 204
Pettiford, Oscar 78, 160, 161, 173, 196, 270, 275, 282, 283
Plank, Conny 255, 262, 263, 297
Plummer, Christopher 206
Porter, Cole 141, 230
Powell, Bud 266
Preston, Eddie 263, 264, 334
Priester, Julian 124, 333, 335, 336
Priestley, Brian 120
Procope, Russell 42, 43, 67, 77-80, 82, 122-125, 160, 161, 183, 195, 197, 227, 240-243, 253, 257, 263, 264, 281, 333-336
Prudente, Vincent 80, 279
Putnam, George 332

Queen Elizabeth II 188, 291-292
QRS piano rolls 19, 40, 195

Raglin, Alvin "Junior" 43, 78, 122, 123, 173, 196, 197
Rainbow Grill 221, 256, 296
Rasky, Harry 207, 208, 212, 219-221, 239
Razaf, Andy 12
RCA Victor 43, 55, 78, 90, 95, 121, 123, 136, 156, 159, 197, 198, 263
Red Baron Records 160, 287, 288, 294, 297
Redman, Don 61, 64, 87, 106
Reinhardt, Django 267
Reno Sweeny Ballroom 160
Rhenus Studio 263, 297
Ricard, Flip 79
Richards, Johnny 125
Roach, Max 67, 180, 181, 188, 197, 198
Roberts, Luckey 20, 165
Roberts, Marcus 194
Robeson, Paul 12
Robinson, Prince 82, 88
Rodgers, Richard 141
Rosenberger, Walter 334, 335
Rosenthal, Ted 194
Rosolino, Frank 49
Rouse, Charlie 108, 113, 123
Royal, Ernie 123
Rubin, Al 124, 334, 335
Rubinstein, Arthur 174
Rully, Ron 277, 278
Russell, Tony 241

Saal, Hubert 311
St. Peter's Lutheran Church 191
Sancton, Ted 8
Sanders, John 70, 78, 79, 124, 125, 160, 161, 190, 200, 218, 240, 241
Satie, Erik 2
Sax, Adolphe 86
Schiff, Stan 8
Schirmer Music Sales Classical 313, 314, 332
Schubert, Franz 268
Schuller, Gunther 99, 120
Scott, Andrew 9
Scott, Raymond 43
Seale, Archie 15, 23, 40

Index of People and Places

Sears, Al 78, 102, 103, 111-114, 120, 121, 123, 124, 160, 161, 197
Senegal 251, 259
Shakespeare, William 6, 151, 152, 209, 210, 227
Shapiro, Nat 40, 51, 77
Shatner, William 206
Shaw, Artie 82, 90, 121, 267
Shaw, Mack 40, 195
Shefter, Bert 43
Shepard, Ernie 42, 79, 160, 198
Sheridan, Phil 277
Sherrill, Joya 298
Shiels, Alan 8
Shiels, Judy 8
Shirley, Don 179
Simkiw, George 277-278
Simon, George T. 111, 121
Sinatra, Frank 63, 143
Sissle, Noble 12
Slome, Stanley 302, 333
Smith, Bill 9, 278, 280
Smith, Bob 212, 215, 221, 228, 239
Smith, Jabbo 55, 77, 78
Smith, Joe 121
Smith, Lonnie Liston 183
Smith, Maggie 212
Smith, Paul 125
Smith, Russell 121
Smith, Stuff 125
Smith, Willie "The Lion" 13, 20, 22, 50, 52, 77, 92, 93, 165, 168-170, 187, 193-196, 198, 200
Snowden, Elmer 15, 49, 50
Somerstein, Stephen 303
Snyder, Ron 241
Stark, Bobby 121
Stewart, Rex 42, 43, 78, 90, 93, 96, 98, 121-123, 159, 195, 196
Stewart, Slam 172
Still, William Grant 12
Stimpson, David 8
Stockholm 75, 80, 261
Stokowski, Leopold 23
Stoller, Alvin 125
Stone, Fred 124, 263, 279, 333-336
Storyville Records 121, 254, 263, 271, 285, 301, 333-335
Stratemann, Klaus 278
Stratford Shakespearean Festival 73, 187, 204, 205, 206, 208, 212, 216, 231, 234, 237, 238
   Musicians of the Stratford Festival 234, 242
Strauss, Richard 2
Stravinsky, Igor 268, 319, 324
Strayhorn, Billy 3, 6, 12-13, 35, 40, 45, 63, 67, 73-74, 79, 94, 96, 102, 106, 122-124, 127-161, 174, 177, 187, 192-193, 198-200, 201, 202, 207, 212, 213, 215, 218, 221, 222, 223, 226, 228, 230, 233, 239, 240-242, 247, 248, 250, 256, 262, 263, 275-276, 277, 287, 288, 294, 297, 299, 302, 308
Stuttgart 156, 161
Sun Ra 182
Sunrise Records 147, 273, 275
Switzerland 123, 315

Swope, Martha 319, 323
Sydney 261
Symphony Silicon Valley 314, 315, 333

Tanglewood Music Center 235, 242
Talbot, Bruce 84, 121
Tate, Grady 42
Tatum, Art 194
Taylor, Billy 42, 95, 122, 195, 196, 198
Taylor, Cecil 182, 194
Taylor, Dave 124
Taylor, Malcolm 263, 264, 334
Tchaikovsky, Pyotr Ilyich 221
Tehran 154, 246
Tempo Music, Inc. 131, 313
Ten Blackberries, The 183
Terry, Clark 43, 78, 79, 109, 123-125, 159-161, 195, 217, 219, 240, 241, 283, 287
Texas 26, 91, 92, 246, 300
Timon of Athens 73, 187, 233-236, 242
Thiele, Bob 283, 288
Thiele, Ian 9
Thilo, Jesper 126
Thomas, Joe 90
Thunder Sound Studios 277, 279
Tizol, Juan 41-43, 57, 59, 65, 78, 96, 121-124, 159, 167, 195, 196, 240, 275-276
Togolese Republic 253
Tokyo 198, 249, 250, 261, 298
Toronto 6-10, 203, 252, 269, 277-280, 282, 294, 296, 306, 308, 332-336
Toronto Duke Ellington Society, Chapter 40 (TDES) 6-7, 8, 9, 203
Toscanini, Arturo 36
Towers, Jack 101, 121
Townsend, Irving 218-220, 222, 223, 226, 228, 229, 239
Travis Air Force Base 295
Trenner, Donn 125
Trotman, Lloyd 124, 196
Truman, Harry S. 38
Truman, Margaret 38
Tucker, Mark 5, 39, 40, 76, 77, 121, 158, 178, 179, 194, 239, 262, 294
Turney, Norris 82, 117, 124, 125, 255-257, 263, 264, 279, 289, 320, 333-336

Udkoff, Bob 132, 159
Ulanov, Barry 23, 40, 50-52, 77, 132, 159, 245, 262
Uplands Air Force Base, Ottawa 184, 199
University of Wisconsin 292

Valburn, Jerry 270, 284
Vance, Dick 106, 110
Van Cliburn 237
Van de Leur, Walter 144, 146, 151, 152, 155, 159
Van Gelder, Rudy 137, 138
Voce, Steve 61, 77
Vodery, Will 12

Waller, Thomas Wright "Fats" 20, 22, 89, 174, 193, 267
Warsaw Symphony Orchestra 313, 314

Washington, Dinah 68, 79
Washingtonians 13, 15, 17, 49-51, 82, 85, 87, 88, 121, 164
Watkins, Tony 199, 200, 298
Webster, Ben 6, 32, 33, 43, 78, 84, 89-109, 111, 113, 114, 116, 118-120, 122-126, 141, 159, 196, 253, 270, 283
Wein, George 198
Welding, Pete 70, 77
Wells, Dicky 121
Westin, Lars 132, 159, 247, 252, 262
Westin, Martin 132, 159, 247, 262
Westinghouse High School 129
Westminster Abbey 262, 303
Weston, Randy 194
Wheeler, Ken 241
Whetsol, Arthur 23, 41, 42, 49, 51, 53, 78, 121, 122, 195
Whistler, James McNeill 102
Whiteman, Paul 43
Whittacker, Byng 187
Wiedemann, Dr. Erik 266
Wilbur, Bob 287
Williams, Cootie 23, 26-32, 34, 41-43, 46, 53, 55, 56, 78, 79, 89, 94, 95, 97, 121, 122, 124, 125, 136, 159-161, 167, 174, 195, 196, 214, 243, 258, 263, 264, 278, 281, 333-336
Williams, Francis 43, 78, 79, 123, 124, 160
Williams, Mary Lou 112, 123, 164, 194, 198
Williams, Nelson 123, 263
Williams, Richard 263
Williams, Skippy 111, 196
Williamson, Ken 262
Wilson, Dick 90
Wilson, Robert 77
Wilson, Teddy 91, 93, 194
Winding, Kai 49
Wollman Auditorium, Columbia University 197, 198
Wood, Mitchell "Booty" 46-49, 61, 64, 70, 72-74, 77, 79, 124, 257, 263, 264, 279, 333-336
Woode, Jimmy 69, 77-79, 124, 159-161, 197, 226, 228, 240, 241
Woodman, Britt 43, 69, 70, 77-79, 109, 123-125, 160, 161, 195, 218, 229, 237, 240, 241, 276
Woods, Phil 125
Woodyard, Sam 42, 78-80, 124, 148, 159-161, 182, 185, 190, 197-200, 230, 240-243, 335

Yancey, Jimmy 193
Young, Lester 90, 91, 267
Young, Trummy 41

Zawinul, Josef 125, 183

INDEX OF COMPOSITIONS AND SONGS

Ad Lib on Nippon   248-250, 263
Afrique   255-257, 263, 264, 297
Afro-Bossa Piano Summations   198
Afro-Eurasian Eclipse (CD)   154, 251, 253, 255, 256, 263, 297
Alcibiades' Camp: Ring Dem Bells   236, 242
Alerado   297
All Star Road Band (CD)   288, 297
All the Sad Young Men   142
All Too Soon   100, 102, 119, 122, 177
Amour Amour   190, 191, 200, 228
Anatomy of a Murder (CD)   203
And His Mother Called Him Bill (CD)   156, 159, 161, 192, 197
A-Oodie-Oobie   128
Apes and Peacocks   291
Asphalt Jungle Theme   199

Baby You Can't Miss   200
Bakiff   57
Ballade for Very Tired and Very Sad Lotus Eaters   128, 139, 148, 159
Ballad of the Sad Young Men   142
Bal Masque (CD)   161
Banquet Scene   235, 236, 242
Baptist Mission   21, 40
Bassment   207
Ben Webster Plays Duke Ellington (CD)   126
Be Patient   125
Best of Duke Ellington, The (CD)   121
Bird of Paradise   188-190, 197, 200
Birmingham Breakdown   15, 16, 165, 195
Black and Tan Fantasy   v, 4, 15, 51, 55, 56, 66-67, 77, 79, 167, 191, 200, 236, 242, 256
Black Beauty   7, 165, 166, 186, 195, 200
Black, Brown and Beige   112, 123, 202, 285, 289, 295, 311, 330
Blood Count   155-157, 161
Blue Belles of Harlem   43, 199
Bluebird of Delhi(Mynah)   247, 261, 263, 264
Blue Cloud   155
Blue Harlem   41
Blue Mood   30, 32
Blue Pepper (Far East of the Blues)   259-260, 264,
Blue Rose (CD)   140, 160
Blues I Love to Sing   51
Blues Plucked Again (LP)   172
Bojangles   119, 126, 171, 196
Bolero   302
Boys from Harlem, The   28-29, 42
B. P. Blues   117, 125
British Connexion, The (CD)   42
Brown Berries   16, 40
Bugle Call Rag   85, 86, 88, 121

Cantata No. 140   214
Canteen Bounce   214
Caravan   57, 180, 181, 185, 187, 190, 191, 200
Carnegie Blues   112, 123
Carolina Shout   19, 20, 40, 164, 187, 195, 200
Castle Rock   112, 124
Charlotte Russe   148, 161
Checkered Hat   117
Chelsea Bridge   102, 109, 119, 122
Chinoiserie   251-253, 263
Christmas Night in Harlem   21
Circle of Fourths   208, 218, 219, 224, 232, 233, 241
C-Jam Blues   109, 190, 200
Clarinet Lament   167
Clothed Woman, The   199
C-Minor Prelude   214
Come Sunday   119, 125, 186, 200, 330
Confab with Rab   128
Conga Brava   57, 96, 102, 119, 122
Cool Rock (CD)   282, 296
Cootie's Concerto   30, 32, 42
Cosmic Scene, The (CD)   70
Cotton Tail   97-99, 102, 119, 122, 125
Creole Love Call   51, 236, 242

Danny Boy   91
Dancers in Love   174, 177, 191, 194, 197, 200
Dance No. 5   63, 78
Dance: Skillipoop/The Mooche   236, 242
Daybreak Express, 214
Day Dream   102, 136-140, 146, 148, 150, 158-160, 213
December Blue   177, 197
Degas Suite, The   238, 242, 290, 295, 321, 333
Depk   247, 248, 263
Didjeridoo   252, 253, 263
Diminuendo in Blue and Crescendo in Blue   18, 37, 55, 98, 113, 124, 150, 240, 324, 330, 331
Do Nothing Till You Hear From Me   119, 199, 200
Don't Get Around Much Anymore   199
Drop Me Off in Harlem   3, 23, 24, 41
Drum Is a Woman, A   202, 209, 232
Duke's Big Four (CD)   199

East St. Louis Toodle-Oo   15-17, 41, 51, 58, 165, 167
Echoes of Harlem   28-32, 42, 167
Echoes of the Jungle   55, 56, 78,195, 200
Ellington Uptown (CD)   43, 78, 271-273

Falls, The   33, 108, 290, 305-307, 310, 313, 314, 324-327, 334, 335
Far East of the Blues   259, 260, 264

Far East Suite, The (CD) 154, 155, 158, 161, 246-249, 259, 262-264
Feeling of Jazz, The (CD) 296, 335
Flaming Sword, The 134
Flamingo 200
Fleurette Africaine 181, 188, 197
Flower Is a Lovesome Thing, A 146, 147, 160, 161
Freakish Lights 156, 161

Giggling Rapids (GRAP) 305, 315, 321, 334
Go Harlem 21
Goutelas Suite 292, 297
Great American Songbook 141, 142
Greatest There Is, The 108, 123
Great Paris Concert, The (CD) 42
Great Summit, The (CD) 25
Great Times! (CD) 173, 196, 198, 275, 283

Half the Fun 151, 158, 161, 211, 213, 218, 232, 238, 240, 241, 242
Happening, The 113, 124, 202, 240, 276
Happy as the Day is Long 84, 86, 121
Happy Birthday Duke (CD) 195, 296
Happy-Go-Lucky-Local 108, 116, 124, 200, 214
Happy Horns of Clark Terry, The (CD) 125
Happy Reunion (CD) 286, 297
Hark the Duke's Trumpets 204, 210, 240
Harlem Air Shaft 17, 32-34, 43, 214
Harlem Choc'late Babies on Parade 21
Harlem Flat Blues 17, 41
Harlem Hotcha 21
Harlemania 41
Harlem Number Man 21
Harlem Rhythm 29, 42
Harlem River Quiver 16, 40, 41
Harlem Romance 41
Harlem Speaks 25-27, 42
Harlem Strut 21, 40
Harlem Symphony 21-22, 40
Harlem Twist 17, 41
Harlem Woogie 21
Hawk Talks, The 163, 195
Hi-Fi Ellington Uptown (LP) 273
Historically Speaking, The Duke (CD) 78
Honeysuckle Rose 200
How High the Moon 104-107, 110-111, 123
Hundred Dreams Ago, A 182
Hy'a Sue 61, 78, 114, 124

Igoo 249
I Got Rhythm 97
I'm Beginning to See the Light 2, 119, 125, 199, 200
In a Jam 90, 122
In My Solitude 199, 200
Intimacy of the Blues, The 158, 296
Intimate Ellington, The (CD) 264, 297
Intimate Interlude 257, 264
Intimate Piano Session, An (CD) 191, 199, 298
In the Beginning God 200
In the Shade of the Old Apple Tree 56, 57, 78
In the Wee Small Hours of the Morning 142
In Triplicate 118, 125

Isfahan 154-156, 161
Janet 185, 199
Jaywalker, The 298
Jeep's Blues 150, 174, 200
Jig Walk 164, 195
Johnny Hodges All Stars With the Duke Ellington All Stars and the Billy Strayhorn All-Stars, The (CD) 124, 239, 240, 275, 294
John Sanders' Blues 190, 200
Jungle Blues 56
Jungle Jamboree 56
Jungle Nights in Harlem 15, 18, 41, 56, 256
Just A-Sitting, and A-Rocking 109, 119
Just Squeeze Me (and Please Don't Tease Me) 2

Kinda Dukish 163, 177, 199, 200
King Porter Stomp 88, 121
Ko-Ko 58-60, 63, 66, 78, 171, 196

Lake, The 204, 303, 305, 316, 317, 322-324, 334
La Mer 308
Lady Mac 219, 233, 241
Lately 211, 240, 241
Leap Frog 85
Le Sucrier Velours 190, 191, 200, 291, 292
Liberian Suite 62, 63, 78
Lightning Bugs and Frogs 291
Li'l Farina 55
Little African Flower 188, 200
Little Max, A 180
Lotus Blossom 148, 156, 191-193, 197, 199, 200
Lots o' Fingers 167, 186, 194, 195, 199
Love Scene 235, 236, 242
Love You Madly 200
Lullaby of Birdland 214
Lush Life 3, 40, 141-146, 159, 160, 239, 287, 294, 297

Madness in Great Ones 215, 216, 233, 236, 238, 240-242
Mainstream (Riba) 327, 328, 335
Marcia Regina 321, 333
Meander, The 305, 321, 333, 334
Meditation 178, 191, 200
Melancholia 175, 177-179, 185, 188, 190, 191, 196, 197, 199, 200
Merry Go Round (aka Harlem Rhythm) 42
Minnie the Moocher 72, 79
Misty 200
Mkis (aka Soul-Soothing Beach) 263
Money Jungle (CD and composition) 180-182, 197, 198
Mooche, The 166, 195, 236, 242, 256, 312
Mood Indigo 58, 64, 79, 134, 147, 191, 199, 200, 239, 297
Mother Her Majesty the Sea, The 302, 329, 336
Multi-Colored Blue 147
Mural From Two Perspectives, A 190, 191, 200
My Love Is As a Fever (Sonnet CXLVII) 230, 241
My People 298, 301, 333

Neo-Hip-Hop Kiddies Community, The 305, 310, 328, 329, 335, 336

Index of Compositions and Songs

New Mood Indigo 297
New Orleans Suite (CD) 117, 124
New World A-Coming 174, 190, 191, 194, 196, 199, 200
New York City Blues 199
New York New York 280, 298
New York New York (CD) 280, 297
Night Creature 294, 312
Night Shepherd, The 191, 200
Nobody Was Looking 199
Northern Lights 291
Nutcracker Suite 221

O Mistress Mine 228
Once in a Blue Mood 182, 183, 197
Ornithology 105, 110, 111

Paris Blues 131, 186, 200
Parlor Social De Luxe 195
Passion Flower 136, 138-141, 146, 148, 149, 150, 160, 177,
Peace Piece 179
Peer Gynt Suite 73, 79
Perdido 57, 99, 283
Perfume Suite, The 175, 197
Piano in the Foreground (CD) 185
Pianist, The (CD) 198, 296
Piano Reflections (CD) 177-179, 182, 185, 187, 188, 192, 194, 196-198
Pitter Panther Patter 172, 173, 196
Portrait of the Lion 168, 170, 195, 196
Prelude to a Kiss 177, 200, 214
Pretty Girl 151, 161, 211, 240, 256
Pretty Little Girl 153, 161

Queen's Suite, The (CD) 188, 203, 285, 291-292, 297, 316
Queer Notions 89, 121

Reflections in D 177, 178, 179, 185, 188, 197, 199, 200, 312
Relaxin' 281, 282
Reminiscing in Tempo 168, 175, 179, 195
Retrospection 177, 178, 196
Rhapsody Junior 188
Riba 305, 310, 314, 327-329, 335
Riff Staccato, (Otto Make That) 112, 123
Ring Dem Bells 236, 242
Rite of Spring 319
River, The 5, 7, 8, 198, 277, 290, 295, 299-305, 307-321, 323-325, 327-336
Rockin' in Rhythm 164
Rocks in My Bed 119, 125
Round About Midnight 31
Rumpus in Richmond 43
Run, The 290, 305, 310, 320-321, 333, 334

Sacred Concerts 191, 237, 254, 257, 262, 303
St. James Infirmary Blues 183
St. Louis Blues 23, 75, 80
Satin Doll 2, 177, 185, 187, 191, 199, 200
Second Portrait of the Lion, The 170, 196
Sepia Panorama 171, 196
Shakespeare and All That Jazz (CD) 229, 241, 294

Single Petal of a Rose, The 119, 126, 188, 199, 200, 291, 292
Skillipoop 187, 200, 235, 236, 242
Skin Deep 271-273
Soda Fountain Rag 168, 191, 195, 200, 280
Solar 105
Solveig's Song 73-74, 79
Sonnet 238, 242
Sonnet for Caesar 223, 230, 231, 233, 241
Sonnet for Hank Cinq 208, 223, 229, 231-233, 237, 241
Sonnet for Sister Kate 69, 79, 223, 230-233, 242
Sonnet in Search of a Moor 223, 226-228, 231, 232, 241, 242
Sophisticated Lady 2, 172, 199, 200
Soul-Soothing Beach 190, 191, 200, 254-256, 263, 264
Soul Flute 257, 258, 264
Soul of Ben Webster, The (CD) 116
Spring, The 302, 303, 305, 318, 319, 329, 333
Stampede, The 89
Star-Crossed Lovers, The 151, 153, 161, 209, 211, 213, 215, 217, 232, 238, 240, 242
Star Dust 101, 102, 122
Stepping Into Swing Society 119, 125
Springtime in Africa 182, 197
Stompy Jones 119
Stud (= Neo-Hip-Hop Kiddies Community) 305, 328, 335
Such Sweet Thunder (CD, suite and movement) 69, 79, 151, 153, 158, 161, 201, 203, 207-209, 217, 221-223, 232-234, 238-242
Summertime 182, 197
Sunset and the Mocking Bird 291
Swamp Drum 276
Swampy River 165, 195
Sweet and Pungent 45, 46-47, 48, 49, 72, 77, 203
Sweet as Bear Meat 132

Taffy Twist 327, 335
Take All My Loves (Sonnet XL) 229, 241
Take the 'A' Train 12-13, 127, 130, 185, 187, 199, 200, 304
Telecasters, The 208, 218, 232, 241
Thanks for the Beautiful Land on the Delta 117, 124
Things Ain't What They Used to Be 119, 200
This One's For Blanton (CD) 173, 196, 199
Tiger Rag 28, 42
Timon of Athens March 235, 242
Timon of Athens Suite 234
Togo Brava Suite 191, 254-258, 263, 264, 289, 290, 298, 334
Tone Parallel to Harlem, A 13, 17, 22, 34-38, 43, 151, 201, 203, 214
Tonk 188, 200
Toto (Afrique) 255-257, 264
Trombone Butter (= Trombone Cholly) 68, 69, 79
Truckin' 89, 90, 122

Ultra Violet (= A Flower is a Lovesome Thing) 147
Up and Down Up and Down (I Will Lead

Them Up and Down)   151, 216-217, 232, 236, 240, 241
Up in Duke's Workshop (CD)   297
UWIS Suite   292, 297

Vancouver Lights   281-282
Village of the Virgins   303, 305, 314, 328-330, 336
Violet Blue (= A Flower is a Lovesome Thing)   147, 161
Vortex, The (= The Whirlpool)   305, 314, 324, 325, 326-327, 335

Warm Valley   102, 134-136, 138, 158, 159, 181, 186, 197, 200, 213
White Christmas   283
Whiteman Stomp   89
Wig Wise   181, 194, 197